Japanese Linguistics

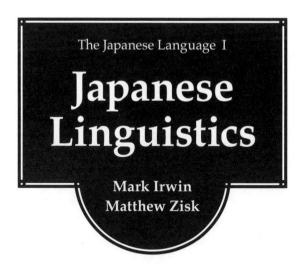

The Japanese Language I

Japanese Linguistics

Mark Irwin
Matthew Zisk

英語で学ぶ日本語学 1　日本語学

Asakura Publishing

First published in Japan in 2019
by Asakura Publishing Company, Ltd.
6-29, Shin'ogawa-machi, Shinjuku-ku,
Tokyo 162-8707, Japan

Copyright © 2019 by Mark Irwin and Matthew Zisk

ISBN 978-4-254-51681-4

All rights reserved. No part of this publication may be reproduced, stored in a retrieval system, or transmitted in any form or by any means, electronic, mechanical, photocopying, recording or otherwise, without prior written permission.

Table of Contents

List of Tables and Figures   viii
List of Abbreviations   xi
Glossing Labels   xiii
Preface   xiv

Chapter 1 Introduction   1
  1.1 Origins and Affiliation   1
  1.2 Typology   4
  1.3 A Brief History of Japanese   7
  1.4 The Modern Language   10

Chapter 2 Phonology and Phonetics   13
  2.1 Fundamentals of Japanese Phonology   13
  2.2 Consonants   15
  2.3 Vowels   17
  2.4 Mora and Syllable   19
  2.5 Phonotactics   20
  2.6 Pitch Accent   23
  2.7 Pitch Accent in Compounds   25
  2.8 Phonological Play   27
  2.9 Phonology through Time   29

Chapter 3 Grammar and Syntax   33
  3.1 Parts of Speech and Word Order   33
  3.2 Nouns, Pronouns and Formal Nouns   38
  3.3 Verbs: Morphophonology   42
  3.4 Verbs: Transitivity, Volition and Aspect   45
  3.5 Adjectives, Adverbs and Adnouns   50
  3.6 Predication and Copulas   53
  3.7 Verbal Suffixes I: Final Suffixes   56
  3.8 Verbal Suffixes II: Non-final Suffixes   65
  3.9 Auxiliaries   69

3 Verbs of Giving and Receiving and Benefactive Auxiliaries 73
3.11 Conjunctions 77
3.12 Particles 79
3.13 Derivational Particles 88
3.14 The Notion of Topic and *wa* versus *ga* 91
3.15 Grammar through Time 94

Chapter 4 Orthography and Writing 99
4.1 Writing Systems 99
4.2 Chinese Characters: Origins 101
4.3 Chinese Characters: Writing 103
4.4 Chinese Characters: Reading 106
4.5 Chinese Characters: *Kokuji* 109
4.6 Hiragana and Katakana 111
4.7 The Roman Alphabet 115
4.8 Chinese and Arabic Numerals 117
4.9 Punctuation 119
4.10 Script Mixing 121
4.11 Braille 123
4.12 Orthographic Licence and Orthographic Play 126
4.13 Writing Styles 129
4.14 Public Signage 131

Chapter 5 Lexicon and Word Formation 134
5.1 Vocabulary Strata 134
5.2 Mimetics 136
5.3 Derivation and Affixation 138
5.4 Compounding 140
5.5 Rendaku 142
5.6 Truncation 145
5.7 Personal Pronouns 147
5.8 Numerals and Classifiers 150
5.9 Homonymy, Polysemy and Heteronomy 153
5.10 Slang and Jargon 155
5.11 Discriminatory Vocabulary 157

Chapter 6 Language and Society 159
6.1 Gender, Age and Social Class 159
6.2 Register and Role Language 162
6.3 Honorifics 165
6.4 Anti-Honorifics 169
6.5 Language in Subculture 172

6.6	Greetings and Partings	175
6.7	Non-Verbal Communication	177
6.8	Attitudes to Language	179
6.9	Names	181

Chapter 7 Language Contact and Dialects 185

7.1	Sino-Japanese	185
7.2	Foreign Borrowings	188
7.3	English Borrowings	190
7.4	Japanese Pidgins and Creoles	192
7.5	Language Murder	195
7.6	Japanese Words in Foreign Languages	197
7.7	Japanese Dialects and Dialect Divisions	199
7.8	Dialect Diffusion	201
7.9	Eastern and Western Dialects	205
7.10	Tōhoku Dialects	207
7.11	Kyūshū Dialects	211

Chapter 8 Education, Research and Policy 216

8.1	Government Language Policy	216
8.2	Kanji and Kana Reform	218
8.3	Loanword Reform	220
8.4	Loanword Prohibition	222
8.5	The *Kokugo* Curriculum	224
8.6	Prescriptive Grammar in Education	227
8.7	Classical Japanese and *Kanbun* Education	231
8.8	Japanese as a Second Language Education	233
8.9	Language Tests and Examinations	235
8.10	Dictionaries and Lexicography	237
8.11	Language Software	241
8.12	Japanese Research on the Japanese Language	243
8.13	Non-Japanese Research on the Japanese Language	246

Further Reading	249
Bibliography	258
List of URLs	271
English-Japanese Glossary	272
Index	280

List of Tables and Figures

Fig. 1.1	Genealogical tree of Japonic languages
Table 1.1	Possible numeral cognates between Japanese and Goguryeo
Fig. 1.3	The linguistic periodization of Japanese
Table 2.2	The Japanese consonant phonemes
Fig. 2.3	The Japanese vowel phonemes
Table 2.4	Examples of Japanese syllables
Table 2.5.1	Possible moras
Table 2.5.2	Phonotactics by vocabulary stratum
Table 2.7	Major compound accent types
Fig. 2.8	A pentagonal iyokan
Table 2.8	Number mnemonics
Table 2.9.1	Old and Middle Japanese consonant phonemes
Table 2.9.2	Semi-vowel sound changes
Fig. 3.1	Major and minor parts of speech
Table 3.2.1	Commonly used *kosoado* demonstratives and interrogatives
Table 3.2.2	Commonly used formal nouns
Table 3.3	Verb classes
Table 3.4	Intransitive-transitive verb pairs
Fig. 3.7	Japanese verbal suffix string structure
Table 3.7.1	Commonly used final suffixes across verbs, adjectives and copulas
Table 3.7.2	*Onbin* forms of consonant-stem verbs
Table 3.8	Non-final verbal suffixes
Table 3.9	Commonly used auxiliaries
Fig. 3.10	Core verbs of giving and recieving
Table 3.10	Verbs of giving and receiving/benefactive auxiliaries
Table 3.11	Commonly used conjunctions
Table 3.12.1	Commonly used syntactic particles
Table 3.12.2	Commonly used thematic particles
Table 3.12.3	Commonly used restrictive particles
Table 3.12.4	Commonly used discourse particles
Table 3.13.1	Syntactic properties of case marker and derivational *no*
Table 3.13.2	Commonly used derivational particles
Table 3.15.1	Old and Middle Japanese verb suffix groups
Table 3.15.2	Old and Middle Japanese verb classes
Table 3.15.3	Some examples of archaisms in fossilized expressions
Table 4.1	Conventional script domains

Fig. 4.2	The character 樂 *yuè*, *lè* 'music, fun' across seven scripts
Fig. 4.3.1	A fresh bottle of Tetsu saké
Fig. 4.3.2	Script styles used in personal seals
Fig. 4.3.3	Some of the many variants of 邊 in *Konjaku mojikyō*
Table 4.4	The multi-strata system of *on-yomi*
Fig. 4.4	Chinese manuscript with Japanese glosses
Table 4.6	Hiragana and katakana with their respective kanji etyma
Table 4.7	Major differences between romanizations
Fig. 4.7.1	Ministry of Construction road sign
Fig. 4.7.2	Elementary school romanization chart
Fig. 4.8	Japanese postcard with both Chinese and Arabic numerals
Fig. 4.10	Extract from the Penal Code of Japan prior to its 1995 revision
Fig. 4.11	Braille on a Washlet control panel
Table 4.11	Japanese braille cells
Fig. 4.12	*Henohenomoheji*
Table 4.13	Copulas across media in BCCWJ
Fig. 4.14.1	Global standard Japanese electronic toilet icons for 'bidet' and 'rear'
Fig. 4.14.2	Road sign icons in Japan
Fig. 4.14.3	Multilingual sign at railway station
Fig. 4.14.4	Amusing mistranslation
Fig. 4.14.5	Multilingual emergency exit sign
Fig. 5.1.1	Japanese vocabulary strata through time
Table 5.1	Hybrid compounds
Fig. 5.1.2	Vocabulary strata proportions in two magazine surveys
Table 5.2	Sound symbolism
Table 5.3	Major derivational affixes by vocabulary stratum
Table 5.6	Truncation types
Table 5.7	Personal pronouns
Table 5.9	Homonyms, polysemes and heteronyms
Table 6.1	Examples of gender differences
Table 6.2	Register in conversation
Fig. 6.2.1	Ramu-chan's use of the made-up particle *Qča*
Fig. 6.2.2	Funasshi's use of the made-up particle *naQšii*
Table 6.4	Verbs with separate honorific and anti-honorific counterparts
Fig. 6.5	Katakana in graphics pattern table of *Dragon Quest*
Table 6.6	Japanese greetings
Fig. 6.7.1	'Female lover' gesture
Fig. 6.7.2	'Come here' gesture
Fig. 6.7.3	Apology gesture
Fig. 6.7.4	*Tegatana* gesture
Fig. 6.8	A dialect tag

List of Tables and Figures

Table 7.1	Phonotactics of SJ morphemes
Fig. 7.2	Borrowing by donor language across time
Fig. 7.5	Objectification of the Ainu
Fig. 7.7	Tōjō's dialect divisions
Fig. 7.8.1	*kao~cura* (ABA diffusion)
Fig. 7.8.2	*fusuma~karakami* (ABAB diffusion)
Fig. 7.8.3	*uroko~koke* (East vs. West + flying sparks AB diffusion)
Fig. 7.8.4	*šimoyake~yukiyake* (North vs. South AB diffusion)
Fig. 7.9.1	Isoglosses along the Itoigawa-Hamanako line
Fig. 7.9.2	Accent types across dialects
Table 7.9	Accent patterns of 2-mora nouns in Tokyo and Keihan $n+1$ type dialects
Fig. 7.10.1	Tōhoku dialects
Fig. 7.10.2	*Yappe Taisō* on NHK Sendai
Fig. 7.10.3	T-shirt with *gaɴbaq-pe miyaⁿgi* slogan
Fig. 7.11.1	Kyūshū dialects
Table 7.11.1	Sato dialect case/topic marking system
Table 7.11.2	Sato dialect verb classes not found in Standard Japanese
Fig. 7.11.2	Kyūshū dialect stickers found on LINE
Table 8.3	The 20 least comprehended loanwords
Fig. 8.4	De-anglicization of cigarette brands
Fig. 8.6.1	Standard classification of parts of speech in school grammar
Table 8.6	Conjugational classes and forms in school grammar
Fig. 8.6.2	Role of the 50-sounds table in conjugational class names
Table 8.7	Spelling versus pronunciation in historical kana usage
Fig. 8.9.1	Notoriously difficult questions from the Level 1 *kanken*
Fig. 8.9.2	More practical questions from the Level 1 JT
Fig. 8.10	*Ruijumyōgishō*, Kanchiin manuscript
Table 8.10	Antiquated slang expressions from a Japanese-English dictionary

List of Abbreviations

§	unit	E1	initial element in compound
~	or, alternating with	E2	second element in compound
*	nonexistent or ungrammatical utterance/form, reconstruction	EJU	Examination for Japanese University Admission for International Students
?	questionable utterance/form		
→	becomes, yields	EMJ	Early Middle Japanese
←	derived from	Eng.	English
[m]	*m* as a phone or sound	EVD	evidentiality
/m/	*m* as a phoneme	F	falling pitch
<m>	*m* as a graph	Fig.	Figure
+	compound boundary	G	glide
-	syllable or affix boundary	H	high pitch
=	particle/copula boundary	IME	input method editor
.	mora boundary	IPA	International Phonetic Alphabet
/	clause break	JLPT	Japanese-Language Proficiency Test
μ	mora		
ø	null (phoneme, morpheme, affix, etc.)	JSL	Japanese as a Second Language
		JT	Japanese Test
↗	rising intonation	L	low pitch
↘	falling intonation	L1	native language
†	obsolete	L2	second language
‡	role language	LC	Loanword Committee
♂	male gender	lit.	literally
♀	female gender	LMJ	Late Middle Japanese
ASP	aspect	MDL	modality
BCCWJ	Balanced Corpus of Contemporary Written Japanese	MEXT	Ministry of Education, Culture, Sports, Science and Technology
BCE	before current era	MJ	Middle Japanese
BJT	Business Japanese Proficiency Test	MOD	modifier
		MoJ	Modern Japanese
C	consonant	NA	nominal adjective
CC	Classical Chinese	NINJAL	National Institute for Japanese Language and Linguistics
CE	current era		
CJ	Classical Japanese	NLC	National Language Council
CMP	case marker particle	NLIC	National Language Investigation Committee
CV	consonant-vowel		
E	East(ern dialects)	NMoJ	Near-Modern Japanese

NP	noun phrase	SNL	Council for Cultural Affairs Subdivision on National Language
NVC	non-verbal communication		
OJ	Old Japanese		
PRED	predicate	SOV	subject-object-verb
RPG	roleplaying game	SUB	subordinator
SG	school grammar	V	vowel
SJ	Sino-Japanese (stratum)	VP	verb/adjective phrase
SKIP	System of Kanji Indexing by Patterns	W	West(ern dialects)
		WWII	World War II
		YPJ	Yokohama Pidgin Japanese

Glossing Labels

See also Tables 3.7.1, 3.8, 3.9, 3.12.1–3.12.4, 3.13.2.

ABL	ablative		HON	honorific (title)
ACC	accusative		HPFX	honorific (prefix)
ACVB	ablative converb		HUM	humble
ADN	adnominal (pre-modern)		IMP	imperative
ADNLZ	adnominalizer		IRCOM	irreversible completive
ADV	adverbial		ITOP	inclusive topic
ADVLZ	adverbializer		LOC	locative
AFF	affirmative		NCJT	negative conjectural
AHON	anti-honorific		NCVB	negative converb
ALL	allative		NEC	necessitive
AVS	adversative		NEG	negative
CAUS	causative		NMNLZ	nominalizer
CAUSL	causal		NOM	nominative
CCL	conclusive (pre-modern)		NPST	nonpast
CJT	conjectural		PASS	passive
CLS	classifier		PCJT	past conjectural
COM	comitative		POL	polite
COMP	complementizer		POT	potential
CONC	concessive		PREP	preparative
COND	conditional		PROG	progressive
CONF	confirmative		PROH	prohibitive
COP	copula		PROV	provisional conditional
CTOP	conditional topic		PST	past
CVB	converbal (*-te* form)		PURP	purposive
CVBLZ	converbalizer		Q	interrogative
DAT	dative		REP	representative
DES	desiderative		RESP	respectful
ENUM	enumerative		RETRO	retrospective
EPST	empirical past (pre-modern)		SIM	simultaneous
EVDNM	evidential nominalizer		SPEC	speculative
EX	exemplative		TER	terminative
EXCL	exclamative		TOP	topic marker
FOC	focus marker		VBLZ	verbalizer
GEN	genitive			

Preface

General treatments of Japanese linguistics written in English are not in particularly short supply. All, however, are pitched squarely towards post-graduates and researchers. Moreover, many are not really the general treatments they purport to be, instead weighted heavily towards one linguistic subfield (usually syntax). Not a few have passed their sell-by date and most are beyond the budget of an undergraduate student. Still others are poorly edited or indexed and hard to find one's way around, or are, without putting too fine a point on it, dull as dishwater. In writing this volume, the authors' aim was to produce a well-balanced general treatment of Japanese linguistics retailing at an affordable price; a volume whose content includes not only the usual standard fare, but also an historical overview of phonology and grammar and how this relates to the modern language; a volume whose coverage includes areas never previously seen in general treatments in English (indicated by * below); and a volume aimed at the undergraduate with some knowledge of basic linguistics. Our notional undergraduate is not just the Japanese non-native, studying either in their home country or in Japan, but also the Japanese-speaking one who, more and more in recent years, is required to study (even Japanese linguistics) in English. As most such undergraduates are not English native speakers, we include in this volume an *English-Japanese Glossary* of important linguistic terminology.

The volume is divided into eight chapters, containing a total of 86 short units. Although these 'bite-size' units can be read in any order—and the volume can thus do double duty as a 'mini-encyclopaedia' or handy classroom teaching material—the chapters are arranged thematically. Copious cross-references are provided.

Chapter 1 *Introduction* considers the origins and typology of Japanese and offers a brief historical overview from prehistoric to modern times. Chapter 2 *Phonology and Phonetics* moves from the fundamentals of Japanese phonology, the consonants and vowels, to more complex notions of the mora, syllable and phonotactics. It also examines the bane of the L2 learner, pitch accent, looks at phonological play* and concludes with phonological changes through time. Chapter 3 *Grammar and Syntax* is the longest in the volume. Beginning with an overview of parts of speech and word order, the chapter treats nouns, pronouns, verbs, adjectives and copulas (with especial focus on their morphophonology and vast array of suffixes), as well as auxiliaries, conjunctions and particles. It also includes units dealing solely with two further banes of the L2 learner, benefactives and the notion of topic. The chapter concludes with a look at grammar through time. Chapter 4 *Orthography and Writing* opens with an overview of the complex Japanese writing system, examines kanji from the four angles of origin, writing, reading and *kokuji* 'national characters'*, then moves on to hiragana and katakana, the Roman alphabet, Chinese and Arabic numerals and punctuation. Script mixing and writing styles are also covered, as are orthographic licence and play*, Japanese braille* and public signage*. Chapter 5 *Lexicon and Word Formation* looks at vocabulary strata in general, and mimetics in particular; then derivation, compounding, rendaku and truncation. After two particularly complex aspects of the Japanese lexicon, personal pronouns and numerals, are examined, the unit covers homonymy, heteronymy and polysemy*, and closes with a look at slang* and discriminatory vocabulary*. Chapter 6 *Language and Society* explains the complexities of gender, age, social class, register and role language*, then moves on to honorifics and anti-honorifics*, language in subculture*, greetings, non-verbal communication*, attitudes towards language, and names*. In the first half of Chapter 7 *Language Contact and Dialects*, the results of external contact are explored: Sino-Japanese vocabulary, foreign and especially English borrowings, Japanese pidgins and creoles*, language murder* and Japanese words in foreign languages*. The second half of the chapter examines internal contact: after looking at Japanese dialect divisions and dialect diffusion in general, the salient differences between Eastern and Western dialects are examined before the chapter closes with an overview of the dialects spoken in the northern and southern reaches of the main islands, Tōhoku* and Kyūshū*. The final chapter of the book, Chapter 8 *Policy, Education and Research*, treats loanword prohibition*, as well as government language policy in general and kana, kanji and loanword reform* in particular. It also looks at Japanese as a second language education*, language tests and examinations*, native speaker education (the *kokugo* curriculum)*, prescriptive grammar* and the curriculum of Classical Japanese and *kanbun* 'Classical Chinese'* taught in schools. It moves on to analyses of Japanese dictionaries* and software* and closes with an overview of research on the Japanese language, both by Japanese* and non-Japanese* researchers.

    For a user-friendly reading experience, we refrain from including references in the text. Instead, at the end of the volume, *Further Reading* cites the authors' sources and offers recommendations for future research. A *Bibliography* is also included.

    Throughout the volume, Japanese, when treated metalinguistically, is written in italics using an 'innovative phonemicization', as illustrated in Table 2.2 and Fig. 2.3 in Chapter 2. When treated non-metalinguistically, Japanese words are written in Hepburn romanization. Thus, the famous working class district of Tokyo is written *šitamači* when the subject of linguistic discussion, but Shitamachi elsewhere. When necessary, phonemic transcriptions are written inside slashes, phonetic transcriptions inside square brackets and orthographic transcriptions inside angled brackets: /šitamači/ ~ [ɕitɑmɑcɕi] ~ <shitamachi>. When necessary, compound boundaries are indicated by a plus sign, mora boundaries by a dot and syllable boundaries by a hyphen: Narita Airport may thus be *narita+kuukoo*, *na.ri.ta.ku.u.ko.o* or *na-ri-ta-kuu-koo*. Korean words appear in Revised romanization; Mandarin in pinyin.

Example phrases and sentences are provided together with interlinear glosses. These glosses provide morpheme-by-morpheme translations of the Japanese, including grammatical morphemes such as verbal suffixes and particles. Grammatical morphemes are given 'glossing labels' designating their primary function (NOM for 'nominative', ACC for 'accusative') and, when bound, are segmented from their stems by use of a hyphen for affixes and an equal sign for particles and copulas. When not referring to a specific form, all verbs, adjectives, copulas and verbal suffixes are cited in their nonpast, or dictionary, form throughout the main text. A list of these labels is provided in *Glossing Labels* and, together with a list of the forms they represent, in Tables 3.7.1, 3.8, 3.9, 3.12.1–3.12.4 and 3.13.2 also.

We would like to acknowledge the huge debt of gratitude we owe to Nic Tranter of Sheffield University for taking the time to read through and comment on earlier drafts of this manuscript. Our book is the better for his input. We would also like to acknowledge Kuroki Kunihiko, Heiko Narrog, Sasaki Kan, Shimoji Michinori and Eamon Watters (in strict alphabetical order) for their valuable comments on earlier drafts of selected chapters. We would like to thank all the good folk at Asakura Publishing for their manifold technical assistance and for putting up with our tardiness; and our wives for putting up with our late nights in the office and 'native speaker questions'. Any errors or inconsistencies that may remain are, of course, entirely our own.

Mark Irwin & Matthew Zisk
Yamagata, autumn 2018

CHAPTER 1 Introduction

1.1 Origins and Affiliation

Where the Japanese language comes from is one of the great questions of not just Japanese linguistics, but historical linguistics as a whole. While most languages of the world can be grouped into larger language families, such as Indo-European, Austronesian or Afroasiatic, each sharing a common ancestor, there is to this day no established theory as regards the roots of Japanese. Although for many years Japanese was considered to be a language isolate (a language without a family), more recent scholarship places Japanese in a language family together with the Ryūkyūan languages, spoken on the Amami and Ryūkyū Islands to the far south of Kyūshū, and Hachijō, spoken on Hachijō Island, approximately 300 kilometres south of Tokyo. Ryūkyūan is further broken down into Southern Ryūkyūan and Northern Ryūkyūan, the former consisting of Macro-Yaeyama (Yonaguni, or Dunan, and Yaeyama) and Miyako, and the latter consisting of Okinawan and Amami. All of these Ryūkyūan languages are mutually unintelligible (§7.7). Collectively, Japanese, Ryūkyūan and Hachijō are known as the Japonic, or Japanese-Ryūkyūan, language family (Fig. 1.1).

Several dates have been proposed for the separation of Japonic into Ryūkyūan and Japanese, with the most recent scholarship placing their separation in the 7th

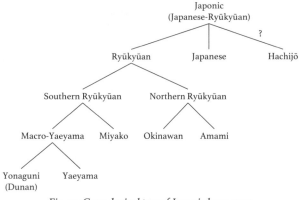

Fig. 1.1: Genealogical tree of Japonic languages

or 8th century. This does not necessarily coincide with the migration of Ryūkyūan speakers to the Ryūkyū Islands, who may in fact have remained in Kyūshū for several centuries before migrating. While there has been a recent surge in Ryūkyūan studies, research on Hachijō is still sparse and the question of whether Hachijō is to be considered a branch of Japonic, or a sub-branch of Japanese, is still very much a matter of debate. Likewise, the exact number of independent Ryūkyūan languages varies from scholar to scholar, as the distinction between language and dialect is often vague (§7.7). Finally, while the notion of a Japonic language family is mainstream in the West, it has had trouble gaining traction in Japan, where the Ryūkyūan languages are still generally classified as dialects of Japanese for socio-political reasons (§7.5, §7.7).

As to the greater question of where Japonic hails from, there is no lack of theories, ranging from the probable to the completely absurd. Perhaps the theory best known in the West is the Altaic hypothesis, which places Japonic in the Altaic language family, along with Turkic, Mongolic, Tungusic and, sometimes, Koreanic (Korean and Jejueo, a language spoken on Jeju Island, 85 km south of the Korean peninsula). The Altaic hypothesis dates back to the 19th century, but saw its heyday in the mid-to-late 20th century with many advocates in both Europe and the US (§8.13). Due to a large number of inconsistencies, however, few scholars now support the Altaic hypothesis or, in some cases, the existence of an Altaic language family at large.

Another prominent theory both inside and outside of Japan is the Japonic-Koreanic hypothesis, which argues for an affinity between Japonic and Koreanic. Given the close proximity of Japan and Korea, as well as the typological similarities between the two language families (both are agglutinative, follow SOV word order and mark case by means of postpositional particles: §1.2, §3.1, §3.12), it is only natural that a large number of scholars should draw such a conclusion. A relationship between the two families was suggested as far back as the 18th century by Arai Hakuseki (1657–1725) and Tō Teikan (1732–1797) and lists of possible cognates have been produced again and again throughout the 20th and 21st centuries. Many of these lists include pronouns, numerals, verbal suffixes and particles, which together build a strong argument. However, the overall lack of cognates among basic vocabulary, such as those appearing in the Swadesh list (a list of 100 'core' words found in nearly all world languages), raises serious questions regarding any common affinity. Given the long cultural ties between the Japanese archipelago and the Korean peninsula, it is equally possible that any similarities simply arose through many centuries of contact.

Another recent theory for the origin of Japonic suggests a link with Goguryeo, an extinct language of the Korean peninsula believed to have been spoken in the eponymous kingdom, founded in the 1st century BCE and a major power in East Asia until its fall in 668 CE. Though extinct for over 1,300 years, we can find approximately 130 Goguryeo toponyms (§6.9) in *Samguk sagi* 'History of the Three

numeral	Goguryeo reconstruction	Old Japanese	Modern Japanese
3	密 *mit	mi_1	mi
5	于次 *yuci	itu	icu
7	難隠 *nanən	nana	nana
10	德 *tək	to_2~to_2wo	too

Table 1.1: Possible numeral cognates between Japanese and Goguryeo

Kingdoms' (1145), an historical record written in Classical Chinese about the three ancient kingdoms of Goguryeo, Silla and Baekje. Similarities between Japonic toponyms and Goguryeo with respect to the numerals 'three', 'five', 'seven' and 'ten' (Table 1.1) were noticed as far back as the early 20th century by the Japanese linguist Shinmura Izuru (1876–1967). Recently, longer lists of possible cognates have been proposed by linguists in the West. Even more recently, Japanese has been compared with other extinct languages of the Korean peninsula, such as Silla, Baekje and Gaya, although the data for these languages (if they can even be considered languages in the first place) is even more fragmentary than that of Goguryeo, making a thorough comparison impossible. The greatest problem with the Japonic-Goguryeo hypothesis is that Goguryeo is a reconstructed language. All of the toponyms from *Samguk sagi* are written in Chinese characters, some phonographically and others semantographically (§1.3, §4.4) and, while we do have a relatively good knowledge of Middle Chinese phonology, there is little data on Sino-Korean (the Korean readings of Chinese characters) from this period, making accurate reconstruction of Goguryeo a complicated task. Even if we were to reject the Japanese-Goguryeo hypothesis at large, given the striking correspondences between native numerals (§5.8), there is good reason to assume there was a Japonic language, or at least a language in deep contact with Japanese, spoken in the Korean peninsula at some point in time, either contemporaneously with, or predating, the Goguryeo kingdom.

Less mainstream origin theories have classified Japanese, together with Indonesian and Malaysian, as an Austronesian language; together with Tamil, as a Dravidian language; as an Austroasiatic language, alongside Vietnamese and Khmer; or as a member of Austro-Tai, a proposed macro-family consisting of Austronesian, Tai-Kadai and Miao-Yao. It has also been suggested that Japanese is a creole or mixed language (§7.4). Some of the more pseudo-scientific theories have suggested a link between Japanese and Hebrew, or between Japanese and Latin. One Japanese scholar in the 1950s even proposed a link between Japanese and the Sino-Tibetan language of Lepcha. Few of these theories have gained any traction in academia, outside of the monographs of their original proposers. A major problem that plagues all origin theories is that the reconstruction of Proto-Japonic is still very much a work in progress. This means that, when making comparisons, researchers are forced to rely on Old Japanese data, or on their own *ad hoc*

Proto-Japonic reconstructions, essentially putting the cart before the horse. As our understanding of Proto-Japonic advances, so most likely will our understanding of the origin of Japonic as a whole.

1.2 Typology

The field of linguistics dealing with commonly shared features of the world's languages, classifying them according to a range of criteria, is known as linguistic typology. Languages can be classified typologically according to phonology, syntax, morphology, lexicon or other criteria. While it is a common belief—especially in Japan—that the Japanese language is unique (§6.8), when compared with other languages, we find that Japanese is actually quite unexceptional. Put at its typologically simplest, Japanese is a predominantly CV, moraic, SOV, head-final, agglutinative language. We will examine what each of these features mean in turn below.

The phonemes, or indivisible units of sounds (§2.1), postulated for any given human language can each be assigned a number of different features, the most pervasive of which are consonant (C) and vowel (V). There is a wide range of variation in the quantity of phonemes across languages. The Rotokas language of Papua New Guinea, for example, has just six consonants and five vowels, while the Taa (or !Xóõ) language of Botswana and Namibia has been analysed as having as many as 129 consonants and 28 vowels. The average number of consonants is around 23, with the average number of vowels five or six. Japanese falls right into this average with 21 consonants and five vowels (Table 2.2, Fig. 2.3).

The rules governing how phonemes can be strung together are known as a language's phonotactics (§2.5). For example, while all languages tolerate CV strings, some may ban CC clusters or syllable-final C. With a few exceptions, Japanese tolerates neither of these and is thus said to be a predominantly CV language. A CV unit in Japanese is known as a mora (§2.4) and all moras take approximately the same length of time to enunciate: *i-i* 'good' is pronounced approximately twice as long as *i* 'stomach'. Languages in which the mora is the smallest unit of prosody are called moraic languages and include Hawaiian and Tamil. They are relatively few —ancient Greek, Latin and Sanskrit are also held to have been at least partly moraic. Japanese phonology and phonotactics, including a more thorough discussion of mora and syllable, are explored in Chapter 2.

We turn now to syntax. A basic transitive sentence in any human language can be broken down into a subject (S: the entity under discussion), object (O: the statement concerning S) and verb (V: the action or state imposed upon O—in Japanese, adjectives are also morphologically verbs: §3.5). These can be ordered in six possible ways: SVO, SOV, OSV, OVS, VSO, VOS. Japanese is rigidly SOV (§3.1). In (1), for example, the subject *kai=ga* 'Kai' comes first, followed by the object *nihoNgogaku=o* 'Japanese linguistics', then the verb *manaN-da* 'studied'. The particles *ga* and *o*

(§3.12) mark the subject (nominative case) and object (accusative case), while the verbal suffix *-da* (also *-ta*: §3.7) marks the past tense.

(1) kai=ga nihoŋgogaku=o manaN-da
    Kai=NOM Japanese.linguistics=ACC study-PST
    'Kai studied Japanese linguistics.'

SOV languages account for roughly half human languages and include tongues as areally diverse as Mongolian, Hindi and Quechua. In the 1960s, the American linguist Joseph Greenberg (1915–2001) published a list of 'linguistic universals', many of which associate a particular word order with a specific grammatical or syntactic variable. In subsequently modified form, the modern theory of 'constituent order' predicts that SOV languages will, amongst other things, have adjectives and genitives that precede their nouns, as well as postpositions (known in Japanese as particles: §3.12, §3.13) instead of prepositions. Statistical studies have shown that approximately 60% of SOV languages, including Japanese, follow all three of these universal principles.

Another syntactic parameter commonly used to classify languages is what is known as head-directionality. In linguistics, a 'head' is the central element in a phrase that determines the phrase's syntactic category (noun phrase, verb phrase). For example, the phrase *the small black cat* is a noun phrase with *cat* as its head and *walk slowly down the street* is a verb phrase with *walk* as its head. Typological studies have found that in some languages heads have a tendency to come at the beginning of a phrase (head-initial), while in others they have a tendency to come at the end (head-final). English is generally held to be head-initial (although recent statistical studies have found that it is closer to a 50/50 mix of head-initial and head-final structures), while Japanese is strongly head-final. This is exemplified in (2), where heads are in bold and modifiers underlined.

(2) kaori=ga <u>daigaku=de</u> <u>saN+neNkaN</u> <u>nihoŋgogaku=o</u> **manaN-da**
    Kaori=NOM <u>college=LOC</u> <u>three+years</u> <u>Japanese.linguistics=ACC</u> **study-PST**
    'Kaori **studied** <u>Japanese linguistics</u> <u>in college</u> <u>for three years</u>.'

Morphologically speaking, human languages can be divided into two broad types. The first type is the analytic language (or isolating language), like Thai or Yoruba, where a word typically consists of a single morpheme. Such a language has no 'endings' on its nouns or verbs and its syntax relies heavily on rigid word order, adpositions (prepositions and postpositions) or auxiliaries (§3.9). The second type is the synthetic language. These can be further subdivided in various ways, but the two most frequently cited are the fusional and the agglutinative language. Both of these use suffixes attached to the stems of nouns, verbs or adjectives to express grammatical meaning, have a relatively free word order and may eschew adpositions or auxiliaries. In a fusional language—examples include Punjabi or Finnish—while a given suffix may express multiple meanings, it will typically be impossible to state which part of the suffix carries which meaning. For example, the Latin ending *-ōs*, found with many second declension nouns, expresses both plurality and accusativity, but one cannot say that *ō* expresses accusativity (the dative and ablative singular are *-ō*, the accusative singular *-um*) or that *s* expresses plurality (the nominative plural is *-ī*, while the genitive plural is *-ōrum*). On the other hand, in an agglutinative language—the subdivision to which Japanese, and also Turkish or Korean, belong—suffixes consist of a string of clearly divisible, semantically transparent, morphological units. In *ik-ase-ta-kaQta* 'wanted to make go', the three suffixes following the stem *ik-* 'go' mean, unambiguously, 'make', 'want' and 'past tense', respectively. The rich agglutinative morphosyntax of Japanese is explored in Chapter 3.

Turning finally to the lexicon, cross-linguistically Japanese possesses a relatively simple system of colour terms and numerals, but a complex system of kinship terms. Only the four basic colours, red (*aka*), black (*kuro*), white (*širo*) and blue (*ao*), possess distinct native terminology. All other terms are either semantic extensions of pre-existing words, mostly plant names (*midori* 'green ← sprout', *murasaki* 'purple ← purple gromwell'), or borrowings from Chinese or Western languages (*koN* 'navy blue' ← Middle Chinese *komH*, *piNku* ← English *pink*). Of these four basic colours, *aka* and *kuro* are believed to have originally expressed the notions of brightness and darkness (a notion *aka-i* still expresses in Western Japanese: §7.9), while *širo* and *ao* expressed those of clarity and paleness. Five stages have been proposed for the acquisition of basic colour terms in the evolution of a language: terms for dark and bright colours (black and white: stage 1), followed by the acquisition of a term for one of the warm primaries (red or yellow: stage 2), then a term for one of the cool primaries (green or blue: stage 3), and so on. The Japanese four basic colours fall right into this pattern. Interestingly, we find that *ao* 'blue' also encompasses what English speakers perceive as green, a fact apparent in such expressions as *aošiNgoo* 'green light' and *aoyasai* 'green vegetables'. The colour referred to as *ao* is termed 'grue' from a typological perspective and can be found in other East Asian languages, such as Korean and Vietnamese.

Japanese has three sets of numerals: native, Chinese and foreign (§5.8). All three of these systems are base 10, by far the commonest base in human languages. The native system, however, is highly defective. While there are native numerals for numbers up to 10, numbers higher than this are rarely used outside of compounds (§5.4), idioms or names (§6.9). This seems to have been the case historically also. Furthermore, the sets *hito* 'one' ~ *futa* 'two', *mi* 'three' ~ *mu* 'six' and *yo* 'four' ~ *ya* 'eight' all display vowel alternation between each member of the same set, suggesting that early stages of the language may have used an alternate counting system grounded on multiples rather than base.

Japanese possesses kinship terms for family members not discriminated in English or most other European languages. Distinctions are made, for example, between elder and younger siblings (*ani* 'elder brother' ~ *otooto* 'younger brother', *ane* 'elder sister' ~ *imooto* 'younger sister'), a pattern common throughout East Asian languages. Most European languages, in contrast, discriminate siblings by sex only. Japanese also possesses distinct prefixes for both great- and great-great-grandchildren: *hi-mago* 'great-grandchild', *yaša-go* (← **yaši-mago* ~ *yašiwa-go*) 'great-great-grandchild'. All kinship terms have plain and polite forms (§6.3). The plain forms are typically used when speaking of kin to non-kin, while the polite forms are employed in all other cases (when addressing kin, speaking of kin amongst other kin or speaking of non-kin): *čiči* 'my father (addressing non-kin)' ~ *otoosaɴ* 'father (all other cases)'. A commonly found areal feature elsewhere in East Asia, many of the polite forms have undergone semantic extension and may be employed to address or reference non-kin in general on an age and gender basis. For example, *ojiisaɴ* can refer specifically to one's grandfather or, by extension, to elderly men in general, while *oneesaɴ* can refer to one's older sister specifically or to young or middle-aged women in general. Making an already complex system even more complicated, alternate kanji orthographies (§4.4) exist for aunts or uncles who are older and aunts or uncles who are younger than one's parent: 伯母 *oba* for 'aunt = parent's older sister' and 叔母 *oba* for 'aunt = parent's younger sister'.

1.3 A Brief History of Japanese

The Japanese language is typically broken down into three major linguistic periods, starting with Old Japanese (OJ), the earliest recorded state of the language, developing into Middle Japanese (MJ), the intermediate stage of the language, and ending with Modern Japanese (MoJ), the language of today. Although where to draw the boundaries between each period remains a subject of debate, most scholars define OJ as the language of the 8th century, or Nara period (710–794), with MJ running from the 9th to the 16th century and MoJ from the 17th century onward. MJ is further subdivided into Early Middle Japanese (EMJ), the language of the Heian period (794–1185), and Late Middle Japanese (LMJ), the language of the Kamakura (1185–1333), Muromachi (1136–1573) and Azuchi-Momoyama (1573–1603) periods. MoJ, meanwhile, is further subdivided into Early Modern Japanese (EMoJ), the language of the Edo period (1603–1868); Near-Modern Japanese (NMoJ), from the Meiji Restoration of 1868 until the end of WWII (1945); and Contemporary Japanese, the language of the post-WWII period (1945–present). See Fig. 1.3 for an overview of these linguistic periods, along with their corresponding historical periods. In the current unit, we cover the major sources of the Japanese language, as well as its sociohistorical background. For an overview of phonological and grammatical history, see §2.9 and §3.15.

Prior to the 8th century information is scant. Our oldest source of Japanese words can be found in the late 3rd century CE Chinese history, *Sānguózhì* 'Records

linguistic period		dates	corresponding historical period
Old Japanese (OJ)		8th C	Nara (710–794)
Middle Japanese (MJ)	Early Middle Japanese (EMJ)	9th–12th C	Heian (794–1185)
			Kamakura (1185–1333)
	Late Middle Japanese (LMJ)	13th–16th C	Muromachi (1336–1573)
			Azuchi-Momoyama (1573–1603)
Modern Japanese (MoJ)	Early Modern Japanese (EMoJ)	17th–mid-19th C	Edo (1603–1868)
	Near-Modern Japanese (NMoJ)	late 19th C–1940s	Meiji–pre WWII (1868–1945)
	Contemporary Japanese	late 1940s–present	post WWII–present (1945–)

Fig. 1.3: The linguistic periodization of Japanese

of the Three Kingdoms'. In its account of the Japanese archipelago, *Sānguózhì* records a number of Japanese personal and place names (§6.9) using Chinese characters phonographically (for their sounds only). Little of what is recorded has any linguistic value, however. There have been a number of pre-8th century artefacts found in Japan, such as bronze mirrors and swords, bearing Chinese character inscriptions. As with *Sānguózhì*, though, phonographic transcriptions here are limited to personal and place names, and we have no transcriptions of Japanese on the sentence, or even phrase, level. As written sources are sparse at best, attempts at reconstructing pre-8th century Japanese must focus on internal reconstruction and on comparative studies of Japanese and Ryūkyūan. Efforts to reconstruct a proto Japanese-Ryūkyūan language, or Proto-Japonic (§1.1), are currently a major area of focus both inside and outside Japan and we can expect our knowledge to grow in coming years.

By the 8th century, we have our first comprehensive corpus of Japanese, consisting of histories such as *Kojiki* 'Account of Old Matters' (711) and *Nihon shoki* 'Chronicles of Japan' (720), as well as the 20-volume poetic anthology *Man'yōshū* 'Collection of Myriad Leaves' (c. 750). OJ predates the creation of hiragana and katakana and all native texts of this period are written entirely in kanji used both phonographically and semantographically (to represent their Japanese equivalents). The phonographic usage is commonly referred to as man'yōgana and is the origin of the modern-day hiragana and katakana scripts (§4.6).

In terms of vocabulary, the OJ corpus is comprised almost entirely of native words (§5.1), typically composed of one or two moras (§2.4), with words of three or more moras generally analysable as compounds (§5.4). Sino-Japanese (SJ: §7.1) is rarely found in OJ, with only a dozen or so examples accounted for in our sources. It should be borne in mind, though, that the OJ corpus is overwhelmingly skewed towards native poetry, where SJ is traditionally impermissible. Given that kanji had been in use for some time and Classical Chinese (CC) texts were being heavily studied by the elite during this period, we can assume that SJ was employed to a greater extent in educated registers (§6.2).

An increasing number of SJ loanwords were introduced into the language during the MJ period, vastly increasing the lexicon, while at the same time a great deal of Chinese-influenced expressions (so-called 'imitations': §7.1) were coined using native words. Much of this Chinese influence can be attributed to a practice known as *kanbun kundoku* 'text transposition', in which CC texts were translated—or, more precisely, 'transposed'—character-by-character into Japanese through a system of lexical and morphosyntactic glosses in manuscripts (see §4.4 for further discussion and §8.7 for a modern example). In the native stratum, many monomoraic OJ words were replaced with compounds during this period, partly due to the pernicious homonymy (§5.9) caused by the many sound changes that occurred during the transition from OJ to EMJ (§2.9). OJ $ki_1 \sim ki_2$ (see §2.9 for the difference between the two vowels), for example, could mean any of 'tree', 'mallet', 'saké', 'clothing', 'stronghold', 'unit of measurement', 'scallion', 'fang', 'yellow' or 'coffin'. In MoJ, all except 'tree' survive only in compounds, several undergoing rendaku (§5.5): *kine* 'mallet', *miki* 'sacred saké', *kimono* 'kimono', *miyagi* 'Miyagi', *hiki* 'classifier' (§5.8) for animals', *negi* 'scallion', *kiba* 'tooth', *kiiro* 'yellow', *hicugi* 'coffin'.

One of the greatest innovations of the MJ period was the development of the hiragana and katakana scripts, both of which make their first appearance as shorthand forms of man'yōgana in Japanese glosses of CC texts (§4.4). During the EMJ period, courtly literature, such as the renowned *Genji monogatari* 'Tale of Genji' (1008), was written in hiragana with small amounts of kanji, while CC-influenced genres, such as the collection of Buddhist and secular narratives *Konjaku monogatarishū* 'Collection of Tales from Times Now Past' (1120), tended to be written in a mixture of kanji and katakana. Entering the LMJ period, script-mixing (§4.10) became standard, with the majority of literary works written in either a mixture of kanji and hiragana, or kanji and katakana: mixing of all three scripts did not become common until EMoJ.

The written language of the EMJ period is commonly referred to as 'Classical Japanese' (§8.7) and remained in use, despite the massive changes wrought on the spoken language, up into the early 20th century. This applies to orthography as well: the system of kana spellings developed in the early 13th century by the calligrapher Fujiwara no Teika remained in use up until the end of WWII (§8.2). This system was later revised by the scholar Keichū (1640–1701), but in contrast to what one would assume, Keichū did not modernize the Teika system, but instead modified it to reflect an even earlier stage of the language. Due to the rigid prescriptiveness of written language throughout the LMJ period, little is known of the spoken language of the first half of this period. Our knowledge increases substantially in the 16th century, however, due in no small part to the labours of the mostly Portuguese-speaking Jesuits (§8.13) who, arriving in Kagoshima in the 1540s, provided the first Roman alphabet transcriptions of spoken Japanese. Much of our knowledge of the phonology and grammar from this period is thus based on Jesuit works. It is also during this period that we see the first European loanwords (§7.2)—from Portuguese, Latin and Spanish—enter the language.

By the MoJ period, Japanese had been greatly enriched both by European loanwords (mainly Dutch in EMoJ, but English, French, German, Russian and other languages by NMoJ: §7.2, §7.3) and, once again, SJ, which served as the building blocks for translations of Western scientific and cultural terminology (§7.1). This massive increase in both European loanwords and SJ gave rise to the stratified lexicon that we see in Japanese today (§5.1). The gap between written and spoken language (§4.13) remained stark throughout the EMoJ period (and right up until WWII in more formal written registers), but began to narrow in the late 19th century with the initiation of the *genbun itchi* 'unification of speech and writing' movement. Around the same time, the government began its rigorous promotion of the 'standard language', or *hyōjungo* (§7.7). This, combined with the *genbun itchi* movement and the continued influx of European loanwords, helped forge the language that we know today.

1.4 The Modern Language

Modern Japanese is spoken as a native language by approximately 125 million people. While there is no official figure for L1 Japanese speakers, the number can be deduced by deducting foreign-born residents and recently naturalized citizens from the general population of Japan (126.4 million in 2018) and adding on a presumed few million expatriate L1 citizens and what little survives of L1 speakers in the former Japanese Empire. Whatever the exact figure, Japanese currently ranks around ninth in the world in terms of L1 speakers, although the fast-declining population means that it is almost certain to drop out of the top ten by around 2030. To put its L1 speaker numbers in perspective, there are approximately three times as many English or Spanish L1 speakers worldwide and more than seven times as many Mandarin L1 speakers. Compared to these three languages, and most others in the top ten, Japanese is unusual in that close to 100% of its L1 population live in one single, largely monolingual, nation state.

In terms of L2 speakers, Japanese is a lot weaker. Although the most recent figures place the number of L2 learners of Japanese in Japan at just under 300,000 and those overseas at approximately 3.6 million (§8.8), 'Japanese as a foreign language' is a fairly recent phenomenon dating back, in the main, to the boom years of the 1980s economic bubble. When are factored in, however, the millions—possibly tens of millions, figures are hard to come by—of L2 speakers who learned informally, or in many cases were forced to learn, Japanese during the decades of the Japanese Empire, it is clear that the number of L2 speakers has dropped over the last century. These millions have died while failing to pass the language on to their children for cultural and political reasons. Most L2 learners in the 21st century are university students, and most are L1 speakers of Mandarin, Cantonese or Korean. From all points west of China, Japanese fails to top the list of L2 choices and is frequently absent from the primary and secondary education curriculum. With Japan's declining economy, with the rise of China and with even its current core learner group threatened by Japan's poor relations with China and the two Koreas, any claim that the L2 future of Japanese is a dazzling one must be taken with a grain of salt.

With only a very small number of exceptions, all L2 learners of Japanese learn the 'standard language', or *hyōjungo* (§7.7), generally defined as that variety spoken by well-educated, well-heeled native speakers living in downtown Tokyo. In reality, very few L1 Japanese speakers use this variety in their daily lives (§7.9–§7.11), although nearly all can understand it and most can make a passable stab at it when dealing with L2 speakers. This is not the case, however, with written Japanese (§4.1). Here, the Standard is practically the only variety found, certainly in mainstream literature.

L2 learners must also contend with the still widespread belief that Japanese is difficult. There is no question that this is true as far as the written language is concerned, but this is not necessarily the case for the spoken language. The sound system of Japanese is comparatively simple (§2.2, §2.3) and contains few sounds L2 learners find difficult to pronounce. Leaving aside the issues of pitch accent (§2.6, §2.7) or vowel length (§2.2), Japanese pronunciation is actually remarkably easy for L1 speakers of English or Spanish, for example. If one ignores the many obscure and quasi-archaic grammatical constructions found in bureaucratese—although unfortunately beloved of the Japanese-Language Proficiency Test (§8.9)—then Japanese grammar is no more difficult than most, its SOV (subject-object-verb) word order being cross-linguistically the most common (§1.2), and its agglutinative morphology (§1.2, §3.1) largely transparent. Japanese syntax and morphology are remarkably easy for L1 speakers of Hungarian or Mongolian, for example.

That L2 learners of Japanese still believe the spoken language is difficult is perhaps due to their unconscious absorption of L1 speaker attitudes. That the Japanese language is bizarre and challenging, that its L1 users are weird and wonderful, and that its L2 learners are doomed to failure before they even bother trying is a product of *nihonjinron* (§6.8), in its heyday in the 1970s and 1980s famously described as 'allegations of uniqueness'. Unfortunately, it is not yet completely dead. Some tracts published by well-known academics have ascribed mystical powers to the language's 'unique' SOV word order, its 'unique' CV (consonant-vowel) sound system (§2.4), its 'unique' love of borrowing words (§7.1–§7.3) and just about any other 'unique' feature one can possibly imagine. Even now, not a few elderly professors find it offensive that non-L1 speakers, like the authors of this volume, should be researching—and, god forbid, writing about—*their* unique language. The reader of this book, if an L2 learner, is studying *nihongo* 'the language of Japan' (§8.8). Meanwhile, the L1 reader of this book has, like all other schoolchildren in Japan, learnt *kokugo* 'the national language' (§8.5). The two are identical. Few L1 speakers of Japanese have paused to consider the palpable divisiveness of this.

So why bother learning Japanese? Why bother reading this book? Because Japanese *is* unique. As, when taken as a whole, are all languages. Being unique is normal and what the *nihonjinron*istas chose to ignore. Japan's 1,300 years of literature and poetry deserve to be read in the original. Japan's leading-edge research in many facets of technology and its output of film, manga, anime and video games (§6.5) deserve direct engagement. Although the Japanese writing system is a challenge, it will open the door to Mandarin and Cantonese. These, we believe, are reasons enough.

Chapter 2 Phonology and Phonetics

2.1 Fundamentals of Japanese Phonology

In linguistics, the study of speech sounds is known as phonetics. Phonetics is further divided into the study of sound production—articulatory phonetics—and sound perception—auditory phonetics. Within the discipline of phonetics, a speech sound is termed a phone. By means of perceived meaningful contrasts, however, speakers organize and systematize the phones of their native language into abstract elements known as phonemes. The study and interpretation of these phonemes is known as phonemics or phonology.

It is standard practice for phones to be written using the character set of the International Phonetic Alphabet (IPA). On the other hand, since phonology is a matter of interpretation, and a given language may possess multiple phonemicizations based on the varying theories and hypotheses of a range of scholars, phonemes may be written using non-IPA characters. In practice, however, IPA characters are generally employed for phonemes too. It is frequently the case, therefore, that a given IPA character, let's say *p* whose value is more or less that of *p* in English, stands for both the phone *p* in a phonetic context and the phoneme *p* in a phonemic context. In order to avoid ambiguity, it is linguistic convention that phones are written between square brackets, while phonemes are written between slashes. A further convention dictates that *p* as a written letter, what is known in linguistic terminology as the grapheme *p*, be written between angled brackets. Thus, a clear and unambiguous three-way contrast can be maintained between the different domains: [p] = the phone *p*, /p/ = the phoneme *p*, <p> = the grapheme *p*.

With the foregoing in mind, some examples should help to make clearer the difference between a phone and a phoneme. First, from English. The *p* in the word *pit* and the *p* in the word *spit*, while written identically as <p>, are actually two different phones. The *p* of *pit* is accompanied by a very brief puff of air, known as aspiration and written using a superscript *h*. *Pit* is thus typically transcribed phonetically as [pʰɪt]. The *p* of *spit*, on the other hand, has no aspiration and *spit* is typically transcribed phonetically as [spɪt]. Non-linguists—the vast majority of the native English-speaking population—will be wholly unaware of such a phonetic distinction. To them, the *p* of *pit* and the *p* of *spit* are perceived as the same phoneme, /p/, something acquired unconsciously while a very young child. This conclusion is based on the fact that there is no contrast between [p] and [pʰ] in English:

there are no minimal pairs [pʰɪt] ~ [pɪt] or [spʰɪt] ~ [spɪt] and, in linguistic terminology, [p] and [pʰ] are said to be allophones—or variations—of the phoneme /p/. A young child immersed in a Japanese-speaking environment also acquires a single phoneme /p/, since Japanese too possesses no [p] ~ [pʰ] contrast. The same very young child immersed in a Korean-speaking environment, on the other hand, does acquire two different phonemes /p/ and /pʰ/, since Korean does have meaningful contrasts for these same phones.

To take a Japanese example now, the initial *r* sounds in the words *raiu* 'thunderstorm' and *roba* 'donkey' are perceived by native speakers of Japanese as the same phoneme, /r/. To a speaker of English—and many other languages—the initial *r* in *raiu* 'thunderstorm' can sound, depending on the Japanese speaker, like English *l*. Since Japanese has no phoneme /l/, the 'scope' of its phoneme /r/ is much wider than that of English /r/, and may on occasion encroach on what, to an English-speaking ear, is '*l*-space'. Conversely, a Japanese speaker finds it difficult to distinguish the myriad of English minimal pairs such as *climb~crime* or *rain~lane*—/r/ and /l/ are separate phonemes in English—perceiving them both as the 'wider' Japanese phoneme /r/. This is the source of the notorious inability of Japanese speakers to 'get their English *r* and *l* right'.

Since phones and phonemes (collectively these can also be termed 'segments') come in many forms, it is convenient to group them into natural classes according to their 'distinctive features'. The most well-known of these, which even the non-linguist is aware of, are the features 'consonant' and 'vowel'. Distinctive features, like phones, are written between square brackets: [b] or [g] are thus said to be [+consonant] and [–vowel], while [u] or [o] are [–consonant] and [+vowel]. Other commonly found distinctive features are based on place ([bilabial], [nasal]) or manner of articulation ([stop], [glide]), voicing ([voice]) or tongue position for vowels ([high], [back]). The consonants of Japanese will be examined in §2.2, while vowels will be treated in §2.3.

Segments can be grouped into blocks. In English, this block is known as the syllable. In Japanese, the major block is the mora, although the syllable also has a minor role. Mora and syllable will be covered in §2.4. Japanese has two cross-linguistically unusual phonemes known as the 'mora consonants', also treated in §2.4. Phonotactics are the set of rules governing which segments can appear where in a mora or syllable, as well as the order and combinations in which segments are permitted to occur. In Japanese, for example, an independent mora can never end in a consonant, only in a vowel; and, while vowels can be strung together *ad infinitum*, consonants are restricted to a string of three maximum, with even this being extremely rare. Japanese phonotactics are examined in §2.5.

Suprasegmentals refer to features of speech which are superimposed upon segments. In Japanese the most important suprasegmental feature is pitch accent, which will be examined in §2.6 and §2.7. Phonological play—punning, palindromes, secret language and mnemonics—will be examined in §2.8. The chapter closes with an historical overview of Japanese phonology through time (§2.9).

2.2 Consonants

The consonant phonemes of Standard Japanese are illustrated in Table 2.2. There is little inter-dialect variation as regards consonant phonemes and most Japanese dialects (§7.7–§7.11) show a broadly similar make-up. As discussed in §2.1, a given language may possess multiple phonemicizations based on the differing hypotheses put forward by researchers. The phonemicization introduced here may be termed 'innovative', in that it takes into account the changes that have been wrought on the Japanese system since the mid-20th century by the massive influx of loanwords (§7.2, §7.3).

Table 2.2 contains 21 consonant phonemes arranged in a 6×5 grid: horizontally according to place of articulation and vertically according to manner of articulation. When two symbols appear in the same cell, this reflects a voiceless/voiced pair. Moving in order from the front of the mouth to the back of the throat, thus from left to right across the table, the five places of articulation found in Japanese are: bilabial (sounds articulated using both lips), alveolar (sounds articulated at the alveolar ridge, the roof of the mouth just behind the top teeth), alveolo-palatal (the front of the hard palate in the middle of the roof of the mouth) or palatal (the back of the same), velar (the soft palate at the back of the roof of the mouth) and glottal (sounds articulated using the glottis or vocal cords). The mora consonants, appearing in the rightmost column and separated from the rest of the table by a dotted line, take on the place of articulation of the following phoneme. Japanese has a preference for sounds produced towards the front of the mouth, with bilabials and alveolars together accounting for more than half of all consonant phonemes.

Turning now to manner of articulation, and thus moving from top to bottom of the chart, the six categories may be grouped into two major classes, containing three members each. The first major class, the obstruents, contains the topmost three categories: plosives, affricates and fricatives. Obstruents are articulated by means of some form of obstruction in the vocal tract. This obstruction can be total or it can be in some way restricted. In plosives the obstruction is total. A restricted obstruction results in a turbulent airflow and gives rise to fricatives. A combination of a plosive followed immediately by a fricative is known as an affricate. The second major class, the sonorants, contains the remaining three categories shown in the lower half of the chart: nasals, taps and glides. Nasals are sounds articulated by means of airflow through the nasal passage, while taps use the tip of the tongue. Glides, or semi-vowels, are consonants whose quality is phonetically that of a vowel. In Japanese, obstruents outnumber sonorants nearly 3:1 (or nearly 2:1 if voicing is ignored) and the distinction between the two major classes is an

	bilabial	alveolar		(alveolo-)palatal	velar	glottal	moraic
plosive	p b	t d			k g		
affricate		c		č j			Q
			z				
fricative	f	s		š		h	
nasal	m	n					N
tap		r					
glide				y	w		

Table 2.2: *The Japanese consonant phonemes*

important one: only obstruents have a voiced/voiceless distinction. This means that, in kana orthography, only obstruents can appear with voicing diacritics (*dakuten*: §4.6). It also means that only obstruents undergo rendaku (§5.5), a pervasive phenomenon found in compounding (§5.4).

Most of the phoneme symbols in Table 2.2 should be easily recognisable—and their phonetic values easily surmised—from the Roman alphabet. These symbols, along with those used for the vowels introduced in §2.3, will be used throughout this volume. We suggest you memorize their values. Those whose phonetic values are not obvious, or which possess important allophones, will be discussed in the remainder of this unit.

The voiced velar plosive /g/ is typically [g], although for some speakers it may be the velar nasal [ŋ], pronounced as in English *ng*, or even the velar fricative [ɣ], as in Spanish *amigo*. These two allophones occur chiefly word-internally and possess a strong sociolinguistic component: they can function as an overt marker of regional identity or age (§6.1, §7.10, §7.11). The affricates /c č j/ are realized [ts cɕ ʥ], that is to say with a pronunciation similar to English *ts*, *ch* and *j*. The fricative /š/ is pronounced [ɕ], close to English *sh*, while /z/ can be pronounced either as the fricative [z] or the affricate [dz], depending on its position in the word and the nature of the preceding segment. The fricative /f/ is [ɸ], the voiceless counterpart of [β] found in, for example, Spanish *nuevo*. Before /i y/, /h/ is [ç], as in German *ich*, but [h] elsewhere. Some of the affricates and fricatives just discussed have restrictions on their phonotactics (§2.5), in particular which vowels they can precede. The tap /r/, generally [ɾ], may become a trill [r], akin to that found in Spanish *burro*, in situations where a speaker wishes to sound threatening (§6.4).

We come finally to the two mora consonants /N/ and /Q/. Known as the mora nasal, /N/ has a wide range of allophones which vary according to the following phoneme: a nasalized dorso-velar glide transcribed in IPA as [ũ̯]—notoriously difficult for L2 learners to pronounce—before the fricatives /f h s š/, glides /y w/ and all vowels; [m] before the remaining bilabials /m p b/; [ŋ] before the remaining velars /k g/; [N] before a pause; and [n] before everything else (/n t d c z č j r/). The mora obstruent, /Q/, on the other hand, is articulated identically to the consonant which follows it: /Qt/, for example, is a long, or geminate, /t/, similar to that found in Italian or Finnish: [tː]. When /Q/ occurs before a vowel or a pause, it is realized as the glottal stop [ʔ], as in the *t* of *get* pronounced in a London accent.

2.3 Vowels

Most dialects of Japanese (§7.7–§7.11), including the Standard (§7.7), possess five vowel phonemes distributed almost maximally across the available acoustic space (the human mouth) so that the distance between each is large. Distinctions between vowels are therefore fairly clear-cut and generally unambiguous. These vowel phonemes are shown as white diamonds in Fig. 2.3, which represents the human mouth (the top of the chart is the roof of the mouth, the left the front). Cardinal vowels are used cross-linguistically as a reference by linguists. Those relevant to the discussion follow-

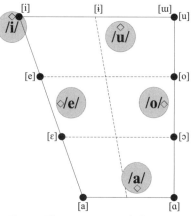

Fig. 2.3: *The Japanese vowel phonemes*

ing are indicated by black dots, along with their phonetic values (§2.1).

The five vowel phonemes of Japanese can be distinguished by assigning only three features (§2.1), [high] [low] [front], to each, as follows:

/i/ [+high, –low, +front]   /u/ [+high, –low, –front]
/e/ [–high, –low, +front]   /o/ [–high, –low, –front]
   /a/ [–high, +low, –front]

The high front vowel /i/ is typically realized as the cardinal vowel [i], pronounced very close to the vowel in English *bee*. The mid front vowel /e/ lies approximately halfway between the two cardinal vowels [e] and [ɛ], though is slightly centralized. The low vowel /a/ is realized approximately halfway between the cardinals [a] and [ɑ], thus a little further forward in the mouth than the vowel found in *spa* in most varieties of English. Similar to its front counterpart, the mid back vowel /o/ too lies halfway between two cardinal vowels, this time [o] and [ɔ], and is close to the vowel found in Spanish *no* 'no'. The fifth vowel phoneme, the high vowel /u/, is a more central vowel than the cardinal vowel [u] but, crucially, exhibits a distinct lack of lip rounding in the Standard. It is thus approximately halfway between the unrounded cardinals [ɨ] and [ɯ].

Unlike English, where vowel quality varies greatly across dialects and is a salient marker of a speaker's origins, such variation is far less apparent across Japanese dialects. Variation is restricted mainly to the high vowels /i/ and /u/: the former may undergo lowering to /e/ (*i-i* 'good' may be pronounced *ee*), and the latter may exhibit more rounding. Both these phenomena appear more frequently in Western Japanese (§7.9). In addition, /i/ and /u/ are collapsed into one vowel in the famous Zūzū dialects, found widely in rural Tōhoku: see §7.10 for examples.

Each of the five vowel phonemes possesses a long counterpart, pronounced in exactly the same manner but around 2.5 times as long. These long vowels are transcribed phonemically in this book as *ii*, *uu*, *ee*, *oo* and *aa*. Myriad minimal pairs exist and, like tones in Mandarin, are the source of embarrassing mistakes for L2 learners: *obasaN* 'middle-aged woman, aunt' ~ *obaasaN* 'old woman, granny', *uNko* 'poo' ~ *uNkoo* 'operation'. Vowels may also come in sequences of two or more different vowels. Although all possible two-vowel sequences exist, those ending in a high vowel are most common, while those ending in /a/ are rare. Only three of these sequences are generally held to be diphthongs and all end in /i/: /ai/ as in *taikai* 'competition', /oi/ as in *čoičoi* 'occasionally', /ui/ as in *ruisui* 'analogy'. The orthography of long vowels does not always match the pronunciation: see §4.6 for more detail.

Of the five vowels, the two high vowels /i/ and /u/ are the weakest and prone to devoicing. Also known as vowel reduction, this is a complex phenomenon which varies in intensity by individual speaker and may also vary according to social situation. It is widespread in Tokyo and in the Standard, but less commonly found in Western Japanese (with the exception of Kyūshū dialects: §7.11). Put at its simplest, a high vowel is reduced—and may even be elided altogether—when sandwiched between two voiceless consonants. Thus, *sute-ru* 'discard' or *fuke-ru* 'get late' sound like *steru* and *fkeru*, while Susukino, the famous nightlife district of Sapporo, can be heard as *sskino*. Vowel reduction also occurs between a voiceless consonant and a pause, although here the level of reduction exhibits greater variation. The copula *des-u* (§3.6), for example, is typically pronounced *des*, while the *-(i)mas-u* forms of verbs (§3.8) are generally *-(i)mas*. Both of these typically appear sentence-finally and thus prior to a pause.

The weak high vowels are also those employed most often in the process known as epenthesis, in which syllables ending in a consonant are given an extra vowel when borrowed into Japanese (§7.2, §7.3). In recent borrowings from Western languages, examples include *fureezu* 'phrase' from English, *borušiči* 'borsht' from Russian or *šunookeru* 'snorkel' from German (epenthetic vowels in bold). Non-high epenthetic vowels are only found to any extent after /t/ and /d/: *teNto* 'tent', *toreNdo* 'trend'. The same two high vowels were used for purposes of epenthesis when Chinese characters and their readings were borrowed well over a millennium ago (§4.4). For this reason the overwhelming majority of kanji deriving from original Chinese monosyllables with a final consonant, end in a high vowel: 一 *iči* 'one', 軸 *jiku* 'axis', 爆発的 *bakuhacuteki* 'explosive' (§7.1).

2.4 Mora and Syllable

The notion of syllable is found in most languages of the world but is slippery to define: here we will go no further than to say it is a unit of sound shorter than the word but longer than the phoneme. If you are a native speaker of English you will perceive the word *automatic* as having four syllables (though where syllable boundaries are drawn will vary from speaker to speaker), while *library* may have two or three (but never one or four). Japanese too possesses syllables, but for native speakers they are not the natural 'timing unit'. Instead Japanese speakers perceive words like *ebi* 'shrimp' or *itadakimasu* 'let's eat' as having two or six moras, respectively.

The mora is known colloquially as a *haku* and is written with the kanji for 'beat', 拍. Its definition, however, is even more slippery than that of the syllable. One famous definition put forward by a Western scholar working in the 1960s was 'something of which a long syllable consists of two and a short syllable consists of one.' What is clear, however, is that all moras take more or less the same time to utter, something which is not true for the syllable. In Japanese, then, moras are said to be isochronous—taking an equal amount of time. Moras come in two types: independent moras, which can form a syllable on their own, and mora consonants (Table 2.2), which cannot. The latter come in two forms, the mora obstruent Q and the mora nasal N. Most moras, however, are independent and take the form in (1), where C is a consonant, G is a glide (the semi-vowels $y \sim w$: §2.2), V is a vowel and brackets indicate optionality. Although the mora can thus consist of anything from one (V: *u* 'cormorant') to three phonemes (CGV: *kyo* 'scheme, behaviour'), CV moras with two phonemes, such as *te* 'hand', dominate.

(1) (C)(G)V   (2) (C)(G)V(V)($_N{}^Q$)

The syllable, in Japanese or any other language, is held to consist of three parts: an onset (initial C, if present), a coda (final C, if present) and a nucleus (everything else in between). Like the mora, a glide can be present between the onset and the nucleus. The syllable in Japanese thus takes the form in (2), where the coda, if present, must be a mora consonant $_N{}^Q$. Most syllables in Japanese are as in (1): typically, therefore, a mora and a syllable correspond to an identical string of segments. Such syllables are said to be 'light' and constitute approximately 70% of syllables in the language. Syllables containing a long vowel or diphthong—(C)(G)VV syllables—or a mora consonant coda—(C)(G)V$_N{}^Q$ syllables—are composed of two moras (equal to one foot, a cross-linguistic unit of prosody) and are said to be 'heavy'. Examples of heavy syllables with a long vowel or diphthong are *kyoo* 'today' or *koi* 'carp'; examples of heavy syllables with an $_N{}^Q$-coda are *haQ* 'yes (humble, archaic)' or *paN* 'bread'. Syllables with both a long vowel or diphthong and an $_N{}^Q$-coda—(C)(G)VV$_N{}^Q$ syllables—are composed of three moras and said to

division by		English gloss	number of	
mora	syllable		moras	syllables
ji	*ji*	haemorrhoids	1	1
ta.n	*tan*	phlegm	2	1
ge.ri	*ge-ri*	diarrhoea	2	2
pu.u.n	*puun*	sudden powerful smell	3	1
be.n.pi	*ben-pi*	constipation	3	2
se.ki.ri	*se-ki-ri*	dysentery	3	3
ka.n.čo.o	*kan-čoo*	enema	4	2
ši.q.ki.n	*šiq-kin*	incontinence	4	2
i.gu.su.ri	*i-gu-su-ri*	stomach medicine	4	4
ta.i.fu.u.ka.re.e	*tai-fuu-ka-ree*	Thai curry	7	4

Table 2.4: *Examples of Japanese syllables*

be 'super-heavy'. Common examples are *roon* 'loan' or *wain* 'wine'. Further examples of syllables are illustrated in Table 2.4, where word syllable count is contrasted with word mora count. Here, mora boundaries are marked with a period, syllable boundaries with a hyphen.

Why is this distinction between mora and syllable important? Many phonological and morphological phenomena found in Japanese operate on the principle of the mora, including various forms of truncation (§5.6). The mora is also the unit used in traditional poetry, as well as its modern offshoots. This is illustrated in the *senryū* in (3), which follows the 5–7–5 mora pattern employed in *haiku*. That said, although their number is comparatively few, other phenomena operate on the principle of the syllable. The most important of these, though still operating in the main on the principle of the mora, is pitch accent: §2.6, §2.7 for the Standard; §7.9–§7.11 for dialects.

(3) *i.ya na hi.to*   Someone that you hate
    yo.ko ka.ra mi.te.mo   When viewed from the side is still
    i.ya na hi.to   Someone that you hate

2.5 Phonotactics

In its broadest sense, phonotactics is concerned with the sequential arrangement of phonemes. In its narrowest sense, phonotactics is concerned with positing phonotactic rules and with defining what are licit and what are illicit phoneme combinations—and hence licit and illicit moras, syllables and words. The most important of these rules, as we have seen in §2.4, is that a mora must take the form either of a (C)(G)V sequence or of ${}_N{}^Q$ (a mora consonant N~Q). This means that consonant clusters in Japanese are severely restricted: they can only be formed when a mora consonant ${}_N{}^Q$ is followed by a C(G)V mora (${}_N{}^Q$.C) or by another mora consonant (${}_N{}^Q{}_N{}^Q$). These restrictions on consonant clusters account for the phenomenon in loanwords (§7.2, §7.3) known as epenthesis, whereby the consonant clusters found frequently in donor words are dealt with by means of inserting a vowel: see §2.3 for further discussion. The ${}_N{}^Q$.C type of consonant cluster is quite common: *te.N.ki* 'weather', *iQ.ta* 'went'. The ${}_N{}^Q$.${}_N{}^Q$ type, on the other hand, is rare, never occurring in the order Q.N (only as N.Q), and carrying the further restriction that the mora boundary between N.Q must correspond to an affix (§5.3) or particle boundary (§3.12, §3.13). Thus, *bu.ra.u.N-Q.po.i* 'brownish', *ro.N.do.N-Q.ko* 'Londoner', *ka.N=Q.te* 'did you say *can*?', where -*Qpoi* '-ish' and -*Qko* 'person (diminutive)' are productive suffixes, and *Qte* is a complementizer particle (§3.13).

The consonants stand in marked contrast to the vowels. If you have studied Japanese for a while, you will probably have noticed that the language is quite 'vowelly', in the sense that there appear to be no restrictions on stringing together long sequences of vowels. This is quite true and, in principle, there is no such restriction. The word *iia-oo* 'let's talk (together)' contains a cluster of five vowels and it is not difficult to find words with a string of four, such as *ubaia-u* 'scramble over', *keiei* 'administration' or *hoooo* 'the Pope'. In this sense, the phonotactics of Japanese are almost the polar opposite of languages such as English, German or Russian, which are highly 'consonanty' and where long strings of vowels, while licit, are unnatural.

Table 2.5.1 shows the 20 possible onset consonants, including the zero onset ø (the *y*-axis), combined with the five vowels and the 10 possible glides+vowels (the *x*-axis). With the mora consonants accorded their own cells bottom right, we find that there exist 292 possible moras in Japanese. The semi-vowels *y*~*w* are said to have a defective distribution, in that they can never appear before their corresponding vowel: *yi*~*wu* are illicit. There exist restrictions on the consonants after which, and the vowels before which, the *y*- and *w*-glides can appear. The *y*-glide is never found after other glides, nor after *c*~*č*~*d*~*j*~*s*~*š*~*t*~*z*. Additionally, it is never found before the front vowel *i* (Fig. 2.3). The *w*-glide too is never found after other glides, nor after *h*, and only very rarely after other consonants. It is never followed by *u*. All these illicit moras, along with *hu*, also illicit, are shown in black in Table 2.5.1. They account for 32% of the mora inventory. Not all licit moras occur with equal frequency. Many are overwhelmingly restricted to the loanword stratum, occurring with low frequency (*če*~*še*~*we*~*ti*), or occurring very rarely only when uttered by the more innovative speaker (*ci*~*si*~*fya*~*ye*). The *w*- and *ye*-glides are especially problematic and are realized by many speakers as two individual moras: *gwi* → *gu.i*. All these low frequency licit moras are marked in grey in the table and account for 33% of the mora inventory. The remaining checked cells, at 36%, form the phonotactic 'core' of the language.

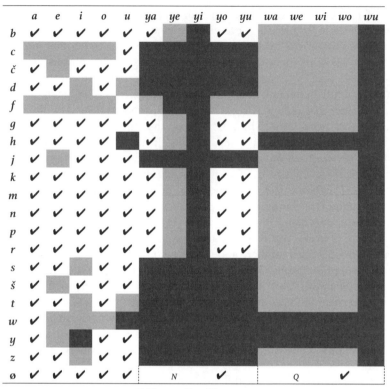

Table 2.5.1: Possible moras

At the level of the word, some mora strings, although perfectly licit phonotactically, do not occur: *kegu* and *tona* are examples and are termed accidental gaps. Those combinations, like *ksiyi* or *častro*, which are phonotactically illicit, are termed systematic gaps. It is difficult to say what the most common mora in Japanese is, as results differ depending on medium and phonemicization. However, an analysis of the *Asahi Shinbun* newspaper has shown that, ignoring moras with glides, the five most frequent are N > *ru* > *ka* > *no* > *ku*; the five least frequent 'core' (checked in Table 2.5.1) moras, *pe* < *pi* < *nu* < *pu* < *po*. The five most frequent consonants (ignoring the mora consonants) are *k* > *r* > *n* > *t* > *s*; the five least frequent *p* < *f* < *w* < *č* < *b*. The vowel frequency order is *u* > *a* > *i* > *o* > *e*.

Vocabulary stratum (§5.1) and phonotactics are closely linked: indeed, some scholars define, or partly define, a given vocabulary stratum by means of phonotactic rules. The native stratum, for example, bans *p*, except after a mora consonant in a few scattered examples: *kaQpara-u* 'snatch', *omoNpakar-u* 'consider'. It disallows words beginning in *r* and, with a few exceptions (§2.9), words with internal *h~f*, words beginning in a voiced obstruent (*b, d, g, z*) or words having more than one

stratum	initial *p*	medial *p*	initial voiced obstruent	more than one voiced obstruent	initial *r*	word-internal *h~f*	Q + voiced obstruent
native	✗	◇	◇	◇	✗	◇	✗
mimetic	✔	◇	✔	✔	◇	◇	◇
Sino	✗	✔	✔	✔	✔	✔	✗
foreign	✔	✔	✔	✔	✔	✔	✔

Table 2.5.2: *Phonotactics by vocabulary stratum*

voiced obstruent. The mimetic stratum is somewhat more tolerant, permitting words beginning in, and containing more than one, voiced obstruent. Though examples are few, it also permits words with internal *p~h~f*, words beginning in *r* and Q*b*~Q*d*~Q*g*~Q*z* strings. The Sino-Japanese stratum (§7.1) allows widespread word-initial *r* and word-internal *h~f*, though bans word-initial *p*. The foreign stratum is rule-free and tolerates all licit moras. The foregoing discussion may be summed up in Table 2.5.2, where the symbol ◇ indicates 'few examples'. Phonotactics can thus reveal a lot: read by column, the table can be a useful guide to pinpointing a given word's etymology. A word with initial *p*, for example, can only be mimetic or foreign; a word with internal *h~f* is unlikely to be native or mimetic.

2.6 Pitch Accent

Pitch accent differs from tone: in the former, variation in pitch is restricted at the most to one or two positions within a word, while in the latter, variations in pitch typically affect every syllable or mora in a word. Pitch accent languages are not particularly common cross-linguistically, but include Shanghainese, Swedish, Lithuanian and Japanese. Within Japanese, pitch accent differs across dialects, and indeed a few dialects arguably do not have a pitch accent system at all (§7.9–§7.11). The description of pitch accent which follows is that of Standard Japanese.

Each mora (§2.4) in a Japanese word has either a high (H) or low (L) pitch, indicated in the examples to follow by overline or underline. 'Crab', for example, is ka̅ni̲, 'dove' is h̅a̅to̲, 'incident' is j̅i̅ke̅N, 'adult' is o̲to̅na̅, 'pressure' is a̲cu̅ryo̅ku̅ and 'terrifying' is o̲so̅ro̅ši̅i̅. Apart from words of one mora, such as h̅i̅ 'day' or e̅ 'picture', a switch in pitch must occur at least once: there exist no polymoraic words with pitch patterns such as *ra̲ba̲ or *ra̲ba̲da̲. The longer a word is, the more likely a pitch switch is to occur more than once but, crucially, twice is the limit. While a word such as *ra̲ba̅da̲ba̲ is possible, there exist no words showing pitch patterns with three or more switches, such as *ra̲ba̅da̲ba̅ or *ra̲ba̅da̲ši̅i̅. This suggests that pitch patterns are not simply random but rule governed. This is indeed the case, with the pitch pattern being entirely predictable provided one knows the location of the accent.

The accent is where a steep drop in pitch level from H to L occurs. An accent is not, however, compulsory: a word may not show a steep drop in pitch level from H to L and thus possess no accent. If it does show a steep drop in pitch level from H to L, this may occur only once and a word may only have one accent. In unaccented words, all moras are H, except for the initial mora, which is L: ka‾sa‾ 'scab', ka‾zaru‾ 'decorate', ka‾takuna‾ 'stubborn'. In accented words, where its position is henceforth shown in bold, the accented mora is H, after which the pitch falls and all succeeding moras are L. All moras before the accented H mora are also H, except for the initial mora which is L (oso‾ro‾šii), unless it is the initial mora itself which is accented (ha‾to). It follows, thus, that there are *n*+1 possible pitch patterns for a word with *n* moras: an accent on any of the word's *n* moras, plus the no-accent option. For 3-mora words we have, for example, su‾ramu 'slum', sune‾ru 'sulk', sube‾ri 'sliding, skiing' and the unaccented su‾zuki‾ 'sea bass'. We dispense henceforth with indicating high and low pitch using over- and underline.

The astute reader will have noticed that the accented *suberi* and the unaccented *suzuki* have the identical pitch pattern LHH. When combined with a particle (§3.12, §3.13) such as *mo*, however, they differ: *suberi=mo* (LHHL) ~ *suzuki=mo* (LHHH). While this is the case with most particles, and indeed with the most common particles, such as *wa~ga~o~ni~kara~de*, some particles cause the accent location to shift. When *bakari~sae~nado*, for example, combine with an unaccented noun, the accent shifts to the first mora of the particle. Thus, with an accented noun we have the expected *suberi=bakari* (LHHLLL), but with an unaccented noun we find *suzuki=bakari* (LHHHLL). With *no* and *gurai* the behaviour is even more complex. Similar shifts in accent are found with compounds (§2.7).

Sadly, there are, no rules of thumb for knowing which words are accented and which are not, nor, in the case of accented words, for predicting accent location. One exception is personal names which, if accented, are always accented on the antepenultimate (third mora from the end). There do exist, however, some rough guidelines for the L2 learner, for whom the mastery of accent is a formidable hurdle. Verbals (§3.1) may be divided into two groups, those whose dictionary forms are unaccented and those whose dictionary forms are accented on the penultimate mora. Various rules govern the movement (in the case of accented dictionary forms) or insertion (in the case of unaccented dictionary forms) of the accent location across verbal suffix strings (§3.7, §3.8).

With native Japanese words (§5.1), statistical studies have shown that approximately 70% of words are unaccented. For the 30% or so which do have an accent, this generally falls on the initial mora in 2-mora words, but on the antepenultimate in longer words. With loanwords (§7.2, §7.3), on the other hand, unaccentedness is unusual, while longer words are generally accented on the antepenultimate mora.

Across all vocabulary strata, some of the possible *n*+1 pitch patterns are thus quite rare, most notably accent on the final mora: *atama* 'head', *šičigacu* 'July'.

Cases where the same word has two or more possible accent patterns are not uncommon. In some instances, the distinction may be between an old-fashioned and a more modern pattern (older *sukuutaa* ~ newer *sukuutaa* 'scooter, moped'), while in others it is in apparent free variation (*hifu* ~ *hifu* 'skin'). Given the difference across dialects both in accent location and in the pitch pattern rules they yield, interference must also have a role to play. There are examples of homonym (§5.9) doublets or triplets distinguished only by their accent. Doublets include *ki* 'spirit, chi' ~ *ki* 'tree' or *čikaku* 'near' ~ *čikaku* 'perception', while *haši* 'bridge' ~ *haši* 'chopsticks' ~ *haši* 'edge' is a well-known example of a triplet. It should not be presumed, however, that accent is a powerful mechanism for distinguishing between homonyms. Research has shown that only around 14% of homonyms are distinguished by accent. An example of a triplet where all three homonyms have an identical accent pattern is *tako* 'octopus' ~ *tako* 'kite' ~ *tako* 'callus'. Examples of four, five, or even more, identical homonyms can be found, particularly in the Sino-Japanese vocabulary stratum (§7.1).

2.7 Pitch Accent in Compounds

Japanese compounds (§5.4) exhibit what is termed culminativity: a compound can have at most one accented mora. This is despite the fact that, as explained in §2.6, each of the elements of which a compound is composed may possess an individual accent. The fact that typically at least one element has to alter its pitch pattern makes pitch accent in compounds extremely complex and a minefield for the L2 learner—a minefield rendered even more perilous by the fact that Japanese L2 textbooks (§8.8) typically ignore the subject, despite the frequency of compounds in everyday speech. For reasons of space, in this unit we will examine accent only in noun+noun compounds, while eschewing much technical detail.

Five tendencies—the word 'rule' cannot be employed—may be distilled from the mass of research carried out on the subject. These are labelled as Types I–V in Table 2.7. Since four of these depend on the nature of the second element (E2) in the compound and only one, whose applicability is not particularly wide-ranging, on the first element (E1), it may be stated as an overarching principle that it is the E2 accent that governs accent placement in the compound as a whole. Shaded cells in the table indicate which element 'sets the conditions'. The mora (μ) which is accented is shown by means of the figures 0 to −4, where 0 indicates unaccented, −1 final accent, −2 penultimate accent, and so on.

We begin with the only tendency where it is E1 that sets the conditions: Type I. Here, there is a strong tendency for 2μ+2μ compounds, whose E1 is unaccented, to be unaccented themselves. For example, when the unaccented *hana* 'nose' appears

type	E1		E2		compound accent location	tendency
	accented mora	mora count	accented mora	mora count		
I	0	2	any	2	unaccented	strong
II	any	any	any	1~2	E1 final syllable	weak
III	any	any	-2, -3, -4	3~4	E2 accent preserved	strong
IV	any	any	any	5+	E2 accent preserved	strong
V	any	any	0, -1	3~4	E2 initial mora	strong

Table 2.7: Major compound accent types

before the accented *uta* 'song' or *kuso* 'excrement', we obtain the unaccented compounds *hana+uta* 'humming' and *hana+kuso* 'snot'.

The rather weak tendency expressed as Type II is that, when E2 is short (1μ~2μ) then compound accent is placed on the final syllable (§2.4)—not mora—of E1. Let us take the place name Yamagata (itself analysable as a compound) as an example. Unbound, this is accented as *yamagata*. When combined with the 1μ E2 *ši* 'city' or the 2μ E2 *eki* 'station', it yields the compounds *yamagata+ši* 'Yamagata City' and *yamagata+eki* 'Yamagata Station'. Here, as the Type II tendency predicts, the accent is on the final syllable of E1, *ta*. Should, however, the final syllable of E1 consist of more than 1μ, for example the place name Sendai, ordinarily accented *seNdai*, then the accent locus is thrown forward to the first mora of that syllable, in this instance to the *da* of E1: *seNdai+ši* 'Sendai City' and *seNdai+eki* 'Sendai Station'. There are, however, so many exceptions, caveats and rules within rules that Type II has minor pedagogical worth.

Types III, IV and V are much more useful, albeit applicable to fewer compounds. When E2 has 3μ~4μ and its accent is non-final (Type III), or when E2 has 5μ+ (Type IV), then the E2 accent is preserved as that of the compound as a whole. An example of Type III is *jiNkoo* 'artificial' + *činoo* 'intelligence' → *jiNkoo+činoo* 'AI'; of Type IV *supoocu* 'sports' + *direkutaa* 'director' → *supoocu+direkutaa* 'director of sports'. Type V states that when E2 has 3μ~4μ and is either unaccented or accented finally, then the accent shifts to the initial mora of E2. For example, *kakutei* 'confirmation' + *šiNkoku* 'tax return' (both E1 and E2 are unaccented) → *kakutei+šiNkoku* 'final tax declaration'.

The foregoing discussion applies only to compounds with a clear modifier-head structure (the overwhelming majority), not to copulative compounds (§5.4) where, semantically, either element is analysable as the head. With these compounds, the accent of E2 is deleted and that of E1 preserved: *haru* 'spring' + *aki* 'autumn' → *haru+aki* 'spring and autumn'. This applies equally to reduplicative copulative compounds: *yama* 'mountain' + *yama* 'mountain' → *yama+yama* 'mountains'. With reduplicative mimetics (§5.2), the location of the accent is generally on the initial mora of E1: *surasura* 'smooth' or *surasura=to* 'smoothly'. When followed by a copula (§3.6), however, a reduplicative mimetic deaccents: *surasura=da* 'it is smooth'.

Finally, a quick look at compound numerals (§5.8), an area even more complex than what we have already discussed. Two main types of compound accent are found: those where the accent of the rightmost, and those where the accent of the leftmost, element is preserved. The former include the 50, 500, 80, 800 series (*gojuuiči* '51'); the latter include the 30, 300, 40, 400, 70, 700, 90, 900 series (*saNjuuiči* '31'). Longer numerals may contain two accented moras and are thus not two compounds, but two distinct prosodic words. When numerals combine with classifiers (§5.8), yet more complexities arise which space precludes us from discussing.

2.8 Phonological Play

Like any language, cases of phonology-based games and puzzles, or the appropriation of phonology for metalinguistic purposes, occur in Japanese. In the short space available, we will be able to cover only a selection of such cases.

Fig. 2.8: *A pentagonal iyokan*

Punning, or *dajare*, is a rich vein of phonological play. Some puns are intended as jokes, the poorer of which, like *sukii=ga suki* 'I like skiing' or *ikura=wa ikura* 'how much is the salmon roe?', are typically termed *oyajigyagu* 'old duffer jokes'. Other puns, however, have attained mainstream cultural or commercial status. Sea bream (*tai*), for example, is often served at up-market 'celebratory' (*omedeta-i*) feasts; iyokan, a kind of citrus fruit (Fig. 2.8), are cultivated for the examination market using pentagonal frames to create *gokaku=no iyokaN* 'pentagonal iyokan' (≈ *gookaku=no i-i yokaN* 'good hunch you'll pass'); and 5-yen (*go-eN*) coins are thrown into offertory boxes at shrines to invoke 'destiny' (*goeN*), while 10-yen coins are avoided because whatever one is wishing for will only come to pass 'far' (*too-i* ≈ *too* '10') in the future.

Palindromes, or *kaibun*, are another example of phonological play. These work at the level of the mora (§2.4) and range from the short individual word, such as *to.ma.to* 'tomato' or *ši.N.bu.N.ši* 'newspaper', to craftily complex sentences, such as *sa.ku.ra to.r-u=no.ni pa.pa=ni no.r-u=to ra.ku=sa* 'picking cherry blossoms is easier when sitting on dad's shoulders'.

Both puns and palindromes are found across many cultures. Not so is the widespread use of phonological mnemonics, in particular those used to memorize numbers, especially in phone numbers and advertising. At their most basic level, each of the digits 0–10 has at least one native and at least one Sino-Japanese (§7.1) pronunciation, as shown in Table 2.8. Foreign stratum pronunciations may also be

	native	Sino-Japanese	foreign
0	**ma**ru	**re**i	**oo**
1	**hi**to	**i**či	**wa**N
2	**fu**ta	**ni**~ji	**cu**u
3	**mi**cu	**sa**N	**su**rii
4	**yo**N~**yo**cu	**ši**	
5	**i**cucu	**go**	
6	**mu**cu	**ro**ku	
7	**na**na	**ši**či	
8	**ya**cu	**ha**či	
9	**ko**kono	**kyuu**~**ku**	
10	**to**o	**juu**~**ji**Q	**te**N

Table 2.8: *Number mnemonics*

appropriated, although these are typically restricted to 0–3 and 10. Not a great deal of scope for pithy taglines is offered by these pronunciations, however, and so in practice only the initial mora (indicated in bold in the table) of a given pronunciation suffices. This widens the possible mapping considerably, especially with the native numerals. Numeral mapping may be expanded still further by the possibility of affixing to an initial mora a further unrelated mora (2 = *fuyu* 'winter', 1 = *ima* 'now'), with vowel lengthening an especially common strategy (1717 = *i-i=naa i-i=naa* '[expression of envy]'). When orthographic ruses are thrown into the mix, such as adding or deleting *dakuten* diacritics (§4.6) and rebuses—*wa* for 0 (a wheel, *wa*, is round like the numeral 0) or 8 (the topic particle *wa* is written は <ha>: §4.6)—a memorable phrase can be created for almost any numeral string through phonological mapping. Examples include phone numbers (*hai ik-oo ik-oo* 'yes, let's go let's go' for 811515, the last six digits of a well-known Yamagata City taxi firm's telephone number), memorable dates (*i-i kuni* 'good country' for 1192, the year of the founding of the Kamakura shogunate) and, often amusingly forced, in mathematics (*fujisaNroku oomu nak-u* 'a parrot squawks in the Mount Fuji foothills' for 2.2360679, the square root of 5).

There exist a number of games and secret languages that operate on the level of the mora. The most widely played mora-based game is *shiritori*, where a player must make a word beginning with the final mora of the word uttered by the previous player. Uttering a word ending in the mora nasal N (§2.4) results in forfeiting the game: *jigoku* 'hell' → *kura* 'warehouse' → *raišuu* 'next week' → *ucubyoo* 'depression' → *ooeN* 'aid, moral support' → !OUT!.

Similar to Pig Latin in English, the *babibu* secret language can be analysed as utilizing both phonological and orthographic play (§4.12). Here, the 'secret' mora *b*V is inserted after each mora, with V being a vowel identical to that of the previous mora: *yamaji* 'mountain path' → *yabamabajibi* or *jigoku* 'hell' → *jibigobokubu*. The orthographic component of the game is apparent in the fact that the mora obstruent Q (§2.4) is rendered as *cu* (← kana orthography っ <cu>); glides (§2.4) written with minuscule *kana* are granted full moraic status; and the long vowels *oo* and *ee* are rendered *ou* and *ei* when spelling dictates. Meanwhile, the mora nasal N is followed by the 'default' secret mora *bu*. Thus, *miQcu* 'three' → *mibicubucubu*, *šare* 'fashion' → *šibiyabarebe*, *kirei* 'pretty, clean' → *kibirebeibi* and *waNtaN* 'wonton' → *wabaNbutabaNbu*. The ultimate *babibu* word is perhaps the delivery service *taQkyuubiN* 'Takkyūbin' which has it all: this becomes *tabacubukibiyubuububibiNbu*.

2.9 Phonology through Time

Quite a few of the phonological phenomena discussed in this chapter can be better comprehended through examining the phonology of earlier periods of the language—Old Japanese (OJ) and Middle Japanese (MJ). Whilst necessarily brief, in this unit we cover some of the major phonological developments pertinent to Modern Japanese (MoJ). We also point the reader to §1.3, where a brief sketch of each of the historical periods of the language is provided, and to §3.15 where a brief history of Japanese grammar is given.

Japanese vowel phonemes—as illustrated in Fig. 2.3—have remained largely unchanged since the beginning of the 9th century, only *u* differing in its surface realization: it was formerly more rounded and thus closer to modern Western Japanese (§7.9, §7.11). Before the 9th century, however, as documented in texts by the use of two sets of man'yōgana (§1.3, §4.6), the OJ vowels *i~e~o* possessed what is known in the Japanese linguistic tradition as the *kō-otsu* 'group A/B' distinction (indicated by a subscript $_1$ for *kō*-type and a subscript $_2$ for *otsu*-type). For example, *ko$_1$* in OJ *ko$_1$pi$_2$* (MoJ *koi*) 'love' was written with a range of different Chinese characters, including 子~古~兒~故, while *ko$_2$* in OJ *ko$_2$ko$_2$ro* 'heart' was written with a different set of characters, including 許~己~来~木. The A/B distinction was not present after all OJ consonants, but restricted to a select group: i_1~i_2 and e_1~e_2 are found after *k~g~p~b~m*, with o_1~o_2 after *k~g~s~z~t~d~n~y~r*. The phonemic significance of these distinctions is one of the great debates of Japanese linguistics. Traditionally, it has been suggested that OJ possessed eight distinct vowels (or diphthongs). In recent years, however, an increasing number of scholars have suggested that some of the distinctions are based on the presence or absence of glides (§2.4), not on the actual phonetic value of the vowels themselves.

In comparison to MoJ, the consonant phonology of earlier stages of the language was considerably less complex. As illustrated in Table 2.9.1, where an arrow → indicates 'from MJ onwards', OJ had only 13 consonant phonemes, while MJ had 16 (compare with Table 2.2). The OJ voiceless alveolar fricative *s* is generally

	bilabial	alveolar	palatal	velar	moraic
plosive	p b	t d		k g	
fricative	→f	s z			→ Q
nasal	m	n			→ N
tap		r			
glide			y	w	

Table 2.9.1: *Old and Middle Japanese consonant phonemes*

held to have possessed three allophones in OJ: [ts] before the back vowels *a~o* (MoJ *asa* 'hemp' and *soko* 'base' were OJ *a*[ts]*a* and [ts]*o₂ko₂*), [ɕ] or similar before the front vowels *i~e* (MoJ *kase* 'shackle' was OJ *ka*[ɕ]*e*) and [s] before *u*. Conversely, unlike MoJ, OJ *t* is generally believed to have exhibited no allophonic variation, being realized as [t] even before the high vowels *i~u*: MoJ *čiči* 'father' and *nacu* 'summer' were OJ [t]*i*[t]*i* and *na*[t]*u*. By the end of the MJ period, both *s* and *t* had developed the allophonic variation they exhibit in the modern language, although the [ɕ]-allophone of *s* before *e* lingered on for some time and indeed may still be found in peripheral dialects today (§7.10, §7.11).

MoJ *h~f* were *p* in OJ, so MoJ *haha* 'mother' was, interestingly, *papa* in OJ (§2.5.2). When word-initial, *p* slowly shifted to *f* between the 9th and 16th centuries, and then, from the very beginning of the MoJ period, lenited further to *h* everywhere except before *u*. The shift *p* → *h* would have been initiated, and terminated, not just at different times in different dialects but possibly also according to socio-economic group, profession or caste. Although exactly when and where it first began is a highly controversial topic, we do know for certain that it had been completed among speakers in the far south by the 16th century because the Portuguese-speaking Jesuits (§1.3, §8.13) who arrived in Kagoshima in the 1540s transcribed this consonant by means of a Roman alphabet <f>.

Far less controversial is that from the 10th century, non-initial *p* in native stratum words disappeared before *u* and become *w* elsewhere: *ap-u* 'meet' → *a-u*, *kapa* 'river' → *kawa*, *kopi* 'love' → *kowi* (→ *koi*), *pape* 'housefly' → *fawe* (→ *hae*), *kapo* 'face' → *kawo* (→ *kao*). There are a small number of exceptions to this change, perhaps caused by orthographic restoration or dialect borrowing. The word for 'mother' *haha*, mentioned earlier, is one: the MoJ form is not, as it 'should' be, *hawa. Other exceptions include *afure-ru* (*aure-ru) 'overflow', *ahiru* (*airu) 'duck' and *hofur-u* (*hoor-u) 'slaughter'.

What is known in the Japanese tradition as the *sei-daku* 'clear-muddy' distinction was in OJ quite different from what it is today. Instead of the voiced/voiceless distinction found in MoJ, the distinction was one of prenasalization: in place of MoJ *p~b*, *t~d*, *k~g*, *s~z*, OJ had *p~ᵐp*, *t~ⁿt*, *k~ᵑk*, *s~ⁿs* (we phonemicize the *daku* variants as *b~d~g~z* throughout this unit). Both members of an OJ *sei-daku* pair are believed to have been allophonically (§2.1) voiced in intervocalic position: MoJ

chronology	'sound'	'man'	'countryside'	'barbarian'	'branch'	'smile'
Old Japanese	oto₂	woto₂ko₁	winaka	emi₁si	yeda	wemi
Early Middle Japanese	woto	wotoko	winaka	yemisi	yeda	wemi
Late Middle Japanese	woto	wotoko	inaka	yemisi	yeda	yemi
Modern Japanese	oto	otoko	inaka	emiši	eda	emi

Table 2.9.2: Semi-vowel sound changes

sugata 'shape' was OJ *su[ⁿg]a[d]a*. When exactly the *sei-daku* distinction shifted from prenasalization to voicing is not entirely clear, but we can infer it was already well underway by the time of the Jesuits, who note that vowels were nasalized before *g~d* but make little or no mention of *b~z*. The Jesuits also make no mention of intervocalic voicing, so we can assume that this feature of the language was lost or in decline by the end of the MJ period. Despite the passing of more than a thousand years, the *sei-daku* distinction has not shifted from prenasalization to voicing in all varieties of the language: the older 'version' is still found in Tōhoku dialects (§7.10) to this day.

Phonotactically, though quasi-illicit in MoJ (§2.5), *y* could appear before *e* in OJ (MoJ *ebi* 'shrimp' was OJ *ye₁bi₁*), while *w* could appear not just before *a*, as in MoJ, but also before *e~i~o* (MoJ *emi* 'smile', *inošiši* 'wild boar', *otoko* 'man' were OJ *wemi*, *wino₂sisi*, *woto₂ko₁*). Beginning around the 10th century and extending into the 14th, a series of sound changes involving these two semi-vowels occurred, as illustrated in Table 2.9.2: *o* merged with *wo*; *wi* with *i*; and *e*, then *we*, with *ye*.

OJ possessed strict phonotactic restrictions on native words. These could not begin in *b~d~g~z*—*daku* members of the *sei-daku* pair—nor could they begin in *r*. Syllable structure (§2.4) was strictly limited to CV syllables, with V syllables tolerated only word-initially. Compounds were typically modified to avoid VV strings, although it should be borne in mind that the vast bulk of the OJ corpus is poetry and any such modification could well have been a poetic licence to fit the metre: **waga+imo* 'my+beloved' → *wagimo* 'my beloved' (vowel elision), **naga+iki₁* 'long+breath' → *nageki₁* 'cry of sorrow' (vowel coalescence), **paru+ame₂* 'spring+rain' → *parusame₂* 'spring drizzle' (consonant epenthesis: §5.3). By Early Middle Japanese (EMJ), under the influence of Sino-Japanese (SJ: §7.1) and the shift from a syllable- to a mora-based phonology, VV strings had come to be tolerated, as they are today (though see below). Native words beginning in *b~d~g~z* are still rare, though include *ba* 'place' and *gara* 'pattern'. They are for the most part derogatory (*zama* 'bad state': compare *sama* 'state, condition'), derived from mimetics (*debu* 'fatty' ← *debudebu* 'chubby') or have been brought about by the elision of an initial vowel (*de-ru* ~ *das-u* 'leave' ← OJ *ide-ru* ~ *idas-u*).

A major phonological development beginning in EMJ was the emergence of *onbin* 'euphony', a series of sporadic sound changes manifesting itself in a number of different ways. These included simple elision (*tukitati* → *tuitati* 'first day of the month'), elision accompanied by nasalization and voicing (*kagupasi* → *kaNbasi* 'fragrant') or elision accompanied by gemination (*poris-u* → *poQs-u* 'desire': §2.2). While generally not productive in MoJ, *onbin* is still found in the *-te* and *-ta* forms of verbs (*yom-u* 'read' → *yoN-de* ~ *yoN-da*; *a-u* 'meet' → *aQ-te* ~ *aQ-ta*: Table 3.7.2) and, in Western Japanese (§7.9), the adverbial of adjectives (Eastern *širo-ku nar-u* ~ Western *široo nar-u* 'become white': §3.7, §7.9). The phenomenon of *onbin* gave birth to the mora consonants (§2.2), shown in the rightmost column of Table 2.9.1, which in turn led to the appearance of heavy syllables (§2.4), although it is likely that mimetics (§5.2) already possessed both these in earlier periods.

Onbin was not the only factor to influence syllable structure. The massive influx of Chinese loanwords (§7.1) also played a crucial role. In addition to possessing heavy syllables, SJ also had post-consonantal glides. These took the form of both *y*-glides (*kya*, *kyu*, *kyo*) and *w*-glides (*kwa*, *kwi*, *kwe*), the former appearing in the written record from the early 9th, the latter from the 11th century. By Late Middle Japanese, a number of previously illicit VV strings (see above) introduced through *onbin* and SJ had coalesced into long vowels: *iu* → *yuu*, *eu* → *yoo*, *ou* → *oo*, *au* → *åå*. The last of these, *åå*, was transcribed as <ŏ> by the Jesuits and is thought to have been a long open-mid back rounded vowel [ɔː], similar to that found in English *caw*. The distinction between *oo*~*åå* is known as the *kai-gō* 'open-closed' distinction in traditional Japanese linguistics. It had collapsed into *oo* by the 17th century, though can still be encountered in some Niigata and Nagano dialects and also in some Kyūshū dialects (albeit here with yet further change: §7.11).

CHAPTER 3 Grammar and Syntax

3.1 Parts of Speech and Word Order

Japanese, in common with all languages, is composed of a number of different parts of speech, or word classes, which can be classified in a variety of ways. In this analysis, we divide Japanese parts of speech into major parts of speech and minor parts of speech, the former expressing lexical meaning—referencing actual objects, actions or attributes—with the latter carrying out grammatical functions. Major parts of speech tend to be open classes (they contain large amounts of words which are easily supplemented), with minor parts of speech being closed classes (containing fewer words which are not easily supplemented). Both of these criteria are not without issue. Some word classes may possess lexical meaning, but have low productivity, such as Japanese verbal adjectives and adnouns. Likewise, a part of speech classified as major may possess grammatical subcategories. This is the case, for example, with formal nouns (§3.2), a subcategory of the Japanese noun.

Another common classification divides Japanese parts of speech into free forms and bound forms, the former being capable of occurring independently, with the latter 'bound' to, or dependent on, other words in a sentence. One well-known analysis that adheres to such a classification is the prescriptive 'school grammar' (§8.6) taught in primary and secondary schools. It is worth noting that Japanese lacks parts of speech which exist in English and many other languages (articles like *the* and *a*), while possessing parts of speech that may not exist in other languages.

Major parts of speech can be divided into three classes: nominals, verbals and modifiers. In the simplest terms, nominals denote things, both physical and abstract; verbals denote actions or attributes; while modifiers modify—add extra context to—nominals and verbals. From a syntactic point of view, nominals form a noun phrase (NP: a single noun or a phrase headed by a noun) which acts as an argument (subject, object) or predicate (the statement concerning the subject) of a sentence. When forming the predicate, nominals require a linking verb, or copula (similar to English *be*). Verbals, on the other hand, either modify a NP or act as a predicate, but cannot form arguments on their own. Finally, modifiers modify both NPs and verbals, but cannot act as arguments or predicates. Below, we will look at each of these three major classes and their subclasses in turn. The foregoing is summarized in Fig. 3.1. Not every word class given in Fig. 3.1 is tenable from a morphological or syntactic perspective, and several of these classes are merely

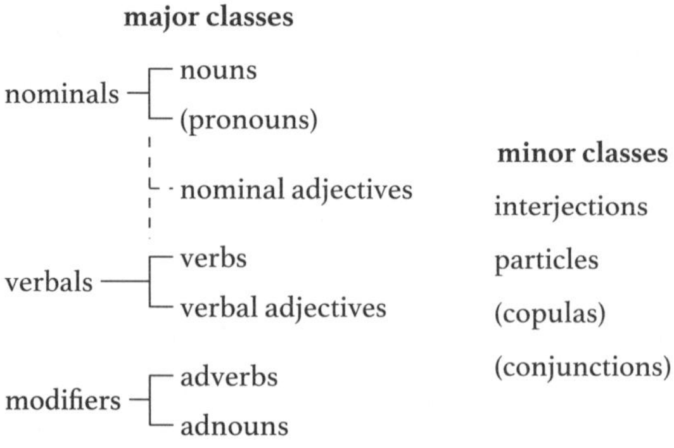

major classes

```
nominals ┬─ nouns
         ├─ (pronouns)
         └· nominal adjectives

verbals ┬─ verbs
        └─ verbal adjectives

modifiers ┬─ adverbs
          └─ adnouns
```

minor classes

interjections
particles
(copulas)
(conjunctions)

Fig. 3.1: Major and minor parts of speech

functional or semantic divisions. In such cases, the word class in question is placed in brackets. Nominal adjectives, which lie between nominals and verbals, are indicated by a dotted line.

Nominals consist of nouns and pronouns. Nouns are a lexical open class accounting for roughly 90% of Japanese vocabulary, while pronouns are more restricted in membership and more grammatical in nature. Nouns express concrete objects (*samurai* 'samurai', *očimuša* 'fallen warrior') or abstract notions (*bušidoo* 'way of the warrior', *seqpuku* 'ritual disembowelment'). They can be further broken down into common nouns, which express more generic concepts as in the examples above, and proper nouns, which refer to unique concepts such as names (§6.9).

Pronouns are nouns that can be substituted for other NPs. Unlike English, in which certain pronouns undergo inflection to indicate grammatical case (*I*, *me*, *my*, *mine*), Japanese pronouns are morphologically indistinguishable from other nouns. Japanese pronouns come in three flavours: personal, demonstrative and interrogative. Personal pronouns indicate grammatical person (*wataši* 'I', *anata* 'you'), while demonstratives indicate concepts in general (*kore* 'this', *koko* 'here') and interrogatives mark indefinite variables (*dare* 'who', *doko* 'where'). Nouns will be covered in §3.2, together with demonstratives, interrogatives and a third type of noun, known as the formal noun, which expresses grammatical meaning. Personal pronouns will be given their own coverage in §5.7, as well as being touched upon in §6.1 and §6.2.

The second major word class, verbals, includes verbs and verbal adjectives. Verbs are words that denote an action (*tabe-ru* 'eat', *ik-u* 'go') or state of being (*ar-u* 'be', *sobie-ru* 'tower over'), while verbal adjectives denote a quality (*ucukuši-i* 'beautiful', *kawai-i* 'cute'). Verbs and verbal adjectives take on grammatical meaning through agglutination (§1.2), a process in which morphemes, the smallest divisible units of meaning in a language, are strung together without undergoing phonological change. The verb stem (the base of a word to which affixes are added) *tabe-*, for example, has no grammatical meaning on its own, but can take on a plethora of meanings through the addition of verbal suffixes: *tabe-sase-rare-ta-i* 'want to be made to eat → want to be (force) fed' ('eat' + causative + passive + desiderative + nonpast).

In addition to verbal adjectives, Japanese possesses a second class of adjective, known as nominal adjectives, which straddle the categories of nominal and verbal. While verbal adjectives take agglutinative suffixes to modify NPs (*aka-i kuruma* 'a red car') or form predicates (*kuruma=ga aka-i* 'the car is red'), nominal adjectives are required to take the particle *na* (§3.5) when modifying NPs (*kirei=na heya* 'a clean room') and a copula (§3.6) when forming predicates (*mori=wa šizuka=da* 'the forest is quiet'). Thus, while adjectives from a semantic stance, morphologically speaking, nominal adjectives are closer to nominals than they are verbals. Verbs are dealt with in §3.3 and §3.4, with verbal suffixes covered in §3.7 and §3.8. Adjectives (verbal and nominal) are examined in §3.5. A special group of verbs and adjectives that express grammatical meaning, auxiliaries, is looked at in §3.9, with verbs of giving and receiving and benefactive auxiliaries covered in §3.10.

The final major class, modifiers, consists of adverbs and adnouns. Adverbs are words that modify verbs, adjectives and other adverbs, or entire verbal clauses and sentences. They express 'how' (*akuseku* 'diligently'), 'when' (*sugu* 'soon, shortly') or 'to what extent' (*iqpai* 'a lot, excessively') an action, event or condition occurs. Adnouns are a class of words that modify nouns, similar to adjectives, but cannot take suffixes or act as a predicate on their own: *arayuru* 'all', *taišita* 'extreme'. While both adverbs and adnouns express lexical meaning, the latter are a closed class consisting predominantly of fossilized forms derived from other parts of speech. Adverbs and adnouns will be covered, together with adjectives, in §3.5.

It is possible to classify minor parts of speech in a number of different ways. Here we will use a four-way classification: interjections, particles, copulas and conjunctions. Interjections are words that express a speaker's emotion (*waa* 'wow!', *yaqpari* 'as expected'), reaction to the addressee (*maji* 'you're kidding, right!?', *ee* 'I'm listening'), call attention (*sateto* 'onto the next subject', *hora* 'look!') or simply act as fillers (*eeqto, ano*). As their use is typically straightforward, we do not devote a separate unit to interjections in this volume.

Particles are short bound words which express the relationships between, or add extra context to, words in a sentence. A major function of particles is to mark case, a grammatical category indicating a noun's syntactic role in a phrase, clause or sentence. The particle *ga*, for example, marks the subject (nominative case), while *o* marks the object (accusative case) of a sentence: *misaki=ga* (subject) *suteeki=o* (object) *tabe-ta* (verb) 'Misaki ate a steak'. Particles can also mark derivation (*ni*: adverbializer; *no*: adnominalizer), topics (*wa, mo*), add emphasis (*ka, koso*: indefinite and definite emphasis, respectively), impose restrictions (*bakari, dake*: both 'only'), draw analogies (*sae, sura*: both 'even'), express speaker judgement (*yo, zo*: both exclamatives) or elicit information (*ne*, *na*, both confirmatives). Particles will be dealt with more fully in §3.12, with derivational particles given particular coverage in §3.13. The difference between the particles *wa* and *ga*, a notoriously difficult hurdle for L2 learners, will be touched upon in §3.14, along with the notion of topic.

Copulas are used to link noun predicates with their subjects or topics. These include the neutral copula *da*, its polite counterpart *des-u* and the analytic *de ar-u*, all roughly equivalent to English *be*. Etymologically, all copulas are fusions of particles with existential verbs (§3.4) and, similar to particles, are bound to their hosts. Thus, distributionally, copulas could be treated as a subcategory of particles. Unlike particles, however, copulas inflect, possessing many of the same forms as verbs: and it is for this reason that we give them special treatment in this description. Copulas will be covered in §3.6, along with the notion of 'predication'.

Finally, conjunctions are words that connect elements of a sentence (words, phrases or clauses), or entire sentences. These include, among others, coordinating (*oyobi* 'and', *aruiwa* 'or'), causal (*dakara* 'therefore', *šitagaǫte* 'accordingly') and adversative (*šikaši* 'however', *tokoroga* 'on the contrary') conjunctions. Similar to adnouns, all conjunctions are derived from other parts of speech, but are overall more etymologically transparent, making it difficult in many cases to draw a line between conjunctions and other parts of speech. Furthermore, from a syntactic stance, many conjunctions are better treated as conjunctive adverbs, similar to English *however* or *moreover*. For the above reasons, a large number of scholars do not posit the conjunction as an individual word class, but rather as a subcategory of adverbs. Conjunctions will be covered in §3.11.

The various parts of speech introduced above do not exist in a vacuum. They are put together in speech, or writing, by means of morphosyntax (morphology and syntax) to form a sentence: a unit of meaningful information. While single-word sentences, or holophrases, such as *kaji* 'fire!' or *sugee* 'wow!', are not rare in Japanese, in the majority of cases, to be meaningful, a sentence must contain a subject and predicate (although it is common for subjects to be omitted when understood by context: further below). To illustrate, consider the word *boku* 'I (male preferential)'. Used by itself out of context, this word communicates little. If we add the nominative case marker particle *ga*, to give *boku=ga*, we are no better off. But add extra information—*boku=ga tabe-ta* 'I ate'—and we have a fully-fledged sentence. The subject, in this case *boku*, is the actor; the predicate, *tabe-ta*, tells us about this actor. The predicate may include an object, indicated by a case marker particle (1), and any number of adverbial modifiers (2). In addition, both the subject and object may take adnominal modifiers (3) and the clause as a whole may take any number of subordinate clauses (4), or act as the subordinate clause of a main clause itself.

(1) boku=ga   raameɴ=o   tabe-ta
    I=NOM   ramen=ACC   eat-PST
    'I ate **ramen**.'

(2) kinoo   ičibaɴ   naka=no   i-i   yuujiɴ=to
    yesterday   most   relationship=GEN   good-NPST   friend=COM

    hisašiburi=ni   futari=dake=de   raameɴ=o   tabe-ta
    long.time=ADVLZ   2.people=only=LOC   ramen=ACC   eat-PST
    'I ate ramen **yesterday together with my best friend, just the two of us, for the first time in a while**.'

(3) onaka=no   sui-ta   yuuki=ga   futari-buɴ=no
    stomach=GEN   be.empty-PST   Yūki=NOM   2.people-portion=ADNLZ

    raameɴ=o   tabe-ta
    ramen=ACC   eat-PST
    '**Hungry** Yūki ate **two portions of** ramen.'

(4) karamiso+raameɴ=o   tabe-ta-ku   naq-ta=kara   /
    spicy.miso+ramen=ACC   eat-DESS-ADV   become-PST=CAUSL

    ryuušaɴhai=ni   iq-te   /   tabe-ta
    Ryū.Shanghai=DAT   go-CVB   eat-PST
    'I had a craving for spicy miso ramen / so I went to Ryū Shanghai (name of ramen restaurant) / and ate some.'

As can be observed from (1)–(4), where *boku* is the subject, *raameɴ* the object and *tabe-ta* the verb, Japanese sentences follow SOV (subject-object-verb) word order, with adverbial modifiers preceding the verb and adnominal modifiers preceding the subject or object (§1.2). Although a degree of flexibility in word order is permitted, it usually indicates a shift in focus. Thus, (5) emphasizes the fact that it was the speaker—and no one else—who ate the ramen. Such inversion is especially common when topicalizing (§3.14) the object of a sentence. This is achieved by replacing the accusative case marker particle *o* with the topic marker particle *wa*, as in (6). In addition to SOV (1)–(4) and OSV (5)–(6), both SVO (7) and OVS (8) sentences are also heard in casual speech. Technically ungrammatical, they are rarely used in formal speech or writing. VSO or VOS sentences are rarely encountered in any register.

(5) raameɴ=o   boku=ga   tabe-ta   'It was me who ate the ramen.'
    ramen=ACC   I=NOM   eat-PST

(6) raameɴ=wa   boku=ga   tabe-ta   'As for the ramen, it was me who ate it.'
    ramen=TOP   I=NOM   eat-PST

(7) boku=ga   tabe-ta,   raameN=o   'I ate it—the ramen, that is.'
    I=NOM   eat-PST   ramen=ACC

(8) raameN=o   tabe-ta,   boku=ga   'Ate ramen, me.'
    ramen=ACC   eat-PST   I=NOM

Adnominal modifiers possess the most rigid constraints, typically only occurring directly before the modified noun or another modifier (9). Adverbial modifiers, on the other hand, display the largest degree of freedom. The adverb *yoku* 'frequently', for example, can come anywhere before the verb it modifies—it can precede the verb (*yoku tabe-ru*), the object (*yoku raameN=o*) or even the subject (*yoku boku=ga*)—with little difference in meaning. Subordinate clauses typically precede the main clause, with the final verb of the sentence governing the tense, aspect or mood of the entire sentence. Thus, in (9) the causative -*(s)ase-ru* and past tense -*ta* suffixes following the final verb of the sentence, *tabe-ru*, apply to *cure-te* (the converbal, or '-*te* form', of *cure-ru* 'take (along with)': §3.7) as well.

(9) onaka=ga   sui-te   uejini+ši-soo=daQta
    stomach=NOM   be.empty-CVB   starve.to.death+do.ADV-EVDNM=COP.PST

    yuuki=o   ryuušaNhai=ni   cure-te   /   raameN=o   tabe-sase-ta
    Yūki=ACC   Ryū.Shanghai=DAT   take-CVB   ramen=ACC   eat-CAUS-PST
    'I took **hungry and about to starve to death** Yūki to Ryū Shanghai / and fed him (lit. let him eat) some ramen.'

(10) A: raameN=o   tabe-ta=no=wa   dare=da   'A: Who ate the ramen!?'
        ramen=ACC   eat-PST=NMNLZ=TOP   who=COP.NPST
     B: boku=da   'B: [It was] me.'
        I=COP.NPST

Subject dropping is a well-known areal feature of East Asian languages and Japanese is no exception. While example (1) is perfectly legitimate, in actual conversation the subject *boku=ga* would typically be dropped when understood through context, as in (2), (4) and (9). Likewise, the object, and in more casual speech, the verb, may also be dropped, or replaced with a copula, when understood through context, as in (10). One may argue that the subjectless sentence is actually the default rather than the exception, Japanese being a topic-prominent language (§3.14).

3.2 Nouns, Pronouns and Formal Nouns

As discussed in §3.1, Japanese nominals consist of nouns and pronouns, with pronouns capable of being further broken down into personal, demonstrative and interrogative. Below we will deal with nouns in general, followed by demonstrative pronouns, interrogative pronouns and a third type of noun expressing grammatical meaning, formal nouns, leaving the discussion of personal pronouns, which display a large degree of gender and register-based variation, to §5.7 (see also §6.1, §6.2).

Japanese nouns are fairly straightforward in their morphology. Unlike most European languages, Japanese nouns are not marked for gender (masculine, feminine, neuter), do not bear a countable/uncountable distinction (Eng. *I hate chicken* (the meat) ~ *I hate chickens* (the living bird, cowards)) and do not undergo inflection to indicate grammatical case (nominative, accusative, genitive) or number (singular, plural, dual). Instead, to mark case, a Japanese noun is followed by a case marker particle. For example, the noun *inu* 'dog' takes the case marker particle *ga* (*inu=ga*) to express the nominative case (subject) and *o* (*inu=o*) to mark the accusative case (object). We will deal with case and case marker particles in detail in §3.12. While nouns do not typically mark plurality, there are four pluralizer suffixes, *-tači* ~ *-ra* ~ *-domo* ~ *-gata*, each carrying their own connotations: see §5.7 for more detail. Apart from personal pronouns, these suffixes are not obligatory for marking plurality—lifeform nouns and demonstratives can be singular or plural depending on context without the need for a pluralizer. Less commonly, nouns undergo reduplication to mark plurality, although this process is largely unproductive in the modern language: see §5.3 for examples.

Demonstratives and interrogatives make up a four-tier system, known in Japanese as *kosoado*, comprising proximal (close to speaker: *kore* 'this', *koicu* 'this bloke'), medial (close to addressee: *soko* 'there', *sočira* 'there, that person, you (polite)'), distal (distant from both speaker and addressee, 'yon' in some English dialects: *are* 'that over there, yon', *aQči* 'over there ~ yonder, that man over there ~ yon man') and indefinite (*doko* 'where', *dare* 'who'). The term *kosoado* comes from the roots *ko~so~a~do*, which are shared across proximals, medials, distals and indefinites. In addition to pronouns, the *kosoado* system also contains sets of adverbs (*koo* 'this way', *soNnani* 'that much', *dooŠite* 'what way, why') and adnouns (*ano [hito]* 'that [person] over there', *doNna [hito]* 'what kind of [person]': §3.5). Complementing the *do* set, there exist sets of interrogatives starting in *i* and *na*: *icu* 'when', *ikucu* 'how many, how old' (both nouns), *ikura* 'how much', *ikaga~ikani* 'how' (both adverbs), *nani~naN* 'what' (both nouns), *naze~naNde* 'why' (both adverbs). See Table 3.2.1 for a list of commonly used *kosoado* demonstratives (proximal/medial/distal) and interrogatives (indefinite).

Demonstrative usage can be separated into two broad categories: spatial deixis, already dealt with above, in which the physical surroundings of the speaker or addressee are referenced, and discourse deixis, in which previous or current discourse is referenced. Here, we will take a brief look at discourse deixis, this being the most confusing for L2 learners. As a general rule, in speech, proximals reference information that is new to the addressee (1), medials information previously introduced by the addressee but new to the speaker (2) and distals information

word class	reference	proximal	medial	distal	indefinite
noun	thing	kore	sore	are	dore
	place	koko	soko	asoko	doko
	place, person (casual)	koqči	soqči	aqči	doqči
	place, person (polite)	kočira	sočira	ačira	dočira
	place, person (polite)	—	—	kanata*¹	donata
	person	—	—	kare*¹	dare*¹
	person (anti-honorific: §6.4)	koicu	soicu	aicu	doicu
adverb	way, method	koo	soo	aa	doo
		koošite	soošite	aašite	doošite*²
	degree	koɴnani	soɴnani	aɴnani	doɴnani
adnoun	thing, place, person	kono	sono	ano ~ kano*¹	dono
	attribute	koɴna	soɴna	aɴna	doɴna

*¹ *kare~dare~kanata~kano* are remnants of an older system in which distal demonstratives were expressed by the stem *ka* and interrogatives by *ta* (→ *da*). The form *anata* 'you', a variant of *kanata*, is no longer used as a demonstrative and only as a personal pronoun (§5.7) in the modern language.
*² in addition to 'what way', *doošite* also carries the meaning 'why'.

Table 3.2.1: *Commonly used* kosoado *demonstratives and interrogatives*

shared by both the speaker and addressee (3). In addition, distals may be used when reminiscing about (or attempting to recall) past experiences (4) or when referring to awkward or socially taboo situations in a circumlocutive manner (5). In writing, proximals present a new topic, while medials refer to previous discourse. Distals are rarely used in writing outside of quotations and monologue.

(1) koɴnani   gaɴbaq-ta=noni   kat-e-na-kaqta
    this.much try-PST=CONC   win-POT-NEG-PST
    'I tried this much and I still couldn't win.' (new to addressee)

(2) A: kinoo   juuni-jikaɴ=mo hatarai-ta B: sore=wa   taiheɴ=da
       yesterday 12-hour=ITOP   work-PST   that-TOP severe=COP.NPST
    A: 'Yesterday, I worked for 12 hours.'   B: 'That's rough.' (new to speaker B)

(3) ano   hito=wa   totemo i-i   hito=da=ne
    that   person=TOP   very   good-NPST   person=COP.NPST=CONF
    'She's (lit. that person's) a really good person.' (shared by speaker and addressee)

(4) ano   toki   moqto gaɴbar-eba   yo-kaqta=noni
    that   time   more   try.hard-PROV good-PST=CONC
    'If only I'd tried harder back then (things might've been different).' (reminiscing)

3.2 Nouns, Pronouns and Formal Nouns

form	lexical meaning	grammatical functions, notes and examples
aida[=ni]	interval	• SUB: simultaneous (dekake-te i-ru aida=ni 'while we were out')
amari[=ni]	remainder	• SUB: excessiveness (acu-sa=no amari=ni 'due to the excessive heat') • has negative implications
cuide=ni	chance	• SUB: supplementary action (ik-u cuide=ni yor-u 'stop by (on the side) when going')
cumori	intention	• MDL: intention (ik-u cumori=da 'intend to go, plan to go')
hazu	nock (of an arrow)	• MDL: necessity or probability (ik-u hazu=da 'should go', soko=ni i-ru hazu=da 'is probably there'; see also example in text)
kagiri	limit	• SUB: limitative (kare-ra=ga ik-u kagiri 'as long as they go'; see also example in text)
koto	(abstract) thing	• NMNLZ • MDL: confirmation (ik-u koto=da 'be sure to go') • also used as an exclamative discourse particle (§3.12)
kuse=ni	habit	• SUB: concessive (make-ta kuse=ni akirame-na-i 'even though they lost, they still won't give up') • has negative implications
mama[=de]	condition	• ASP: stative (doa=o ake-ta mama=da 'the door's been left open') • SUB: stative condition (pajama=o kita mama 'while wearing pyjamas')
mono~moɴ	(physical) thing	• NMNLZ • necessity or realization (ik-u mono=da 'should really go') • also used as an exclamative discourse particle (§3.12) • moɴ is casual
sei[=de]	consequence	• SUB: causal (ame=ga fuq-ta sei=de okure-ta 'was late because it rained') • has negative implications
soo	etymology disputed	• EVD: hearsay (ik-u soo=da 'I've heard she'll go')
tame[=ni]	advantage	• SUB: purposive (hašir-u tame=ni raɴniɴgušuuzu=o kaq-ta 'bought running shoes to go running with') • SUB: causal (hašiq-ta tame cukare-ta 'got tired from running')
toki	time	• SUB: temporal condition (ik-u toki 'when I go')
tokoro[=de]	place	• NMNLZ • ASP: prospective (see example in text) • SUB: temporal condition (doa=o ake-ta tokoro 'on opening the door')
toori[=ni]	passage	• SUB: similitude (ue=de nobe-ta toori 'as stated above', iw-are-ta toori=ni su-ru 'do as you're told')
wake	reason	• MDL: reasoning (sore=de i-i wake=da 'that's fine, for obvious reasons') • often in the negative (ik-u wake=ga na-i 'no way I'll go')
yoo[=ni]	appearance	• EVD: visual evidence (see example in text) • SUB: purposive (okure-na-i yoo=ni su-ru 'try to not be late') • nominal adjective after EVD usage (ik-u yoo=na ki=ga su-ru 'have a feeling that he'll go')

ASP = aspect, EVD = evidentiality, MDL = modality, NMNLZ = nominalizer, SUB = subordinator

Table 3.2.2: *Commonly used formal nouns*

(5) are=no   keqka=wa   doo   naq-ta=no
    that=GEN results=TOP how   become-PST=Q
    'How were the results of the you-know-what?' (circumlocutive)

Finally, we turn our attention to formal nouns. Formal nouns are nouns that have been bleached of their lexical meaning to carry out a grammatical function, a process commonly referred to as grammaticalization. Such nouns follow the nonpast, past, negative and desiderative forms of verbs and adjectives (§5.7, §5.8) or, in some cases, a noun phrase (NP) with the adnominalizer particle *no* (§3.13), forming a NP with the formal noun as its head. Most formal nouns are also lexical nouns—that is, in addition to being used to mark a grammatical function, they can still be used in their original lexical sense: *aida*, for example, can be used to express the lexical meaning 'interval' or to form a simultaneous subordinate clause: *ne-te i-ru aida* 'while I was sleeping'.

The majority of formal nouns act as subordinators, following the head of a clause and marking it as subordinate: *kagiri* 'limit' in *šiQ-te i-ru kagiri* 'as far as I know'. A few simply act as nominalizers, turning the preceding verb or adjective into its nominal equivalent: *koto* 'thing' in *kaNgae-ru koto* 'thinking thing → thoughts'. Yet others mark modality (speaker intention or judgement concerning a proposition: *hazu* 'nock (of an arrow)' in *tanoši-i hazu* 'it should be fun'), aspect (the state of an action in terms of progression: *tokoro* 'place' in *ima ik-u tokoro=da* 'I'm about to go') or evidentiality (speaker assessment of evidence that an event will occur: *yoo* 'appearance' in *ik-u yoo=da* 'it appears he'll go'). A number of formal nouns, such as *tokoro* (subordinator + nominalizer + aspect marker) or *mono* (nominalizer + modality marker), straddle multiple categories. When acting as subordinators, formal nouns typically take the derivational particles *ni* and *de* (§3.13). These particles may be optional (*aida* ~ *aida=ni* are both licit) or mandatory (*cuide=ni*, but not **cuide*), depending on the noun. A list of common formal nouns (not intended to be comprehensive) is given, along with examples, in Table 3.2.2.

Nouns also take a large array of derivational suffixes to form other parts of speech. While an in-depth discussion of these suffixes is beyond the scope of this volume, a few of the more common suffixes include the adjectivizers *-raši-i* ~ *-Qpo-i* and the nominal adjectivizer *-mitai*, all meaning, roughly, '-like': *otoko-raši-i* 'manly', *mizu-Qpo-i* 'watery', *e-mitai=na fuukei* 'picturesque scenery'. These three suffixes are of especial interest as they can also follow predicates in general (including verbs and adjectives, but not copulas) to express evidentiality: *dare=mo ik-ana-i-mitai* 'it seems that nobody will go'. When following predicates, *-raši-i* and *-Qpo-i* lose their inflections. Thus, while *ašita=wa ame-rašii* 'they say it'll rain tomorrow' is licit, **ašita=wa ame-raši-ku na-i* 'they say it won't rain tomorrow' is not.

3.3 Verbs: Morphophonology

Japanese verbs belong to one of four major classes: consonant-stem (*ik-u* 'go', *hašir-u* 'run'), in which the stem of the verb ends in *k*, *g*, *s~š*, *t~č~c*, *n*, *b*, *m*, *r*; vowel-stem (*oki-ru* 'wake up', *tabe-ru* 'eat'), in which the stem ends in *i* or *e*; S-irregular, in which the stem alternates between *se~ši~su~s* (*se-zu* ~ *ši-te* ~ *su-ru* ~ *s-are-ru*, all forms of 'do'); and K-irregular, in which the stem alternates between *ko~ki~ku* (*ko-zu* ~ *ki-te* ~ *ku-ru*, all forms of 'come'). The consonant- and vowel-stem classes comprise the bulk of Japanese verbs, with the S- and K-irregular classes containing only a single verb each: *su-ru* 'do', *ku-ru* 'come' and compounds thereof. Due to a series of historical sound changes (namely the weakening of intervocalic *p* to *w*, or its disappearance entirely: §2.9), some verbs with stems ending in the vowels *a~i~u~o* in the modern language actually function as consonant-stem verbs: *a-u* 'meet' ← Old Japanese (OJ) *ap-u*, *i-u ~ yu-u* 'say' ← OJ *ip-u*, *su-u* 'suck' ← OJ *sup-u*, *omo-u* 'think' ← OJ *omop-u*. We will refer to such verbs as 'old *p*-stems' in the discussion below. Such old *p*-stems are easily distinguishable from vowel-stem verbs by observing their nonpast form: while vowel-stem verbs take the suffix *-ru*, old *p*-stems take *-u*: *i-ru* 'be' (vowel-stem) ~ *i-u* 'say' (old *p*-stem). What is problematic, and must be memorized, is the distinction between consonant-stem verbs ending in *ir-u* or *er-u* and vowel-stem verbs, which appear identical in the nonpast: *kir-u* 'cut' ~ *ki-ru* 'wear' (*kiru*), *her-u* 'decrease' ~ *he-ru* 'elapse' (*heru*).

Verbs are typically given in dictionaries, and discussed metalinguistically, in what is known as the dictionary, or canonical, form. This is the stem of the verb plus the nonpast suffix: *-u* for consonant-stems (*ik-u*, *hašir-u*), *-ru* for vowel-stems (*oki-ru*, *tabe-ru*) and irregulars (*su-ru*, *ku-ru*). Sino-Japanese (SJ: §7.1) and foreign borrowings (§7.2, §7.3) can only function as verbs through derivation (§5.3), typically as so-called nominal verbs. These are nouns followed by the verb *su-ru* 'do': *beNkyoo+su-ru* 'study, lit. do studying', *raNniNgu+su-ru* 'go running, lit. do running'. This use of *su-ru* is sometimes referred to as a light verb, since it relies on the preceding noun for semantic content. SJ nouns may also take the suffixes *-ji-ru* (vowel-stem) ~ *-zu-ru* (S-irregular): *šiN-ji-ru* 'believe', *too-zu-ru* 'throw'. Less commonly, the suffix *-s-u* (consonant-stem) is found: *ai-s-u* 'love', *yaku-s-u* 'translate'. Historically, all of these suffixes are derived from *su-ru*. A small number of SJ and foreign borrowings may also take the suffix *-r-u* and function as consonant-stem verbs: 牛耳 *gyuuji* 'leader, lit. cattle ears' → *gyuuji-r-u* 'control', *memo* 'memo, note' → *memo-r-u* 'take notes'. In the rare case of a foreign borrowing already ending in *ru*, this *ru* may be reanalysed as *r-u*: *guuguru* 'Google' → *gugur-u* 'to google'.

Japanese verbs take a number of suffixes to express grammatical meaning (tense, aspect, modality, etc.) and follow a relatively simple set of morphophonological rules when doing so. Historically, sequences of vowels (VV) or consonants (CC) were illicit in native stratum vocabulary (§2.9, §3.15): barring morphological adaption, consonant-stem verbs could not take suffixes beginning in a consonant and vowel-stem verbs suffixes beginning in a vowel. With the exception of old *p*-stems and a small number of irregular forms, these restrictions still stand. Take, for example, the form *ikitai*, a combination of the stem *ik-* 'go' and the desiderative suffix *-ta-i*. In order for this string to be phonotactically licit, a vowel (in this case, *i*) must be inserted between the stem and suffix. Likewise, in the form *taberareru*, a combination of *tabe-* 'eat' and the passive suffix *are-ru*, a consonant (in this case, *r*) must be inserted to resolve the illicit structure. We refer to these inserted segments as union vowels and consonants. There exist two union vowels (*a~i*) and three

verb class	stem structure	morphophonological rules
consonant-stem	final C- or final V(w)-	• *-te* form, *-ta* form and their reflexes undergo *onbin* (§2.9, Table 3.7.2) • old *p*-stems add *w* to the stem before all negative suffixes, passive and causative (*a-u* → *aw-ana-i, aw-are-ru*, etc.) • final *r* is dropped in honorific verbs ending in *sar-u ~ šar-u ~ zar-u* when taking *-(i)mas-u* or *-i* (*kudasar-u* → *kudasa-i*) • takes *-e-ru* to form potential (*ik-e-ru*) • takes *-e* to form imperative (*ik-e*)
vowel-stem	final *e- ~ i-*	• takes *-rare-ru ~ -re-ru* to form potential (*tabe-rare-ru ~ tabe-re-ru*) • takes *-ro* (Eastern Japanese) or *-yo* (Western Japanese) to form imperative (*tabe-ro ~ tabe-yo*)
S-irregular	*se- ~ ši- ~ su- ~ s-*	• *se-* before archaic/Western negative (*se-nu ~ se-N*), archaic negative converb (*se-zu[ni]*) and formal imperative (*se-yo*) • *su-* before all suffixes with union consonant *r* other than passive (*su-ru, su-reba*, etc.) • *s-* before passive (*s-are-ru*) and causative (*s-ase-ru*) • *su-* or *s-* before necessitive (*su-rubeki ~ s-ubeki*) • *ši-, su-* or *s-* before negative conjectural (*ši-mai ~ su-rumai ~ s-umai*) • *ši-* before all other suffixes (*ši-te, ši-ta, ši-mas-u*, etc.) • no potential form (*deki-ru* used instead) • takes *-yo* (formal) or *-ro* (casual) to form imperative (*se-yo ~ ši-ro*)
K-irregular	*ko- ~ ki- ~ ku-*	• *ko-* before negative suffixes, passive, causative, potential, imperative and conjectural-hortative (*ko-na-i, ko-rare-ru, ko-sase-ru*, etc.) • *ku-* before all suffixes with union consonant *r* other than passive (*ku-ru, ku-reba*, etc.) • *ko-, ki-* or *ku-* before negative conjectural (*ko-mai ~ ki-mai ~ ku-rumai*) • *ki-* before all other suffixes (*ki-te, ki-ta, ki-mas-u*, etc.) • takes *-rare-ru ~ -re-ru* to form potential (*ko-rare-ru ~ ko-re-ru*) • takes *-i* to form imperative (*ko-i*)

Table 3.3: Verb classes

union consonants (*r~s~y*), which vary according to suffix. Whether these union vowels and consonants belong to the stem at the lexical level (*iki-* and *taber-* are allomorphs of *ik-* and *tabe-*), are independent affixes ('stem extenders': *ik-i-, tabe-r-*) or belong to the suffix (*ik-ita-i, tabe-rare-ru*), is a largely unresolved matter. Here, for ease of description, we treat them as part of the suffix and place them in brackets: *-(i)ta-i* (desiderative), *-(r)are-ru* (passive). When taking the suffixes *-te* (*-te* form), *-ta* (past) and their reflexes, consonant-stem verbs do not all take a single union vowel, but instead undergo a set of systematic sound changes known as *onbin* (§2.9, Table 3.7.2). Verbal suffixes will be discussed in further detail in §3.7 and §3.8.

A small number of other irregularities exist for consonant-stem verbs:

(1) Honorific verbs (§6.3) ending in *sar-u* ~ *šar-u* ~ *zar-u* lose their stem-final *r* when taking the polite suffix *-(i)mas-u* or the polite imperative *-i*: *gozar-u* → *goza-imas-u* 'be (polite)', *iraQšar-u* → *iraQša-i* 'welcome (lit. please come)!'. The polite imperative irregularity (and the polite imperative itself) is restricted to *kudasar-u*, *iraQšar-u* and *nasar-u*.

(2) When taking a suffix starting in *a*, or with a union vowel *a*, the stem-final element of old *p*-stems switches to *w*: *i-u* + *-(r)are-ru* → *iw-are-ru* 'be said' (passive), *i-u* + *-(a)zu* → *iw-azu* 'don't say, and' (archaic negative converb).

All verbs, regardless of class, typically take the same set of suffixes, the two major exceptions being the potential and the imperative. The potential emerges as *-e-ru* after consonant-stem verbs (*ik-e-ru* 'can go'), but *-rare-ru* ~ *re-ru* (the second form being a recent development: §3.8) after vowel-stem (*tabe-rare-ru* ~ *tabe-re-ru* 'can eat') and K-irregular verbs (*ko-rare-ru* ~ *ko-re-ru* 'can come'). S-irregular verbs, meanwhile, have no potential—the verb *deki-ru* 'be able to do, come to completion' is supplemented instead. The other major exception is the imperative. This emerges as *-e* after consonant-stems (*ik-e* 'go!'), but *-ro* ~ *-yo* after vowel-stem (*tabe-ro* ~ *tabe-yo* 'eat!') and S-irregular verbs (*se-yo* ~ *ši-ro* 'do!'). For vowel-stem verbs, the imperative form *-ro* is an Eastern feature and *-yo* a Western feature (§7.9). For S-irregulars, however, *-ro* is simply the casual and *-yo* the formal, or literary, form. K-irregulars take the imperative *-i* (*ko-i*), as do the small number of honorific verbs listed in (1) where they express a polite command. Table 3.3 summarizes the morphophonological rules of the four verb classes—examples are not intended to be exhaustive.

3.4 Verbs: Transitivity, Volition and Aspect

In §3.3, we illustrated how, from a morphophonological standpoint, Japanese verbs can be broken down into consonant-stem, vowel-stem and S- and K-irregular verbs. A number of other criteria exist for classifying verbs, the most common being transitivity, volition and aspect, each of these being grammatical categories, or distinctions which add grammatical meaning to words. Transitivity determines whether or not a verb can take a direct object—a physical object or concept that the agent of the verb (the subject) acts upon. The verbs *tabe-ru* 'eat' and *nom-u* 'drink', for example, are transitive, taking food or drink as their direct objects. The verbs *hare-ru* 'become clear' and *kumor-u* 'become cloudy', on the other hand, are intransitive—a change in state from cloudy to clear, or vice versa, is not an action that acts upon some physical object or concept. Existential verbs (verbs which express a state of existence) such as *ar-u* 'be (for inanimates)' or *i-ru* 'be (for animates)' are also prime examples of intransitive verbs as none of these verbs can take an object.

Volition marks whether the action of a verb is conducted under the will of the actor or not. The verb *cukur-u* 'make', for example, is volitional, as the act of making something is usually intentional. The verb *otos-u* 'drop', meanwhile, is non-volitional—one does not typically drop things intentionally. Finally, aspect marks the state of an action in terms of progression: whether the action is just starting, ongoing, completed or repeated. This is in contrast to tense, which marks the specific point in time at which an action occurs: in the past, present or future. We will look at how aspect ties in with the meaning of verbs in the second half of this unit.

The grammatical categories defined above are not always mutually exclusive: it is possible for one usage of a verb to be transitive or volitional, with another being intransitive or non-volitional. For example, *tabe-ru* can be used in the sense 'make a living' (1), in which it would arguably be difficult to insert a direct object. Likewise, *otos-u* can be used in the sense 'place the winning bid (in an auction)' (2) or 'fail (a student)' in which case the will of the actor is most definitely involved. And, of course, one could think of any number of scenarios in which a normally involuntary action would be conducted voluntarily, and vice-versa: one could 'drop' one's pen intentionally to slip a note under the table at a meeting for nefarious reasons, or one could plan to make dinner for two, but accidently cook enough for four. Thus, volition is intrinsically linked with context, rather than simply being a semantic attribute.

(1) koNna   kyuuryoo=dewa   tabe-te   ik-e-na-i
    this.kind salary=COND   eat-CVB   go-POT-NEG-NPST
    'I can't make a living on such a salary.' (intransitive)

(2) yafuoku=de   juumaN-eN=de   čuukoša=o   otoši-ta
    Yahoo!.Auctions=LOC   100,000-yen=LOC   used.car=ACC   drop-PST
    'I won a second-hand car for ¥100,000 on Yahoo! Auctions.' (volitional)

(3) yuzuho=ga   amido=o   ake-ta
    Yuzuho=NOM   screen.door=ACC   open-PST
    'Yuzuho opened the screen door.' (transitive)

(4) kaze=de   amido=ga   ai-ta
    wind=LOC   screen.door=NOM   be.opened-PST
    'The screen door opened from the wind.' (intransitive: force of nature)

(5) A: oi   amido=ga   ai-te-ru=yo
       hey   screen.door=NOM   be.opened-CVB.PROG-NPST=EXCL
       'Hey! The screen door's open!' (intransitive: unknown third party)

    B: aQ   gomeN.   boku=ga   ake-ta=N=da
       oh   sorry   I=NOM   open-PST=NMNLZ=COP.NPST
       'Oh, sorry. I opened it.'

3.4 Verbs: Transitivity, Volition and Aspect

A small number of verbs are both transitive and intransitive in their primary sense: *hirak-u* 'open' or 'be opened', *owar-u* 'finish' or 'be finished'. Such ambitransitive verbs are, however, far less common than they are in, for example, English. Japanese is well-known for possessing transitive and intransitive variants of the same verb. The verbs *ake-ru* 'open' and *ak-u* 'be opened', for example, form a transitive-intransitive pair, the former taking a door, window or other closed interface as its direct object (3), with the latter unable to take a direct object. In (4) the screen door is opened by the wind, while in (5) it is unclear how it was opened.

Historically, transitive verbs were derived from intransitive verbs, and vice versa, through modification of the stem, in many cases accompanied by a change in verb class (Table 3.3) from consonant- to vowel-stem, or vice versa. While such derivational processes are no longer productive in Modern Japanese (nor were they in any attested stage of the language), a number of 'patterns' can be observed where the intransitive, transitive or both variants of an intransitive-transitive verb pair are morphologically marked before the stem boundary. These patterns can be divided into three major groups: transitivizing, or causative, in which the transitive form is marked (*ak-u* 'be opened' ~ *ake-ru* 'open (something)'); detransitivizing, or anticausative, in which the intransitive form is marked (*ware-ru* 'be cracked' ~ *war-u* 'crack (something)'); and equipollent, in which the transitive and intransitive forms are both marked (*hajimar-u* 'be started' ~ *hajime-ru* 'start (something)'). One characteristic observed across multiple intransitive-transitive pairs is that the stem-endings of intransitive verbs tend to include *r*, while *s* is common in transitive verbs (*nor-u* 'ride in, be placed on' ~ *nose-ru* 'place in, place on'). From an etymological standpoint, *r* appears to be linked to anticausativity and *s* to causativity: compare the passive *-(r)are-ru* and causative *-(s)ase-ru* verb suffixes (§3.7). Table 3.4 gives a list of common patterns for intransitive/transitive verb pairs. The stem-ending ø indicates 'none', while superscript C and V indicate consonant-stem and vowel-stem verbs.

All verbs are intrinsically linked with aspect in one way or another. The English verb *eat*, for example, expresses an action that can be thought of in terms of progression (progressive *I'm eating ramen* or perfect *I've eaten ramen*), while *know* expresses a state of being (*I know how to eat ramen*). The latter cannot be used in the progressive, at least in its primary sense of recognizing or being familiar with: **I'm knowing how to eat ramen*. There exist a number of classifications of Japanese verbs based on aspect, the most famous being those proposed by the linguists Kindaichi Haruhiko (§8.11) and Kudō Mayumi.

Kindaichi divides verbs into four groups based on how their aspectual meaning changes when taking the perfect-progressive auxiliary *-te i-ru* (§3.9). These are stative, durative, spontaneous and 'Type IV'. Stative verbs express a state of being, unbound to progression, and include the verbs *ar-u* 'exist' and *i-ru* 'be', which cannot take *-te i-ru*, just as *know* cannot typically take *-ing*. Durative verbs express an action that is capable of being carried out over a period of time such as *yom-u*

intransitive ending	intransitive	transitive ending	transitive
transitivizing (anticausative/transitive marked)			
ø^C	ugok-u 'move (on one's own)'	(w)as	ugokas-u 'move'
	mado-u 'get lost'		madowas-u 'mislead'
	sawag-u 'be noisy'	(w)ase	sawagase-ru 'disturb'
	a-u 'match'		awase-ru 'make match'
	ak-u 'be opened'	e	ake-ru 'open'
	horob-u 'be annihilated'	os	horobos-u 'annihilate'
	uruo-u 'become moist'	s	uruos-u 'moisten'
ø^V	ne-ru 'sleep'	kas	nekas-u 'put to sleep'
		kase	nekase-ru 'put to sleep'
	ni-ru 'resemble'	se	nise-ru 'make resemble'
detransitivizing (causative/intransitive marked)			
(w)ar	cunagar-u 'be connected'		cunag-u 'connect'
(w)are	umare-ru 'be born'		um-u 'give birth to'
oe	kikoe-ru 'be audible'	ø^C	kik-u 'listen, hear'
or	cumor-u 'pile up'		cum-u 'load'
e	ware-ru 'be cracked'		war-u 'crack'
e	mie-ru 'be visible'	ø^V	mi-ru 'look, see'
equipollent (transitive and intransitive marked)			
(w)ar	hajimar-u 'be started'	e	hajime-ru 'start'
	kawar-u 'be changed'		kae-ru 'change'
(w)are	wakare-ru 'be divided'	e	wake-ru 'divide'
	toraware-ru 'be captured'		torae-ru 'capture'
e	make-ru 'lose'	(w)as	makas-u 'defeat'
	furue-ru 'be shaken'		furuwas-u 'shake up'
	obie-ru 'be frightened'	yakas	obiyakas-u 'frighten'
	hie-ru 'get cold'	yas	hiyas-u 'chill'
i	iki-ru 'live'	(w)as	ikas-u 'let live, make the most of'
	oki-ru 'wake up'	os	okos-u 'wake (somebody) up'
	cuki-ru 'be used up'	us	cukus-u 'use up'
ie	kie-ru 'disappear'	es	kes-u 'erase'
ir	majir-u 'be mixed in'	e	maze-ru 'mix'
or	nukumor-u 'get warm'	e	nukume-ru 'warm up'
ore	umore-ru 'get buried'	e	ume-ru 'bury'
r	cukamar-u 'be caught'	e	cukamae-ru 'catch'
	nokor-u 'remain'	s	nokos-u 'keep'
	nor-u 'ride in, be placed on'	se	nose-ru 'place in, place on'
re	koware-ru 'be broken'	s	kowas-u 'break'

Table 3.4: Intransitive-transitive verb pairs

3.4 Verbs: Transitivity, Volition and Aspect

'read' or *fur-u* 'rain'. Spontaneous verbs express an instantaneous action that occurs once and then ends: they include *šin-u* 'die' or *kie-ru* 'disappear, go out'. When taking *-te i-ru*, durative verbs express the progressive (*yoɴ-de i-ru* 'reading', *fuq-te i-ru* 'raining'), while spontaneous verbs express the perfect, or resultative (*šin-de i-ru* 'dead', *kie-te i-ru* 'disappeared, turned off'). Type IV verbs express an attribute or quality, similar to adjectives, when used together with *-te i-ru* and rarely appear in their nonpast form without *-te i-ru*: *sobie-te i-ru* 'tower over', *sugure-te i-ru* 'excel'.

Kudō, on the other hand, divides verbs into two main groups: static and dynamic. Static verbs express a state of being, attribute or quality, similar to Kindaichi's stative and Type IV verbs, while dynamic verbs express a physical action. Dynamic verbs are said to express aspect in the traditional sense, while static verbs express no aspect: they are not bound to progression. Kudō divides dynamic verbs into three aspectual categories: subject-acting-and-object-modifying (SA+OM), subject-modifying (SM) and subject-acting (SA), where subject refers to the agent of a transitive or sole argument of an intransitive verb and object refers to the direct object, or patient, of a transitive verb. SA+OM verbs modify the state of the object through the subject's actions (*ake-ru* 'open', *otos-u* 'drop'), while SM verbs modify only the state of the subject (*agar-u* 'rise', *koware-ru* 'break'). SA verbs, meanwhile, express an action by the subject that does not (directly) modify the state of the object (*ugokas-u* 'move (something)', *kag-u* 'sniff'). When taking *-te i-ru*, SA+OM verbs express the progressive (6) or perfect (7). Meanwhile, SM verbs can express only the perfect (*agaq-te i-ru* 'risen', *koware-te ir-ru* 'broken') and SA verbs (typically) only the progressive (*ugokaši-te i-ru* 'moving', *kai-de i-ru* 'sniffing').

(6) ima   doa=o   ake-te   i-ru=kara   čoqto   maq-te
    now   door=ACC   open-CVB   PROG-NPST=CAUSL   a.little   wait-CVB
    'I'm opening the door now so hold on a bit.' (progressive)

(7) doa=o   ake-te   i-ru   hoo=ga   aɴšiɴ+su-ru
    door=ACC   open-CVB   PROG-NPST   way=NOM   feel.easy+do-NPST
    'Having the door open makes me feel at ease.' (perfect)

(8) ano   hoɴ=wa   moo   yoɴ-de   i-ru
    that   book=TOP   already   read-CVB   PROG-NPST
    'I've already read that book.' (perfect)

(9) reineɴ=yori   ame=ga   fuq-te   i-ru
    average.year=ABL   rain=NOM   rain-CVB   PROG-NPST
    'It's been raining more than usual this year.' (perfect)

Neither of these classifications is without its flaws, with a large number of verbs straddling multiple categories in Kindaichi's classification in particular. Both *yon-de i-ru* (8) and *fuq-te i-ru* (9), for example, can express the perfect, given context. When comparing transitivity, volition and aspect, we find that the majority of Kindaichi's stative, spontaneous and Type IV verbs are intransitive and non-volitional, while the bulk of his durative verbs are transitive and volitional. Meanwhile, SA+OM verbs are transitive and SM verbs intransitive by definition (the former take an object while the latter do not), with SA verbs being a mix of the two. Volition plays little role in Kudō's classification.

3.5 Adjectives, Adverbs and Adnouns

Adjectives, adverbs and adnouns are all classes of words expressing attributes or qualities. Adjectives and adnouns express the qualities of objects or concepts (nouns), while adverbs express those of actions or states of being (verbs). Japanese has two types of adjective, verbal and nominal, both of which display different morphosyntactic properties than, for example, their English counterparts. Cross-linguistically, there are three universal pragmatic functions (or 'propositional speech acts'): reference (identifying an object or concept), predication (describing an action or state of said reference) and attribution (also called 'modification': describing the properties of said reference). Some languages, such as English, make a three-way distinction between these functions: nouns are used for reference, verbs for predication and adjectives for attribution. In other languages, attribution is carried out by the same class of words used for reference or predication. This is the case for Japanese, where verbal adjectives have more in common with verbs, and nominal adjectives more in common with nouns, than they do with English adjectives.

We look first at verbal adjectives. These take the ending *-i* to form the nonpast (predicative) or adnominal (attributive) (§3.7). While English adjectives are required to take a linking verb, or copula (§3.6), when forming the predicate of a sentence, Japanese verbal adjectives carry out predication on their own (although it is common practice to attach the copula *des-u* to the end of a verbal adjective to express politeness: §3.6, §6.3). This can be seen from (1), in which *aka-i* 'red' expresses a state of being—the state of being red. While we have provided the gloss 'red' for *aka-i*, a more accurate translation would be 'is red', with *aka-i* functioning as a verb. Such morphosyntactic properties have led a number of Japanese linguists to call words such as *aka-i* 'qualitative verbs' instead of 'adjectives', a term also used in Chinese and Korean linguistics. At the same time, however, when *aka-i* acts as an adnominal modifier, as in (2), it can be argued that *aka-i* does not express a state of being, but merely an attribute—red colour. Thus, taking the abovementioned pragmatic functions into consideration, verbal adjectives are no less 'adjective-like' than their English counterparts: rather, in addition to carrying out attribution, they can also carry out predication.

3.5 Adjectives, Adverbs and Adnouns

(1) riNgo=ga aka-i
    apple=NOM red-NPST
    'The apple is red.'

(2) nacuki=ga aka-i riNgo=o tabe-ta
    Natsuki=NOM red-NPST apple=ACC eat-PST
    'Natsuki ate a red apple.'

(3) riNgo=ga aka-i → kiwi=ga aka-ku na-i
    apple=NOM red-NPST kiwi.fruit=NOM red-ADV nonexistent-NPST
    'Apples are red.' (positive) 'Kiwis aren't red.' (negative)

Similar to verbs, verbal adjectives take a series of suffixes (§3.7) to express grammatical meaning. These suffixes are, for the most part, identical in function to the suffixes found after verbs. That is, parallel to the nonpast verb suffix *-(r)u*, there is the nonpast adjective suffix *-i*, while parallel to the past verb suffix *-ta*, there exists the past adjective suffix *-kaQta* (see Table 3.7.1 for a list of corresponding forms). While most adjective suffixes have corresponding verb suffixes, the reverse does not hold true—verbal adjectives cannot take suffixes expressing grammatical meanings requiring an action, such as passive, causative, potential or imperative. Another major exception is the negative, which is formed through suffixation for verbs (stem + *-(a)na-i*), but as an analytic (syntactically separate) form for verbal adjectives, as in (3). Unlike verbs, the stems of verbal adjectives may be used independently to express exclamation: *taka* 'that's damn expensive!', *sugo* 'that's amazing!', *samu* 'it's freezing!'. Often, a mora obstruent (realized as a glottal stop [ʔ]: §2.2) is added to the end of the stem for emphasis: *taka-Q, sugo-Q, samu-Q*.

In stem form, single-mora (§2.4) verbal adjectives are rare, with only three (ignoring adjective-type verbal suffixes: §3.8) employed to any extent in the modern language: *yo-i ~ i-i* 'good', *na-i* 'nonexistent', *ko-i* 'thick'. The pair *yo-i ~ i-i* is of particular interest, as *i-i*, in addition to sounding more casual, is defective, appearing in nonpast form only (**i-ku* or **i-kaQta* do not exist in the Standard). When taking the evidential suffix *-soo* (§3.7), the single-mora adjectives *yo-i* and *na-i* (but not *ko-i*) optionally take the allomorph *-sasoo* and, while prescriptively illicit, this allomorph can also be found after *-(a)na-i*: *yo-sasoo* 'seems good', *na-sasoo* 'seems unlikely', *ik-ana-soo ~ ik-ana-sasoo* 'it seems she won't go'. The origin of this allomorph is not entirely clear, but it seems to have arisen for prosodic reasons.

There are four nominalizer suffixes, *-sa ~ -mi ~ -me ~ -ge*, that may follow the stems of verbal adjectives to turn them into nouns or, in the case of *-me ~ -ge*, nominal adjectives. Overall, *-sa* places an emphasis on degree or quantity (*geemu=no tanoši-sa* 'fun points of the game', *yama=no taka-sa* 'height of the mountain'), with *-mi* expressing a number of different meanings dependant on the adjective it follows (*geemu=no tanoši-mi* 'points of the game to look forward to', *yama=no taka-mi* 'peaks of the mountain'). Etymologically, *-mi* appears to have derived from verbs such as *tanošim-u* 'have fun' and *kurušim-u* 'be in pain' and until recently was not productive in Modern Japanese. This has changed in recent years, however, with *-mi* now used among younger speakers to express a feeling of vagueness or ambiguity and as a marker of youth identity (§6.1): *cura-mi* 'kind of painful'. The latter two suffixes, *-me* and *-ge*, express tendency ('tends to') and visual evidentiality ('appears to'), respectively: *naga-me=na* (~ *naga-me=no*) *hanaši* 'longish talk', *tanoši-ge=ni wara-u* 'laugh in a fun looking way'. A single irregular form, *ko-ime*, is employed when attaching the suffix *-me* to the single-mora stem *ko* of the adjective *ko-i* 'thick', seemingly for prosodic reasons similar to *sa* above.

We turn now to nominal adjectives. Just as verbal adjectives share functionality with verbs, nominal adjectives function in a similar way to nouns. When forming the predicate, they take the same copulas as nouns, *da* ~ *des-u* ~ *de ar-u*, as illustrated in (4). Unlike nouns, however, nominal adjectives can act as adnominal modifiers by taking the particle *na* (← Middle Japanese copula *nar-i*: §3.13, §3.15), as in (5), or as adverbs by taking the particle *ni* (§3.13), as in (6). In L2 textbooks (§8.8), nominal adjectives are commonly referred to as '*na* adjectives', while verbal adjectives are referred to as '*-i* adjectives'. Nominal adjectives can take the nominalizer *-sa* (*šizuka-sa* 'quietness', *sumuuzu-sa* 'smoothness'), but rarely take other nominalizers outside of a small number of idiomatic expressions (*šiNsecu-mi* 'kindness', *tokui-ge* 'proud look'). Recently, however, similar to verbal adjectives, *-mi* may be employed after nominal adjectives by younger speakers: *baka-mi* 'kind of stupid'. In addition to the standard nominal adjective, there is a further group of nouns in Japanese, sometimes referred to as '*no* adjectives', that can function as adnominal modifiers by taking the particle *no* (§3.13): *midori=no yasai* 'green vegetables', *mikaN=no sakuhiN* 'uncompleted work'. A number of nouns, such as *saikoo* 'best' and *saiaku* 'worst', can take either *na* or *no* to form the adnominal, with little or no difference in meaning. Likewise, a number of nominal adjectives possess verbal adjective counterparts: *ooki* ~ *ooki-i* 'big', *čiisa* ~ *čiisa-i* 'small'. Just as Sino-Japanese (SJ: §7.1) and foreign borrowings (§7.2) form nominal verbs together with *su-ru* (see §3.3 for examples), nominal adjectives are also frequently formed from the non-native lexicon: *šiNsecu (na)* 'kind', *baka (na)* 'idiotic', *tocuzeN (na~no)* 'sudden' (all SJ); *riizunaburu (na)* 'reasonably priced', *šai (na)* 'shy', *burauN (no)* 'brown' (all foreign).

(4) mori=ga šizuka[=da ~ des-u ~ de ar-u]
 forest=NOM quiet[=COP.NPST ~ COP.POL-NPST ~ CVBLZ exist-NPST]
 'The forest is quiet.'

(5) koko=wa šizuka=na mori=da
 here=TOP quiet=ADNLZ forest=COP.NPST
 'This is a quiet forest.'

(6) mori=no naka=o šizuka=ni arui-ta
 forest=GEN inside=ACC quiet=ADVLZ walk-PST

'I walked through the forest quietly.'

Moving on to adverbs, Japanese adverbs function similarly to adverbs in English, their main function being the modification of verbs, adjectives, other adverbs, clauses or sentences. Just as with adjectives, however, there exist a number of complications regarding which words should be defined as adverbs. The greatest is that, in addition to modifying verbs and adjectives, some Japanese adverbs can take the particle *no* to modify nouns: *sukoši=no gamaN* 'a little bit of perseverance', *kanari=no naNmoN* 'quite a difficult problem'. In general, though, such adnominal usage is the exception rather than the rule, with the majority of adverbs unable to take nouns as arguments: *sugu owar-u* 'finish soon', never **sugu=no šiai* 'soon game'. Some adverbs modify verbs and adjectives directly without taking any particles (*daitai owaQ-ta* 'mostly finished'), while for others it is necessary to employ *ni* (*tadači=ni hajime-ru* 'start immediately', not **tadači hajime-ru*). Still others may be used with or without *ni* (*sugu owar-u* ~ *sugu=ni owar-u*: both 'finish soon'). Furthermore, a number of adverbs take *to* (§3.13) instead of *ni* to form arguments: *iroiro=to komar-u* 'be troubled in many ways'. Similar to *ni*, *to* can be mandatory or optional. Overall, *to* is most common in mimetic adverbs (§5.2): *gerogero=to nak-u* 'croak (of a frog)', *korori=to šin-u* 'roll over dead'.

A final class of modifiers, known as *rentaishi* in Japanese and sometimes referred to as 'adnouns' in the English literature must also be mentioned. Adnouns are, in essence, defunct forms of nouns, verbs and adjectives that function as adnominal modifiers in the modern language, though without taking any adnominalizer particles. Examples deriving from verbs include *itaranu* 'unsatisfactory' (← *itar-anu* 'lit. do not reach') or *taišita* 'extraordinary' (← *tai+ši-ta* 'lit. did big'), while examples deriving from nouns include *kono* 'this', *sono* 'that' or *ano* 'that (over there)' (← *ko~so~a* + genitive case marker particle *no*: see also §3.2). Several adnouns originate as 'imitations', or direct translations of, Classical Chinese (CC: §1.3, §7.1). One example of such a word is *aru* 'a certain' (as in *aru hito* 'a certain person', *aru toki* 'a certain time'), which derives from Middle Japanese *ar-u* 'exist' (adnominal), an imitation of CC 有 and 或, both of which, in addition to possessing the sense 'exist', also possess the sense 'a certain'.

3.6 Predication and Copulas

The question of what constitutes a sentence has been a topic of hot debate since the early days of Japanese linguistics. One of the key issues in this debate has been the concept of predication, or *chinjutsu* 'lit. statement' in Japanese, a term originally proposed by the early 20th century Japanese linguist Yamada Yoshio (§8.13) to describe the process in which the various components of a clause or sentence are 'unified' by the speaker or writer to form a coherent utterance. Apart from inversions such as *ik-e, omae* 'go, you!', predication always occurs at the end of a clause or sentence in Japanese. While in English and other European languages the presence of a verb is a necessary criterion for predication, in Japanese, predication can be carried out by verbs, verbal adjectives or, in the case of noun phrases (NPs) and nominal adjective predicates, a special group of words known as copulas, to be covered in this unit. Standard English sentences such as 'this *is* an interesting book' or 'this *is* wonderful', for example, require the linking verb *be* (in its third person singular form here) in order to be grammatical. The same two sentences in Japanese achieve predication through the use of a copula (1) or an adjective (2).

(1) *kore=wa   omoširo-i   hoN=**da***
     this=TOP   interesting-NPST book=COP.NPST
     'This **is** an interesting book.'

(2) *kono   hoN=wa   **omoširo-i***
     this   book=TOP   **interesting-NPST**
     'This book **is interesting**.'

Prescriptively speaking, Japanese sentences with a NP or nominal adjective predicate are required to take a copula. There are two main copulas in Modern Japanese, *da* and *des-u*, as well as two analytic copular constructions formed through combining the particle *de* (§3.13) with existential verbs (§3.4). The more common of the two analytic copulas is *de ar-u* (*de* + *ar-u* 'exist'); the less common is the super-polite *de gozar-u* (*de* + *gozar-u* 'exist (super-polite)'), which regularly appears in the polite form *de goza-imas-u*, in which the final *r* of the stem *gozar-* is dropped (§3.3). Use of each of the four copulas varies according to style and politeness: *da* is the casual or neutral form, used when speaking to social equals or inferiors; *des-u* is the polite form, used when speaking to superiors and strangers, or in formal scenarios in general; *de ar-u* is rarely encountered in speech, but rather reserved for politeness-neutral writing styles such as academic writing and prose (where *da* may also be employed); and *de gozar-u* is reserved for highly formal situations and is frequently formulaic (*sayoo=de goza-imas-u* 'that is correct', *kyooŝuku=de goza-imas-u* 'I am terribly sorry to bother you'). See §4.13 for a discussion on copula usage in writing styles and §6.3 for a discussion on polite forms in general. While *da* and *des-u* typically only come at the end of clauses and sentences, the two analytic copulas, *de ar-u* and *de gozar-u*, can also be used as adnominal modifiers: *seNsei=de ar-u otoosaN* 'my father, who is a teacher'.

From an etymological standpoint, both *da* and *des-u* are derived from earlier analytic constructions. The former is a truncation (§5.6) of the particle *de* and *ar-u* (*de ar-u* → *dea* → ⁽*⁾*dya* → *da*) with the latter most likely being a truncation of *de* and *goza-imas-u* (*de goza-imas-u* → *des-u*). It has also been proposed that *des-u* is a truncation of *de ar-imas-u* or *de sooro-u*, both analytic copulas of the Early Modern period (§1.3, §3.15). However, a variant form of *des-u*, *deges-u*, is observed in late Edo

3.6 Predication and Copulas

Japanese and similar forms can be found today in Tōhoku (§7.10) and Kyūshū (§7.11) dialects (*degas-u*: Miyagi, *degos-u*: Aomori, *degowas-u*: Kagoshima), all giving support to the *de goza-imas-u* theory. In Western Japanese (§7.9), the copula *ya*, and among older speakers (§6.1) and especially in role language (§6.2), the copula *ja*, are also commonly used. Similar to *da*, both these copulas are derived from *de ar-u* (*de ar-u* → *dea* → ⁽*⁾*dya* → *ja~ya*). In the analytic copulas *de ar-u* and *de gozar-u*, the particle *de* is not fully merged with the following verb and may be followed by the topic markers *wa* and *mo*: *de=wa ar-u*, *de=mo gozar-u* (both treated in this volume as compound particles: *dewa~demo*; see §3.13 for further discussion). In casual speech, *dewa* is often contracted to *ja*, not to be confused with the Western copula *ja* noted above.

The copula can be deleted in holophrases (one-word sentences), such as *kaji* 'fire!' or *jišiN* 'earthquake!', and in certain literary styles such as poetry and legalese (§4.13). In casual speech, copulas are also commonly omitted, especially in sentences lacking discourse particles: *kare=wa i-i hito=da* 'he's a good person'. When discourse particles come into play, the rules get trickier. Copula deletion is compulsory before certain particles, while a marker of female speech before others: see §3.12 and §6.1 for further discussion.

Just as particles are a bound word class, copulas are also bound, never occurring on their own, but always following NPs, nominal adjectives, as well as (with *des-u*) verbal adjectives. Exceptions do exist, such as the copula-derived conjunctions *dakara~desukara* 'therefore' or *daga~desuga* 'however' (§3.10) and the interjections *dayone~desuyone* 'I know, right', but all of these could be considered marginal lexicalized forms. As all copulas are derived from particle-verb sequences and are bound to the preceding word in the same sense as particles, a more accurate term for copula would be 'particle-verb'. Moreover, similar to pronouns in regard to nouns (§3.2), copulas could be said to comprise a functional subcategory of particle rather than a word class proper. For the above reasons, we segment copulas from their preceding forms using an equal sign, similar to particles, throughout this volume.

Of the four copulas, *des-u*, *de ar-u* and *de gozar-u* all function as consonant-stem verbs, capable of taking verbal suffixes (§3.7). While nearly all verb suffixes are licit after *de ar-u* and *de gozar-u*, *des-u* is defective, capable of taking only the more common suffixes, such as the nonpast (*des-u*), past (*deši-ta*) and the irregular conjectural *deš-oo* (these restrictions are similar to those imposed on the polite verb suffix *-i-mas(u)*: Table 3.8). The copula *da* possesses a number of inflected forms, arising from inflections of *de ar-u*: *daQta* (past: ← *de aQ-ta*), *daroo* (conjectural: ← *de ar-oo*), *daQtaroo* (past conjectural: ← *de aQ-taroo*). See Table 3.7.1 for a list of the different forms of *da* and *des-u*. The copulas *da ~ des-u ~ de ar-u* possess no negative form, with analytic structures used instead: *de[wa] ar-imase-N ~ ja ar-imase-N* for *des-u*, *de[wa] na-i ~ ja na-i* for *da*, *de[wa] na-i* for *de ar-u*.

While, strictly speaking, the use of copulas after verbs and verbal adjectives should be illicit, given that this would result in 'double predication', recent developments have allowed for such constructions to express politeness. The use of *des-u* after verbal adjectives, both in nonpast and past form was considered sub-standard up until the mid-20th century, but is now Standard Japanese: *oiši-i=des-u* 'is delicious (polite)', *oiši-kaǫta=des-u* 'was delicious (polite)'. This applies to adjective-type verbal suffixes and auxiliary adjectives (§3.9) as well: *ik-ana-i=des-u* 'don't go (polite)', *ik-ita-i=des-u* 'want to go (polite)', *oiši-ku na-i=des-u* 'not delicious (polite)'.

One final point of interest is the conjectural form of the copulas, *daroo* ~ *deš-oo* ~ *de ar-oo*, which have all attained a suffix-like usage in the modern language, capable of following both the past and nonpast forms of verbs, adjectives and other copulas: *iǫ-ta=daroo* 'probably went', *ik-ana-i=daroo* 'probably won't go', *kare=daǫta=daroo* 'it was probably him'.

3.7 Verbal Suffixes I: Final Suffixes

Being an agglutinative language (§1.2, §3.1), Japanese verbs, verbal adjectives and copulas (§3.6) all take a large arsenal of suffixes to express syntactic and grammatical meaning. These suffixes can be broadly classified into two types: mandatory final suffixes, which appear at the end of a suffix string, and optional non-final suffixes, which appear between the primary stem of a verb and its final suffix, forming what could be called a 'secondary stem'. Fig. 3.7 offers a basic schematization of this string structure, with bold indicating mandatory components. We will cover final suffixes in this unit, leaving the discussion of non-final suffixes to §3.8.

Final suffixes are commonly referred to as inflectional suffixes: suffixes which simply add grammatical meaning and do not change the word class or lexical meaning of the base form. This term is problematic, however—at least in its textbook definition—as there are examples of final suffixes that do exhibit a clear change in word class, such as the adverbial *-ku*, which follows verbal adjectives turning them into adverbs (*haya-i* 'quick' → *haya-ku* 'quickly'), or the nominalizer *-(i)*, which follows verbs turning them into nouns (*aruk-u* 'walk' → *aruk-i* 'walking'). While we do not adopt the term 'inflectional suffixes' in this volume, we do

	stem	non-final suffix(es) (secondary stem)	final suffix
verb:	***tabe* 'eat'** —	*sase* (causative) — *rare* (passive)	— ***ta* (past)**
verbal adjective:	***tanoši* 'fun'** —	*gar* (verbalizer) — *ana* (negative)	— ***i* (nonpast)**

Fig. 3.7: Japanese verbal suffix string structure

3.7 Verbal Suffixes I: Final Suffixes 57

meaning	label	verbs	verbal adjectives	*da*	*des-u*
adnominal-conclusive suffixes					
archaic/Western negative	NEG	*-(a)nu ~ (a)N*			
conjectural-hortative	CJT	*-(y)oo*	*-karoo*	*daro[o]*	*deš-o[o]*
necessitive	NEC	*-(r)ubeki*			
negative conjectural	NCJT	*-(r)umai ~ mai*			
nonpast	NPST	*-(r)u*	*-i*	*da*	*des-u*
past	PST	*-ta*	*-kaQta*	*daQta*	*deši-ta*
past conjectural	PCJT	*-taro[o]*	*-kaQtaro[o]*	*daQtaro[o]*	*deši-taro[o]*
conclusive suffixes					
imperative	IMP	*-e ~ -ro ~ -yo ~ -i*			
prohibitive	PROH	*-(r)una*			
converbs					
adverbial	ADV	*-(i)*	*-ku*	*ni*[*1]	
archaic concessive	CONC	*-(r)utomo*	*-kutomo*	*tomo*[*1]	
archaic negative	NCVB	*-(a)zu[ni]*	*-karazu*		
concessive	CONC	*-temo*	*-kutemo*	*demo*[*1]	
concessive-simultaneous	SIM	*-(i)nagara*	*-inagara*	*nagara*[*1]	
emphatic-iterative conditional	COND	*-tewa ~ -ča*	*-kutewa ~ -kuča ~ -kya*	*dewa~ja*[*1]	
negative *-te* form	NCVB	*-(a)naide*			
perfective conditional	COND	*-tara*	*-kaQtara*	*daQtara*	*deši-tara*
provisional conditional	PROV	*-(r)eba*	*-kereba*		
purposive	PURP	*-(i)ni*			
representative	REP	*-tari*	*-kaQtari*	*daQtari~nari*[*1]	*deši-tari*
simultaneous	SIM	*-(i)cucu*			
-te form	CVB	*-te*	*-kute*	*de*[*1]	*deši-te*
temporal ablative	ACVB	*-tekara*			
temporal conditional	COND	*-(r)uto*	*-ito*	*dato*	*des-uto*
nominalizers					
evidential nominalizer	EVDNM	*-(i)soo*[*2]	*-ge*[*2 *3] *-soo*[*2 *3]		
(de)verbal nominalizer	NMNLZ	*-(i)*			
idiomatic nominalizer	NMNLZ		*-mi*		
instrumental nominalizer	NMNLZ	*-(i)kata* *-(i)yoo*			
qualitative nominalizer	NMNLZ		*-sa*		
tendential nominalizer	NMNLZ	*-(i)gači*[*2]	*-me*[*2]		

[*1] the corresponding copula forms for each of these suffixes are supplemented with particles, given in the table: see §3.12 and §3.13 for further discussion.
[*2] derive nominal adjectives.
[*3] also follow nominal adjectives.

Table 3.7.1: Commonly used final suffixes across verbs, adjectives and copulas

occasionally use the term 'inflections' to collectively refer to a verb, verbal adjective or copula's suffixed forms. Final suffixes can be broadly divided into four groups: adnominal-conclusive suffixes, conclusive suffixes, converbs and nominalizers. Adnominal-conclusive suffixes come before a noun phrase (NP) as its modifier, or at the end of a clause or sentence, in which case they are sometimes followed by discourse particles (§3.12). Conclusive suffixes come at the end of a sentence or clause, rarely taking discourse particles and unable to modify a NP. Converbs form subordinate or cosubordinate (further below) clauses, while nominalizers change a verb or adjective into a noun. A list of the most common final suffixes for verbs and verbal adjectives, as well as the corresponding forms for the copulas *da* and *des-u*, is given in Table 3.7.1, along with the glossing labels (PST = past, NPST = nonpast) used for each form throughout this volume.

Ignoring mostly obsolete and dialect (§7.7–§7.11) forms, there are eight adnominal-conclusive suffixes in Modern Japanese (hereafter, unless otherwise stated, only verb suffixes will be given in the main text; see Table 3.7.1 for the corresponding verbal adjective suffixes and copulas). The nonpast, or dictionary form (§3.3), *-(r)u* expresses present (1a), habitual (1b) or future tense (1c), while the past *-ta* expresses past (1d) or past-in-future (1e). The conjectural-hortative *-(y)oo* expresses a supposition about the present (1f) or future (1g), an invitation or expression of will (hortative/volitional: 1h) or, together with the speculative discourse particles *ka* or *kana* (§3.12), speculation (1i). The first of these three usages is literary and archaic in tone, as is its corresponding verbal adjective suffix *-karoo* (1j). This is not the case for the copula conjecturals *daroo* ~ *deš-oo*, however, which in addition to following noun-predicates, also commonly follow the nonpast and past form of verbs and adjectives (*ik-u=daroo* 'shall go', *iQ-ta=deš-oo* 'probably went': see §3.6 for further discussion). In addition to being used sentence-finally, all of the above suffixes can be also used adnominally to modify NPs: *iQ-ta hito* 'person who went' (past), *yar-ubeki koto* 'thing that needs to be done' (necessitive).

The past conjectural *-taroo*, as its name suggests, expresses a supposition about the past (1k). Similar to the present conjectural, this form is literary and archaic in tone, but there exists a colloquial variant *-taro*, which when accompanied by rising intonation, expresses a confirmative question: *iQ-taro↗* '(you) went, yeah?'. The necessitive *-(r)ubeki* expresses obligation or necessity (necessitive: 1l) and the negative conjectural *-(r)umai* ~ *-mai* a supposition that something will not occur (1m). The necessitive is irregular after S-irregular verbs, emerging as *su-rubeki* ~ *s-ubeki*, while the negative conjectural is irregular after vowel-stem verbs, S-irregular and K-irregular verbs, emerging as *tabe-rumai* ~ *tabe-mai*, *su-rumai* ~ *s-umai* ~ *ši-mai* and *ko-mai* ~ *ku-rumai* ~ *ki-mai*. When used conclusively, the necessitive typically takes a copula (1l) and, while frowned upon by prescriptivists, it may also be found after the negative suffix *-(a)na-i* (§3.8) in the speech of younger cohorts: *ik-ana-i(=)beki* 'mustn't go, shouldn't go'. Thus, distributionally, this suffix shares a number of properties with particles and seems to be undergoing reanalysis in the modern

3.7 Verbal Suffixes I: Final Suffixes

language. The last adnominal-conclusive suffix on our list, *-(a)nu*, expresses negation (1N). This suffix is archaic in tone and generally limited to the written language. Its variant *-(a)N*, however, is widespread in Western Japanese, often in the forms *-(a)heN ~ -hiN* (a merger of *wa se-N*: *ik-i=wa se-N* → *ik-aheN*; §7.9).

There are only two conclusive suffixes in Modern Japanese, both expressing commands: the imperative and the prohibitive (or negative imperative). The imperative *-e ~ -ro ~ -yo ~ -i* expresses a command (2a), while the prohibitive *-(r)una* expresses prohibition (2b). The imperative has four allophones: *-e* after consonant-stem verbs, *-ro* (Eastern) or *-yo* (Western) after vowel-stem and S-irregular verbs, and *-i* after K-irregular verbs and a small number of honorific verbs (see §3.3 for further discussion). With the exception of *-i* when used after honorific verbs, all of these command forms are typically informal when used in speech, often bearing anti-honorific connotations (§6.4). All conclusive suffixes, except for the *-yo* allomorph of the imperative, can take the discourse particle *yo* (exclamative/assertive), but no other discourse particles; imperative *-yo* cannot take any discourse particles at all.

(1)
   a. *wakar-**u*** — 'understand, know' (present)
   b. *maitoši furaNsu=ni ik-**u*** — 'go to France every year' (habitual)
   c. *raigecu doicu=ni ik-**u*** — 'go to Germany next month' (future)
   d. *kyoneN supeiN=ni iQ-**ta*** — 'went to Spain last year' (past)
   e. *koNdo iQ-**ta** toki* — 'next time I go (lit. next time I went)' (past-in-future)
   f. *imagoro ame=wa fuQ-te i-**yoo*** — 'it's probably raining now' (present conjectural)
   g. *ašita=wa ame=ni nar-**oo*** — 'it'll most likely rain tomorrow' (future conjectural)
   h. *tai=ni ik-**oo*** — '[let's go ~ I think I'll go] to Thailand' (hortative/volitional)
   i. *itaria=ni ik-**oo**=ka[na]* — 'I wonder if I should go to Italy' (speculative)
   j. *kore=de yo-**karoo*** — 'this'll be fine' (conjectural)
   k. *kaNkoku=ni iQ-**taroo*** — 'she probably went to Korea' (past conjectural)
   l. *ik-**ubeki**=da* — 'I must go, I should go' (necessitive)
   m. *ašita yuki=wa fur-**umai*** — 'it shouldn't snow tomorrow' (negative conjectural)
   n. *šir-**an**-u ma=ni* — 'without noticing' (archaic/Western negative)

(2)
   a. *ik-**e** ~ tabe-**ro*** — 'go!' ~ 'eat!' (imperative)
   b. *sawar-**una*** — 'don't touch!' (prohibitive)

Converb is a term used in linguistic typology to refer to a non-finite verb form (not inflected for tense, person or number) marking adverbial subordination. The most versatile of the Japanese converbs is *-te*, which has been given various appellations in the literature including gerund, sequential converb and perfective converb. Here, we will simply call this converb the '*-te* form'. In addition to marking subordinate clauses, the *-te* form can also mark what is known as a cosubordinate (or 'coordinate-dependent') clause, a type of clause falling somewhere between a coordinate and subordinate clause, in the sense that it is syntactically dependent on a main clause (it inherits tense, aspect and mood from the main clause) but at the same time logically equivalent in status—coordinate—to the main clause (it can take its own independent subject). In (3), the highlighted portion of the sentence is a subordinate clause, providing the circumstances under which the ramen and dumplings were ordered. In (4), on the other hand, the highlighted portion is a cosubordinate clause, inheriting its tense from the main clause, but at the same time taking its own independent subject and thus existing on the same logical level as the main clause.

(3) raameɴya=ni   iQ-te   / raameɴ=to   gyooza=o   tanoɴ-da
    ramen.shop=DAT   go-CVB   / ramen=and   dumplings=ACC   order-PST
    'I went to a ramen shop **and** ordered ramen and dumplings.' (subordinate)

(4) ryuuta=ga   raameɴya=ni   iQ-te   / ryoota=ga   šokudoo=ni   iQ-ta
    Ryūta=NOM   ramen.shop=DAT   go-CVB   / Ryōta=NOM   cafeteria=DAT   go-PST
    'Ryūta went to a ramen shop **and** Ryōta went to the cafeteria.'
    (cosubordinate)

(5) sušiya=ni   ik-i   / maguro=to   kaɴpači=o   tabe-ta
    sushi.shop=DAT   go-ADV / tuna=and   amberjack=ACC   eat-PST
    'I went to a sushi restaurant **and** ate tuna and amberjack.' (subordinate)

(6) mariko=ga   kacuo=o   tanom-i   / emi=ga   saamoɴ=o
    Mariko=NOM   skipjack.tuna=ACC   order-ADV / Emi=NOM   salmon=ACC
    tanoɴ-da
    order-PST
    'Mariko ordered some skipjack tuna **and** Emi ordered some salmon.'
    (cosubordinate)

A similar structure to the *-te* form is the converb *-(i)*, also bearing multiple appellations in the literature including adverbial, infinitive, continuative and imperfective converb. Here we adopt the term 'adverbial' for the sake of convention, although this term is not without issue: all converbs are, by definition, adverbials. The adverbial takes the form *-i* after consonant-stem verbs, but is morphologically null (the stem forms the adverbial on its own) after vowel-stem, S-irregular and K-irregular verbs (*ik-i* 'go, and', but *tabe-ø* 'eat, and', *ši-ø* 'do, and', *ki-ø* 'come, and').

3.7 Verbal Suffixes I: Final Suffixes

Similar to -*te*, the adverbial also forms subordinate (5) and cosubordinate (6) clauses, but is more formal than -*te*, generally restricted to written language. In addition to acting as a converb, -*(i)*, but not -*ku*, is also used to mark the first element in a verbal compound: *hašir-i+das-u* 'break into a run' (see also §3.9 and §5.4).

There are approximately 10 other converbs, including so-called 'secondary converbs' (mergers of the primary converbs with particles). Primary converbs include -*(a)naide*, the negative of the -*te* form, which marks a negative (co)subordinate clause (7); -*(a)zu* ~ -*(a)zuni*, a more archaic form of the negative -*(a)naide*, typically restricted to writing (8); -*(i)cucu*, which expresses a simultaneous (co-occurring) action (9); and -*tari*, which presents one representative result of a multiple outcome scenario (10). This final form, -*tari*, is supplemented by the particle *nari* (← obsolete copula *nar-i*: §3.15), which, in addition to following NPs and nominal adjectives, also follows the nonpast/past of verbs and verbal adjectives (11). Such *nari* constructions are slightly archaic in tone and limited for the most part to the written language. In addition to forming (co)subordinate clauses, both -*te* and -*naide* can be used sentence-finally to express imperative (12a) and prohibitive (12b) meaning. While more polite than the conclusive suffix command forms (2a, 2b), -*te* and -*naide* are still broadly casual in tone and usually followed by *kudasai* 'please' (← *kudasa-i* 'give (respectful)' + imperative) when used in polite speech (§6.3).

(7) *yuuhaN=o   tabe-naide   ne-ta*
    supper=ACC   eat-NCVB   sleep-PST
    'She went to bed **without** eating supper.' (negative subordinate)

(8) *dokomo   yor-azu[ni]   kaeQ-ta*
    anywhere   stop.by-NCVB return.home-PST
    'He went home **without** stopping anywhere.' (negative subordinate)

(9) *tabe-cucu   yase-ru   daieto=ga   i-i*
    eat-SIM   lose.weight-NPST   diet=NOM   good-NPST
    'I like a diet where you can eat and lose weight **at the same time**.' (simultaneous)

(10) *iQ-tari   ik-ana-kaQtari   su-ru*
     go=REP   go-NEG-REP   do-NPST
     '**Sometimes** I go, **sometimes** I don't.' (representative)

(11) *ik-u=nari   kaer-u=nari   haya-ku   kime+nasa-i*
     go-NPST=REP   return.home-NPST=REP   fast-ADV   decide+do.RESP-IMP
     '**Whether** you're going **on or** coming back home, make up your mind now.' (representative)

(12) a. *čoQto maQ-te*   'wait a moment!' (imperative)
     b. *sono koto iw-anaide*   'don't say that!' (prohibitive)

There are three conditional converbs: *-(r)uto*, *-(r)eba* and *-tara*. These are supplemented by the particle *nara[ba]*, derived from the conditional of the obsolete copula *nar-i*, which follows NPs, nominal adjectives or the nonpast/past of verbs and verbal adjectives. The differences between each of these conditionals are subtle and space precludes us from going into a detailed discussion. Put at its simplest, *-(r)uto* expresses a temporal condition, where the consequent occurs along with (13) or immediately after (14) the antecedent; *-(r)eba* indicates what is known as a provisional condition ('provided that A, B') (15); *-tara* a perfective condition (bound to the completion of another action) (16); and *nara[ba]* an assertive condition (the speaker's assertion of a predicted outcome) (17). These are only general rules of thumb, though, and in many examples, more than one conditional is licit: *-tara* could be used in any of (13)–(16), while *-(r)uto* could replace *-(r)eba* in (15) and *-(r)eba* could replace *-(r)uto* in (13). In addition, the converb *-(r)utomo* (etymologically related to but not derived from *-(r)uto*: §3.15), while archaic after verbs, is found after verbal adjectives (*-kutomo*) where it expresses a concessive clause ('even though') or condition ('even if') (18) or a lower (19a) or upper (19b) limit.

Secondary converbs of *-te* include *-tewa* (also found in the contracted form *-ča*), *-temo* and *-tekara*. The former two are conditionals, *-tewa* expressing an emphatic (contrastive or absolute) condition, often with negative connotations (20), and *-temo* a concessive clause or condition (21). In addition, *-tewa* can also be used to express iteration of two or more actions in succession (22). These converbs are also used to express prohibition (23a) and permission (23b) in set constructions, and the verbal adjective counterpart of *-tewa*, *-kutewa* (contracted to *-kuča* or *-kya*), expresses necessitation when following the negative form of verbs (24). The last of the *-te* converbs, *-tekara*, expresses a temporal ablative (starting at a specific point in time) subordinate clause (25). Secondary converbs of *-(i)* include *-(i)nagara*, which expresses a simultaneous action (26) or concessive clause or condition (27), and *-(i)ni*, which expresses the purposive (purpose of an action: 28). This list is not comprehensive and various other secondary converbs may be encountered.

(13) doa=o   ake-**ruto**   oto=ga   nar-u
     door=ACC   open-COND   sound=NOM   ring-NPST
     'The door squeaks **when** I open it.' (temporal condition: co-occurrence)

(14) doa=o   ake-**ruto**   neko=ga   tobikakaQ-te   ki-ta
     door=ACC   open-COND   cat=NOM   pounce=CVB   come-PST
     '**As soon as** I opened the door, a cat came pouncing onto me.' (temporal condition: immediate)

(15) doa=o   ake-**reba**   kaze=ga   tooQ-te   suzuši-i
     door=ACC   open-PROV   wind=NOM   pass-CVB   cool-NPST
     'Open the door **and** a nice breeze will flow through.' (provisional condition)

3.7 Verbal Suffixes I: Final Suffixes

(16) doa=o muriyari=ni ake-**tara** koware-čaQ-ta
door=ACC forceful=ADV open-COND break-CVB.IRCOM-PST
'I opened the door forcefully **and** it broke.' (perfective condition)

(17) doa=o ake-**ru=nara[ba]** eakoN=o keši-ta hoo=ga
door=ACC open-NPST=COND air.conditioner=ACC turn.off-PST way=NOM
i-i
good-NPST
'**If** you're going to open the door, then you should turn off the air conditioner.' (assertive condition)

(18) cura-**kutomo** saigo=made akirame-na-i
tough-CONC end=TERM give.up-NEG-NPST
'**No matter** how tough it is, I won't give up until the end' (concessive)

(19a) haya-**kutomo** roku-ji (19b) oo-**kutomo** gojuQ-ko
early-CONC six-o'clock many-CONC 50-CLS
'at the earliest, 6 o'clock' (lower limit) 'at the most, 50' (upper limit)

(20) kaQte=ni doa=o ake-rare-**tewa** komar-u
without.consideration=DAT door=ACC open-PASS-COND be.troubled-NPST
'**If** you go opening doors without asking, we're going to have a problem.' (emphatic condition)

(21) nani=o ši-**temo** dame=da
what=ACC do-CONC no.good=COP.NPST
'**No matter** what I do, things never work out.' (concessive)

(22) oki-**tewa** tabe-ru. tabe-**tewa** mata ne-ru
wake.up-COND eat-NPST eat-COND again sleep-NPST
'I wake up **and** I eat. I eat **and** I go back to sleep (again and again).' (iterative)

(23a) yaQ[-**tewa** ~ **ča**] ik-e-na-i (23b) yaQ-**temo** i-i
do-COND go-POT-NEG-NPST do-CONC good-NPST
'You **may not** do that.' (prohibitive) 'You **may** do that.' (permissive)

(24) yar-ana[-**kutewa** ~ -**kuča** ~ -**kya**] ik-e-na-i
do-NEG-COND go-POT-NEG-NPST
'I **must** do that' (necessitive)

(25) hirugohaN=o tabe-**tekara** ik-u
lunch=ACC eat-ACVB go-NPST
'I'll go **after** eating lunch.' (temporal ablative)

(26) keitaideNwa=o   mi-**nagara**   aruk-u   koto=wa   abuna-i
     cell.phone=ACC   look-SIM   walk-NPST   thing=TOP   dangerous-NPST
     'It's dangerous to look at your mobile **while** you walk.' (simultaneous)

(27) uso=da=to   šir-**inagara**   yoku   sono   koto=o   i-u
     lie=COP.NPST=COMP   know-SIM   well   that   thing=ACC   say-NPST
     'You have a nerve saying that, knowing it's a lie.' (concessive)

(28) eiga=o   mi-**ni**   ik-imase-N=ka
     movie=ACC   see-PURP   go-POL-NEG=Q
     'Would you like to go and see a movie with me?' (purposive)

There exist no less than five nominalizers each for verbs and adjectives. The default verbal nominalizer -*(i)*, identical in shape to the adverbial but possessing a different accent pattern (§2.6), forms a verbal noun (a verb-like noun capable of taking an object: *mač-i* 'waiting' in *basu+mač-i* 'waiting for the bus') or deverbal noun (a full-fledged noun: *kaer-i* 'return' in *kaer-i=no šiNkaNseN* 'return shinkansen'). The suffixes -*(i)yoo* and -*(i)kata* act as instrumental nominalizers, turning a verb into a noun expressing method or means. While -*(i)yoo* is typically restricted to negative statements (29a), no such restriction exists for -*(i)kata* (29b). Finally, the suffixes -*(i)soo* and -*(i)gači*, both of which form nominal adjectives, express evidentiality. The former expresses the notion that something appears as if it is going to happen, or looks a certain way (visual evidential: 29c), while the latter indicates a tendency towards a certain state or action (tendential: 29d). In addition to attaching to verbs, *soo* can also attach to the stems of verbal and nominal adjectives (30a, 30b) and a select number of nouns (30c). Likewise, *gači* can also attach to select nouns (30d). Nominalizers exclusive to adjectives, which include -*sa*, -*mi*, -*ge* and -*me*, are covered in §3.5.

(29) a. yar-**iyoo**=ga na-i   'there's no **way to** do it' (instrumental)
     b. yar-**ikata**=o ošie-te   'teach me **how to** do it' (instrumental)
     c. ame=ga fur-**isoo**=da   '**looks like** it's going to rain' (visual evidential)
     d. yar-**igači**=na misu   '**commonly made** mistake' (tendential)
(30) a. tanoši-**soo**=da   '**looks like** fun' (visual evidential)
     b. šizuka-**soo**=na bašo   'a quiet **looking** place' (visual evidential)
     c. šiNpai-**soo**=na kao   'a worried look' (visual evidential)
     d. eNryo-**gači**=na taido   'a reserved attitude' (tendential)

In the discussion above, the observant reader may have noticed that -*te*, -*ta* and their various reflexes (-*taro[o]*, -*tara*, -*tari*, -*tewa*, -*temo*) do not take a fixed union vowel when attaching to consonant-stem verbs like the other consonant-initial suffixes, but instead trigger systematic sound changes in the stems of the verbs to which they attach. This is due to a set of sound changes known as *onbin* 'sound euphony', which began in approximately the 9th century (§2.9). Although

stem-final consonant	onbin rules				voicing of -te ~ -ta	examples
	stem-final consonant					
	→ ši	→ (ø)i	→ Q	→ N		
s~š	✔					sas-u → saši-te
k		✔				kak-u → ka(ø)i-te
g		✔			✔	kog-u → ko(ø)i-de
t~č~c			✔			kac-u → kaQ-te
r			✔			ar-u → aQ-te
ø (old p-stems)			✔			a(ø)-u → aQ-te
b				✔	✔	yob-u → yoN-de
m				✔	✔	yom-u → yoN-de
n				✔	✔	šin-u → šiN-de

Table 3.7.2: Onbin *forms of consonant-stem verbs*

consonant-stem verbs originally took the union vowel *i* before *-te* or *-ta*, this vowel now only emerges after verbs ending in *s~k~g* (for consistency, in examples throughout this volume, we include this union vowel in the stem of its respective verb). *Onbin* forms surface as either dropping of the stem-final consonant (*kak-u* → *ka(ø)i-te* 'write') or replacement of the stem-final consonant with a mora consonant (§2.2): *ka-u* → *kaQ-te* 'buy', *yob-u* → *yoN-de* 'call'. Both are accompanied by voicing of *-te ~ -ta* to *-de ~ -da* when the stem ends in *b~g~n~m*: *oyob-u* → *oyoN-de* 'extend', *oyog-u* → *oyoi-de* 'swim', *šin-u* → *šiN-de* 'die', *yom-u* → *yoN-de* 'read'. Further confusing an already complicated picture are irregular verbs such as *ik-u* 'go', whose stem alternates to *iQ-* (*iQ-te*, not *ii-te*), and *to-u* 'ask' and *ko-u* 'beg', whose stems alternate to *too-* and *koo-* (*too-te*, *koo-te*). A small number of verbs, such as *so-u* 'be parallel to, follow' and *o-u* 'bear', possess two *onbin* forms: *soQ-te ~ soo-te*, *oQ-te ~ oo-te* are all acceptable. The *onbin* forms of consonant-stem verbs are summarized in Table 3.7.2.

3.8 Verbal Suffixes II: Non-final Suffixes

The second type of verbal suffix (Fig. 3.7), non-final suffixes, are formed through derivation, a word-building process in which the word class or lexical meaning of the base form is modified, usually through affixation (§5.3). All non-final suffixes are actually verbals in and of themselves: that is, non-final suffixes do not close the suffix string, but create secondary stems upon which further affixes can be built. Non-final suffixes follow the same paradigms laid out for verbs and verbal adjectives in §3.3 and §3.5 and may be either verb-type (forming the same classes and taking the same suffixes as verbs) or adjective-type (taking the same suffixes as

meaning	label	form	slot	type	final suffixes
\multicolumn{6}{c}{suffixes attaching to verbs}					
causative	CAUS	-(s)ase-ru	1	verb	• all final suffixes
passive	PASS	-(r)are-ru	2	verb	• all final suffixes
potential	POT	-e-ru ~ -[ra]re-ru	2	verb	• all final suffixes
anti-honorific	AHON	-(i)yagar-u	3	verb	• all final suffixes
desiderative	DES	-(i)ta-i	4	adjective	• all final suffixes, but rarely nominalizers
negative	NEG	-(a)na-i	4	adjective	• all final suffixes, but rarely nominalizers
polite	POL	-(i)mas-u	4	verb	• -(r)u, -ta, -te, -tewa, -temo, -tekara, -(y)oo (irregular: -(i)maš-oo), -(a)N (irregular: -(i)mase-N), -(r)uto, -tara, -taroo, -tari, -e
suffixes attaching to adjectives					
emotive verbalizer*¹	VBLZ	-gar-u	5*²	verb	• all final suffixes

*¹ also attaches to a select number of nominal adjectives and -(i)ta-i.
*² resets suffix string to zero (may take any non-final suffix starting from slot 1).

Table 3.8: Non-final verbal suffixes

verbal adjectives). Non-final suffixes are commonly referred to as derivational suffixes and, while it is true that all non-final suffixes are derivational, a number of final suffixes (such as -ku or -sa) are also derivational in nature making the use of the term problematic (see §3.7 for further discussion).

Non-final suffixes are much less numerous than final suffixes and, in the modern language, limited almost entirely to verbs. This was not always the case, however, and in earlier stages of the language non-final suffixes were just as, or more, numerous than final suffixes: indeed, many modern final suffixes derive from non-final suffixes (§3.15). There are eight non-final suffixes in Modern Japanese, seven of which attach to verbs and one of which attaches to adjectives. These are summarized in Table 3.8.

The verb suffixes -(a)na-i and -(i)ta-i, both of which are adjective-type, express the negative (1a) and desiderative (1b). The remaining verb suffixes are verb-type. The most versatile of these, -(r)are-ru, in addition to expressing the passive (1c), can also express malefactive meaning (1d) or show respect towards an actor (1e). The suffix -(s)ase-ru expresses the causative (1f) or permissive (1g), while -e-ru ~ -[ra]re-ru are both potentials, the former attaching to consonant-stem (1h) and the latter to vowel-stem and K-irregular (1i) verbs: see also §3.3. Finally, -(i)mas-u is used to create the polite form of verbs (1j) (§6.3), while -(i)yagar-u forms the anti-honorific (1k) (§6.4).

3.8 Verbal Suffixes II: Non-final Suffixes

Two recent developments, particularly among younger cohorts (§6.1), that deserve attention are *ra-nuki* '*ra*-dropping' and *sa-ire* '*sa*-insertion'. The former refers to the dropping of the initial mora *ra* in the potential of vowel-stem verbs: *tabe-rare-ru* 'can eat' → *tabe-re-ru*. The latter refers to the insertion of *sa* (for consonant-stem verbs) or *isa* (for S-irregular verbs) before *se-ru* in the causative: *ik-ase-ru* 'make go, let go' → *ik-asase-ru*; *s-ase-ru* 'make do, let do' → *š-isase-ru*. Both phenomena are typically considered 'improper Japanese' by prescriptivists (although *ra-nuki* has been gradually gaining acceptance, even finding its way into L2 textbooks: §8.8), but from a linguistic standpoint could be viewed as shifts towards semantic or morphological transparency. That is, *ra-nuki* results in the elimination of pernicious homonymy (§5.9) between the potential and passive (both are *-rare-ru* after vowel-stem verbs in the Standard), while *sa-ire* brings the structure of the causative after consonant-stem and S-irregular verbs closer to that of other verb classes. In terms of linguistic change, *ra-nuki* seems to be a type of economization (phonetic reduction to improve efficiency), while *sa-ire* is held to arise from analogy: when taking the causative, the consonant- and S-irregular stems are analysed as final C*a*- and *ši*- respectively: both the so-called 'irrealis' ending of school grammar (§8.6). This results in all verb classes taking the same suffix *-sase-ru* (*ika-sase-ru*, *tabe-sase-ru*, *ši-sase-ru*, *ko-sase-ru*), thus eliminating the need for the *-ase-ru* allomorph. Whether this 'irrealis analysis' takes place on the subconscious level or is a result of prescriptive hypercorrection is unclear.

(1) a. *ik-**ana**-i* 'don't go' (negative)
    b. *tabe-**ta**-i* 'want to eat' (desiderative)
    c. *gojira=ni tabe-**rare**-ta* 'was eaten by Godzilla' (passive)
    d. *ame=ni fur-**are**-ta* 'was rained on' (malefactive)
    e. *seNsei=wa ik-**are**-mas-u=ka* 'will you go, professor?' (respectful)
    f. *yasai=o tabe-**sase**-ru* '**make** eat vegetables' (causative)
    g. *okaši=o tabe-**sase**-ru* '**let** eat candy' (permissive)
    h. *ik-**e**-ru* '**can** go' (potential)
    i. *tabe-[ra]**re**-ru ~ ko-[ra]**re**-ru* '**can** eat' ~ '**can** come' (potential)
    j. *ik-**imas**-u* 'go' (polite)
    k. *tabe-**yagar**-u* '**fucking** eat' (anti-honorific)

The sole adjective non-final suffix, *-gar-u*, attaches to the stems of emotive adjectives turning them into verbs of feeling or emotion: *tanoši-i* 'fun' → *tanoši-gar-u* 'feel (that something is) fun', *uQtooši-i* 'annoying' → *uQtooši-gar-u* 'feel annoyed'. This suffix also attaches to a select number of emotive nominal adjectives (*iya* 'be disinclined' → *iya-gar-u* 'feel disinclined', *zaNneN* 'regrettable' → *zaNneN-gar-u* 'feel regretful'), as well as to the desiderative of verbs (essentially an adjective), in which case it expresses the desire of a second/third person animate (*ik-ita-gar-u* 'you/he/she/it/they want(s) to go', *tabe-ta-gar-u* 'you/he/she/it/they want(s) to eat'). In addition to *-gar-u*, there are many other verbalizer suffixes which attach to adjectives and, in some cases, nouns as well. These include -*m-u*, which expresses a state of being (*tanoši-m-u* 'have fun', *kuruši-m-u* 'be in pain') and -*bur-u*, which expresses putting on an act (*era-bur-u* 'act important', *gakuša-bur-u* 'act like a scholar'). None of these, however, are productive to any extent in the modern language and thus not included in Table 3.8.

There are a number of rules concerning the order in which non-final suffixes may occur. With just one exception, the causative appears in slot 1 of a string, followed by the passive or potential (never co-occurring) in slot 2. The anti-honorific appears in slot 3, followed by the desiderative, negative or polite form (none ever co-occurring) in slot 4, and finally the emotive verbalizer in slot 5. After the emotive verbalizer, a suffix string is 'reset' to zero, overturning the causative's leftmost prominence and permitting such forms as *ik-ita-gar-ase-ru* 'make want to go' or *tabe-ta-gar-ase-ru* 'make want to eat'. This becomes possible because the desiderative essentially yields an adjective stem, which is then derived back into a verb through the emotive verbalizer. These five slots are summarized in Table 3.8, along with a list of rules concerning the further suffixation of each form.

The slots are a list of possibilities, not actualities. Thus, while a 'maxed out' suffix string might look something like (2), in practice this form would never be encountered. Likewise, not all combinations of suffixes, even if in the correct order, are possible: the grammaticality of both ?*ik-e-ta-i* 'want to be able to go' (potential+desiderative) and ?*ik-e-yagar-u* 'fucking can go' (potential + anti-honorific), for example, are questionable, while *ik-iyagar-imas-u* 'fucking go (polite)' is grammatically licit but highly sarcastic in tone. Interestingly, the 'resetting' of the string by -*gar-u* may allow for the same non-final suffix to occur more than once in the same string: once in the 'inner stem' of the initial verb and once in the 'outer stem' of the derived emotive verb (3). The practicality of such a 'double causative' form, though licit, is questionable, however. While unable to co-occur in the same string, the desiderative and negative are often used together in the analytic construction -*(i)ta-ku na-i* (§3.9) to express the undesirable: *ik-ita-ku na-i* 'don't want to go', *tabe-ta-ku na-i* 'don't want to eat'.

(2) ?*tabe-sase-rare-ta-gar-iyagar-imas-u*
    eat-CAUS-PASS-DESS-VBLZ-AHON-POL-NPST
    'Fucking want to be made to eat.' (polite)

(3) *haha=ga   kodomo=ni   keNka=o   yame-sase-ta-gar-ase-ta*
    mother=NOM   child=DAT   fight=ACC   stop-CAUS-DESS-VBLZ-CAUS-PST
    'The mother **made** the child want to **make** the fight stop.'

Most non-final suffixes can take all (or at least the majority of) final suffixes. The exception is the polite suffix -*(i)mas-u*, which is restricted to select suffixes. Two of these are irregular: the negative -*(i)mase-N*, where -*(i)mas-u* switches to an S-irregular pattern (§3.3) and takes the archaic/Western negative -*(a)N* (§3.7, §7.9);

and the conjectural-hortative *-(i)maš-oo*, seemingly a contraction of *-(i)maši-yoo*, also following an S-irregular pattern. While one is highly selective. The imperative *-(i)mas-e* only appears after *iraQšar-u ~ kudasar-u ~ nasar-u*: *iraQša-imas-e* 'welcome', *kudasa-imas-e* 'please', *o-yasum-i+nasa-imas-e* 'good night' (all forms being superpolite and the latter two strongly female preferential: §6.1). The copula *des-u* possesses the same irregular conjectural *deš-oo*, while also being restricted to mostly the same suffixes as *-(i)masu* (see §3.6 and Table 3.7.1 for further discussion).

3.9 Auxiliaries

Japanese verbs and, to a lesser extent, verbal adjectives are commonly strung together to form compounds (§5.4), with the final element acting as the head (§1.2) of the compound and all preceding elements being its dependents, or modifiers. For 2-element (E1+E2) compounds, when the dependent is a verb, the compound takes the shape [E1 adverbial (§3.7) + E2]: *nom-i+aruk-u* 'drink+walk → go on a pub crawl', *tabe+yasu-i* 'eat+easy → easy to eat'. When, however, the dependent is an adjective, the compound takes the shape [E1 stem + E2]: *ama+zuQpa-i* 'sweet+sour → bittersweet', *tabe+sugi-ru* 'eat+exceed → overeat'. In cases such as *tabe+yasu-i* and *tabe+sugi-ru*, in which the head can be construed as expressing grammatical meaning (in this case, facility and excessiveness), we commonly refer to the heads as auxiliaries. Auxiliaries may be verbs (*tabe+sugi-ru*) or adjectives (*tabe+yasu-i*) and, in addition to forming compounds, they may also follow the *-te* form of a verb, or the adverbial of verbal adjectives, to form a complex predicate: *tabe-te i-ru* 'have eaten, are eating' (perfect-progressive), *omoširo-ku na-i* 'not interesting' (negative). In the ensuing discussion, to distinguish such complex predicate-forming auxiliaries from compound-forming auxiliaries, we add *-te* in front of auxiliaries which follow the *-te* form of a verb and *-ku* in front of those which follow the adverbial of verbal adjectives. Auxiliaries can be broken down into five groups based on grammatical category: aspectual, diathetic (pertaining to voice), benefactive, modal and negative.

Aspectual auxiliaries are by far the most common of the five. The most frequent, and perhaps most versatile, is *-te i-ru*, which can express the progressive (1a), perfect (1b), habitual (1c) and stative (1d) aspects. Similar to *-te i-ru* is *-te ar-u*, which expresses stative aspect (1e), though only for inanimate objects: **tookyoo=ni suN-de ar-u* 'live in Tokyo' is illicit. Two other frequently used aspectual auxiliaries are *-te ok-u* and *-te šima-u*. The first expresses an action done in preparation (1f), a temporary measure (1g) or an action done at the request of another (1h). Meanwhile, *-te šima-u* indicates an action that is irreversible once completed (1i). In casual speech, *-te i-ru*, *-te o-ku* and *-te šima-u* are commonly contracted to *-te-ru*, *-tok-u* and *-ča-u* (or, less frequently, *-čima-u*), with the allomorphs *-de-ru ~ -dok-u ~ -ja-u ~ -jima-u* occurring in the relevant *onbin* environment (Table 3.7.2).

auxiliary category	form	lexical meaning	grammatical functions, notes and examples[1]
aspectual	cukus-u	'expend'	• expended completive (*i-i+cukus-u* 'say everything you have to say')
	cuzuke-ru	'continue'	• continuative (*iki+cuzuke-ru* 'continue living, stay alive')
	das-u	'take out'	• sudden inchoative (*wara-i+das-u* 'burst out laughing')
	hajime-ru	'start'	• inchoative (*kak-i+hajime-ru* 'begin writing')
	kake-ru	'hang'	• incompletive (*šin-i+kake-ru* 'be dying, be about to die')
	kir-u	'cut'	• completive (*tabe+kir-u* 'finish eating entirely')
	kom-u	'be crowded'	• intensive (*siɴji+kom-u* 'firmly believe')
	makur-u	'roll up'	• iterative (*yar-i+makur-u* 'do again and again')
	naos-u	'fix'	• revisional (*kak-i+naos-u* 'write over again, rewrite')
	nogas-u	'miss'	• missed completive (*deɴša=o nor-i+nogas-u* 'miss the train')
	owar-u ~ oe-ru	'finish'	• terminative (*tabe-owar-u* 'finish eating', *yom-i+oe-ru* 'finish reading')
	sokona-u	'lose'	• failed completive (*ik-i+sokona-u* 'fail to go')
	sugi-ru	'exceed'	• excessive (*nom-i+sugi-ru* 'drink too much') • can also follow adjective stems (*kura-sugi-ru* 'too dark')
	-ku nar-u	'become'	• translative (*aka-ku nar-u* 'turn red') • follows adjectives
	-te ar-u	'exist'	• inanimate perfect ('be done')
	-te i-ru	'be'	• progressive ('be doing') • perfect ('have done') • habitual ('do regularly'), stative ('be in the state of') • contracted to *-te-ru ~ -de-ru* in casual speech • glossed as PROG
	-te ik-u	'go'	• departing action (*kore=kara omoširo-ku naꞯ-te ik-u* 'things are going to get interesting from here on out') • nonpast contracted to *-te ku* in casual speech
	-te iraꞯšar-u	'be'	• respectful form of *-te i-ru* • contracted to *-teraꞯšar-u ~ -deraꞯšar-u* in casual speech
	-te ku-ru	'come'	• arriving action (*acu-ku naꞯ-te ki-ta* 'it's got hot out')
	-te mair-u	'come'	• humble form of *-te ku-ru*
	-te ok-u	'put'	• preparative ('do in advance') • temporary ('do for now') • compliant ('do for somebody') • contracted to *-tok-u ~ -dok-u* in casual speech
	-te or-u	'be'	• humble form (or Western form: §7.9) of *-te i-ru* • contracted to *-tor-u ~ -dor-u* in casual speech
	-te šima-u	'put away'	• irreversible completive ('do and cannot take back') • contracted to *-ča-u ~ -ja-u* or *-čima-u ~ -jima-u* in casual speech • glossed as IRCOM

[1] when already given in the text above, examples are omitted from the table.

Table 3.9: Commonly used auxiliaries

(1) a. *ima tabe-**te i-ru***   'ea**ting** now' (progressive)
     b. *moo tabe-**te i-ru***   '**have already** eaten' (perfect)
     c. *mainiči saɴpo ši-**te i-ru*** 'go for a walk every day' (habitual)
     d. *tookyoo=ni suɴ-**de i-ru***   'live in Tokyo' (stative)
     e. *nani=ka kai-**te ar-u***   'something is written' (inanimate stative)

3.9 Auxiliaries

auxiliary category	form	lexical meaning	grammatical functions, notes and examples*¹
diathetic	a-u	'match up'	• reciprocal ('do back and forth'), harmonious ('do together')
	-ku su-ru	'do'	• causative verbalizer ('make be/do') • follows adjectives
benefactive		see Table 3.10 for a list of benefactive auxiliaries	
modal	e-ru ~ uru	'attain'	• potential (ar-i+e-ru ~ ar-i+uru 'possible (lit. can exist)') • uru (← u-ru) is an archaic form of the nonpast (§3.15)
	gata-i	'solid'	• universal labourative ('hard for anyone to do')
	kane-ru	'combine'	• negative potential (i-i+kane-ru 'cannot say')
	nasar-u	'do'	• respectful auxiliary (turns a verb into a respectful form: §6.3) • quasi-obsolete • used overwhelmingly in imperative, which may be contracted to na in casual speech
	niku-i	'detestable'	• physical labourative ('hard to do physically') • non-frequentative ('doesn't occur frequently')
	-te hoši-i	'want'	• desire or wish towards a second/third party ('want you/him/her/it/them to do, wish would happen')
	-te mi-ru	'see'	• attemptive ('try to do') • exploratory ('discover when doing')
	-te mise-ru	'show'	• demonstrative ('show that I can do')
	yasu-i	'peaceful'	• facilitative ('easy to do') • frequentative ('occurs frequently')
	zura-i	'painful'	• intimate labourative ('physically or mentally painful to do')
negative	-ku na-i	'nonexistent'	• negative • follows adjectives
	-te na-i	'nonexistent'	• negative of -te ar-u • homonymous in casual speech with -te-na-i, contracted form of te i-na-i (negative of -te i-ru)

Table 3.9 (continued)

f. biiru=o hiyaši-te ok-u   'chill a beer **in advance**' (preparative)
g. doa=o ake-te ok-u   'leave the door open **(for now)**' (temporary)
h. yorošiku=to cutae-te ok-u 'I'll give them your regards' (compliant)
i. kaQ-te šima-u=yo   'I'm buying it **(and you can't stop me)**' (irreversible)

Diathetic auxiliaries include *a-u*, which expresses an action conducted by two or more parties, either reciprocally (2a) or in harmony (2b), and the causative verbalizer *-ku su-ru*, which changes an adjective into a causative verb (2c). The more analytic form *ni su-ru* can be found after noun phrases (NPs) and nominal adjectives: *dameniNGeN=ni su-ru* 'make into a hopeless loser', *kirei=ni su-ru* 'make pretty, make clean'. Benefactives, which indicate for whose benefit an action is performed, are covered separately in §3.10.

Modal auxiliaries include *-te mi-ru*, expressing attempt (3a) or discovery (3b); *-te mise-ru*, an attempt to prove something (3c); and *-te hoši-i*, a desire or wish on the part of the speaker towards a second or third party (3d). Modal auxiliaries also include a group of auxiliaries expressing ease or difficulty that we will call facilitatives and labouratives. There is one facilitative, *yasu-i*, and three labouratives, *niku-i*, *zura-i* and *gata-i*, each with subtly different connotations. The facilitative *yasu-i* comes from the adjective *yasu-i*, originally meaning 'peaceful, easy', and indicates an action is easy (3e) or frequently occurs (3f). The three labouratives come from the adjectives *niku-i* 'detestable', *cura-i* 'painful' and *kata-i* 'solid, hard'. The first indicates an action is physically difficult (3g) or infrequently occurs (3h); *-cura-i* an action that is not only difficult but also causes some degree of physical or mental discomfort (3i); and *kata-i* an action whose occurrence is objectively or universally problematic (3j–3k). Modal auxiliaries are unique in that they contain a large number of verbal adjectives, while the other categories of auxiliaries consist primarily of verbs.

(2) a. *kiso-i+a-u*   'compete **back and forth**' (reciprocal)
    b. *yorokob-i+a-u*   'rejoice **together**' (harmonious)
    c. *tanoši-ku su-ru*   '**make** something fun' (causative verbalizer)

(3) a. *yaQ-te mi-ru*   'give it a try' (attemptive)
    b. *doa=o ake-te mi-ruto*   'upon opening the door...' (exploratory)
    c. *yaQ-te mise-ru=zo*   'I'll **show you** I can do it!' (demonstrative)
    d. *gaNbaQ-te hoši-i*   'I **want** you to try your best' (wish towards 2nd/3rd party)
    e. *tabe+yasu-i*   '**easy to** eat' (facilitative)
    f. *byooki=ni nar-i+yasu-i*   '**frequently** get ill' (frequentative)
    g. *hone=ga oo-kute tabe+niku-i*   'it's bony and **hard to** eat' (physical labourative)
    h. *byooki=ni nar-i+niku-i*   '**rarely** get ill' (non-frequentative)
    i. *ik-i+zura-i*   '**difficult to** get to' (due to physical/mental reservation)
    j. *soozoo+ši+gata-i*   '**hard to** imagine' (universally problematic)
    k. *ar-i+gata-i*   'much appreciated (lit. **hard to** exist)'

    The negative auxiliary *na-i* 'lit. nonexistent' can follow the *-te* form of verbs or the adverbial of verbal adjectives. When following the *-te* form, *na-i* can actually be one of two forms: the negative of *-te ar-u* (*nanimo kai-te na-i* 'nothing is written') or a contraction of *-te i-nai* to *-te-na-i* (*saikiN roNbuN=o kai-te-na-i* 'I haven't written any papers recently'). In many cases, it is impossible to distinguish between the two forms given their pernicious homonymy (§5.9). Unlike verbs, which have a distinct negative suffix *-(a)na-i*, verbal adjectives form the negative by taking *na-i* or the polite negative form of the verb *ar-u*: *oiši-ku na-i* ~ *oiši-ku ar-imase-N* 'not delicious'. Both of these forms mirror the analytic forms *de[wa] na-i* ~ *de[wa] ar-imase-N* used as a negative copula after NPs and nominal adjectives (§3.6). Similar to the copula negative, the adjective negative may take *wa~mo* between *-ku* and *na-i*, but always with contrastive meaning: *oiši-ku=wa na-i* 'not particularly delicious', *mazu-ku=mo na-i* 'also not disgusting'. The super-polite *gozar-u* forms (§6.3) may also be put in the negative (*oišuu goza-imase-N*), but are largely obsolete.

Unlike English auxiliaries such as *may* or *can*, which have undergone full grammaticalization (§3.2), being bleached of their lexical meaning, with nearly all Japanese auxiliaries, the lexical meaning of the form in question can still be inferred to a certain degree. For example, *-te i-ru* (← *i-ru* 'be') can be interpreted as '*be* doing', *-te ok-u* (← *ok-u* 'place, lay down') as '*placing* or *laying down* an action in advance or for the time being' and *-te šima-u* (← *šima-u* 'put away') as '*putting away* an action (so that it cannot be reversed)'. Table 3.9 gives a list of the major auxiliaries, along with their lexical and grammatical meanings. It is by no means comprehensive and for a more detailed overview we direct the reader to the literature cited in Further Reading at the end of this volume. Unless stated otherwise, the auxiliaries in the chart follow only verbs. While verbal suffixes and particles are given glossing labels (Tables 3.7.1, 3.8, 3.12.1–3.12.4, 3.13.2) in the examples throughout this volume, with the exception of a few of the more major forms (indicated in the chart), we simply gloss auxiliaries with their lexical meaning.

3.10 Verbs of Giving and Receiving and Benefactive Auxiliaries

Japanese verbs of giving and receiving (G&R) form a three-way system of those expressing centrifugal giving (transfer of an object outwards from the giver), centripetal giving (transfer of an object inwards towards the receiver) and reception (emphasis on the act of receiving). Their meanings are expressed by the core verbs *age-ru* 'give (centrifugal)', *kure-ru* 'give (centripetal)' and *mora-u* 'receive', each of which possesses honorific (§6.3) and, in the case of *age-ru*, anti-honorific (§6.4) counterparts. Unlike English G&R verbs, the actions carried out by the three core G&R verbs and their counterparts are in nearly all cases beneficial to the recipient and G&R verbs are rarely used in negative contexts. Fig. 3.10 schematizes the usage of the three core G&R verbs, with the exchange of objects taking place between the speaker (A) and a second or third party (B). See also Table 3.10 for an overview.

With *age-ru*, although the giver may be the speaker (1) or a second/third party (2), the receiver is limited to a second/third party—a speaker can never use *age-ru* when they are the receiver. When the giver and receiver are both a second/third party, the benefit gained is neutral to the speaker (2). The verb *age-ru* possesses a humble honorific counterpart *sašiage-ru* and an anti-honorific counterpart *yar-u*, which is used towards equals and inferiors (3a) or non-human lifeforms, such as animals (3b) or plants (3c). Just as with many anti-honorific forms, *yar-u* does not necessarily express contempt. When used towards equals and inferiors it is often

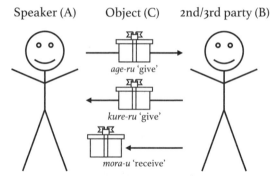

A=*ga* B=*ni* C=*o age-ru* 'A gives C to B' (centrifugal)
B=*ga* A=*ni* C=*o kure-ru* 'B gives C to A' (centripetal)
A=*ga* B=*ni* C=*o mora-u* 'A receives C from B' (reception)
Fig. 3.10: Core verbs of giving and recieving

form	direction	honorific level	notes
age-ru	centrifugal giving	neutral	• -*te age-ru* may be contracted to -*tage-ru* ~ -*dage-ru* in casual speech • benefactive use towards superiors rude
sašiage-ru	centrifugal giving	respectful	• benefactive use hyper-polite and possibly rude
yar-u	centrifugal giving	anti-honorific	• used towards inferiors, animals and plants
kure-ru	centripetal giving	neutral	• has anti-honorific imperative *kure*[e]
kudasar-u	centripetal giving	respectful	• final *r* drops before -(*i*)*mas-u* and -*i* (§3.3)
mora-u	reception	neutral	• rarely used with 2nd/3rd party receiver
itadak-u	reception	humble	• rarely used with 2nd/3rd party receiver

Table 3.10: Verbs of giving and receiving/benefactive auxiliaries

just a marker of casual or rough speech and when used towards non-human lifeforms it is arguably politeness neutral.

(1) *maitoši   tomodači*=*ni   taɴjoobi*+*purezeɴto*=*o   *age-ru*
     every.year   friend=DAT   birthday+present=ACC   give-NPST
     'Every year, I give my friend a birthday present.' (beneficial to friend)

(2) *seito-tači*=*ga   *seɴsei*=*ni   *čokoreeto*=*o   *age-ta*
     student-PL=NOM   teacher=DAT   chocolate=ACC   give-PST
     'The students gave their teacher some chocolate.' (beneficial to teacher)

(3a) *kodomo*=*ni   *okaši*=*o   *yaQ-ta*
     child=DAT   sweets=ACC   give.AHON-PST

3.10 Verbs of Giving and Receiving and Benefactive Auxiliaries

'I gave my kid some sweets.' (towards inferior)

(3b) inu=ni   esa=o   yaq-ta
     dog=DAT   food=ACC   give.AHON-PST
     'I gave my dog his food.' (towards animal)

(3c) hana=ni   mizu=o   yaq-ta
     flower=DAT water=ACC   give.AHON-PST
     'I watered the flowers (lit. I gave the flowers water).' (towards plant)

The verb *kure-ru*, in addition to expressing giving from a second/third party to the speaker (4), can also express giving to members of the speaker's ingroup (friends, family, co-workers), as in (5). When the receiver is a member of the speaker's ingroup, the benefit gained usually impacts (even if indirectly) the speaker as well. As the agent is always a second/third party and never the speaker, *kure-ru* possesses no humble honorific counterpart but instead a respectful honorific counterpart *kudasar-u*. While there is no anti-honorific counterpart, the stem of *kure-ru*, *kure* (sometimes lengthened to *kuree*), can be used to express a rough command: *sake=o kure[e]* 'give me the booze!'

(4) tomodači=ga   suteki=na   purezento=o   kure-ta
    friend=NOM   wonderful=ADNLZ   present=ACC   give-PST
    'My friend gave me a wonderful present.' (beneficial to speaker)

(5) šokuba=no   hito=ga   haha=ni   keeki=o   kure-ta
    workplace=GEN   person=NOM   mother=DAT   cake=ACC   give-PST
    'A person where my mother works gave her a cake.' (beneficial to member of speaker's ingroup)

With *mora-u*, the agent (in this case the receiver) is almost always the speaker (6). One exception is in situations in which the speaker is speaking from the perspective of the addressee, as in (7). Given that the speaker is typically the agent, *mora-u* possesses the humble honorific counterpart *itadak-u*, but no respectful form.

(6) tomodači=ni   suteki=na   purezento=o   moraq-ta
    friend=DAT   wonderful=ADNLZ   present=ACC   receive-PST
    'I got a wonderful present from my friend' (beneficial to speaker)

(7) A. kore   takeši-san=kara   moraq-ta   tokei.   kawai-i=deš-o
       this   Takeshi-HON=ABL   receive-PST   watch   cute-NPST=COP.POL-CJT
       'I got this watch from Takeshi. It's cute, isn't it?

    B. sore   takeši=ja   na-kute   ore=kara   moraq-ta=daroo
       that   Takeshi=COND   nonexistent-CVB   I=ABL   receive-PST=COP.CJT
       'That's not from Takeshi, it's from me, you know.' (from addressee's perspective)

In addition to being used independently, as illustrated in (1)–(7), *age-ru*, *kure-ru*, *mora-u* and their (anti-)honorific counterparts are often used as auxiliary verbs (§3.11) to indicate that the recipient of an action benefits from such action. Such auxiliaries are commonly referred to as 'benefactives'. The auxiliaries *-te age-ru* ~ *-te yar-u* express benefactivity from the perspective of the giver (8)–(9), while *-te kure-ru* ~ *-te kudasar-u* and *-te mora-u* ~ *-te itadak-u* express benefactivity from the perspective of the recipient (10)–(11). While *-te yar-u* bears the same anti-honorific connotations as *yar-u* above, *-te age-ru* is rarely used towards superiors as it can sound condescending or arrogant to imply directly that one's action is benefiting a superior. The auxiliary *-te sašiage-ru*, while grammatically licit, is rarely used in practice as it can sound hyper-polite and sarcastic (12). Similar to *-te i-ru* contracting to *-te-ru* ~ *-de-ru* (§3.11), *-te age-ru* may be contracted to *-tage-ru* ~ *-dage-ru* (*yaQ-tage-ru* 'do for you', *hakoN-dage-ru* 'carry for you') in casual speech.

(8) kyoo=wa   wataši=ga   yuuhaN=o   cukuQ-te   age-mas-u
    today=TOP I=NOM   dinner=ACC   make-CVB   give-POL-NPST
    'Today, I'll cook dinner for you.' (beneficial to addressee)

(9) beNtoo=o   sukoši   wake-te   yar-oo=ka
    lunch=ACC   a.little   split-CVB   give.AHON-CJT=Q
    'How about I split my lunch with you?' (beneficial to addressee; anti-honorific)

(10) yuuhaN=o   cukuQ-te   kure-te   arigatoo=ne
     dinner=ACC   make-CVB   give-CVB   thank.you=CONF
     'Thanks for cooking me dinner!' (beneficial to speaker)

(11) eki=made   mukae-ni   ki-te   itadak-e-mas-u=ka
     station=TERM   pick.up-PURP   come-CVB   receive.HUM-POT-POL-NPST=Q
     'Could you come and pick me up at the station?' (beneficial to speaker; humble)

(12) ?čikara=o   kaši-te   sašiage-maš-oo=ka
     helping.hand=ACC   lend-CVB   give.HUM-POL-CJT=Q
     'Could I lend you a hand?' (beneficial to addressee; hyper-polite)

While it is possible to use G&R verbs in a negative sense, or even benefactive auxiliaries (in this case, 'malefactives'), doing so implies, in most cases, condescension, frustration or sarcasm. In examples (13)–(14), *mora-u* and *kure-ru* express the notion that the speaker has received something burdensome or unwanted: (14) makes use of the adverb *yokumo* 'well' for added sarcastic effect.

(13) kodomo=kara   kaze=o   moraQ-ta
     child=ABL   cold=ACC   receive-PST
     'I got a cold from my kid.' (slightly condescending)

(14) suzuki-seNsei   yokumo   aNna   waru-i   seiseki=o   cuke-te
     Suzuki-teacher   well   that.kind bad-NPST   grade=ACC   mark-CVB
     kure-ta=na
     give-PST=CONF
     'Prof. Suzuki's got a nerve giving me such a bad grade!' (sarcastic)

3.11 Conjunctions

One of the first questions that arises when discussing conjunctions in Japanese is whether or not they exist in the language in the first place. From a strictly syntactic perspective, most scholars would give a firm 'no', but from a functional viewpoint, the problem is not so simple. A quick look at any Japanese grammar will show that there is no lack of constructions for linking words or clauses. All such constructions, however, are either derived from, or are semantic extensions of, other parts of speech such as nouns, verbs or particles (§3.12, §3.13). While it is frequently the case cross-linguistically that conjunctions are grammaticalizations (§3.2) of other word classes, in the case of Japanese many of the underlying forms still retain a fair deal of their original meaning. It is thus difficult to state whether or not these constructions have developed fully into conjunctions or not. Further complicating the question is the fact that most so-called conjunctions can also be treated as conjunctive adverbs (§3.1, §3.5).

Take *sošite* '(and) then', for example. Etymologically, this is a reduction of *soošite* 'in that way' (§3.2), from *soo* 'that way' and *ši-te*, the *-te* form (§3.7) of *su-ru* 'do'. In fact, the full form of this conjunction is still common in Modern Japanese, as in (1). While the *soošite* and *sošite* variations of (1) bear slightly different connotations—*soošite* implies that going bankrupt was the cause of the father losing his money, while *sošite* simply indicates that the father lost his money *after* going bankrupt—both *soošite* and *sošite*, in their essence, express a causal relationship between the two sentences. The same type of causal relationship, however, can also be expressed simply by using a converb such as *-te*, as in (2). Thus, since *soošite* and *sošite* each contain *-te* in their underlying forms, from a syntactic standpoint one could argue that *soošite* and *sošite* function not as conjunctions proper but as subordinate adverbial clauses (§3.7), or conjunctive adverbs.

(1) čiči=no   kaiša=ga   toosaN+ši-ta.
    father=GEN   company=NOM   bankruptcy+do-PST

    [soošite~sošite]   okane=ga   na-ku   naQ-ta
    [in.that.way ~ then]   money=NOM   nonexistent-ADV become-PST
    'My father's company went bankrupt. [**That's how ~ Then**] he lost his money.'

(2) čiči=no   kaiša=ga   toosaN+ši-te
    father=GEN   company=NOM   bankruptcy+do-CVB

   okane=ga   na-ku   naQ-ta
   money=NOM   nonexistent-ADV   become-PST
   'My father's company went bankrupt **and** he lost his money.'

This is but one example—and similar arguments can be made for all of the so-called conjunctions in Japanese. The underlying form is not always as apparent as it is in the case of *sošite*. Take, for example, the words *šikaši* 'however', *oyobi* 'and' and *aruiwa* 'or'. Each of these can be traced back to lexical nouns and verbs: *šikaši* is a truncation of *šikašinagara*, itself a merger of *šika* 'that way' (now obsolete) and *ši-nagara* 'while doing'; *oyobi* the adverbial form (§3.7) of the verb *oyob-u* 'reach'; and *aruiwa* a merger of the verb *ar-u* 'exist', the obsolete emphatic particle *i* (§3.15) and the topic marker *wa* (§3.12, §3.14). Each of these words was grammaticalized far before the modern period, however, and it would be a stretch to say that the average native speaker is conscious of their underlying forms and etymologies. While *šikaši* is perhaps better treated as a conjunctive adverb (similar to English *however*), *oyobi* is used to coordinate words within a single clause (*gureetoburitaN oyobi kitaairuraNdo reNgooookoku* 'United Kingdom of Great Britain and Northern Ireland'), while *aruiwa* may be used for adverbial subordination (3) or coordination within a single clause (4). Thus, one could argue that it is only proper to use the word 'conjunction' for words that mark coordination within a single clause, such as *oyobi* and *aruiwa*, and for which the etymology is opaque. Such words make up only a small portion of conjunctive expressions in Japanese, however, and interestingly all arise from direct translations, or 'imitations', of Classical Chinese (see §7.1 for further discussion).

(3) roNbuN=wa   nihoNgo=de   tookoo+ši-te   kudasai.
    paper=TOP   Japanese   submit+do-CVB   please

   aruiwa   eigo=demo   ukecuke-mas-u
   alternatively English=CONC   accept-POL-NPST
   'Please submit papers in Japanese. Papers in English will **also** be accepted.'
   (adverb-like)

(4) roNbuN=wa   nihoNgo   *aruiwa*   eigo=de   tookoo+ši-te   kudasai
    paper=TOP   Japanese   **or**   English=LOC   submit+do-CVB   please
    'Please submit papers in Japanese **or** English.' (conjunction-like)

From an etymological standpoint, Japanese conjunctions can be divided into the seven categories listed in Table 3.11. Of these, the underlying forms of the examples in I–VI are all easily inferable by native speakers: like *soošite* and *sošite*, the particles, nouns or verbs of the underlying forms retain to some extent their original meaning and function. The underlying forms of the examples in VII, on the other hand,

	category	examples and etymologies
I	reanalysed particles (§3.12)	• *de* 'so' (← converbalizer particle: §3.13) • *demo* 'but' (← concessive converbalizer particle: §3.13) • *ga* 'but' (← adversative conjunctive particle: §3.12)
II	reanalysed verbal suffixes (§3.7–§3.8)	• *kedo[mo]~keredo[mo]* 'but' (← obsolete concessive adjective suffix *-keredo[mo]* or combination of obsolete hearsay past and concessive verb suffix *-(i)ker-edo[mo]*: §3.15)
III	inflections of verbs (verbs + final suffixes: §3.7)	• *šitagaQte* 'accordingly' (*šitaga-u* 'obey, follow' + *-te*) • *towaie* 'nevertheless' (complementizer *to* (§3.13) + topic marker *wa* (§3.12) + imperative of *i-u* 'say')
IV	copula-based constructions (§3.6)	• *dakara* 'therefore' (copula *da* + ablative case marker particle (CMP) *kara*: §3.12) • *dakedo* 'however' (*da* + *kedo*) • *nara~naraba* (← conditional *nar-aba* of obsolete copula *nar-i*: §3.15)
V	demonstrative-based constructions (§3.2)	• *soošite~sošite*[*1] • *sokode* 'thereupon' (*soko* 'there' + *de*) • *kokoni* 'hereupon' (*koko* 'here' + dative CMP *ni*)
VI	other noun-based constructions	• *tokoroga* 'however' (*tokoro* 'place' + adversative *ga*) • *tokorode* 'incidentally' (*tokoro* + *de*) • *iQpoo* 'on the one/ other hand' (originally 'one direction')
VII	etymology not easily inferable	• *šikaši*[*1] • *oyobi*[*1] • *aruiwa*[*1] • *naiši* 'or' (Sino-Japanese: §7.1) • *sunawači* 'namely' (originally 'moment of completion, immediately') • *cumari* 'namely' (← *cumar-u* 'be clogged') • *tadaši* 'however' (← *tada* 'only' + obsolete emphatic particle *ši*: §3.15) • *moQtomo* 'though' (← *motomo* 'true, truly')

[*1] see text for examples and discussion of etymology

Table 3.11: Commonly used conjunctions

are not easily inferable without knowledge of their etymologies, making these forms the closest to actual conjunctions.

3.12 Particles

The definition of what constitutes a particle is one of the most heated debates in Japanese linguistics. At the core of this debate lies the question: are particles actually words? The orthodox view in Japan, based on 'school grammar' (§8.6), defines particles as non-inflecting 'bound words' (*fuzokugo*) and posits six categories of particle based on syntactic properties. Such a definition seems, however, to fly in the face of the traditional definition of a word as 'the smallest string of meaning-bearing sounds that can be used in isolation'. For this reason, some scholars reject the notion of particles as words altogether, treating them as a type of affix, while others choose to treat them as 'clitics', a type of morpheme that is somewhere in between a word and an affix in that it possesses a degree of syntactic freedom but is phonologically dependent on its host. Both of these theories are not without issues, however. When put through certain 'tests' for 'affix-hood' or 'clitic-hood', particles show indecisive results. It must also be remembered that the definition of what constitutes a word is one of the most contested topics in linguistics.

Here, we will go no further than to define particles as short bound words that attach to the ends of other words, phrases and particles, or in some cases the ends of clauses and sentences, to express grammatical meaning. We group them into four main categories based on both their syntactic and semantic features: syntactic, thematic, restrictive and discourse. The most commonly found forms are listed in Tables 3.12.1–3.12.4, which are not intended to be comprehensive, but merely representative. A number of particles straddle multiple categories. For a more in-depth analysis, we direct the reader to Further Reading at the end of this volume.

Syntactic particles indicate the syntactic relationship between two elements in a sentence. These are the most diverse type of particle and can be subdivided into case marker, derivational and conjunctive particles. For reasons of space, case marker and conjunctive particles will be covered in the current unit, with derivational particles (particles that mark a shift in word class or syntactic function other than case) given special treatment in §3.13. Case marker particles (CMPs), of which there are 11, follow noun phrases (NPs) and mark case (§3.1). The main usages of each CMP are exemplified in (1), with more minor usages given in Table 3.12.1. Three CMPs, *ga*, *o* and *ni*, mark the nominative (subject: 1a), accusative (object: 1b) and dative (indirect object: 1c), respectively. Of these, *ga* also marks the direct object of desiderative and potential (§3.8) verb forms (1d, 1e), *o* also marking the ablative (movement away from a location: 1f) and prosecutive (movement across a surface: 1g) with certain verbs. Meanwhile, *ni* marks about another eight different cases including the allative (movement towards a location: 1h), locative (existence at a location: 1i) and temporal (occurrence at a time: 1j). The remaining eight CMPs are used as follows: *de* and *nite* (an older variant of *de*, mostly restricted to written language) mark the locative (1k) and instrumental (the means by which an action is performed: 1l), *e* the allative (1m: a function it shares with *ni*), while *kara* and *yori* mark the ablative (1n), *made* the terminative (movement up to a certain point: 1o), *no* the genitive (possession: 1p) and *to* the comitative (action together with others: 1q).

(1)   a. *minami=**ga** tabe-ru*   'Minami eats' (nominative)
     b. *piza=**o** tabe-ru*   'eat pizza' (accusative)
     c. *takuma=**ni** hon=o age-ru*   'give a book to Takuma' (dative)
     d. *nacumi=wa buta=**ga** tabe-ta-i*   'Natsumi wants to eat pork' (desiderative object)

e. *riN=wa airuraNdogo=ga hanas-e-ru*
   'Rin can speak Irish' (potential object)
f. *heya=o de-ru*   'step out of the room' (ablative)
g. *kooeN=o aruk-u*   'take a stroll through the park' (prosecutive)
h. *hoNkoN=ni ik-u*   'go to Hong Kong' (allative)
i. *šiNgapooru=ni i-ru*   'be in Singapore' (locative)
j. *rokuji=ni oki-ru*   'wake up at six' (temporal)
k. *ie=de yasum-u*   'rest up at home' (locative)
l. *te=de tabe-ru*   'eat with one's hands' (instrumental)
m. *herušiNki=e ik-u*   'go to Helsinki' (allative)
n. *berufasuto[=kara ~ =yori]* 'from Belfast' (ablative)
o. *keNburiǰi=made*   'as far as Cambridge' (terminative)
p. *taketo=no aifooN*   'Taketo's iPhone' (genitive)
q. *mari=to saNpo+su-ru*   'go for a walk with Mari' (comitative)
r. *imooto=no sačiko*   'my younger sister Sachiko (lit. younger sister's Sachiko)' (appositive genitive)

In addition to marking the genitive, *no* also marks what is known as the appositive genitive, a case marking syntactic parallelism between two nouns in a NP (1r). It is sometimes contracted to *n* in casual speech before *t~č~d~n* and occasionally in other environments also: *boku=n toko* 'my place'. When following another mora nasal, it may be lost entirely: *obaačan=ø či* 'grandma's house'. When used to mark the genitive, it is common for the head NP (the possessee) of a genitive construction formed by *no* to be omitted when understood through context (*kore=wa taisei=no hon=da* → *kore=wa taisei=no=da* 'this is Taisei's (book)'). Aside from a small number of exceptions, most notably the highly versatile *ni*, which can follow various forms of verbs and adjectives (*sum-u=ni i-i bašo* 'good place to live (lit. living is good place)', *yasu-i=ni koši-ta koto=wa na-i* 'cheaper is better (lit. being cheap is not surpassed)') and *made*, which can follow the nonpast of verbs (*šigoto=ga owar-u=made* 'until I finish work'), CMPs always follow NPs or other particles. They cannot typically follow, or be followed by, other CMPs. The exceptions are *kara* and *made*, which are commonly followed by other CMPs: *kore=kara=ga hoNbaN=da* 'now it's time for the real deal', *go-ji=made=ni owar-ita-i* 'I'd like to finish by 5 o'clock'. In such examples, the particles *kara~made* form a NP expressing point of origin or termination together with the preceding noun, and may thus be more appropriately treated as derivational particles. Headless genitive constructions formed with *no* may also be followed by other CMPs: *taisei=no=ga hoši-i* 'I want Taisei's'.

Conjunctive particles come in two types: nominal-linkers and clause-linkers. Many conjunctive particles are derived from CMPs, with others derived from thematic particles, verbal suffixes and copulas, many of which are obsolete (§3.15). The three main nominal-linkers are *ka*, *to* and *ya*: *ka* indicates a disjunctive relation ('or':

subclass	form	label	grammatical functions, notes and examples[*1]
case marker (CMP)	*de*	LOC	• locative (existence at) • instrumental (method or means) • temporal (time: *goji=de owari* 'ending at five o'clock') • causal (cause: *byooki=de taore-ru* 'be struck down by illness')
	e	ALL	• allative (movement towards) • dative (indirect object: *oya=e tegami=o okur-u* 'send a letter to one's parents') • may replace other uses of *ni* in certain dialects/registers
	ga	NOM	• nominative (subject) • desiderative/potential accusative (marks direct object of desiderative/potential verb forms), various other accusative usages
	kara	ABL	• ablative (movement away from) • temporal ablative (from a certain time: *nigacu=kara* 'from February') • causal (*hacumei=wa hicuyoo=kara umare-ru* 'inventions are conceived from necessity')
	made	TER	• terminative (movement up to a certain point) • temporal terminative (up to a certain time: *saNgacu=made* 'until March')
	ni	DAT	• dative • allative • locative • temporal • translative (transformation in state: *gakusei=ni nar-u* 'become a student') • comparative (comparison: *raibaru=ni masar-u* 'be superior to one's rival') • agentive (agent of passive/causative verb: *sagiši=ni damas-are-ru* 'be deceived by a con artist', *kaiša=ni zaNgyoodai=o šiharaw-ase-ru* 'make the company pay overtime') • causal (*daitooryoo=no boogeN=ni odorok-u* 'be surprised by the president's abusive language') • purposive (purpose: *kaimono=ni dekake-ru* 'go out shopping')
	nite	LOC	• locative • instrumental • temporal • causal
	no~N	GEN	• genitive (possession) • appositive genitive (apposition)
	o	ACC	• accusative (direct object) • ablative • prosecutive (movement across a surface)
	to	COM	• comitative (action together with others) • translative (*moNdai=to nar-u* 'become a problem') • comparative (*icumo=to onaji* 'same as always')
	yori	ABL	• ablative • temporal ablative (*goji=yori* 'from five o'clock') • referential comparative (marks a reference for comparison: *yamagata=wa yonezawa=yori hiro-i* 'Yamagata is bigger than Yonezawa')

[*1] when given in the text or easily inferable, examples are omitted.

Table 3.12.1: Commonly used syntactic particles

3.12 Particles 83

subclass	form	label	grammatical functions, notes and examples*¹
conjunctive 1: nominal-linker	ka		• disjunctive ('A or B') • ← interrogative ka
	ni		• additive ('in addition to A, B') • ← CMP ni
	to		• closed copulative (closed set 'A and B') • ← CMP to
	ya		• open copulative (open set 'A and B') • ← obsolete interrogative particle ya (§3.15)
conjunctive 2: clause-linker	ga	AVS	• adversative ('A but B': girigiri=daQta=ga ma=ni aQ-ta 'it was tight, but we made it in time') • preliminary ('concerning A, B': seNjicu hanaši-ta keN=des-u=ga 'concerning the issue we talked about the other day...') • ← CMP ga
	kara	CAUSL	• causal ('because A, B': ame=ga fuQ-ta=kara šiai=wa čuuši=to naQ-ta 'the game was cancelled due to rain') • ← CMP kara
	kedo[mo] ~ keredo[mo]	AVS	• adversative • preliminary • see Table 3.11 for etymology
	monoo	CONC	• concessive ('even though A, B': kaer-eba yo-kaQta=monoo saigo=made i-ta 'although I should have gone home, I stayed till the end') • merger of mono 'thing' and CMP o • literary and archaic
	monono	CONC	• concessive • merger of mono and CMP no • literary
	nara[ba]	COND	• assertive conditional ('in case of A, B') • see Table 3.11 and §3.15 for etymology • see §3.7 for an example
	nari	REP	• archaic representative ('whether A or B') • ← nar-i (§3.15) • see §3.7 for an example
	node	CAUSL	• causal • more formal than kara • merger of derivational no and de (§3.13)
	noni	CONC	• concessive • merger of derivational no and ni (§3.13)
	ši	ENUM	• enumerative ('A, moreover B': tabako=mo suw-ana-i=ši osake=mo nom-ana-i 'I don't smoke and I don't drink')
derivational			see Table 3.13.2 for a list of derivational particles

Table 3.12.1 (continued)

inu=ka neko 'dogs or cats'), while *to* and *ya* indicate a copulative one ('and'). Of the latter two, *to* marks a closed or complete set, *ya* an open or representative one: *inu=to neko* 'dogs and cats (only)', *inu=ya neko* 'dogs and cats (and other animals left unsaid)'. An additional nominal-linker, *ni*, marks addition to a set: *inu=ni neko* 'in addition to dogs, cats'. Clause-linkers include *ga* and *kedo[mo]~keredo[mo]* 'but'; *kara* and *node* 'because'; *ši* 'moreover'; *nara[ba]* 'in case of'; *nari* 'whether'; and *monono, monoo* and *noni* 'even though'. A number of clause-linkers also function as conjunctions, capable of occurring at the beginning of a sentence. See §3.11 for

84   Chapter 3   Grammar and Syntax

subclass	form	label	grammatical functions, notes and examples[1]
emphatic	ka	FOC	• indefinite focus ('however so many/much') ← interrogative ka
	koso	FOC	• definite focus ('X and only X')
topic marker	mo	ITOP	• inclusive topic (marks inclusive topic: 'as for X, also') • intensive focus (marks intensity, ubiquity or, together with a negative predicate, complete absence)
	nara[ba]	CTOP	• conditional topic (marks a topic meeting a certain condition: maQto=nara deki-ru 'Matt can do it (lit. if Matt, can do)') • see Table 3.11 and §3.15 for etymology
	Qtara	TOP	• anti-honorific topic (marks general topic; derogatory in tone: maaku=Qtara 'that no good Mark') • truncation of complementizer to (§3.13) and iQ-tara 'if I were to say'
	Qte	TOP	• casual topic (marks general topic; casual in tone: kore=Qte nani 'what's this?') • ← complementizer Qte (§3.13)
	wa	TOP	• topic (marks general topic: 'as for X') • contrastive (adds exclusive meaning: see §3.14 for examples)

[1] when given in the text or easily inferable, examples are omitted.

Table 3.12.2: Commonly used thematic particles

further discussion on such conjunctions and §3.7 for a discussion on *nara[ba]* and *nari*.

Thematic particles have two main functions: marking the topic of a sentence (topic marker particles) and adding emphasis, or focus, to a specific word or phrase in a sentence (emphatic particles). Topic marker particles include *wa* and *mo*, the former marking a general topic and the latter an inclusive one: *mana=wa nihoNjiN=da* 'lit. as for Mana, she's Japanese', *kana=mo nihoNjiN=da* 'lit. as for Kana, she's also Japanese'. In addition to following NPs, *wa* and *mo* also follow CMPs (but **o=wa → wa*), in which case *wa* often takes on a contrastive, or non-exhaustive, meaning: *kyoota=ni=wa age-ru* 'I'll give it to Kyōta (and I may or may not give it to others)'. See §3.14 for a more in-depth discussion of thematic and contrastive *wa*. Other less common topic markers include *Qte*, *Qtara* and *nara[ba]*. Emphatic particles consist of *koso* and *ka*, of which the former marks definite focus (*kare=koso* 'him, he's the one!') and the latter, in combination with an interrogative (§3.2), marks indefinite focus (*dare=ka* 'someone', *naN-kai=ka* 'a few times or so'). The inclusive topic marker *mo* may also be used in conjunction with an interrogative or a numeral+classifier (§5.8) to mark focus, in which case it expresses intensity (*naN-kai=mo* 'time after time', *saN+kai=mo* 'a whopping three times'), ubiquity (*doko=mo onaji=da* 'it's the same everywhere') or, together with a negative predicate, complete absence (*iQ+kai=mo na-i* 'not even once', *dare=mo i-na-i* 'nobody's here').

Restrictive particles place limits on the extent of the modified word (limitative particles) or indicate exemplary cases (analogical particles). Limitative particles may express isolation (*bakari, dake, nomi, šika*: all 'only'), extent (*hodo* 'as much as', *made* 'as far as'), approximation (*goro, kurai~gurai*: all 'about') or, in the case of *nagara*, a simultaneous state (*namida=nagara* 'while in tears'). The limitative *made* is a semantic extension of the terminative CMP *made*, while *nagara* may also function as a verbal suffix (§3.7). There are seven analogical particles, employed as follows: *nado* marks examples in general (*riNgo=to oreeNji=nado* 'apples and oranges, etc.'); *demo* (see also the identical derivational particle: §3.13), *sae, sura* and *daQte* mark extreme examples or minimal requirements (*kare=demo deki-ru* 'even he can do it', *okane=sae ar-eba* 'if only I had money'); and *naNka* and *naNte* add humble or derogatory (anti-honorific: §6.4) meaning to an example (*oča=naNka ikaga=deš-oo=ka* 'how about some tea?', *kare=naNka* 'him, that no good'). Restrictive particles are also called adverbial particles, as in many cases the modified word acts in a similar way to an adverb (§3.5).

Discourse particles are also known as sentence-final particles, since they commonly occur sentence-finally (2). However, this term is not entirely accurate, as some may be used as fillers mid-sentence as well (3). They supply essential pragmatic information and can be broadly divided into two types: those indicating speaker judgment or stance and those seeking to elicit information from the addressee.

(2) *nihoN=no   nacu=wa   acu-i=des-u=ne*
    Japan=GEN   summer=TOP   hot-NPST=COP.POL-NPST=CONF
    'Summers in Japan sure are hot, **aren't they**?'

(3) *kono   hito=ne   jicu=wa=sa*
    this   person=CONF   actually=TOP=EXCL

    ooganemoči=na=N=des-u=yo
    super.rich=ADNLZ=NMLZ=COP.POL-NPST-EXCL
    'This person, **right**, they're actually, **you know**, super rich!'

The former type consists of 10 to 20 different particles, depending on analysis. Three of these, *no, wa* and *ka*, come in two varieties, distinguished by rising (↗) or falling (↘) intonation. Exclamation or assertion can be expressed by any of *koto, mono~moN, no*↘, *sa, wa*↗, *wa*↘, *ya, yo, ze* or *zo*; *ka*↘, *kamo, kana* and *kašira* are used when speculating (*kore=kašira* 'this, I wonder') or expressing possibility (*kore=kamo* 'this, perhaps'); *tomo* expresses the idea of 'indeed' or 'of course' (*wakar-imaši-ta=tomo* 'understood, of course'); while *Qke* shows retrospection (*kagi=o doko=ni oi-ta=Qke* 'now, where did I put my keys?'). The latter type of discourse particle, those seeking to elicit information from the addressee, includes *ka*↗, *kai, dai* or *no*↗ for questions (*ik-imas-u=ka* 'are you going?') and *ne[e]* or *na[a]* for inviting confirmation (*kore i-i=ne* 'this is nice, don't you think?'). In general, discourse particles cannot be combined. The major exceptions are *ne[e]* and *na[a]*,

subclass	form	label*¹	grammatical functions, notes and examples*²
analogical	daQte		• positive analogical (marks an extreme example: aho=daQte kanemoči=ni nar-e-ru 'even fools can make it rich') • truncation of da=tote 'is said that'
	demo		• positive analogical • negative analogical (marks a minimal requirement: sukoši=demo gaNbar-eba 'if you try even just a little') • suggestive (presents a suggestive example: oča=ni=demo ši-mas-u=ka 'shall we have some tea, perhaps?' • ubiquitous (together with an interrogative, marks ubiquity: dare=demo 'anyone', doko=demo 'anywhere') • ← converbalizer demo (§3.13)
	nado	EX	• exemplative ('for example') • humble (adds humble (§6.3) meaning: wataši=nado=ni=wa deki-mase-N 'I couldn't do that' (humble) • anti-honorific (adds derogatory (§6.4) meaning: omee=nado ir-anee 'nobody needs your no good filthy ass')
	naNka	AHON	• humble • anti-honorific • filler • ← nani=ka 'something'
	naNte	AHON	• anti-honorific • truncation of nado and complementizer to (§3.13)
	sae		• positive analogical • negative analogical
	sura		• positive analogical
limitative	bakari		• isolation (aho=bakari 'only fools') • approximation (saN+seNči=bakari 'just about three centimetres')
	dake		• isolation • upper limit ('as much as': yar-e-ru=dake no koto=o yar-u 'do as much as I can') • expectation (before aQ-te: basuke=no seNšu=dake aQ-te aši=ga haya=i 'being a basketball player, she is fast on her feet just as expected')
	goro		• approximation (juu-ji=goro 'at around 10 o'clock') • ← noun koro 'time period'
	hodo		• extent ('as much as', 'so ... that': šin-u=hodo cukare-ta 'so tired I could die') • ← noun hodo 'degree'
	kurai~gurai		• approximation • ← noun kurai 'rank'
	made		• terminative extent ('go as far as': nusumi=made su-ru 'go as far as stealing')
	nagara	SIM	• simultaneous ('while') • concessive ('against one's expectations': kare=nagara yoku hašir-e-ta 'against my expectations, he was able to run quite well') • see also -(i)nagara (§3.7)
	nomi		• isolation • literary
	šika		• inverse isolation (always used with negative: kare=šika ik-ana-i 'only he goes')

*¹ forms without glossing labels are glossed using English equivalents (ka 'or', to 'and') throughout this volume.
*² when given in the text or easily inferable, examples are omitted.

Table 3.12.3: Commonly used restrictive particles

3.12 Particles 87

subclass	form	label	grammatical functions, notes and examples[*1]
information eliciting	dai	Q	• casual interrogative (*doko ik-u=dai* 'where ya goin'?')
	ka↗	Q	• interrogative (*tabe-mas-u=ka* 'would you like to eat?') • may sound rhetorical following the plain form of a verb (*tabe-ru=ka* 'are you gonna eat that?')
	kai	Q	• casual interrogative
	na[a]	CONF	• confirmative (invites confirmation from addressee: *sore=na* 'that, right?') • optative (expresses a wish: *ik-ita-i=na[a]* 'I really wish I could go')
	ne[e]	CONF	• confirmative • filler (*kare=ne[e]...*, *konaida=ne[e]...* 'he, you know..., the other day, you know...')
	no↗	Q	• casual interrogative • ← nominalizer *no* (§3.13)
speaker judgement	ka↘	SPEC	• speculative (wondering aloud: *kore=de i-i=ka* 'this ought to do it, right?') • rhetorical question (*icu=made cuzuk-u=ka* 'how long is this going to continue...?')
	kamo	SPEC	• speculative • probabilitive (expresses probability) • truncation of *ka=mo šir-e-na-i* 'lit. can't even know if'
	kana	SPEC	• speculative • optative (after negative: *haya-ku owar-ana-i=kana* 'can't it just be over with?')
	kašira	SPEC	• speculative • optative (after negative) • both uses female preferential: §6.1 • truncation of *ka šir-an-u* 'lit. don't know if'
	koto	EXCL	• exclamative • imperative (following a verb) • exclamative use female exclusive • ← noun *koto* 'thing' (§3.2)
	mono~moN	EXCL	• exclamative • assertive (*moN* is casual) • *mono* following polite predicates is female exclusive • ← noun *mono* 'thing' (§3.2)
	no↘	EXCL	• exclamative • assertive • imperative (following the nonpast or negative form of a verb: *te=de tabe-na-i=no* 'don't eat with your hands!') • final use female preferential • ← nominalizer *no* (§3.13)
	ǫke	RETRO	• retrospective (attempt to remember)
	sa	EXCL	• exclamative • assertive • speculative • filler • first three uses male preferential
	tomo	AFF	• affirmative ('indeed, of course')
	wa↗	EXCL	• exclamative • female exclusive
	wa↘	EXCL	• exclamative • assertive • both uses gender neutral
	ya	EXCL	• exclamative • relaxed affirmative (*maa i-i=ya* 'sure, that's fine, whatever')
	yo	EXCL	• exclamative • assertive
	ze	EXCL	• exclamative • assertive • both uses male exclusive
	zo	EXCL	• exclamative • assertive • both uses male preferential

[*1] when given in the text or easily inferable, examples are omitted.

Table 3.12.4: Commonly used discourse particles

which can follow most other discourse particles (*ik-u=yo=ne* 'you're going, right?'), and *yo*, which can follow *wa* and *no* in female speech (§6.1).

When taking a noun-predicate, most discourse particles follow a copula (§3.6), although this can be deleted by female speakers. Others (*sa, ya, kamo, kana, kašira, ka*↗, *ka*↘, *kai, dai*) result in compulsory deletion of the copula by both genders (*inu=da=zo* but *inu=sa*: both 'it's a dog, man!'). Meanwhile, *no*↗, a semantic extension of the nominalizer *no* covered in §3.13, requires *na* when following a NP (*kare=na=no*↗ 'him?'), similar to its nominalizer counterpart. Discourse particle usage varies markedly with register and gender: see §6.1 and §6.2 for examples. In spoken Japanese, especially informal conversation, few sentences end without a discourse particle. In the written language, on the other hand, they are less frequent, the exception being *ka*↗ for questions. Whether written or spoken, when the polite form (§6.3) of a predicate is employed, only *ka*↗, *ka*↘, *yo, ne*[*e*], *mono* and *wa*↗ (the latter two being female exclusive) are found to any extent.

3.13 Derivational Particles

In Japanese, a number of particles are used to indicate shifts from one part of speech (§3.1), or syntactic role in a sentence, to another. We will refer to such particles as 'derivational particles'. All derivational particles, with the exception of *na* (further below), are semantic extensions of case marker particles (CMPs) and thus not typically given special treatment in grammars. As derivational particles clearly carry out a different syntactic function from CMPs (derivation instead of case marking), it is only proper they should receive special treatment in the same fashion as conjunctive particles. Derivational particles include *ni*, which acts as an adverbializer, turning a noun phrase (NP) or nominal adjective into an adverb (*majime* 'serious' → *majime=ni* 'seriously': 1a), and *to* which, in addition to acting as an adverbializer, acts as a complementizer, turning a word, phrase or clause into a complement. The *to* adverbializer is commonly used with mimetics (1b), while the *to* complementizer is used with quotations (1c). The *to* complementizer also possesses a casual form *ǫte* (1d).

(1) a. *majime=ni beNkyoo+su-ru*   'study seriously' (adverbializer)
     b. *nikoniko=to wara-u*   'grin widely' (adverbializer)
     c. *kare=wa ik-u=to iǫ-ta*   'he said he'd go' (complementizer)
     d. *kore=wa naN=ǫte i-u*   'what's this called?' (casual)
     e. *yakiniku=no mise*   'Japanese BBQ restaurant' (adnominalizer)
     f. *midori=no madoguči*   'green window (the JR ticket office)' (*no* adjective)
     g. *ik-u=no ~ ooki-i=no*   **'the act of** going' ~ 'big **one**' (nominalizer)
     h. *nigiyaka=na mači*   'bustling city' (adnominalizer)

3.13 Derivational Particles

The particle *no* (and its casual variant N) also functions as a derivational particle with two major functions: (i) turning a NP into an adnominal modifier (1e) or *no* adjective (1f) (§3.5) and (ii) turning a verb/adjective phrase (VP) into a NP (1g). We will refer to (i) as the adnominalizer and (ii) as the nominalizer *no*. The adnominalizer *na* found after nominal adjectives (1h), derived from the obsolete copula *nar-i* (§3.15), can also be treated as a derivational particle with a function similar to *no*. Unlike CMP *no*, adnominalizer *no* commonly follows other CMPs: *otoosan=e=no tegami* 'letter to father', *kimi=to=no deai* 'my first encounter with you'. Similar to CMP *no*, when understood through context, the head of an adnominal construction formed with *no* may be omitted: *otoosan=e=no=ga oo-i* 'there are many (letters) to father'. When following nominal adjectives, nominalizer *no* is required to take *na*: *šizuka=na=no* 'quiet one'. Nominalizer *no* is frequently used before copulas (*no=da* ~ N=*da*, *no=des-u* ~ N=*des-u*, *no=de ar-u*), in which case it nominalizes an entire clause or sentence. In such examples, *no* can follow NPs as well. When following NPs or nominal adjectives, *no*+copula constructions are required to take *na* which, when combined with *no*, often contracts to *naN* in casual speech: *wataši=na=no=des-u* 'it's me' (polite) ~ *wataši=naN=da* 'it's me' (casual). Such *no* + copula constructions express a large array of modal meanings, such as reasoning (2) or discovery (3), and often have no English equivalent.

(2) A: *doošite   ik-ana-i=no*   B: *isogaši-i=N=da*
     why   go-NEG-NPST=Q   busy-NPST=NMNLZ=COP.NPST
    'A: Why aren't you going?   B: Because I'm busy.' (reasoning)

(3) *koko=ni=mo   mosu=ga   aQ-ta=N=da*
    here=DAT=ITOP MOS.Burger=NOM   exist-PST=NMNLZ=COP.NPST
    'So, there was a MOS Burger here too.' (discovery)

(4) *bareebooru[=ga ~ =no]   tokui=na   hito*
    volleyball[=NOM ~ =GEN] talented=ADNLZ   person
    'a person who is good at volleyball'

(5) *pikaso[=ga ~ =no]   kai-ta   e*
    Picasso[=NOM ~ =GEN]   paint-PST   painting
    'a painting by Picasso'

(6) *midori=no   yasai   →   yasai=ga   midori=da*
    green=ADNLZ   vegetable   vegetable=NOM   green=COP.NPST
    'green vegetables → the vegetables are green'

Table 3.13.1 summarizes the syntactic properties of CMP *no* (genitive and genitive appositive) and derivational *no* (adnominalizer and nominalizer), where ✔ indicates grammatically licit, ✗ grammatically illicit and • uncommon or grammatically questionable. The first seven properties refer to where each *no* can occur in a sentence: CMP indicates a CMP other than *no*, COP a copula and NA a nominal

syntactic property	genitive	genitive appositive	adnominalizer	nominalizer
NP=*no* NP	✓	✓	✓	✗
NP=CMP=*no* NP	✗	✗	✓	✗
NP=CMP=*no*[=CMP~COP]	✗	✗	•*1	✓
NP=*no*[=CMP~COP]	•*1	✗	•*1	✗
NP=*na*=*no* COP	✗	✗	✗	✓
NA=*na*=*no*[=CMP~COP]	✗	✗	✗	✓
VP=*no*[=CMP~COP]	✗	✗	✗	✓
no → N	✓	•	•	✓*2
no → *ga*	✓	✗	✗	✗
no → *na*	✗	✗	✓*3	✗
MOD → PRED	✗	✓	✓	✗

*1 only in headless genitive/adnominal constructions (see §3.12 and above for examples).
*2 only preceding copulas and never after another CMP.
*3 only for NP=*no* NP and with a small set of nominal adjectives (see §3.5 for details).

Table 3.13.1: *Syntactic properties of case marker and derivational* no

adjective. Thus, NP=CMP=*no*[=CMP~COP] could indicate *otoosaN=e=no=ga* or *otoosaN=e=no=da*. The next property, *no* → N, marks whether or not *no* can be contracted to N in casual speech. The final three properties mark the possibility of three types of 'conversions'. The first of these, *no* → *ga*, only applies to genitive case marker *no* and is known as the *ga/no* conversion. It indicates that *no* can be substituted with *ga* with little difference in meaning in

- phrases with the structure [NP=*no* VP NP], where VP represents a verb (4) or adjective (5) phrase used adnominally.

The second, *no* → *na*, only applies to adnominalizer *no* and indicates that after certain nominal adjectives, *no* can be substituted with *na* with no difference in meaning (*saikoo=no* ~ *saikoo=na* 'best': see also §3.5). The final property, MOD → PRED, applies to genitive appositive and adnominalizer *no* and indicates that the modifier (MOD) directly preceding *no* could also be used as a predicate (PRED) to describe the modified NP (6).

One final derivational particle requiring discussion is the converbalizer *de*, which follows a NP or nominal adjective and, as in (7) and (8), turns it into an adverbial (co)subordinate clause (§3.7). It also frequently acts as a 'copularizer', fusing with *ar-u* 'exist' or *gozar-u* 'exist (super-polite)' to form an affirmative copula and with *na-i* 'nonexistent' to form a negative copula. Similar to the *-te* form, *de* can take the particles *wa* and *mo* to form secondary converbs. In fact, when forming a negative copula, *de* routinely takes *wa* and this form is contracted to *ja* in casual speech. Aside from the negative copularizer (which takes on little to no contrastive meaning), the meaning of *dewa* and *demo* are nearly identical to that of the converbs *-tewa* and *-temo* (§3.7), the former forming an emphatic condition (9), with the

form	label	grammatical functions and notes
de	CVBLZ	• converbalizer (NP/nominal adjective → converb) • copularizer (forms a copula together with *ar-u*, *gozar-u* or *na-i*: §3.6)
demo	CONC	• concessive converbalizer (NP/nominal adjective → converb)
dewa~ja	COND	• emphatic conditional converbalizer (NP/nominal adjective → converb) • negative copularizer (NP/nominal adjective → converb)
ni	ADVLZ	• adverbializer (NP/nominal adjective → adverb)
no~N	ADNLZ	• adnominalizer (NP → adnoun)
	NMNLZ	• nominalizer (VP → NP)
to~Qte	COMP	• complementizer (word/phrase/clause → complement) • adverbializer (especially after mimetics) • *Qte* is casual and cannot replace adverbializer usage
na	ADNLZ	• adnominalizer (after nominal adjectives) • ← *nar-i* (§3.15)

Table 3.13.2: Commonly used derivational particles

latter a concessive clause or condition (10). See §3.6 for a discussion on the affirmative and negative copulas.

(7) *kyoo=wa   asa=kara   ame=de   hadazamu-i*
    today=TOP   morning=ABL   rain=CVB   chilly-NPST
    'It's been raining and chilly out since morning today'. (subordinate)

(8) *kyoo=wa   ame=de   ašita=wa   yuki=ni   nar-u*
    today=TOP rain=CVB   tomorrow=TOP   snow=DAT   become-NPST
    'Today's forecast is rain, tomorrow's snow'. (cosubordinate)

(9) *sore=dewa   komar-u*
    that=COND   be.troubled-NPST
    'Now that **would be** troubling' (emphatic condition)

(10) *ame=demo   šiai=o   su-ru*
     rain=CONC   game=ACC   do-NPST
     'The game will be held **even if** it rains.' (concessive)

3.14 The Notion of Topic and *wa* versus *ga*

A major topic of debate among Japanese linguistics for the past half century has been the notion of topic—no pun intended. Japanese sentences are often said to lack a grammatical subject in the traditional sense. While the particles *ga* and *wa* (§3.12) are commonly used to mark what could be construed as subjects, there are examples such as (1)–(2), where what appear to be subjects on the surface turn out upon further scrutiny to be in fact something very different. Note that in natural speech, the *ga* in (1b) and (2b) would be pronounced with prosodic prominence (raising of pitch for the point of focus or reduction of pitch for the following material).

(1a) Waiter: nani=ni   nasa-imas-u=ka
             what=DAT do.RESP-POL-NPST=Q
             'What will you be ordering?'

   Customer: boku=**wa** unagi=des-u
             I=TOP   eel=COP.POL.NPST
             'I'll have eel.' (when ordering food)

(1b) Waiter: unagi=wa dočira-sama=deš-oo=ka
             eel=TOP   who-HON=COP.POL-CJT=Q
             'Who ordered eel?'

   Customer: boku=**ga** unagi=des-u
             I=NOM   eel=COP.POL.NPST
             'It was me (who ordered eel).' (when receiving order)

(2a) Aya: otoosaN=**wa** doko=da
            father=TOP   where=COP.NPST
            'Where's dad?'

   Miho: otoosaN=**wa** tenisu
           father=TOP   tennis
           'Dad's out playing tennis.'

(2b) Aya: okaasaN=mo
            mother=ITOP
            'Mum too?'

   Miho: čiga-u.   otoosaN=**ga**   tenisu. okaasaN=wa   šir-ana-i
           wrong-NPST father=NOM   tennis   mother=TOP   know.NEG-NPST
           'No. It's dad who's out playing tennis. I've no idea where mum is.'

In the glosses above we have provided natural sounding translations. Inputting these examples into Google Translate, however, rewards us with the following arguably interesting, but atypical, exchanges:

(1a) 'What would you like?'   'I am an eel.'
(1b) 'Who are the eels?'   'I am an eel.'
(2a) 'Where is Dad?'   'Dad is tennis.'
(2b) 'Mom too?'   'Wrong. Dad is tennis. Mother does not know.'

3.14 The Notion of Topic and *wa* versus *ga*

Either we are dealing with some anthropomorphic eels and dad is the embodiment of all that is tennis (and mum is unaware of the situation), or something has been lost in translation. So what then has been lost? The problem we are dealing with here is that of the topic. In (1a) and (1b), *wa* does not express the grammatical subject, but instead the general topic of each sentence. The topic of (1a) is *boku* 'I', while *otoosaN* 'father' is the topic of (2a). The 'objects' of these sentences, *unagi* 'eel' and *tenisu* 'tennis', are not objects in the traditional sense, but simply attributes related to the topics *boku* and *otoosaN*. Therefore, a more accurate translation would be (1a) 'as for me, eel' or (2a) 'concerning dad, tennis'. Pragmatically, (1a) and (2a) could be analysed as context-based substitutions of the more complete utterances (3)–(4). By replacing *ga* with *wa*, *boku* and *otoosaN* are topicalized, allowing for such utterances as in (1a) and (2a).

The role of *ga* in (1b) and (2b) is slightly more complicated. In these two examples, *ga* appears to be marking *boku* and *otoosaN* as topics. The case is actually the opposite, though. From a pragmatic standpoint, we can think of (1b) as an inversion of (5) and (2b) as an inversion of (6), both of whose English translations are literal. In other words, *unagi* and *tenisu* are actually the topics and *ga* indicates that *boku* and *otoosaN* are attributes associated with these topics. This mental inversion (along with prosodic prominence) leads to the implication that *boku* and *otoosaN* are exhaustive—that is, *ga* works in contrast with *wa* to indicate it is 'I and nobody else' who ordered the eel and that it is 'dad and not mum' who is out playing tennis.

(3) boku=**ga**   unagi=o   tabe-ta-i=des-u
    I=NOM   eel=ACC   eat-DES-NPST=COP.POL-NPST
    'I would like to eat eel.'

(4) otoosaN=**ga**   tenisu=o   ši-ni   iQ-te   i-ru
    Father=NOM   tennis=ACC   do-PURP   go-CVB   prog-NPST
    'Father has gone to play tennis.'

(5) unagi=**wa**   boku=ga   [čuumoN+ši-maši-ta]
    eel=TOP   I=NOM   [order+do-POL-PST]
    '**As for** the eel, I (ordered it)'.

(6) tenisu=**wa**   otoosaN=ga   [ši-ni   iQ-te   i-ru]
    tennis=TOP   dad=NOM   [do-PURP   go-CVB   PROG-NPST]
    '**As for** tennis, dad (is out playing it)'.

(7) karee=**ga**   suki=da
    curry=NOM   liking=COP. NPST
    'I like curry.'

(8) karee=**wa**   suki=da=kedo   kono   buraNdo=**wa**   dame=da
    curry=TOP   liking=COP.NPST=AVS   this   brand=TOP   no.good=COP.NPST
    'I like curry, but this brand is no good.'

There are cases in which *wa* can express contrast as well, in the exact opposite way of *ga* above: by implying that a topic is non-exhaustive. Example (7) simply states that the speaker likes curry, while (8) states that the speaker likes curry, but the brand in question is not to their taste. By using *wa* instead of *ga*, the speaker hints that there is some sort of incompleteness attached to their proposition—that is, the speaker does not wish to imply that the proposition is exhaustive (true in every respect). In (6), this non-exhaustiveness surfaces as a feeling of reservation: the speaker likes curry but not the particular make. A similar implication could be that the speaker likes curry but is not keen on another dish being served for dinner. While *ga* is typically used together with *wa* to express contrast, as in (2a) and (2b), *wa* can take on a contrastive meaning by itself. Due to its contrastive undertones, it would sound odd for someone to say to their lover *kimi=wa suki=da* 'I love you', for example, as it would imply deeper, perhaps unfavourable, connotations such as 'I love you, but I cannot spend my life with you' or 'I love you, as do I my other lovers'.

3.15 Grammar through Time

A number of the morphosyntactic phenomena described in §3.1–§3.14 can be better understood by examining the grammar of earlier periods of the Japanese language. While far from comprehensive, we cover here some of the major grammatical developments relevant to the modern language. We also direct the reader to §1.3, which provides a brief sketch of each of the historical periods of the language, and to §2.9 which covers the history of the language's phonology. Old Japanese (OJ) and Middle Japanese (MJ) examples in this unit are cited using the historical phonemicization in Table 2.9.1.

We start with verbs. In contrast to the four verb classes we see today, OJ and MJ featured seven verb classes: consonant-stem, single vowel-stem, dual vowel-stem, N-irregular, R-irregular, S-irregular and K-irregular. Four of these classes had stems which alternated depending on the suffix they took: dual vowel-stems alternated between final V- ~ *u*- ~ ø- (where V = the vowels *i* or *e*; ø = deletion of the final vowel), while N-irregular alternated between final *n*- ~ *nu*-, S-irregular between *se*- ~ *si*- ~ *su*- ~ *s*- and K-irregular between *ko*- ~ *ki*- ~ *ku*- ~ *k*-. Due to the phonotactics (§2.5) of OJ, which word-internally tolerated only CV moras (§2.4), stems ending in a consonant were required to take a union vowel when affixing consonant-initial suffixes, while stems ending in a vowel took a union consonant when affixing vowel-initial suffixes. This phenomenon is still observed for the most part in Modern Japanese (MoJ) (§3.3). Which suffix triggered which alternation is a complex issue but, put at its simplest, suffixes may be divided into four groups I–IV, with each group triggering different alternations depending on the verb class. Table 3.15.1 gives examples of suffixes (which are not exhaustive) for each group, while Table 3.15.2 (also not exhaustive) shows how these alternations are reflected

3.15 Grammar through Time

group	suffixes
I	• passive -(r)ar-u • causative -(s)as-u • imperative -e ~ -yo • stative -(e)r-i (only follows consonant-stem and S-irregular verbs) • all suffixes with union vowel a: negative -(a)zu, conjectural -(a)m-u, etc.
II	• all suffixes with union vowel i: -te form -(i)te, stative -(i)tar-i, etc.
III	• adnominal -(r)u • realis -(r)e • causal -(r)eba • concessive -(r)edo[mo]
IV	• all suffixes with union vowel r not included in I–III: conclusive -(r)u, necessitive -(r)ube-si, etc.

Table 3.15.1: Old and Middle Japanese verb suffix groups

verb class	stem structure	morphophonological rules (I–IV = suffix groups)
consonant-stem	final C-	• C- before I–IV*¹
single vowel-stem	final V-	• V- (i- ~ e-) before I–IV*¹
dual vowel-stem	final V- ~ u- ~ ø-	• V (i- ~ e-) before I, II: oki-rar-u, tabe-te • u- before III: oku-ru, tabu-re • ø- (final vowel deleted) before IV: ok-u, tab-ube-si
S-irregular	se- ~ si- ~ su- ~ s-	• se- before I: se-rar-u, se-sas-u • si- before II: si-te, si-tar-i • su- before III: su-ru, su-re • s- before IV: s-u, s-ube-si
K-irregular	ko- ~ ki- ~ ku- ~ k-	• ko- before I: ko-rar-u, ko-sas-u • ki- before II: ki-te, ki-tar-i • ku- before III: ku-ru, ku-re • k- before IV: k-u, k-ube-si
N-irregular	final n- ~ nu-	• n- before I, II, IV: sin-ar-u, sin-ite, sin-u • nu- before III: sinu-ru, sinu-re
R-irregular	final C-	• C- before I–IV, but takes allomorphic conclusive -i: ar-i

*¹ identical to MoJ

Table 3.15.2: Old and Middle Japanese verb classes

in each verb class. Only S-irregular and K-irregular verbs retain stem alternation in MoJ, but the phenomenon is still active in some vowel-stem verb classes of Kyūshū dialects (§7.11).

In addition to a more complex set of verb classes, OJ and MJ possessed significantly more verbal suffixes (§3.7, §3.8)—in particular non-final suffixes—than they do today. Often cited are the past/perfect suffixes, of which there were six (or eight including allomorphs) as opposed to the lone -ta (§3.7) in MoJ: -(i)tar-i ~ -(e)r-i expressed the stative or perfect, while -(i)ki ~ -(i)si expressed the empirical past (personally experienced past), -(i)ker-i the hearsay past (past heard from another), -(i)kem-u the past conjectural (supposition about the past), -(i)t-u the volitional perfect (perfect linked to the volition of the actor) and -(i)n-u the non-volitional perfect (naturally occurring perfect). A number of these extinct suffixes can still be observed in fossilized expressions such as *waka-kar-iši koro* 'in my youth', where *-iši* indicates the empirical past. See Table 3.15.3 for a list of such archaisms, given in modern phonemicization. Many non-final suffixes lost their inflections over time evolving into final suffixes (§3.7) in MoJ. Notable examples include MJ *-(i)tar-i* (perfect-stative) → MoJ *-ta* (past) and MJ *-(a)m-u* (conjectural) → *-(a)u* → MoJ *-(y)oo* (conjectural-hortative).

Several major changes started to take place in Late Middle Japanese (LMJ) that brought the system of verb classes closer to its modern form. The two most important were the adnominal-conclusive merger and what is known in the Japanese tradition as *ichidanka* 'monogradization'. The former involved the merger of two distinct verb forms into what we now call the nonpast, or dictionary, form (§3.3). Prior to the merger, dual vowel-stem and the four irregular verb classes had distinct conclusive (sentence-final) and adnominal (noun-modifying) forms: *ok-u* 'wake up' (conclusive) ~ *oku-ru pito* 'awakening person' (adnominal), *sin-u* 'die', *sinu-ru toki* 'time of death'. As far back as OJ, there are examples of the adnominal being used in sentence-final position to express exclamation or a lingering tone of suggestiveness. Over time this usage became widespread, resulting in the eventual loss of the adnominal-conclusive distinction. It is for this reason that a large number of MoJ final suffixes, including the nonpast, can be used both adnominally and conclusively (§3.7). The second important change, *ichidanka*, involved the loss of vowel alternation in the dual vowel-stem class, which resulted in these verbs merging with the single vowel-stem class. Around the same time, N-irregular and R-irregular verb classes merged with the consonant-stem class, bringing the total number of verb classes down to four. These changes did not all occur at once, but rather across many centuries taking place at different speeds across different regions, social classes and registers, finally reaching completion at the beginning of the MoJ period.

Adjectives also endured a number of changes, the most important being the adnominal-conclusive merger, which occurred at approximately the same time as it did for verbs. Prior to the merger, adjectives possessed a distinct adnominal and conclusive form. The former was expressed by *-ki* (*piro-ki kawa* 'broad river, *taka-ki yama* 'high mountain') and the latter by *-si* (*piro-si* 'broad', *taka-si* 'high'), with *-si* suppressed after stems ending in *si* (*tanosi(-ø)* 'fun', not **tanosi-si*). Both these forms merged as *-i*, the MoJ nonpast suffix, though can still be found in archaisms (Table 3.15.3) and personal names (§6.9), in this instance Hiroshi and Takashi. Adjectives had fewer final suffixes than they do today, but this was compensated for by a verbalizer suffix *-kar-i* (a contraction of *-ku* and *ar-i* 'exist'), which allowed adjectives to take semantically compatible non-final verb suffixes. Some of these verbalized forms have developed into inflections in MoJ (Table 3.7.1): *-kar-itar-i* (verbalizer + perfect-stative) → *kaQta* (past), *-kar-am-u* (verbalizer+conjectural) → *karoo* (conjectural-hortative).

3.15 Grammar through Time

MJ form	grammatical function	fossilized expressions
-(u)be-si	necessitive	• kak-ube-kar-azar-u 'absolutely necessary'
goto-si	similitude copula	• no goto-ši 'like' (kooiN ya=no goto-ši 'time flies like an arrow')
i	emphatic particle	• ar-u=i=wa 'or' (§3.11)
-kar-i	adjective verbalizer	• see -(i)ki ~ -(i)si and -(u)be-si
-(i)ker-i	hearsay past	• ni yor-iker-i 'depend on' (hito=ni yor-iker-i=da 'it depends on the person')
-ki	adjective adnominal	• ki + noun (waka-ki seNši 'young warrior', aka-ki cubasa 'Red Wings') • na-ki=ni=ši=mo ar-azu 'it's not impossible that'
-(i)ki ~ -(i)si	empirical past	• waka-kar-iši koro 'in my youth'
-(a)m-u ~ -(a)N	conjectural	• -(a)N koto=o prophetic 'may' (foosu=to tomo=ni ar-aN koto=o 'may the Force be with you') • see §6.5 for a further example
nar-i	copula	• nar-i 'is' (toki=wa kane=nar-i 'time is money'), nar-u adnouns (sei=nar-u 'holy', taN=nar-u 'simply')
-(e)r-i	perfect-stative	• iki-to=ši ik-er-u mono 'all living beings'
-si	adjective conclusive	• ši (toki sudeni oso-ši 'already too late', ijoo na-ši 'no abnormalities, all clear') • see also goto-ši
si	emphatic particle	• tada-ši 'however' (§3.11) • see also -(e)r-i and -ki
tar-i	copula	• tar-u mono 'people who call themselves' (kyooši=tar-u mono 'people who call themselves teachers') • X=no X=tar-u yueN 'what makes X what it is' (hito=no hito=tar-u yueN 'what makes man who he is') • tar-u adnouns (šu=tar-u 'principal', juNzeN=tar-u 'pure')
ya	interrogative particle	• šir-u=ya šir-azu=ya 'whether or not you know it' • see also zo
yo	addressive particle	• šokuN=yo 'gentlemen!', šooneN=yo taiši=o idak-e 'boys, be ambitious!'
-(a)zar-i	negative	• -(a)zar-u=o e-na-i 'must' (ik-azar-u=o e-na-i 'must go')
zo	emphatic particle	• naN=zo=ya 'what exactly' (koofuku=to=wa naN=zo=ya 'what is happiness?'), kami=nomi=zo šir-u 'God only knows'

Table 3.15.3: Some examples of archaisms in fossilized expressions

There existed two classes of nominal adjective in MJ: *nar-i* adjectives and *tar-i* adjectives. The former took the copula (§3.6) *nar-i* (a contraction of *ni ar-i*), the latter the copula *tar-i* (a contraction of *to ar-i*) when modifying nouns (*siduka=nar-u tani* 'quiet valley') or forming predicates (*keNzeN=tar-i* 'manifest'). Both of these copulas occurred after noun phrases (NPs) as well. Over time, *nar-i* lost its inflections, surviving only as *na* after nominal adjectives, as well as in several other fossilized forms: *nara~naraba~nari* (§3.7, §3.11, §3.12). The *tar-i* copula fell out of usage almost entirely, with most *tar-i* adjectives merging with *na* adjectives. Both of these copulas can still be found in archaisms, however, and form a small set of fossilized adnouns (Table 3.15.2). The modern-day copulas *de ar-u* and *da* (the latter derived from the former) first appeared in LMJ, but *des-u* did not appear until the 18th century (see §3.6 for a more detailed overview). A third MJ copula, *goto-si* (*ga goto-si* ~ *no goto-si* after NPs), used to express similitude between subject and predicate, also remains only in archaisms (Table 3.15.3).

While verbs, adjectives and copulas have endured multiple transformations over the course of history, particles have remained relatively unscathed. While there have been additions to the word class—including fossilized forms of extinct verbal suffixes (see the etymology of *kedo*[*mo*] ~ *keredo*[*mo*] in Table 3.11)—relatively few particles have fallen out of use. Those that have can often still be found in archaisms (Table 3.15.3), such as the emphatic particles *zo*, *i* and *si* or the interrogative particle *ya*. The semantics of particles have also remained relatively intact—the exception is *ga*, which has shifted from a genitive to nominative case marker particle. This shift took place in multiple stages over several centuries, with *ga* generally held to have attained its current usage by the end of the LMJ period. The older genitive *ga* can still be found in fossilized expressions such as *wagaya* 'my (humble) abode' (← *wa=ga ya*) or *wagakuni* 'our (beloved) country' (← *wa=ga kuni*), as well as in myriad toponyms (§6.9: Sekigahara, Kasumigaseki, Sakuragaoka). It is most likely this earlier genitive usage that gave rise to the interchangeability of *ga* with *no* (§3.13) and the exhaustive use of *ga* in MoJ (§3.14).

CHAPTER 4 Orthography and Writing

4.1 Writing Systems

The modern Japanese language is written, for the most part, in a mixture of three scripts. These are Chinese characters, known in Japanese as kanji and examined in §4.2–§4.5, and two 'syllabaries' derived from these, hiragana and katakana, explored in §4.6. In addition, the Roman alphabet, first introduced from the mid-16th century by Jesuit missionaries (§1.3, §8.13), has in recent decades come to be used more and more frequently, especially in signage, acronyms and computing (§8.11). The Roman alphabet is discussed in §4.7 and public signage in §4.14. The Greek alphabet is employed to a much smaller degree, its use largely restricted to scientific or mathematical notation. Arabic numerals (§4.8), less commonly Roman numerals, and a range of punctuation marks and typographical symbols (§4.9) are also employed. These scripts are mixed (§4.10) while, like any other language possessing a writing system, Japanese can be written in a variety of different styles (§4.13) with substantial room for individual licence (§4.12). Braille (§4.11) is also employed. Japanese thus possesses a writing system of fiendish complexity and is generally reckoned to be one of the hardest to master. Certainly, no other writing system anywhere on earth employs a core mix of three different scripts.

In modern Japanese, the domains of use of the three major scripts are, by convention, as shown in Table 4.1. Here, script functions are broken down into the five subcategories of native and Sino-Japanese (SJ: §7.1) vocabulary, borrowed vocabulary (§7.2, §7.3), education, names (§6.9) and sociolinguistic and pragmatic usage. In the table, ✔ indicates 'widely used', • 'occasionally used', while ✗ indicates 'hardly ever, or never, used'. Historically, many domains have used different conventions to those found at present: verbal suffixes and particles, for example, now written almost wholly in hiragana, were also written in katakana, depending on genre, until shortly after WWII (§4.10).

With the exception of mimetics (§5.2), and ignoring names, native and SJ vocabulary is generally written in kanji or hiragana, while borrowed vocabulary is widely written in katakana. With names, orthographic practice largely favours kanji or katakana, with hiragana usage found to a lesser degree. The personal and place names of Japan and sinolingual countries are typically written in kanji, while those of non-sinolingual countries are written in katakana. The Korean peninsula straddles the boundary between these two spheres, having gradually moved in

	kanji	hiragana	katakana
native and Sino-Japanese vocabulary			
• nouns (non flora and fauna)	✔	•	✗
• nouns (flora and fauna)	✔	✔	✔
• verb stems (§3.3, §4.10) • adjective stems (§3.5)	✔	•	✗
• verbal suffixes (including 'conjugational endings': §3.7, §3.8, §4.10, §8.6) • particles (§3.12, §3.13)	✗	✔	✗
• other grammatical elements: auxiliaries (§3.9), copulas (§3.6), conjunctions (§3.11), interjections (§3.1), formal nouns (§3.2)	•	✔	✗
• mimetics (§5.2)	•	✔	✔
borrowed vocabulary			
• borrowings from modern Chinese topolects (§7.1)	✔	•	✔
• borrowings from languages other than Chinese topolects (§7.2, §7.3)	•	•	✔
education			
• *kun-yomi* (§4.4) of kanji listed in dictionaries	✗	✔	✗
• *on-yomi* (§4.4) of kanji listed in dictionaries	✗	✗	✔
• foreign language transcriptions	✗	✗	✔
names			
• names of Japanese nationals (§6.9) • Japanese place names (§6.9)	✔	•	•
• nationals of, and place names in, sinolingual countries	✔	•	•
• nationals of, and place names on, Korean peninsula	✔	✗	✔
• nationals of, and place names in, non-sinolingual countries	•	✗	✔
sociolinguistic and pragmatic			
• foreigner talk (§7.4) • broken Japanese • infant babbling	✗	✗	✔
• emphasis	✗	✗	✔
• non-standard language • slang (§5.10)	✗	✗	✔

Table 4.1: Conventional script domains

recent decades from the former to the latter. The abbreviations for foreign countries, many borrowed from Chinese, are exceptions. These are typically still written in kanji and derive from earlier orthographic practice: 米 *bei* 'USA', 英 *ei* 'UK', 豪 *goo* 'Australia', 仏 *fucu* 'France', 露 *ro* 'Russia'.

Of the three scripts, katakana shows the most diversity, employed in a wide range of domains, contrary to the often heard erroneous view that it is only used for loanwords. Katakana also dominates the domains in which it is employed: in many of the domains in which it occurs, it is the sole script used. On the other hand, hiragana is the most fluid, with • 'occasionally used' more common than ✔ 'widely used', squaring with its perception as the Japanese default script. Although many native speakers follow the conventions above in their writing practice, considerable licence exists, particularly in advertising, brand and corporate names, poetry, subculture (§6.5) and social media, as well as in orthographic play (§4.12).

4.2 Chinese Characters: Origins

Throughout most of history, the origin of Chinese characters remained a mystery. Ancient legends attributed their invention to the historian of the Yellow Emperor, Cangjie (c. 2650 BCE), who was said to have had four eyes and invented Chinese characters based on the footprints of birds and beasts. Today, archaeological findings give us a clearer picture of how Chinese characters came into being.

The earliest known form of Chinese characters is oracle bone script, dating back to the latter half of the Shang dynasty (c. 1600–1046 BCE). During the Shang dynasty, it was common to use the bones of animals and turtle shells for divination. A diviner would ask questions to the deities about the weather, crops or the fortunes of the royal family, then apply heat to a bone or shell using a metal rod until cracks formed in the surface. Predictions would be made based on these cracks, then often carved into the bones and shells. Later into the Shang dynasty, it become common to engrave characters on giant bronze vessels, in a slightly more refined style of script known as bronze script. The shape and form of characters in oracle bone script and bronze script are more pictographic than in later scripts, and one can guess the meaning of the simpler characters from their shape alone. Given the complexity of the information recorded, though, we can conclude that both of these scripts were not simply sets of symbols, but fully developed writing systems.

Up until the Han dynasty (206 BCE–221 CE), there was a large variation in script styles. It is a well-known anecdote that, as part of his wars for unification, the First Emperor, Qin Shi Huang (220–210 BCE), ordered his chancellor Li Si to take the many varieties of script and unify them into a single standard, giving rise what is known as small seal script. This script is characterized by its overall complexity and its many rounded shapes and lines and is still frequently used in official seals in China, Taiwan, the Koreas and Japan to this day (§4.3). The life of small seal script as an official script was short, however, with the more simplistic and rectilinear clerical script taking its place shortly after. The name clerical script derives from the belief that this script was developed by low-ranking government officials, or 'clerks', during the Qin dynasty. We now know, though, from archaeological finds of the late 20th century, that clerical script was already in use at least a century before Qin Shi Huang rose to power.

oracle bone   bronze   small seal   clerical   regular   semi-cursive   cursive

Fig. 4.2: The character 樂 *yuè, lè 'music, fun' across seven scripts (oracle bone and bronze script:* 白川 *2012; others:* 高田 *2014)*

Clerical script is defined by a strong wavelike flaring at the ends of its strokes. Over the course of many centuries, clerical script was continually refined, evolving into what is called regular script, the official script used in sinosphere countries today. Examples of regular script have been unearthed dating back to the 3rd century, though the script did not reach its modern form until the time of the Tang dynasty (618–907). In addition to regular script and its predecessors, there are two types of running hand: semi-cursive script, which is legible to most readers and still in use today, and cursive script (or 'grass script'), which requires special training to read and write and is now mostly limited to the calligraphy classroom. See Fig. 4.2 for a comparison of script styles.

Chinese characters are often described as 'ideograms' or 'pictograms'. While it is true that a number of the more basic characters are pictographic in nature, all Chinese characters represent both sound and meaning and thus living, breathing words—not simply detached ideas. It is more appropriate, therefore, to use the term 'logogram' (a character representing a word) than ideogram (a character representing a concept) when describing Chinese characters. In most cases, Chinese characters (as used in China) represent a single monosyllabic word or morpheme; however, there are cases of two characters being used together to express disyllabic morphemes as well: 蝴蝶 *húdié* 'butterfly'. It is also not uncommon for a Chinese character to have multiple readings associated with multiple words (§4.4).

Chinese characters are formed in a variety of ways. The simplest of characters are pictograms, resembling a word through an image of what that word represents. Some examples of pictograms are 木 'tree', whose oracle bone script 𣎴 resembles branches on a tree, or 水 'water', whose oracle bone script 𣱳 resembles flowing water. A type of character similar to—or, more appropriately, a subcategory of—the pictogram is the indicative pictogram. Instead of emulating a physical object or entity, indicative pictograms represent a word through abstract iconification. The character 上 'up', for example, is written as 𠄞 in oracle bone script, with a short line on top of a longer line, indicating the quality of being above. Meanwhile, 下 'down' is written as 𠄟, with the short line under the long one, indicating the quality of being beneath. Other characters combine two or more (indicative) pictograms together to form a single meaning in what is known as a compound pictogram. For example, 林 puts two trees together to represent 'copse, woods' and 森 puts three trees together to represent 'forest'.

By far the most common type of character is the phono-semantic compound. This type of character combines two elements to represent the meaning and sound of a word: a determinative, or radical, which represents the semantic domain of the character, and a phonetic, which represents the sound of the character. For example, the characters 語 *yǔ* 'word' and 詩 *shī* 'poem' contain the radical 言 'say, word' —to indicate their relationship to language—alongside the phonetics 吾 *wú* and 寺 *sì* (while these phonetics are pronounced in Modern Mandarin differently from the characters as a whole, they would have been identical or similar in Old Chinese). 吾 and 寺 express the meanings 'I' and 'temple' when used independently, but when used as phonetics, their meanings are ignored.

Yet other characters originated as pictograms but over time lost their original meaning and became associated with another identical or similar sounding word. These characters are known as phonetic loans. A well-known example is the character 我 'I', which takes the form of a halberd 𰻞 in oracle bone script, but has been used as a personal pronoun since Old Chinese. Phono-semantic compounds and phonetic loans provide a way of expressing abstract concepts that are not easily representable by pictograms.

4.3 Chinese Characters: Writing

As any non-sinolingual L2 learner of Japanese will attest, remembering how to write kanji ('Chinese characters' hereafter; 'kanji' when referring to their usage in Japanese) is one of the most difficult parts of learning the language. This fact holds true for native speakers as well. Since the advent of word processors and personal computers, the need to write kanji by hand in daily life has greatly diminished, leading to a general decline in writing proficiency, especially among the younger smartphone-dependent generation (§8.11). The difficulty involved in writing kanji is not just a modern phenomenon: there have been movements to limit the number of kanji, or even to ban kanji altogether, as far back as the 19th century (§8.2). Despite undergoing several major reforms, however, kanji remain a major pillar of the Japanese writing system to this day. One cannot master Japanese without mastering kanji.

Individual characters are written from left to right, top to bottom, in a series of strokes. The term 'stroke' refers to a single uninterrupted motion of a brush. Even if one changes direction midway through a motion, as is common at corners, the motion is still counted as one stroke. For example, the character 口 'mouth' consists of three strokes: a vertical stroke ｜ that goes from top left to bottom left; an inverted L-shaped stroke ㄱ that goes from top left to top right and then, without interruption, to bottom right; and a horizontal stroke 一 that goes from bottom left to bottom right. The simplest characters consist of a single stroke, such as 一 'one' and 乙 'second', while the most complex character in Morohashi Tetsuji's *Dai kanwa jiten* (§8.10), 龖龘 'loquacious' (4×龍 'dragon'), consists of 64 strokes. Of course, the character 龖龘 is rarely (if ever) used in everyday life, but it can be found in the name of a saké from Nan'yō City, Yamagata (Fig. 4.3.1). When learning kanji, a heavy emphasis is placed on stroke order. While it is not necessary to remember stroke order to write characters, knowing the correct stroke order will help one write more balanced and aesthetically pleasing characters. For this reason, Japanese language tests (§8.9) often include problems requiring students to identify correct stroke order.

Fig. 4.3.1: A fresh bottle of Tetsu saké

As mentioned in §4.2, there are a number of different script styles for writing Chinese characters. The most commonly used script in modern day Japan is regular script. Semi-cursive script, found on signage (§4.14) or menus for artistic effect, is also used in handwriting, but has largely fallen out of use by the younger generation due to the focus on regular script in modern education. Small seal script and, to a lesser extent, clerical script are commonly used in personal seals. An embellished variant of small seal script, referred to as *insōtai* 'seal of fortune script' or *kissōtai* 'good fortune script', is also used in personal seals for good luck and to prevent forgery. An additional style, known as *kointai* 'old seal script', based on *yamato koin* 'Japanese old seal', a script style used in official seals of the 7th to 12th century, is also common in personal seals today. See Fig. 4.3.2 for a comparison of the different script styles used in personal seals.

The total number of Chinese characters in existence is impossible to compute as there are countless historical and regional variants. Although Morohashi lists 51,109 characters in the final edition of his dictionary, the vast majority of these are either obsolete or obscure variants of more common characters: a knowledge of 2,000 to 3,000 characters is regarded as sufficient for everyday purposes in Japan. In order to facilitate the teaching and writing of characters, the Japanese government has issued a number of regulations on kanji usage (§8.2). The most recent of these, the *jōyōkanjihyō* 'list of kanji for daily use', lists 2,136 characters for use in everyday publications. While newspapers and government documents generally

small seal   seal of fortune   old seal   clerical   regular   semi-cursive

Fig. 4.3.2: Script styles used in personal seals (name: 福澤諭吉 *Fukuzawa Yukichi) (hankomori.com)*

tend to adhere to these restrictions, this is not always the case for books, magazines and other non-government publications. In order to be fully literate in Japanese, knowledge of a slightly higher number of characters is required. The Japan Kanji Aptitude Test (§8.9), for example, tests the knowledge of roughly 3,000 characters in its Level Pre-1 test recommended for university students and high school graduates.

In addition to the standard form of a character, there often exist multiple variants. Many characters also have both traditional and simplified forms, the former having been used prior to WWII and the subsequent script reforms: 實~実 'truth, fruit', 舊~旧 'old'. Variants are especially common in toponyms and family names (§6.9). They may range from the simple addition or deletion of a dot or line (京~亰 'capital city', 辻~辻 'crossroads'), through the rearrangement of elements (峰~峯 'mountain peak', 島~嶋~嶌 'island'), to the entire replacement of elements (体~體~躰~骵, all variants of 體 'body', 体 being the simplified form used today). Others may be simplified forms not included in the *jōyōkanjihyō*, such as the ubiquitous ヶ used in place of the classifiers (§5.8) 箇~個: 三ヶ月 saN-ka-gecu 'three months', 五ヶ go-ko 'five (small objects)'. Believed to derive from an abbreviation of the grass radical in 箇, the same character, due to near-homonymy, may also be used to express genitive ga (§3.15) in place names: 自由ヶ丘 'Jiyūgaoka', 聖蹟桜ヶ丘駅 'Seiseki-sakuragaoka Station'. Still other variants may bear no visual resemblance to their standard graphs at all. The *daiji* used to mitigate against forgery (§4.8), such as 壱~壹 for 一 'one' or 萬 for 万 '10,000', all fall into this category.

In extreme cases, a single character may have dozens or even hundreds of variants. For example, the Ministry of Justice lists the following 15 variants for the character 邊 (simplified form 辺), used in the surname Watanabe 渡邊, in the

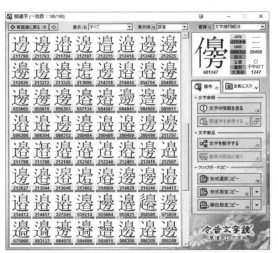

Fig. 4.3.3: Some of the many variants of 邊 *in* Konjaku mojikyō

Family Register Character Unification Database: 辺~边~辺~边~迌~迌~迌~迌~迌~迌~迌~邊~邊~邊.

If this seems excessive, *Konjaku mojikyō* (§8.11), a set of fonts for displaying obscure characters and variants, lists 190 variants for 邊 (Fig. 4.3.3). It has been speculated that when members of the Watanabe clan split off into separate clans, each family slightly modified the character 邊 to distinguish themselves from others. While the number of characters parents can choose from when naming their children is limited (§6.9, §8.2), there is no restriction on the characters one may register for a family name. This has made the digitization process of family registers a long and tedious task. As of 2015, there were a total of 55,271 characters and variants registered in the Family Register Character Unification Database and this number could grow even larger in the future.

4.4 Chinese Characters: Reading

If learning how to write kanji was not hard enough, then learning all of the different readings for each character will provide an immense challenge to any L2 learner wishing to master them. While in China many characters have only one reading, in Japan most (aside from *kokuji*: §4.5) have at least three different readings (even if in many cases some of these readings are obscure). The number of readings even goes up into the double digits for some characters. For example, the *jōyōkanjihyō* (§8.2) gives 12 readings for the character 生 'live, be born' and this number would go even higher if non-standard readings were included (one kanji dictionary gives a total of 21 readings for 生). How did one character come to possess so many different readings? The answer lies in differences between Chinese and Japanese in their morphology and semantics, as well as the process whereby Chinese character readings were transmitted to Japan.

Kanji have two types of readings in Japan: *on-yomi* 'lit. sound reading', which approximate the Middle Chinese pronunciation of a character, and *kun-yomi* 'lit. meaning reading', which are Japanese native equivalents for the word or words expressed by a character. For example, the character 犬 'dog' has the *on-yomi* of *keN*, an adaptation of Middle Chinese *khwen*, and the *kun-yomi* of *inu*, the Japanese word for 'dog'.

There are three major strata of *on-yomi*, each having differing dates of transmission. The earliest stratum, the *go-on* 'Wu readings', were transmitted to Japan around the 5th to 6th century and are traditionally held to have originated from the Wu region, south of the Yangtze River. The Chinese term 吳音 *wúyīn*, on which *go-on* is modelled, however, was used during the Tang dynasty (618–907) to refer to southern or archaic character readings in general, and since the word *go-on* does not appear until the 11th century, it is unclear whether *go-on* refers to Wu in particular, or simply a southern/archaic reading style. When the Japanese first adopted

	go-on	kan-on	tō-on	kan'yō-on
明 'bright'	myoo	mei	miN	—
和 'harmony'	wa	ka	o	—
石 'stone'	šaku~jaku	seki	(ši~šicu)*¹	koku
茶 'tea'	(ja)	(ta)	sa	ča

*¹ 'Ghost readings' (those only appearing in dictionaries) given in brackets

Table 4.4: *The multi-strata system of on-yomi*

Chinese characters, they did so by way of the Korean peninsula, and thus *go-on* are likely heavily influenced by the Sino-Korean readings—that is the Koreanized pronunciation of Chinese characters—of the time. The second stratum of *on-yomi* are called *kan-on* 'Han readings' and were adopted directly from the Tang dynasty capital Chang'an by Japanese envoys and monks sent to China to study Buddhism. *Kan-on* were heavily promoted by the Nara court, with a number of imperial decrees ordering scholars and monks to abandon the by now dated *go-on* in favour of *kan-on* (§8.2). The final stratum of *on-yomi* are called *tō-on* or *tō-in* 'Tang readings' ('Tang' here refers to China in general and not the Tang dynasty), a collective term for all readings transmitted to Japan postdating *kan-on* and predating the modern period. In Modern Japanese, *kan-on* are the most commonly used readings, although *go-on* are still used in many older Sino-Japanese (§7.1) words, especially Buddhist terms. *Tō-on* are the least common and generally restricted to Zen Buddhist terms.

In addition to these three strata of borrowed readings, there is another group of *on-yomi* known as *kan'yō-on* 'customary readings', idiomatic readings arising from misinterpretations and Japanizations of original readings. All these *on-yomi* strata are summarized in Table 4.4. Also borrowed into Japanese over the past century have been a number of readings from various contemporary Chinese topolects (炒飯 *čaahaN* 'fried rice' ← Mandarin *chǎofàn*, 小籠包 *šooroNpoo* 'steamed buns' ← Shanghainese *shiáwlongbaw*, as well as some sinoxenic readings (adapted kanji readings from other sinosphere languages: 越南 *betonamu* 'Vietnam' ← Vietnamese *việt nam*, 平昌 *pyoNčaN* 'Pyeongchang' ← Korean *pyeongchang*). For a discussion on kanji readings in sinosphere personal and place names, see §6.9 and §7.2.

Unlike *on-yomi*, *kun-yomi* were not transmitted to Japan over multiple periods, but rather evolved gradually over time. It is difficult to state exactly when the Japanese began to ascribe kanji to native words. Our earliest examples of *kun-yomi* date back to the 6th century, but are nothing more than rebuses for the names of aristocrats and places: 額田部 'forehead + rice paddy + group' for the clan name Nukatabe, 池辺大宮 'pond+environs+big+palace' for the place name Ikebe no Ōmiya. The use of *kun-yomi* became prevalent in the 8th century, when they began to be utilized in native works of literature, such as *Kojiki* 'An Account of Ancient

Matters' and *Man'yōshū* 'Collection of Myriad Leaves', to record Japanese using kanji only (§1.3). Beginning in the late 8th to early 9th centuries, a practice known as *kanbun kundoku* 'lit. Classical Chinese (CC) meaning reading', known in the West as 'vernacular reading' or 'text transposition', in which Japanese monks and scholars would read CC texts in Japanese through a series of morphosyntactic and lexical glosses (Fig. 4.4; see §8.7 for a modern example), came into widespread use, triggering a massive increase in *kun-yomi*. Thus, *kun-yomi* were a crucial tool both for recording Japanese and interpreting CC texts in Japanese.

Since, in many cases, a single character possesses multiple meanings, or multiple characters possess a synonymous meaning, it is common for a single character to have more than one *kun-yomi*, or multiple characters to share the same *kun-yomi*. Returning to the example of 生, the *jōyōkanjihyō* assigns this character the following 10 *kun-yomi*: (1) *iki-ru* 'live', (2)

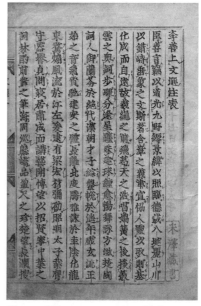

Fig. 4.4: Chinese manuscript with Japanese glosses

(Monzen/Wénxuǎn *'Selections of refined literature'*, 1607 Naoe edition, Yonezawa City Library)

ikas-u 'let live', (3) *ike-ru* 'arrange flowers', (4) *um-u* 'give birth', (5) *umare-ru* 'be born', (6) *hayas-u* 'grow out', (7) *hae-ru* 'be grown out', (8) *o-u* 'cover', (9) *nama* 'fresh', (10) *ki* 'pure'. Viewed the other way around, the reading *hakar-u* 'measure, plan' is assigned to the following six characters, each with a slightly different meaning and different reading in CC: 計 'measure (length, weight or depth)', 量 'measure (weight)', 図 'plan', 測 'guess', 諮 'consult', 謀 'plot against'. While these nuances are lost in spoken Japanese, one can distinguish between the different senses of *hakar-u* in writing through the choice of character. In many cases, these semantic distinctions were introduced to the language through the use of kanji, one of the many ways in which CC has influenced Japanese (§5.9, §7.1).

In addition to the standard *on-yomi* and *kun-yomi*, kanji are often used idiomatically to express words or phrases with no standard kanji notation (or in place of the standard kanji notation) in a form of notation known as *ateji* 'arbitrary notation'. *Ateji* may consist of simple rebuses, in which characters are used phonographically with their meanings ignored: 沢山 *takusaN* 'a lot' ← 沢 *taku* 'stream, swamp' + 山 *saN* 'mountain', 目出鯛 *medeta-i* 'joyous' ← 目 *me* 'eye' + 出 *de* 'exit' + 鯛 *tai* 'seabream' (§2.8). Or they may employ phono-semantic matching, where characters are used both phonographically and semantographically at the same time: 倶楽部 *kurabu* 'club' ← 倶 *ku* 'together' + 楽 *raku* 'fun' + 部 *bu* 'group'. In other cases, *ateji* may be solely semantic: 一寸 *čoQto* 'a little bit' ← 一 'one' + 寸 '*sun* (a unit of measure equal to roughly 3cm)'; 煙草 *tabako* ← 煙 'smoke' + 草 'grass'. This final type of *ateji* is often referred to as *jukujikun* 'compounded reading', indicating a single Japanese word assigned two or more characters read in sequence. Personal names (§6.9) also frequently employ non-standard or archaic readings. For example, 隆~孝~貴~崇~賢~剛~尊 are all read as *taka~takaši* in personal names, despite none of these characters having *taka~takaši* as a standard reading. A quick glance at a kanji dictionary (§8.10) shows that each of these characters has a handful of other readings for use in names as well.

4.5 Chinese Characters: *Kokuji*

In addition to the multitudes of characters borrowed from China, the Japanese also created independently a number of logographic characters in the likeness of Chinese characters. These Japan-made characters are commonly referred to as 国字 *kokuji* 'lit. national characters' and use the same basic components and formation principles as Chinese characters proper. Offshoots of Chinese characters are not limited to Japan and are observed in a number of other sinosphere countries such as Korea, where they are known as *gukja* (the Sino-Korean reading of 国字), and Vietnam, where they are known as *chữ nôm* 'lit. southern characters'.

The vast majority of *kokuji* are compound pictograms (§4.2). Examples include 峠 *tooge* 'mountain pass', which combines the 'mountain' radical 山 with the components 上 'up' and 下 'down' to express a path going up and down a mountain, or 躾 *šicuke* 'discipline (= teaching manners)' which combines the 'body' radical 身 with the component 美 'beauty', conveying the image of a person with proper (beautiful) posture. *Kokuji* may also be phono-semantic compounds (§4.2). Some examples are 塀 *hei* 'wall, fence', formed by combining the 'dirt' radical 土 with the phonetic 屏 *hei* 'enclosure, screen', or 働 *doo*, *hatarak-u* 'work', formed by combining the 'person' radical 亻 with the phonetic 動 *doo* 'move'. While the majority of Chinese characters employ this formation principle, it is relatively rare for *kokuji*. A small number of *kokuji* also combine pictograms with phono-semantic compounds (§4.2), as is the case for 鱩 *hatahata* 'sailfin sandfish', which combines the 'fish' radical 魚 with the phono-semantic compound 神 'god' ('alter' radical 示 + phonetic 申 *šin* 'stretch'). Here, 神 does not express any sound, but simply the meaning 'god-like' (another name for sailfin sandfish is *kaminariuo* 'thunderbolt fish': *kaminari* literally means 'roar of the gods'). A further type of Japan-made logograph, *gōji* 'ligatures', are also commonly classified as *kokuji*. These include the personal names 麿 *maro* (combining the man'yōgana (§1.3, §4.6) 麻 *ma* and 呂 *ro*) and 粂 *kume* (combining the man'yōgana 久 *ku* and 米 *me*), as well as 甃 *bosacu*

'Bodhisattva', an abbreviated ligature formed from the 'grass' radicals (艹) found on both characters in the word 荙 (菩薩 in modern form) *bosacu*. This final example was common in Late Middle Japanese (§1.3) Buddhist literature.

The most common criterion for defining *kokuji* is whether or not the character in question appears in Classical Chinese (CC) literature or dictionaries. This criterion is not always accurate, however, since it is often the case that a character existing in CC may have been reconfigured—or perhaps even created anew in ignorance of its existence—in Japan with a meaning unrelated to its CC counterpart. Some examples are 拵 *koširae-ru* 'construct' (which has the CC counterpart 拵 'put in position') and 鮨 *suši* 'vinegared fish, sushi' (which has the CC counterpart 鮨 'fermented fish paste'). In both of these examples, a parallel can be drawn between the original meaning and the Japanese meaning, leading to the conclusion that the creator probably had knowledge of the original Chinese character. At the same time, though, there are reasons to believe that these characters were coined independently in Japan. While 拵 does exist in CC, it only appears in a small number of dictionaries and there are no examples of its use in actual texts. 鮨 too is quite rare in CC texts outside of dictionaries and the meaning 'sushi' (rather than 'fermented fish paste') can easily be deduced from its two components, 魚 'fish' and 旨 'delicious'. These Japanized usages of Chinese characters, in which it is unclear whether the character was borrowed or coined, are traditionally referred to as *kokkun* 'national meanings'.

As one may assume, *kokuji* are commonly used to express Japanese objects, concepts or flora and fauna that have no Chinese equivalent. There are, for example, a large number of *kokuji* containing the 'tree' radical 木 which are used to express names of trees native to Japan, such as 樫 *kaši* 'evergreen oak' or 榊 *sakaki* 'Cleyera japonica'; as well as carpentry terms, such as 枠 *waku* 'frame' or 杢 *moku* 'carpenter'. There are also a large number of *kokuji* with the 'fish' 魚 radical (鰯 *iwaši* 'sardine' 鯱 *šači[hoko]* 'mythical beast with the head of a tiger and the body of a carp') and 'rice' 米 radical (糀 *kooji* 'Aspergillus oryzae (type of mould used in cooking)', 籾 *momi* 'unhulled rice'). *Kokuji* also exist for metric units (although obsolete), a rare example of *kokuji* being created for foreign loanwords (§7.2). Units of length, for example, take the 'rice' radical 米 *mei* (short for *meetoru* 'metre') as a phonetic and the components 十 '10', 百 '100', 千 '1,000', 分 '1/10', 厘 '1/100' and 毛 '1/1,000' to form the characters 籵 'decametre', 粨 'hectometre', 粁 'kilometre', 粉 'decimetre', 糎 'centimetre' and 粍 'millimetre'. Interestingly, a number of *kokuji*, such as 鱈 *tara* 'cod' or the metric units listed above, have been 'reimported' (§7.1) into Chinese topolects.

While Japanese kanji dictionaries may list hundreds of *kokuji*, many are obsolete and the number in daily use is actually quite small: the *jōyōkanjihyō* (§8.2), for example, lists only 10. This does not stop their appearance in family names and toponyms (§6.9), however, where restrictions on character usage are lax (§4.4). *Kokuji* can also be dialectal (§7.7–§7.11) in nature. Regionally, character variants are common and there are even some examples of made-in-Japan kanji with no CC equivalent. An example of a regional variant is 崔, a shorthand form of 鶴 *curu* 'crane', used in Tsuruoka (鶴岡 → 崔岡) City, Yamagata Prefecture; an example of a regional made-in-Japan kanji is 梛 *nagi* 'Asian bayberry', a character used in the name of the Nagitsuji (梛辻) region in Yamashina, Kyoto.

4.6 Hiragana and Katakana

The Japanese writing system is, in essence, a mixture of logographic (§4.2) and phonographic writing. Kanji fall under the former category, with kana (hiragana and katakana) falling under the latter. Hiragana and katakana are often referred to as 'syllabaries'. This term is not entirely accurate, though, as a syllabary is by definition a set of symbols rendering syllables and kana are used to render moras (§2.4).

Hiragana and katakana are both derived from kanji, the former being a highly cursivized form and the latter an abbreviated form of their respective kanji etyma (bracketed in Table 4.6). Prior to the development of kana, the Japanese employed a method of phonographic writing using kanji phonetically. This system of writing was known as man'yōgana (§1.3) due to its heavy use in the 8th century poetry anthology *Man'yōshū* 'Collection of Myriad Leaves'. The word *kana* literally means 'makeshift letters', while *hira* and *kata* mean 'smooth' and 'partial'. These names derive from the fact that kana were originally considered to be 'makeshift' forms of kanji—*mana* 'lit. true letters'—for use in non-formal writing. It is a common misconception that women developed hiragana while men developed katakana. Evidence shows, however, that both hiragana and katakana were devised by male scribes as shorthand forms for man'yōgana, mostly for use in Japanese glosses of Classical Chinese (CC) texts, during the 9th–10th centuries. Gradually, hiragana came to be used in letter writing, poetry and courtly literature, while katakana remained the more formal of the two, typically restricted to glosses and CC-inspired literature. The reason for hiragana being attributed to women and katakana to men lies simply in the fact that the genre of courtly literature was dominated by women, while CC literature was a subject of study for men.

Modern orthographical practice dictates that kana typically represent a unique mora—put the other way, Japanese words written in kana are, for the most part, 'spelt like they sound'. When kana were first devised, however, there were numerous variants for each kana, derived from multiple kanji. While katakana lost these variants early on, hiragana variants were in use up until the early 20th century. For example, the mora *a* could be written historically as あ (← 安) ~ 𛀂 (← 阿) ~ 𛀅 (← 愛) ~ 𛀃 (← 悪), though can only be written as あ in Modern Japanese. Similarly, *ka* could be written formerly as か (← 加) ~ 𛀎 (← 可) ~ 𛀗 (← 閑) ~ 𛀊 (← 我) ~ 𛀌 (←

			-a		-i		-u		-e		-o	
seion	vowels	ø	あ (安)	ア (阿)	い (以)	イ (伊)	う (宇)	ウ (宇)	え (衣)	エ (江)	お (於)	オ (於)
	unvoiced obstruents	k	か (加)	カ (加)	き (幾)	キ (幾)	く (久)	ク (久)	け (計)	ケ (介)	こ (己)	コ (己)
		s~š	さ (左)	サ (散)	し (之)	シ (之)	す (寸)	ス (須)	せ (世)	セ (世)	そ (曽)	ソ (曽)
		t~c~č	た (太)	タ (多)	ち (知)	チ (千)	つ (川)	ツ (川)	て (天)	テ (天)	と (止)	ト (止)
		h~f	は (波)	ハ (八)	ひ (比)	ヒ (比)	ふ (不)	フ (不)	へ (部)	ヘ (部)	ほ (保)	ホ (保)
	nasals	n	な (奈)	ナ (奈)	に (仁)	ニ (仁)	ぬ (奴)	ヌ (奴)	ね (祢)	ネ (祢)	の (乃)	ノ (乃)
		m	ま (末)	マ (末)	み (美)	ミ (三)	む (武)	ム (牟)	め (女)	メ (女)	も (毛)	モ (毛)
	taps	r	ら (良)	ラ (良)	り (利)	リ (利)	る (留)	ル (流)	れ (礼)	レ (礼)	ろ (呂)	ロ (呂)
	glides	y	や (也)	ヤ (也)			ゆ (由)	ユ (由)			よ (与)	ヨ (與)
		w	わ (和)	ワ (和)	ゐ (為)	ヰ (井)			ゑ (恵)	ヱ (惠)	を (遠)	ヲ (乎)
dakuon (voiced obstruents)		g	が	ガ	ぎ	ギ	ぐ	グ	げ	ゲ	ご	ゴ
		z~j	ざ	ザ	じ	ジ	ず	ズ	ぜ	ゼ	ぞ	ゾ
		d~j	だ	ダ	ぢ	ヂ	づ	ヅ	で	デ	ど	ド
		b	ば	バ	び	ビ	ぶ	ブ	べ	ベ	ぼ	ボ
handakuon		p	ぱ	パ	ぴ	ピ	ぷ	プ	ぺ	ペ	ぽ	ポ
mora nasal		N	ん (无)						ン (尓)			

Table 4.6: *Hiragana and katakana with their respective kanji etyma*

駕) ~ 苏 (← 嘉) ~ 茭 (← 賀) ~ 欸 (← 歌) ~ 哥 (← 哥) ~ 柔 (← 家), but can only be written as か in Modern Japanese.

The modern kana are arranged by mora in Table 4.6, with hiragana on the left and katakana on the right of each cell. There are a total of 73 kana: 47 for *seion* 'clear sounds' (moras without an initial consonant, moras beginning in a consonant other than *p~b~d~g~z~j*), 20 for *dakuon* 'muddy sounds' (moras beginning in *b~d~g~z~j*: voiced obstruents), five for *handakuon* 'half muddy sounds' (moras beginning in *p*) and one for the mora nasal (§2.2). Each *seion,* as well as the mora nasal, possesses unique kana, while the *dakuon* and *handakuon* are rendered through use of the diacritics ゛ and ゜, respectively. The former, known as a *dakuten* 'muddy mark', is appended to the upper right corner of the kana for the corresponding *seion*: か <ka> ~ が <ga>, さ <sa> ~ ざ <za>. The latter diacritic, known as a *handakuten* 'half-muddy mark', is appended to the upper right corner of the kana for the corresponding *h-* or *f-*mora: は <ha> ~ ぱ <pa>, ひ <hi> ~ ぴ <pi>. The distinction between *seion, dakuon* and *handakuon* is not just one of Japanese orthographic tradition, it also plays an important role in the history of the Japanese language (§2.9), in phonotactics (§2.5) and in morphophonological processes such as rendaku (§5.5).

The kana in Table 4.6 comprise all the graphs required to represent the core Japanese moras (checked in Table 2.5.1). The discrepancy between the 73 kana in Table 4.6 and the 102 core moras in Table 2.5.1 is accounted for by (A1)–(A4). The non-core moras (grey in Table 2.5.1) are written with 'kana digraphs', created using

4.6 Hiragana and Katakana

a number of 'spelling devices' described in (B1)–(B8). Also used in select core moras (A1)–(A3), such spelling devices are indicated (in this unit only) by a box: <ti> indicates the orthographic representation of the mora *ti*, while <te.i> indicates the kana used to create the orthographic representation of the mora *ti*. Alternative varieties of such spelling devices may exist which space precludes us from detailing in full: (B8) is but one example of alternate spellings for (B7). Moreover, while a conservative speaker may realize certain spelling devices polymoraically, paralleling majuscule/miniscule orthographic rules, the more innovative speaker will use a single mora, as illustrated also in (B8). This is especially so with spelling devices for glides (B2, B6, B7).

(A) Core mora spelling devices:
  (1) *ša~šu~šo, ja~ju~jo, ča~ču~čo* in Table 2.5.1 do not have unique kana. Instead, they are rendered by placing a miniscule や <ya>, ゆ <yu> or よ <yo> after the kana for the *i*-mora of the relevant consonant: しゅ <ši.yu> for *šu*, じょ <ji.yo> for *jo*, ちゃ <či.ya> for *ča*.
  (2) *y*-glides are rendered by placing a miniscule や <ya>, ゆ <yu> or よ <yo> after the kana for the *i*-mora of the relevant consonant: きゃ <ki.ya> for *kya*, びゅ <bi.yu> for *byu*, にょ <ni.yo> for *nyo*.
  (3) The mora obstruent Q (§2.2) is indicated by a miniscule つ <cu>: いった <i.cu.ta> for *iQta* 'went'.
  (4) Appearing in Table 4.6 are the obsolete kana ゐ <wi> ~ ゑ <we> (§2.9); also を <wo>, used exclusively to write the accusative case marker particle *o* (§3.12).

(B) Non-core mora spelling devices:
  (1) *ca~ce~ci~co, fa~fi~fe~fo, we~wi~wo, si~zi* are rendered by placing a miniscule version of the vowel in question after the kana for the *u*-mora of the relevant consonant: ツァ <cu.a> for *ca*, フェ <fu.e> for *fe*, ウォ <u.o> for *wo*, スィ <su.i> for *si*. Observe that the fossil kana を <wo> (A4) is not used to render *wo* and that スィ <su.i> may also render *swi* (B7).
  (2) *fya~fyo~fyu* are rendered by placing a miniscule や <ya>, ゆ <yu> or よ <yo> after フ <fu>: フョ <fu.yo> for *fyo*.
  (3) *še~če~je*, as well as *ye*-glides, are rendered by placing a miniscule エ <e> after the kana for the *i*-mora of the relevant consonant: シェ <ši.e> for *še*, ピェ <pi.e> for *pye*. The mora *ye* is rendered as イェ <i.e>, with no initial consonant used.
  (4) *ti~di* are rendered by placing a miniscule イ <i> after the kana for the *e*-mora of the relevant consonant: ティ <te.i> for *ti*.

(5) *tu~du* are rendered by placing a miniscule ウ <u> after the kana for the *o*-mora of the relevant consonant: ドゥ <do.u> for *du*.

(6) *wa*-glides are rendered by placing ワ <wa>, or a miniscule ヮ <wa> ~ ァ <a>, after the kana for the *u*-mora of the consonant in question: クワ <ku.wa> ~ クァ <ku.a> ~ クヮ <ku.wa> for *kwa*.

(7) *wi-, we-* and *wo*-glides are rendered by placing either a miniscule ィ <i> ~ ェ <e> ~ ォ <o>, or the digraphs ウィ <u.i> ~ ウェ <u.e> ~ ウォ <u.o>, after the kana for the *u*-mora of the consonant in question: スェ <su.e> or スウェ <su.u.e> for *swe*. The second option here yields trigraphs and, in combination with (A1), even tetragraphs: シュウェ <si.yu.u.e> for *šwe*.

(8) in many cases more than one spelling may exist for a single loanword: スィーツ <su.i.-.cu> ~ スウィーツ <su.u.i.-.cu> ~ スイーツ <su.i.-.cu> for *swi.i.cu ~ su.i.i.cu* 'sweets'.

It is possible to render some illicit moras (black in Table 2.5.1) in kana, but such orthography is generally reserved for transcribing foreign languages, each of which has its own unique conventions (historically both Taiwanese Hokkien and Ainu possessed widely used kana transcriptions). In some loanwords (§7.2, §7.3), what is perhaps best termed a 'spelling conceit' may be encountered. The presence of a *v* in the original etymon, though overwhelmingly realized as [b], is rendered by placing a miniscule version of the vowel in question after the kana ヴ <vu>, coined in the 19th century by the Japanese author and educator Fukuzawa Yukichi (1835–1901): ヴァ <vu.a> for <va>.

As with any writing system, there are a number of quirks, for the most part remnants of *rekishiteki kanazukai* (§8.2), a prescriptive spelling method in use until WWII which reflected the sound system of Early Middle Japanese (§1.3, Table 2.9). The particles *wa* (topic marker) and *e* (allative case marker) (§3.12) are written as は <ha> and へ <he>. In Sino-Japanese (§7.1) vocabulary, the long vowels *ee* and *oo* are typically written <e.i> and <o.u> (せんせい <se.N.se.i> 'teacher', こうとうがっこう <ko.u.to.u.ga.cu.ko.u> 'high school'). Meanwhile, the long vowels found in loanwords—and, optionally, in the mimetic stratum (§5.2) and native stratum interjections (§3.1) as well—are rendered by the use of a horizontal dash (known as *choooNpu* 'long sound mark' or *nobašiboo* 'stretching stick') for the second mora: スタートレック <su.ta.-.to.re.cu.ku> 'Star Trek', ザーザー <za.-.za.-> 'pouring rain', あー <a.-> 'ah!'. In texting and manga this may be replaced by a wave dash 〜 or dashes 〜〜 (§4.9): わ〜〜 <wa.~.~> 'yeeeey!'. An exception is *ee*, which may also be written as <ee> or <ei> in loanwords: バレエ <ba.re.e> 'ballet', メイン <me.i.N> 'main, Maine'.

4.7 The Roman Alphabet

Although, conventionally, Japanese is not written using the Roman alphabet, it can be. Until relatively recently, this was generally done for the convenience of non-native speakers. Despite the fact that native speakers typically find reading Japanese in the Roman alphabet awkward and time-consuming, textbooks for Japanese schoolchildren learning the Roman alphabet have existed since the early 20th century. Historically, there have been movements seeking to abolish both kanji and kana and replace them with a Roman alphabet script (§8.2).

One of these movements, the *Rōmajikai* 'Roman Alphabet Society' established in 1885, gave rise to the first of the three major Roman letter transcription systems used in Japan today. This is the *hebon-shiki* 'Hepburn-style' system, modelled on the romanization used in the Japanese-English dictionary compiled by James Hepburn (§8.10, §8.13), a Christian missionary and physician from Pennsylvania. The second major romanization system was first proposed in 1881 by the physicist Tanakadate Aikitsu (1856–1952). This is the *nihon-shiki* 'Japan-style' system, modelled on kana. The third and final system grew out of the inconsistencies created by the dual use of the divergent systems just discussed. It was essentially a slightly modified form of *nihon* promulgated by the cabinet in 1937 and known as the *kunrei-shiki* 'official-directive-style' system. Although General MacArthur issued an executive order overturning *kunrei* in favour of *hebon* in 1945, *kunrei* was reconfirmed by cabinet directive in 1954 (§8.1). Although it is still the only romanization with legal status in Japan, the 1954 *kunrei* directive was, in effect, a fudge. Its wording made it clear that, in certain cases, both *hebon* and *nihon* would also be permitted. An official directive which sought to remedy confusion thus ended up compounding it.

Hebon is phonetic (§2.1) and based largely on English spelling conventions. Thus, し is <shi>, not <chi> or <schi> had it been based on French or German spelling conventions. Both *kunrei* and *nihon* are based on kana: here し is <si>. The major differences between *hebon*, *nihon* and *kunrei* are shown in Table 4.7. While *kunrei* marks long vowels with a circumflex <ô>, *hebon* usage is highly confused: officially long vowels are marked with macrons; however, the circumflex, an '*h* length mark' <oh>, a double vowel <oo>, kana spelling (or word-processor input) based transcriptions such as <ou>, and no length mark at all may all be found. *Nihon*

kana	し	ち	つ	ふ	じ	しゃ	ちゃ	じゃ	おう	んC	んV
hebon	shi	chi	tsu	fu	ji	sha	cha	ja	ō~ô~oo~oh~o~ou	n~m	n-~n'
nihon	si	ti	tu	hu	zi	sya	tya	zya	ō~ô	n	n'
kunrei	si	ti	tu	hu	zi	sya	tya	zya	ô	n	n'

Table 4.7: Major differences between romanizations

prescribes no rules for long vowels, although in practice macrons or circumflexes are employed. Although in all three transcriptions it is <n> when word-final, transcriptional practice varies when the mora nasal N (§2.4) appears before a consonant (C) or a vowel (V). While *hebon* can use <m> in environments where N is realized as [m] (before *m~b~p*: §2.2), *nihon* and *kunrei* use <n> before all consonants. Before a vowel, the mora nasal may be transcribed as <n-> or <n'> in *hebon*, but only <n'> in *nihon* and *kunrei*.

While phonemic kana-based *nihon* and *kunrei* are easier for Japanese native speakers to use, the fact remains that it was never Japanese speakers, being more comfortable in their own writing system, who were targeted as the end-users of either of these systems. Non-native speakers, when confronted with a *nihon* or *kunrei* romanization such as <siti> for 'seven', are apt to pronounce it something like English *city*, incomprehensible to a Japanese. Further, when it comes to transcribing the recent phonemic distinctions brought about by the massive influx of loanwords since the mid-20th century (§7.2, §7.3), both *nihon* and *kunrei* are unfit for purpose. Both *han* 'group' and *faN* 'fan', for example, must be transcribed identically as <han>. In consequence, *hebon* has become the dominant romanization found today, its use widespread even by government ministries (most notably in road signs: Fig. 4.7.1). Although the domain of *kunrei* continues to narrow, adding even further to the muddle is the fact that young children learn this romanization first in elementary school (Fig. 4.7.2).

Fig. 4.7.1: Ministry of Construction road sign

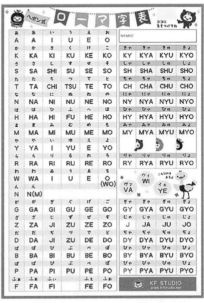

Fig. 4.7.2: Elementary school romanization chart (www.kfstudio.net)

The romanization confusion which reigns today is, on the whole, generally benign. An example, however, of its more insidious consequences are the situation it presents for credit cards and, yet worse, names (§6.9) on passports. Officials working in Japanese passport offices routinely insist on applicants using a *hebon* romanization of their full name with no vowel length marks, although a small number of variants are accepted upon request. This is not the case for credit card and other companies, who generally leave romanization entirely up to the client, with the caveat that diacritics are not permitted. Thus a person with the surname 東海林, pronounced *šooji*, will generally have their passport surname written as *hebon* SHOJI, while their credit card could have SYOZI, SYOOZI, SYOUZI, SYOHZI, SHOZI, SHOOZI, SHOUZI, SHOHZI, SYOJI, SYOOJI, SYOUJI, SYOHJI, SHOJI, SHOOJI, SHOUJI or SHOHJI. Similarly, someone whose given name is 七郎, pronounced *šičiroo*, could write their credit card name as SITIRO, SITIROO, SITIROU, SITIROH, SHITIRO, SHITIROO, SHITIROU, SHITIROH, SICHIRO, SICHIROO, SICHIROU, SICHIROH, SHICHIRO, SHICHIROO, SHICHIROU or SHICHIROH. Given credit card companies appear to tolerate romanization 'script mixing', our hypothetical Mr. 東海林七郎 could spell his card name in any one of 256 different ways. In an age where a discrepancy in spelling across ID documents can trigger 'terrorist flagging' at many airports, this is a serious issue which the Japanese government can no longer ignore as part of its language policy (§8.1).

4.8 Chinese and Arabic Numerals

In addition to being written using kana, Japanese numbers (§5.8) can also be written in Chinese (一二三), Arabic (123) and, to a lesser extent, Roman numerals (I II III). As a general rule, Chinese numerals are more common in vertical script, while Arabic and Roman numerals are more common in horizontal script, but there is considerable leeway.

In general, Chinese numerals conjure up a more conservative image and are favoured in formal contexts, such as legal documents, certification and letter writing. There are contexts in which only Chinese numerals are acceptable, such as in Sino-Japanese (§7.1) words and in certain idioms (一様 *ičiyoo* 'uniform', 十人十色 *juuniNtoiro* 'each to his own'), as well as contexts in which Chinese numerals are preferred (street numbers on addresses written in vertical script on envelopes and postcards). Arabic numerals, on the other hand, tend to be more progressive and favoured in newspapers, magazines and academic writing. Unlike Chinese numerals, there are few contexts in which only Arabic numerals are acceptable, but there are contexts in which they are used almost exclusively (mathematics, timetables at train stations and model numbers on consumer products) and in which they are preferred (postal codes on envelopes and postcards). Arabic and Roman numerals possess both half and full width variants in printed matter: that is, variants the same width as Roman alphabet ASCII characters (123, I II III) and variants the same width as kanji and kana (1 2 3, I II III). While there are no set rules concerning when to use half width or full width, half width numerals tend to be preferred in horizontal script with full width numerals preferred in vertical script. This is mainly for aesthetic reasons, though, and it is common for half width Arabic numerals to be set horizontally in the space of a single full width character in vertical script as well. See Fig. 4.8 for an example of a postcard utilizing both Chinese and Arabic numerals.

Chinese numerals up to 10,000 increase by powers of 10 (十 *juu* '10', 百 *hyaku* '100', 千 *seN* '1,000', 万 *maN* '10,000'), while numbers greater than 10,000 increase by every fourth power of 10 (億 *oku* '10^8', 兆 *čoo* '10^{12}', 京 *kei* '10^{16}').

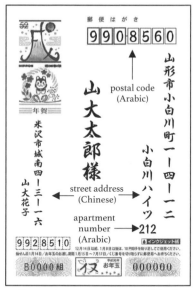

Fig. 4.8: Japanese postcard with both Chinese and Arabic numerals

Thus, when counting larger numbers, one counts in myriads (units of 10,000), a system of counting common in East and South Asian languages. When writing numbers of four digits or more in Arabic numerals, it is common practice to place commas every three decimal places from right to left, as in Western languages. This leads to a discrepancy between the way numerals are written and the way they are read aloud. In order to avoid this discrepancy and facilitate reading, Chinese and Arabic numerals are often used in combination. For example, the number 'ten thousand three hundred and forty' can be written as 10,340, 1万340 (1×10,000+340) or 10千340 (10×1,000+340). Chinese numerals for numbers greater than *kei* '10^{16}' do exist, but are rarely seen in general use. Apart from idioms such as 万が一 *maN=ga iči* 'on the off-chance that (lit. 10,000 to 1)', no power of 10 (including negative powers) other than 1,000 and 100 can be used independently. Instead, they must be preceded by 一 'one', or 1, when their base value is indicated: 一万 ~ 1万 '10,000', not simply 万.

Chinese numerals exist also for decimal fractions, which decrease by powers of ten in the order 分 *bu* '0.1', 厘 *riN* '0.01', 毛 *moo* '0.001', 糸 *ši* '0.0001'. In writing, these are rarely used outside of idioms (九分九厘 *kubukuriN* 'almost entirely (lit. 99%)', 五分五分 *gobugobu* '50/50'), but are heard when reading certain fractions out loud, such as body temperatures (*saNjuuroku-do hači-bu* '36.8°'). In most scenarios, each number in a fraction is read individually following 点 *teN* 'point', similar to English (*kyuujuukyuu teN kyuu kyuu* '99.99'). There is an additional fraction 割 *wari*, synonymous with 分 *bu*, which may be followed by *bu* or *riN*, in which case the latter represent 1/10 and 1/100 of a *wari* (0.01 and 0.001), respectively. The *wari* system is frequent in advertisements for sales and in sporting averages: 2割引き *ni-wari+biki* '20% off' or 打率4割5分7厘 *daricu yoN-wari go-bu nana-riN* '.457 batting average'.

In addition to the standard numerals, a set of circled numerals known as *maru sūji* 'circle numerals' are used to number bullet points in, for example, academic writing, posters or minutes for meetings. Circled numerals are usually Arabic (①②③), but Unicode (§8.11) characters for circled Chinese numerals exist as well (㊀㊁㊂). There is one final set of numerals, 大字 *daiji* 'lit. big characters', a set of complex variants (§4.3) of Chinese numerals used to mitigate against forgery in legal and financial documents and in banknotes. These exist for all numerals up to 10,000, but are typically only used for 'one', 'two', 'three' and 'ten', as these numerals are the easiest to falsify due to their simplicity: 壱~壹 for 一 'one', 弐~貳 for 二 'two', 参~參 for 三 'three', 伍 for 五 'five', 拾 for 十 'ten'.

4.9 Punctuation

Japanese punctuation consists of both elements similar to punctuation in Western languages, such as commas, full stops and brackets, and elements unique to Japanese, such as interpuncts, hook brackets and wave dashes. It is a common misconception that punctuation did not exist, or was rarely used, before contact with Western languages. While it is true that contact with Western languages accelerated the use of punctuation in Japanese—with much modern punctuation borrowed directly from such languages—there are examples of punctuation being used in Japanese glosses of Chinese texts (§1.3, §8.7) as far back as the 8th century and in native texts as far back as the 12th century. It was not until the 17th century that punctuation began to be used on a large scale, however, and not until the early 20th century that the system of punctuation that we see in use today came into being.

Japanese commas and full stops come in two different flavours: the dot and circle (、。), and the comma and period (, .). The former is the more traditional of the two styles, dating back to the 17th century, and used in both vertical and horizontal script. The latter is modelled after Western usage and employed mostly in horizontal script. Rules of usage concerning full stops are, for the most part, the same as those in Western languages: to mark the end of a sentence. An exception is that full stops are not usually used at the end of quotations as they are in English. Commas, on the other hand, have no definitive set of rules concerning their usage and are largely dependent on author and style. Their use can be broken down into three main categories: logical breaks, pauses and rhetorical breaks. Logical breaks consist of breaks following interjections (§3.1) at the start of a sentence, phrasal breaks at the end of a subordinate clause, breaks at the start and end of parenthetical clauses and breaks in between words or phrases in apposition. All of these are typical in standard writing. Commas for pauses are added for overall rhythm when reading aloud and display a large degree of individual licence (§8.13)—some writers may opt to add no pauses at all, while others may add a pause after nearly every particle. Finally, rhetorical break commas are added for emphasis, their usage entirely dependent upon the writer.

There are a total of no less than seven types of brackets in common use in Modern Japanese, with additional less frequently used variants available in Unicode fonts (§8.11). The most commonly used brackets are parentheses ( ), which serve the same function as their Western counterparts: closing off parenthetical clauses or providing intertextual annotations such as cross-references, citation sources and kanji readings. Other brackets shared with Western languages include square brackets [ ] and curly brackets { }, while brackets unique to Japanese (and other sinosphere languages) include tortoise shell brackets 〔 〕, angled brackets 〈 〉, double angled brackets 《 》 and lenticular brackets 【 】, none of which possess officially designated usages but are used in technical writing with various meanings.

Japanese quotation marks 「 」 are actually a form of brackets known as 'hook brackets'. In addition to enclosing intertextual quotations and citations, hook brackets are also used to enclose the titles of papers and articles, to designate ad hoc titles or terminology and to add emphasis to keywords. A variant of hook brackets, known as 'double hook brackets' 『 』, are used to enclose the titles of books, movies, and plays, and to mark quotations or citations within another quotation or citation. Western-style inverted commas ' ' and double inverted commas " " are also used in horizontal script, and occasionally even in vertical script, but are overall less common than their hook bracket counterparts.

Other forms of punctuation include interpuncts ・, wave dashes 〜, horizontal bars — and ellipses …. Interpuncts are used to separate words in apposition or in lists, similar to a backslash: 和語・漢語・外来語 *wago kango gairaigo* 'native words/ Sino-Japanese words/borrowed words'. Or they may be used to mark spaces in foreign names and loanwords (§7.2, §7.3): ジョン・スミス *joN sumisu* 'John Smith', スター・ウォーズ *sutaa uoozu* 'Star Wars'. Wave dashes are used to indicate ranges (12月24日〜25日 'from December 24th to 25th'), points of origin or destination (東京〜 'from Tokyo') and, mostly in texting and manga, long vowels (いいね〜〜 *i-i=neee* 'great!': §4.6). Horizontal bars, —, function almost the same as em-dashes in Western languages, with the addition of being used before and after subtitles. They can, however, be easily confused with the kanji for 'one' 一 or with the vowel length mark ー. Ellipses are frequently encountered, especially in manga and video games, where, in addition to marking omission, they may also express speechlessness. Question marks ?, exclamation marks !, colons : and, to a lesser extent, semicolons ; are also observed in Japanese writing—particularly horizontal script—with little difference in usage to their Western counterparts. In formal writing, question marks and exclamation marks are avoided.

Emphasis in text is marked by what are known as 'round dots' or 'side dots'. These take the form of dots • or sesames ヽ and are placed to the right of the text in vertical script and above the text in horizontal script: 漢字は表語文字である ~ 漢字は表語文字である kaɴji=wa hyoogomoji de aru 'kanji are logograms'. A number of iteration marks, known as *odoriji* 'lit. dancing characters', are used to express the repetition of kanji or kana. Traditionally, kanji iteration marks consisted of the 'same mark' 々 (a simplification of 同 → 仝 'same') and the 'double mark' ゞ (a simplification of 二 'two'). The latter, however, fell out of use after WWII. With kana, the 'single mark' is used to mark the iteration of a single kana: ゝ ~ ゞ for hiragana, ヽ ~ ヾ for katakana, the second variant of each set rendering *dakuon* (§4.6). Thus, はゝ for <ha.ha> or タヾ for <ta.da>. Meanwhile, the '*ku* mark' (〱 ~ 〲), named for its resemblance to the hiragana く, is used to mark the iteration of two or more hiragana letters in vertical script, where it takes the space of two characters. Kana iteration marks are now rarely found, but are still retained to a degree in letter writing among older cohorts.

4.10 Script Mixing

One of the most distinctive features of Japanese writing is the way in which different scripts are mixed together in texts. Script mixing has a long and varied history in Japan. From the earliest documents, kanji and man'yōgana (§1.3, §4.6) were mixed together to form a hybrid script consisting of both semantographic and phonographic elements. After the development of hiragana and katakana, it became standard to mix kanji with hiragana in some genres and kanji with katakana in others. Eventually, all three scripts came to be used together. Entering the modern era, the Roman alphabet (§4.7), Arabic numerals (§4.8) and, to a lesser extent, the Greek alphabet and a number of punctuation marks (§4.9) and symbols (§4.14) were also added to the mix under the influence of Western languages (§7.2, §7.3).

In Modern Japanese, major parts of speech (nominals, verbals and modifiers: §3.1) are typically written in kanji for words possessing kanji notation and hiragana or katakana for those without. Whether or not a word possesses kanji notation largely depends on its lexical domain (§4.1)—there are also a number of domains such as flora and fauna which, though possessing kanji notation, are commonly written in katakana (Table 4.1). On the other hand, verbal suffixes (§3.7, §3.8) and minor parts of speech (particles, copulas, conjunctions and interjections: §3.1) are written mostly in hiragana, or in some cases, katakana. Kana added to the end of verb and adjective stems to render a suffix is called *okurigana* 'dispatched kana'. In theory, this should lead to the stem of a verb or adjective being written in kanji with its suffix in kana. In practice, however, since kana is a moraic writing system and a large portion of Japanese verbs have consonant-final stems (§3.3), it is often orthographically impossible to separate a stem from a suffix using only kanji and kana.

Take, for instance, the consonant-stem verb *ik-u* 'go'. Morphologically speaking, the boundary between stem and suffix comes between *ik-* and *-u*. Due to the orthographic limitations of a moraic writing system, though, this word is written as 行く <i.ku>, with the first mora in kanji and the second in kana. Add to this a number of other quirky conventions originating in a kana-based analysis of the language's morphology and we end up with a system that is far from perfect. Vowel-stem verbs with stems longer than one mora, for example, end up with the final mora of the stem written in kana: 食べる *tabe-ru* 'eat', 起きる *oki-ru* 'wake up'. See §8.6 for a discussion on how such a kana-level analysis of morphology plays a major role in the prescriptive grammar taught in Japanese schools.

There exists another system of notation known as *furigana* 'attached kana', a type of phonetic guide in which kana are added to the top (or in vertical script, the right side) of kanji indicating the Japanese reading. *Furigana* was originally employed in the form of glosses to facilitate the reading of difficult characters in Classical Chinese texts (§4.4) and over time its usage spread to Japanese texts as well. It was especially common in the literature of the 17th to 19th centuries and in late 19th to early 20th century newspapers, magazines and novels, as kanji literacy was much lower at this time than today. After WWII, *furigana* use declined considerably and now is typically only added to difficult kanji or kanji using non-standard readings. There are still several genres of literature, such as children's books or manga and video games (§6.5) for minors, however, in which *furigana* is added to nearly every kanji to improve literacy. *Furigana* is also common in L2 textbooks (§8.8).

As outlined in §4.1, the lexical domains in which each script is employed in Modern Japanese are for the most part well defined. This does not mean, however, that all genres of writing employ all types of scripts and, historically speaking, there has been a wide range of variation in how scripts are mixed together across different genres. From the 17th century, a mixture of kanji (with *furigana*) and hiragana became the norm in mainstream literature, with a mixture of hiragana and a small number of kanji being used in traditional poetry and lowbrow genres (see also §1.3 for an overview of script mixing in the pre-modern period). In Modern Japanese, for the first time, we find a four-way mixture of kanji, katakana, hiragana and the Roman alphabet. While this blend dominates most genres of literature at present, we still find examples of other blends. Many early computer programs and video games, for example, employed only hiragana or katakana in their script due to memory limitations. Even today, simple LCDs on home appliances such as telephones often display only katakana. One example of an official document using an alternate style of script mixing is the Penal Code of Japan (Fig.

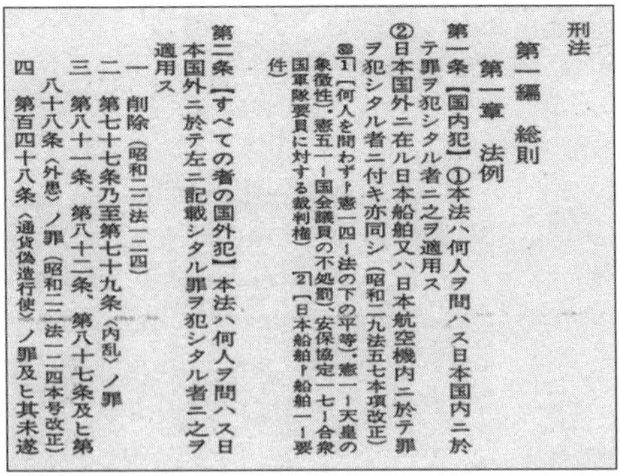

Fig. 4.10: Extract from the Penal Code of Japan prior to its 1995 revision (塩野他 1994)

4.10) which, until a revision in 1995, was written entirely in kanji and katakana, as was common in pre-war legislation.

4.11 Braille

The famous Japanese educator, Nitobe Inazō (1862–1933), once remarked that 'the blind man can be better educated than his more fortunate brethren who are endowed with good sight; for the former, by acquiring the 47 letters of the *iroha* syllabary [the kana], through the Braille system, can read history [...] or anything written in that system; whereas he who has eyesight cannot read the daily papers unless he has mastered at least 2,000 characters [kanji]'.

Braille, as known in its present form of a raised dot binary system, was developed in 1837 by Louis Braille (1809–1852) for the French alphabet and is thought to have been based on night-time messages using lights sent by French troops during the Napoleonic Wars. The Japanese system, known as 点字 *tenji* 'lit. dot letters', was developed in 1890 by Ishikawa Kuraji (1859–1944) at the Kunmōain (the Blind and Mute Academy, now the Tōkyō Mōa Gakkō, the Tokyo School for the Blind and Mute). In 1926, it was possible to vote in national elections using braille ballot slips, while by 1940 the Japan Braille Library had been founded in Tokyo. In 1969 漢点字 *kantenji*, a braille kanji system, was developed, but has not been widely adopted. Today, *tenji* is ubiquitous in daily life, appearing on elevator control panels, at pedestrian crossings, on a range of essential

Fig. 4.11: Braille on a Washlet control pane

products, on warnings (including the well-known ⠔⠹⠳ *osake* on alcoholic beverages), and even on Washlet toilet control panels, as illustrated in Fig. 4.11.

Tenji are written using raised dots within a 2×3 rectangular 'cell' for 64 (= 2^6) possible combinations. For ease of the discussion to follow, these six dots will be numbered as shown in the cell to the right. Like kana script, *tenji* are moraic (§2.4) and, with the exception of the 'prefixes' discussed below, there is a one-to-one correspondence between a *tenji* cell and a kana. Unlike kana but similar to Korean hangul, however, *tenji* are segmental, in that the vowel and consonant portions of the cell are separable units. The five vowels *a~i~u~e~o* are written using dots 1–3, as ⠁ ~ ⠃ ~ ⠉ ~ ⠋ ~ ⠊, while the seven *seion* (excluding glides and vowel only moras: §4.6) are written with dots 4–6: as *k* ⠠, *s~š* ⠰, *t~c~č* ⠼, *n* ⠄, *h~f* ⠤, *m* ⠴, *r* ⠆. We will call the top left dots 123 ⠇ the vowel sector, the bottom right 456 ⠰ the consonant sector. A mora is created by simply locking the two sectors together: *su* is ⠝, *mi* is ⠍, *re* is ⠗. *Sumire* 'violet' is thus ⠝⠍⠗. Observe, however, that the order of the sectors is unnatural: someone reading left to right, or top to bottom, will encounter the vowel (V) before the consonant (C) sector, whereas a mora is CV.

1	2
3	4
5	6

The two mora consonants, N~Q (§2.1), are written ⠍ (as *m* with no vowel) and ⠠, respectively: *seqkeN* 'soap' is ⠎⠢⠦⠴. Thus, Q 'steals' vowel space and, while in kana the symbol for Q and *cu* are the same (differing only in size: §4.6), in *tenji* this is not the case, two completely different cells being employed: ココナッツ *kokonaQcu* 'coconut' is ⠪⠪⠅⠢⠝. Voicing on consonants, indicated by the diacritic known as *dakuten* in kana orthography, is marked by means of a prefix cell ⠐ (hereafter V̲, for voicing). So-called *handakuten*, used to write *p*, is also indicated by a prefix, this time ⠠ (hereafter P̲). Thus, *pagoda* 'pagoda' is ⠠⠓⠐⠅⠐⠞ <P̲.ha.V̲.ko.V̲.ta>, where the underlined first, third and fifth *tenji* are all *(han)dakuten* prefixes—what in kana takes three graphs requires six in *tenji*.

Tenji begin to get quirky with the two glides (§2.4). The first of these, *w*, has its own unique cells: *wa~wo* use no vowel sector dots and are ⠢ ~ ⠣, while the now obsolete *wi~we* use the same consonant sector dots as *wa~wo* but with vowel dot 3 added: ⠦ ~ ⠧. The other semi-vowel, *y*, is treated within the *tenji* system as a vowel, employing dot 2 ⠐. Unlike a vowel, however, *y* cannot exist as an independent mora and must be combined with another vowel. Since *y* already occupies vowel space, this is achieved by 'dropping' the vowel sector as far to the bottom of the cell space as possible: *a* is dropped from 1 to 5 to give ⠈ for *ya*, *u* is dropped from 12 to 56 to give ⠘ for *yu*, and *o* is dropped from 23 to 45 to give ⠨ for *yo*. The y-glides (§2.4) are expressed in *tenji* by using ⠈ as a prefix (hereafter Y̲): *ryo* is written ⠈⠗ <Y̲.ro>. When a y-glide co-occurs with *(han)dakuten*, both prefixes are combined within a single cell to create independent y-glide + *dakuten* ⠘ (Y̲V̲) or y-glide + *handakuten* ⠰ (Y̲P̲) cells. For example, *bya* is ⠘⠓ <Y̲V̲.ha>, while *pyo* is ⠰⠓ <Y̲P̲.ho>.

A long vowel is indicated by means of ⠒ (visually similar to the long sound mark ー: §4.6) and is used regardless of any long vowel rule applicable in kana

4.11 Braille

	0	1	2	3	12	13	23	123
0	space	a 1	Y	Q	u 3	i 2	o 9	e 6
4	V	ra 5	YV	long vowel	ru 4	ri 8	ro 0	re 7
5	wa	na	ya	wi	nu	ni	no	ne
6	P	ka	YP	?	ku	ki	ko	ke
45	wo	ta	yo	we !	cu	či	to	te
46	、	sa		。	su	ši	so	se
56	「」 -	ha	yu	▶English text follows	fu	hi	ho	he
456	N ▶English text ends	ma	▶digits follow	( )	mu	mi	mo	me

Table 4.11: Japanese braille cells

orthography. Thus, the *o* mora of the long *oo* in 党 <tou> 'political party' and 十 <too> 'ten' are written identically: both these words appear in braille as ⠞⠒. Particles whose kana orthography reflects a former pronunciation (§8.2) exhibit quirky behaviour: while は and へ are written as pronounced, as *wa* ⠴ and *e* ⠢, を is written as *wo* ⠔, not *o* ⠒. At the sentence level, Japanese braille employs spaces ⠀, unlike orthography for the sighted. Particles, however, are attached to the nouns they follow with no space cell used—another indication of their boundedness (§3.12).

Punctuation (§4.9) is also indicated by cells, some of which do double duty as moras. These include ⠒ for 。 and ⠢ for ! (also used for *we*). The vowel-only and *r*-mora cells all do double duty as the numerals 0–9. Thus, ⠊ may be *ri* or 8, depending on context. To avoid confusion, a number of cells are assigned to flag a shift in input: ⠼ 'digits follow' or ⠤ 'English text ends'. Major *tenji* cell functions are summarized in Table 4.11, with some minor uses omitted. The eight columns show vowel sectors, the eight rows consonant sectors. In both cases, an empty sector (all dots unraised) is indicated by 0. Observe that the cells in columns 0, 2 and 3 fall outside the overarching system and are employed for a variety of moras, prefixes and other functions. The prefixes Y (*y*-glide), V (*dakuten*) and P (*handakuten*)—and combinations thereof—are shaded, while input shift cells are marked with a ▶.

4.12 Orthographic Licence and Orthographic Play

As has been demonstrated throughout this chapter, Japanese orthography is highly complex and subject to many conventions, as summarized in Table 4.1. But 'conventions' these are, not rules. Despite the hundreds of hours of compulsory education (§8.5) devoted to mastering script choice (kanji or kana), kanji readings (§4.4), kanji choice, *okurigana* (§4.10), punctuation (§4.9) and much else, there still remains considerable leeway for the individual to exploit. In addition, the orthographic component of Japanese compulsory education has changed and evolved over the last century: the number of kanji taught has waxed and waned, with individual kanji added or removed (§8.5). Both inside and outside the classroom, the conventions for *okurigana* and kana choice (hiragana or katakana) have altered (§4.6, §4.10); kana rules underwent a major revision in 1946 (known as the *gendai kanazukai*: §8.2); and around the same time, the direction of horizontal script switched from right-to-left to left-to-right. Someone born in the 1920s, who learnt to write before WWII, possesses a radically different 'mental orthography' to someone born in the 1990s. These generational differences imposed from above, combined with exploitation imposed from below of the leeway inherent in the orthography itself, is what we term here orthographic licence.

Orthographic licence manifests itself in many ways. Some Japanese language users flout orthographic conventions wholesale, in order to make a political point, to attract attention or to irritate. The authors of this volume, during our long tenure in Japan, have encountered Japanese users who restrict their kanji use to Sino-Japanese vocabulary (§7.1), who refuse to use kanji at all, who use katakana in place of hiragana, or who use pre-war kanji graphs (§4.3) and kana spellings (§8.2, §8.7). The extract below, taken from a social media post, illustrates the orthographic practice of a correspondent who falls into the last category.

> 最近知り合った青年に舊漢字・舊假名でメイルを送ったところ、或る相對的方向に偏った、危ない人に<u>思はれてしまひ</u>、極めて遺憾。面識が有るのだから、普通の人間である<u>くらゐ</u>分かる<u>だらう</u>に。

'I was deeply disappointed to find that, after sending an email written in pre-war kanji and kana spellings to a young person I had recently met, this person took me to be a shady figure with a certain political agenda. They know who I am, so they should understand at the very least that I'm just a normal person.'

The kanji in bold, 舊 (→旧), 假 (→仮) and 對 (→対), are written using their traditional, pre-war forms, while the underlined words, 思はれてしまひ (→思われてしまい), くらゐ (→くらい) and だらう (→だろう), all employ historical kana usage. Notice how the author of the post comments on how their use of pre-war kanji and kana spellings gave a newly met acquaintance the impression that he held to a 'certain political agenda', ultra-right conservativism, a group commonly associated with using such orthography.

Other language users limit their licence to the domain of just one script, to kanji only, via a marked bias towards or against certain characters. Yet others overuse the Roman alphabet (§4.7) or emoji, while others underuse kanji. In yet other cases, an apparent instance of orthographic licence may in fact be unconscious, brought about by a low level of orthographic competence. Some written media tolerate orthographic licence more than others. While it is no surprise to find wide-ranging licence in poetry, novels, manga, blogs and social media, it is tolerated much less in bureaucratese, textbooks and national newspapers.

Orthographic licence can be exploited for commercial purposes, as is evident in company names such as トイザらス *toizarasu* 'Toys R Us' (with the *ra* only in hiragana, mirroring the English orthographic play) or the use of pre-war kanji in the names of conservative-leaning schools such as 國學院大學 *kokugakuin daigaku* 'Kokugakuin University'. Such licence can also be felicitous: the name of a brand of *taiyaki* (a fish-shaped cake with red bean filling) sold in Tokyo, for example, is 天下鯛へい *tenka taihei* 'lit. seabreams throughout the world (へい *hei* here is meaningless)', a play on words with 天下泰平 *tenka taihei* 'peace throughout the world'.

In these and similar instances, it is often difficult to draw a line between orthographic licence and orthographic play. The same can be said for *ateji* 'arbitrary notation' (§4.4), which are often employed in a playful manner. The kanji notations 恋水 'lit. love-water' for *namida* 'tear', 宇宙 'outer space' for *sora* 'sky' and 魂 'soul' for *kokoro* 'heart', for example, are all observed in song titles and lyrics. Other examples of playful *ateji* include 夜露死苦 'lit. night-dew-death-pain', which can be read as *yorošiku* 'nice doing business with you', and 愛死天流 'lit. love-death-heaven-flow', read as *aišiteru* 'I love you', both popular slogans among members of adolescent motorcycle gangs. There are examples of *ateyomi* 'arbitrary readings' being applied to kana and the Roman alphabet as well, usually through the use of *furigana* (§4.6): チャット *čaqto* 'chat' read as *ošaberi* 'gossip' in the manga *Install* by Mizuki Mio or W read as *daburu* 'double' in Wきっぷ *daburu kiqpu* 'double ticket'.

Moving on to what is more obviously orthographic play, Japanese is no different from other major languages in having a wide range of orthography-based puzzles and board games, most of which, including crosswords, can utilize either kanji or kana for added variety. Perhaps the most well-known form of orthographic play in Japanese is *kaomoji* 'emoticons (lit. face characters)'. Not to be confused with *emoji* 'picture characters', these are typographic representations of smiles, frowns, crying and other facial expressions. While emoticons are by no means unique to Japanese, the number employed is greater than in most other languages due to their inclusion from the late 1990s in mobile phone texting applications and IMEs (§8.11). While emoticons in the West are typically written at a 90° angle to the text, in Japanese they are written at the same angle, as illustrated in (1). Japanese emoticons usually utilize punctuation (§4.9), the Roman alphabet and symbols, but can employ kanji or kana as well (2). Another form of orthographic play can be found in what are known as *gyaru moji* 'gal characters' (3)–(4): typographic representations of kana using punctuation, symbols, the Roman alphabet and other kana.

(1)   'smile, laughing'   'sadness, crying'   'surprised, confused'
       English   :) :] :D XD   :(:[:c :'(D: :O :o %) :s
       Japanese   (^_^) (^^) \\(^o^)/   (;_;) (T_T) (´ `)   (*_*) (@_@) (° □°)

(2)   (・皿・) 'teeth grinding', (つ^_^)つ 'hug', (=^エ^=) 'cat face'

(3)   レヽ: katakana レ <re> + katakana iteration mark (§4.9) for い <i>

(4)   ナ=:   katakana ナ <na> + equal sign for た <ta>

Given their logographic nature (§4.2), kanji have been employed in orthographic play since the dawn of written records. The kanji wordplay 山上復有山 'lit. mountain on top of another mountain' to express 出 'exit' (which looks like two mountains 山 stacked on top of each other) from *Man'yōshū* 'Collection of Myriad Leaves' (§1.3) is particularly famous. The mock kanji dictionary, *Ono ga bakamura usojizukushi* 'The Ono ga Bakamura Guide to Fake Kanji' (1806), which listed 190 mock kanji, mostly compound pictograms (§4.2), is an example of kanji wordplay at its peak. Examples include 众 *hitogomi* 'crowded' (nine 人 'people' kanji) and 姦 *uwakimono* 'adulterer' (six 色 'colour, erotic' kanji). Modern examples include 欣応 for 慶應 'Keio (University)', after the letters K and O pronounced *kei-oo* in Japanese, and 钃 or 䯊, both kanji-ized visualizations of Gundam robots which trended on social media in 2013. There is even a 'kanji creation' contest hosted annually by the *Sankei Shimbun* since 2009, the winners of the 2017 contest being 冹 'figure skating' (a combination of the 'ice' radical 冫 and 舞 'dance') and 囲 'tissue' (a combination of a box 口 and 紙 'paper' with the first stroke of 紙 poking out of the box).

Orthographic play is also used for pedagogical purposes: young children learning kana, for example, are taught how to use the four kana へのもじ <he.no.mo.ji> to draw a face, known as the *henohenomoheji* へのへのもへじ, shown in Fig. 4.12 with the *dakuten* (§4.6) stylized as perspiration.

Fig. 4.12: Henohenomoheji

4.13 Writing Styles

As is the case with many languages, Japanese shows great variance between the written and spoken language. The gap was even larger in earlier stages of the language, with two highly distinct styles, *kōgo* 'spoken language' and *bungo* 'literary language', being used in tandem until WWII. This gap began to narrow in the late 19th century, as popular authors such as Futabatei Shimei (1864–1909) and Natsume Sōseki (1867–1916) abandoned *bungo* for the more readable *kōgo* in their novels, a movement commonly referred to as *genbun itchi* 'unification of speech and writing' (§1.3). While no longer employed on a large scale, *bungo* remained common in academic writing up until WWII and is still used today, to an extent, for stylistic effect (see §6.5 for an example from a video game). It is also taught as part of the *kokugo* curriculum (§8.5, §8.7).

While *kōgo* changes with each generation, *bungo* is a fossilized form of the language based on Classical Japanese and the *kanbun kundoku* tradition (§1.3, §4.4). One example of the use of *bungo* is the 1887 *Bungoyaku* 'literary translation' of the bible. Examples (1) and (2) are the Japanese translations of John 1:1 given in both the literary translation (1) and the more modern *Shinkaiyaku* 'New Japanese Bible' translation (2). The archaic-flavoured *King James Version* and the more modern *New Living Translation* are given in parallel. Today, texts written entirely in *bungo* are rare, although vocabulary originating in *bungo* (called *bunshōgo* 'literary lexicon') is still common in academic and formal writing.

(1) 太初に　　　　言　　　　あり、　　　　言は　　　　神と
    hajime=ni　　*kotoba*　　*ar-i*　　　*kotoba=wa*　　*kami=to*
    beginning=DAT　word　　exist-ADV　word=TOP　　god=COM

    偕に　　　　　あり、　　　言は　　　　　神なりき。
    tomo=ni　　　*ar-i*　　　*kotoba=wa*　　*kami=nar-iki*
    together=ADVLZ　exist-ADV　word=TOP　　god=COP-EPST.CCL

    'In the beginning was the Word, and the Word was with God, and the Word was God.' (John 1:1, *Bungoyaku* with *King James Version* below)

(2) 初めに、　　　　ことばが　　あった。　　ことばは　　　神と
    hajime=ni　　*kotoba=ga*　*aQ-ta*.　　*kotoba=wa*　　*kami=to*
    beginning=DAT　word=NOM　exist-PST　word=TOP　　god=COM

    ともに　　　　　あった。　　ことばは　　　神で　　　あった。
    tomo=ni　　　　*aQ-ta*.　　*kotoba=wa*　　*kami=de*　*aQ-ta*
    together=ADVLZ　exist-PST　word=TOP　　god=VBLZ　exist-PST

    'In the beginning the Word already existed. The Word was with God, and the Word was God.' (John 1:1, *Shinkaiyaku* with *New Living Translation* below)

Bungo may have fallen out of style, but that does not mean there is no difference between spoken and written language. Today, written Japanese has two main styles: *keitai* 'polite style' (commonly referred to as *desu-masu*-style) and *jōtai* 'neutral style'. In the former, sentences end in the polite copula *des-u* (§3.6) or polite verb suffix *-(i)mas-u* (§3.7); in the latter, sentences end in the neutral copula *da* or *de ar-u* and verbs do not take the polite suffix *-(i)mas-u*. Polite style is the style of choice for formal scenarios such as letters, business e-mails and company websites. It is also preferred in children's books, as it has the effect of softening the overall tone. Neutral style is the unmarked of the two: in genres such as journalism and academic writing, in which politeness is not an issue, neutral style is preferred as it sets a more objective tone. This does not mean, however, that such media never employ polite style and there is a large degree of individual licence (§4.12). For example, an academic book aimed at beginners may use polite style to sound more user-friendly, while an editorial column in a newspaper may do so to give the appearance of relating more to the reader. In each of these cases, however, the use of polite style is a marked stylistic choice. Magazines and non-academic books, both fiction and non-fiction, show great variation in style depending on the intended audience. A magazine on cars or computers, for example, will most likely use neutral style, as its main purpose is to relay detailed information and specifications. A food or fashion magazine, on the other hand, may opt to use polite style to soften the overall tone.

Table 4.13 gives the approximate frequency of the copulas *da*, *de ar-u* and *des-u* (including the inflections given in Table 3.7.1) in the Balanced Corpus of Contemporary Written Japanese (BCCWJ). Taking a look across genres, we find that internet blogs and local bulletins tend to adopt polite style, while technology and engineering books, as well as magazines, show no strong preference. All other

	neutral	polite		
	da	*de ar-u*	*des-u*	*n*
books (literature)	65%	15%	20%	405,995
books (tech and engineering)	28%	36%	36%	53,919
internet blogs	36%	5%	59%	229,546
the law	0%	100%	0%	2,764
local bulletins	10%	11%	79%	15,789
magazines	50%	13%	36%	65,872
newspapers	71%	13%	16%	11,196
poetry	71%	19%	9%	1,600
textbooks	29%	48%	23%	8,338
white papers	1%	97%	1%	24,829

Table 4.13: Copulas across media in BCCWJ

genres prefer neutral style. The use of polite style in internet blogs and local bulletins is presumably because both these media are close to the spoken language and aimed at readers from a broad social spectrum, including social superiors and strangers. Within neutral style heavy genres, we find that literature and newspapers prefer the copula *da*, with textbooks and white papers preferring *de ar-u*. Interestingly, poetry and the law are found to use few copulas. In fact, with the law, there are no sentence-final copulas at all, the only copula observed being the adnominal *de ar-u* (*de ar-u toki* 'when ... is', *de ar-u baai* 'in the case that ... is'). This is due to the fact that poetry follows sentence structure only loosely, while laws tend to be written in a bullet point-type style with sentences ending in structures such as *ši-na-kereba nar-ana-i* 'must do', *to su-ru* 'shall be', *to i-u* 'shall be called' and *deki-ru* 'can do'.

4.14 Public Signage

The study of signs, known as semiotics, was born in the late 19th century and has been heavily influenced by two scholars. The Swiss linguist, Ferdinand de Saussure (1857–1913), held that a sign has as its most basic characteristic a dual relationship between 'signifier', the form of the word or words uttered, and 'signified', the conceptual content. Crucially, the link between signifier and signified is arbitrary. This means there are no inter-linguistic rules governing what shape a signifier is to take: when a small furry animal that likes torturing mice is signified, the signifier may be *cat*, *neko* or any number of other terms wholly unconnected with size, furriness or ability to torture small rodents. The US logician, Charles Peirce (1839–1914), meanwhile, emphasized the role of the reader or listener in 'interpreting' the relationship between sign and object. Whether viewed in Saussurean or Piercian terms, signs come in many different types. In examining public signage in this unit, we will look at two of Peirce's main types: icons and symbols.

Icons are frequently encountered in public signage in Japan and generally appear in the form of pictograms (§4.2): the signifier physically resembles the signified. As icons are extra-linguistic—they do not rely on a specific language—they are often found in signage related to leisure or tourism. In 2018, the icons used on Japanese electronic toilets (see Fig. 4.14.1 for just two examples) were approved as a

Fig. 4.14.1: Global standard Japanese electronic toilet icons for 'bidet' and 'rear'

Fig. 4.14.2: Road sign icons in Japan

global standard. Examples found outside the home include the icons for hot spring ♨, temple 卍, shrine ⛩, hospital ⊕, post office ⊖ or school 文. With the huge rise in foreign tourist numbers since the start of the 21st century, some of these icons will likely be revamped following complaints that they are offensive (the swastika symbol for temple) or incomprehensible (the hot spring symbol resembles a bowl of hot soup). This highlights, in some cases, a lack of universal iconicity: that the Nazi *Hakenkreuz* icon was a deliberately reversed swastika, and that the hot spring icon signifies a pool of steaming water, are both culture-specific notions. The icons for post office and school are not only non-universal, but also semi-symbolic in that they are derived from, or are stylized versions of, linguistic symbols: from the katakana テ <te> for *teišin* 'communications' and the kanji 文 'writing, culture', respectively. Icons are also frequently found on road signs: illustrated in Fig. 4.14.2 are the icons for 'beware of cross-winds', 'school zone', 'no bicycles', 'beware of racoon dogs' and 'road works'. As with tourism and leisure icons, road icons may also be culture-specific. In Japan, racoon dogs have large cute eyes, while workers carrying out roadworks apologize (and bow).

We turn now to the symbol. Here, information, the signified, is provided by written language. Unlike the icon, the symbol is language-specific (leaving out cases where a complete Japanese sign written in kanji may correspond exactly to one written in another sinospheric language: 出口 'exit'). Signs containing symbols are in the overwhelming majority—in Japan, or any other country with near-universal literacy—and, viewed as a whole, they constitute what is termed the 'linguistic landscape'. Signs can be official (signs placed by government bodies, such as street block names, road signs, stations or public buildings) or non-official.

One of the most productive ways of analysing the linguistic landscape is by which linguistic symbols are employed: the language in which a sign is written. Signs can be monolingual or multilingual. In Japan, the majority of monolingual signs are in Japanese, though non-official monolingual signs in a foreign language, mainly in English, can be used for effect (especially in the names of shops, bars and restaurants) or for specific purposes (advertising oriented towards specific ethnic groups). Monolingual Japanese signs may be written using idiosyncratic script, in kana only, for the same reasons: for effect, or geared towards readers presumed to be non-native Japanese speakers with limited literacy. They may also appear in dual orthography: sighted script as well as braille (§4.11).

Multilingual signs in Japan tend to be restricted to large cities and major roads (Fig. 4.7.1) and railway stations (Fig. 4.14.3). Until relatively recently, the foreign language on multilingual official signs was limited to English, though in recent years this has started to include Mandarin (both traditional and simplified) and Korean. Multilingual non-official signs are more likely to include foreign languages other than English, especially in the more ethnic neighbourhoods of large cities. Multilingual signs may be homophonic (the languages used are complete translations or glosses of each other: Fig. 4.14.3), polyphonic (language content is

Fig. 4.14.3: Multilingual sign at railway station

Fig. 4.14.4: Amusing mistranslation

Fig. 4.14.5: Multilingual emergency exit sign

completely independent), or mixed (a complete translation appears for some content, but information is extraneous or omitted elsewhere). In Japan, both homophonic and mixed signs often contain mistranslations and errors, causing amusement, bemusement or offense and thus negating the purpose for which they were originally placed (Fig. 4.14.4). Multilingual signs are almost always hierarchical: the dominant language may be indicated by placing it first, by using larger font size or by employing two different signs where one is more visible than the other. Fig. 4.14.5, for example, exhibits a double hierarchy, with the four languages in question not only appearing in the quasi-standard order of Japanese-English-Mandarin-Korean, but with font size decreasing too. The last two languages appear in such a small font that it could be readily misconstrued as indicating a Mandarin or Korean speaker's life is worth less than an English or Japanese speaker's.

Chapter 5 Lexicon and Word Formation

5.1 Vocabulary Strata

Japanese, in common with languages like Turkish or English, exhibits marked lexical stratification. It is typically analysed as possessing four vocabulary layers: native (also known as *wago* 'Japanese words' or *yamatokotoba* 'Yamato words'), mimetic, Sino-Japanese (SJ) and foreign. The first two of these strata have always been part of the language, while SJ begins to appear in the 5th–6th century with the importation of the Chinese writing system. The most recent stratum is composed of non-Chinese foreign borrowings, which begin to appear from the mid-16th century. The historical perspective is illustrated in Fig. 5.1.1, the jagged line at around the early 8th century indicating the limit of comprehensive written evidence.

The native and mimetic layers are composed of those words indigenous to Japanese. Cross-linguistically, it is well known that core vocabulary is the most resistant, though not immune, to borrowing and it therefore comes as no surprise that a large proportion of Japanese core vocabulary is native stratum. Core vocabulary includes fundamental biological activities (*aruk-u* 'walk', *ase* 'sweat'), kinship terms (*haha* 'mother', *mago* 'grandchild': §1.2), body parts (*ke* 'hair', *hiza* 'knee') and natural phenomena (*ame* 'rain', *cuki* 'moon'). Native vocabulary is not accorded its

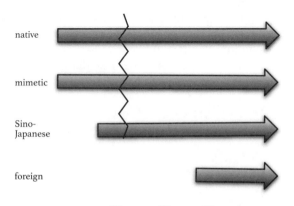

Fig. 5.1.1: Japanese vocabulary strata through time

	native	Sino-Japanese	mimetic	foreign
native		šika+niku 'venison'	maru+poča 'plump'	wa+gomu 'rubber band'
Sino-Japanese	ki+magure 'whim'		kiN+pika 'gilded'	meiwaku+meeru 'spam (email)'
mimetic	poi+sute 'littering'	dotabata+kigeki 'slapstick comedy'		biQkuri+maaku 'exclamation mark'
foreign	koohii+mame 'coffee bean'	eQkusu+seN 'X-ray'	ramu+šabu 'lamb shabushabu'	

Table 5.1: *Hybrid compounds*

own independent unit: it is the default exemplificatory stratum throughout this book. Mimetics are covered in more detail in §5.2.

Both the SJ and the foreign stratum, on the other hand, are products of language contact. SJ words reflect the immense prestige accorded Chinese culture across many centuries and include Buddhist terminology (*sooryo* 'monk', *nehaN* 'nirvana'), Confucian notions (*jiN* 'benevolence', *kookoo* 'filial piety'), political and administrative terms (*daijiN* 'minister', *keN* 'prefecture') and legal terminology (*saibaN* 'trial', *keiyaku* 'contract'). Many were not directly borrowed but later coined in Japan. Foreign borrowings, meanwhile, are composed mainly of loans from English but, prior to the mid-20th century, from Portuguese, Dutch, German, French and Russian. Foreign borrowings in general will be discussed in §7.2, while English loans in particular will be examined in §7.3. SJ is reviewed in greater detail in §7.1.

There exists also a hybrid stratum, compounds (§5.4) whose elements are from more than one vocabulary layer. These are not as infrequent as might be supposed. Some examples are shown in Table 5.1, where the stratum of the initial element is shown on the *y*-axis and that of the second element on the *x*-axis.

Over the past century, across a range of media, a number of surveys have been carried out seeking to quantify the proportions the various strata comprise of the Japanese lexicon. The two largest and most comprehensive surveys examined the vocabulary of a broad-based magazine sample and were published in 1956 and 1994. These are summarized by token count (number of individual words) in Fig. 5.1.2. In the four decades between the two surveys, SJ has overtaken native vocabulary as the largest stratum. What is perhaps more conspicuous is that the proportion of foreign lexemes has quadrupled from 3% to 12%. Caution is required here, however. Magazines are, in general, on the cutting-edge end of the vocabulary spectrum. More conservative print media, such as daily newspapers, show a considerably lower penetration rate of foreign words, as does the everyday speech of older cohorts (§6.1).

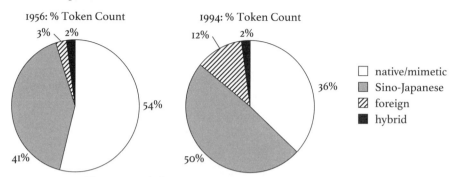

Fig. 5.1.2: *Vocabulary strata proportions in two magazine surveys*

5.2 Mimetics

Also known as onomatopoeia, many mimetic words do not appear in ordinary Japanese dictionaries (§8.10), nor do they show up with any frequency in textbooks for L2 learners (§8.8). They are probably close to impossible for L2 learners to master and even the most advanced student typically fails to fully comprehend their nuances. Although found in English (*clunk, cuckoo, wham*), mimetics in Japanese are far richer and display a large degree of systematization, something less common cross-linguistically, though not unique to Japanese. This systematization, together with their marked phonotactics (§2.5), mean mimetics are generally accorded their own vocabulary stratum (§5.1) by scholars of Japanese linguistics. Although this stratum can be subdivided in several different ways, we will adopt a three-way categorization in this unit: phonomimes (*giseigo* or *giongo*), phenomimes (*gitaigo* or *giyōgo*) and psychomimes (*gijōgo*). Closest to the conventional sense of onomatopoeia are phonomimes, which mimic sounds: *gačaN* 'crash', *zaazaa* 'the sound of pouring rain'. Phenomimes mimic phenomena: *pikapika* 'shiny', *čaračara* 'cheap and flashy, tacky'. Finally, psychomimes mimic psychological conditions: *zukizuki* 'throbbing pain', *bikubiku* 'scared'.

The typical mimetic lexeme, regardless of the subdivision to which it belongs, is formed from either a CV or CVCV root (§2.2, §2.3), which can be altered morphologically in a number of different ways. One of these is intensification, which can be manifested as vowel lengthening or by the affixation of a mora consonant (Q or N: §2.4). Roots can also be altered through reduplication or suffixation (§5.3). Morphologically altered or not, they are then typically followed by the particle *to* (§3.13) or the verb *suru*. As an example, and leaving aside the issue of what it actually 'means', the CV root *ki* can undergo intensification: to *kii* 'door creaking' through vowel lengthening; to *kiQ* 'dirty look' through Q-affixation; to *kiN* 'clang' through N-affixation; and even, through a combination of these, to *kiiQ* 'short creak'

consonant	in CV root	as C₁ in CVCV root	as C₂ in CVCV root
p~b	abruptness, tautness	tautness	explosion, decisiveness
t~d~č~j~c~z	tapping, laxness	laxness	hitting, agreement
k~g	solidity, depth	solidity	opening, expansion
s~z~š~j	smoothness	quietness, runniness	friction
h~f	breathiness	weakness, softness	breathiness
m	vagueness, suppression	murkiness	no apparent symbolism
n	vagueness, suppression	stickiness, sluggishness	elasticity, unreliability
y	—	leisure, unreliability	childishness, haziness
w	emotional expression	emotional expression	softness, haziness
r	—	reverberation, fluidity	fluidity, rolling
vowel			
a		wide range, conspicuousness	
i		straightness, high pitch	
u		small opening	
e		vulgarity	
o		narrow range; conspicuousness	

Table 5.2: Sound symbolism

or *kiiN* 'screech'. These intensified forms may then be reduplicated, as in *kiikii* 'recurring door creak' or *kiNkiN* 'recurring clang'. As an example of a CVCV root, *piči* becomes *pičiQ* 'tight' with Q-affixation; *pičipiči* 'fresh' with reduplication; or *piQčiri* 'snug' with Q-affixation and *ri*-suffixation. Not all roots exhibit all possible morphological variations and the same root can straddle different mimetic subcategories: *kiN* 'clang' (phonomime) ~ *kiQ* 'dirty look' (phenomime).

Intensification, reduplication and suffixation are not arbitrary, but largely systematic. With intensification, Q indicates inflexibility and energy; N flexibility and reverberation; while vowel lengthening indicates instantaneousness in CV roots, but a longer time span when the second vowel in CVCV roots. Thus, the CV roots *puQ* 'fart' ~ *puN* 'reek' ~ *puuN* 'sudden powerful smell'; and the CVCV roots *fuwa* 'fluffy, spongy' ~ *fuwaa* 'very fluffy, very spongy'. Reduplication may indicate repetition (*poNpoN* 'one after another'), speed (*saQsa* 'immediate') or a recurring action (*kiikii* 'recurring door creak'). The most commonly found suffix is *-ri*, added to CVCV roots and denoting a quiet ending. Thus, *garagara* 'clatter' ~ *garari* 'light clatter'.

What is also of great linguistic interest is the non-arbitrariness—what is known as the 'iconicity' (§4.14)—of the individual phonemes (§2.1) that make up the CV or CVCV roots themselves. This form of systematicity is known as 'sound symbolism' and is summarized in Table 5.2. It should not be thought of as a set of hard and fast rules but rather general tendencies. The obstruent pairs (the first four rows in Table 5.2) show additional iconicity in terms of voicing contrast (§2.2). Voiceless obstruents indicate lightness, smallness or fineness; while their voiced counterparts indicate the opposite: *kuukuu* 'pigeon cooing' ~ *guuguu* 'stomach rumbling'.

The symbolism of a vowel remains largely unaltered regardless of the type of root in which it appears and regardless of its position within a root. For consonants, on the other hand, differences are apparent. Sometimes these are semantically related, as is the case with *s~z~š~j*. At other times, however, there appears to be no obvious semantic connection: *k~g* symbolizes solidity when the initial consonant in a CVCV root, but opening or expansion when the second. Observe that *p* almost never occurs as the second consonant in a CVCV root, while *r* and *y* appear in CV roots only very rarely.

5.3 Derivation and Affixation

In other units we look at word building by means of inflection and derivation in verbs, adjectives and copulas (§3.3, §3.5–§3.8). Both inflection and derivation are achieved in Japanese mainly through affixation, although reduplication also plays a minor role in derivation. In this unit we will examine word building strategies at large, in particular derivation. In §3.8, we defined this as a word building process triggering a change in the word class or lexical meaning of the base form—as opposed to inflection, which simply adds grammatical meaning. In this sense, we can say that derivation is a morphological process (it affects the inner properties of a word), while inflection is syntactic (it affects a word's role in a sentence). In Standard Japanese, apart from verbals and copulas, Japanese parts of speech do not inflect and only show morphological derivation. This is not always the case in dialects, however, with inflection used for marking noun cases in a number of Kyūshū dialects (§7.11).

Derivation is prevalent in the major parts of speech (nominals, verbals and modifiers), but rare in minor parts of speech (particles, copulas, conjunctions and interjections) (§3.1). Morphologically, derivational affixes are divided cross-linguistically into six types: prefixes, suffixes, infixes, circumfixes, transfixes and interfixes. Circumfixes (German *ge-wohn-t* 'lived') and transfixes (Arabic *ktb* 'write' → *kitaab* 'book' ~ *kaatib* 'clerk') do not occur in Japanese. Infixes (intra-stem affixes) and interfixes (inter-stem affixes) do, though both are rare. The former include the mora consonants Q~N (§2.4) found in mimetics (§5.2), such as *niQkori* 'grin' (cf. *nikori* 'smile') or *fuNwari* 'light and fluffy' (cf. *fuwa* 'fluffy, spongy'); the latter fossilized forms such as *harusame* 'spring rain'. Suffixes and prefixes, meanwhile, are common. Both suffixes and prefixes are found with nouns, verbs, adjectives and adverbs and vary according to vocabulary stratum (§5.1), with a given affix often

classification	native (N)	Sino-Japanese (SJ)	foreign (F)
prefixes			
emphasis	ma(Q)-, do-	čoo-	za-
degree: 'big'	oo-	dai-	biqgu-, suupaa-
negation		fu-, bu-, mu-, hi-	noo-, NON-
honorific (§6.3)	o-, mi-, ON-	go-, gyo-	
suffixes			
actor	-ya, -te	-ka, -ši, -šu	-maN, -aa

Table 5.3: *Major derivational affixes by vocabulary stratum*

having two or even three different forms. This is illustrated in Table 5.3, using as examples affixes from some major semantic and grammatical classifications.

The vast majority of the time, an affix attaches to a form from the same stratum: *do-inaka* 'hicksville' (N-N), *dai-moNdai* 'big problem' (SJ-SJ). However, examples of hybrid words are not uncommon: *o-deNwa* 'phone (polite)' (N-SJ), *čoo-kawai-i* 'super cute' (SJ-N). Affixes can be productive, as are most in Table 5.3, or unproductive: *mi-* 'honorific' (§6.3). They can also operate at a stage intermediate between productiveness and unproductiveness, whereby new coinages are possible only for a restricted set of words. Examples include *koN-* 'this' (restricted to periods of time: *koN-šiizuN* 'this season') and *-domo* 'plural, humble' (restricted to personal pronouns, *watakuši-domo* 'we, I (humble)', and lifeforms, *cuwamono-domo* 'warriors': §5.7), but also *ko-* 'small' and *-ka* '-er', where it is unclear what restrictions apply and productive tolerance will vary from speaker to speaker. Both affixes and suffixes can occur within the same word: *hi-booryoku-šugi* 'nonviolence (lit. nonviolence-ism)'. Finally, affixes can be peculiarly 'Japanese', in that a translation into a foreign language is difficult: *te-* 'lit. hand' (*te-mijika* 'brief', *te-oči* 'slip-up'), *-doo* 'path, way' (*buši-doo* 'way of the samurai', *karate-doo* 'way of karate'), *-kaN* 'feeling' (*aNšiN-kaN* 'sense of security', *sogai-kaN* 'feeling of alienation'). Adjectives possess four nominalization suffixes, *-sa, -mi, -ge* and *-me*, which are covered in detail in §3.5, while nouns possess a highly productive adjectivization suffix, *-teki: bucuri-teki* 'physical', *wataši-teki* 'as for me (lit. I-like)'. Some affixes serve to switch word class: see §3.2 and §3.8 for more detail.

While suffixes are common with verbs (§3.7, §3.8), the use of prefixes here is highly marginal, confined in the main to youth speech and slang (§5.10) and, in addition, being restricted to a few verb forms only. Perhaps the most flexible prefix is *čoo* 'emphasis', which can be used with nearly all verb forms: *čoo-kuq-ta* 'I totally stuffed myself', *čoo-nom-u* 'I'm going to drink loads'. Here, however, it is also possible to analyse *čoo-* as an adverb (*čoo nom-u*, not *čoo-nom-u*). With deverbal nouns (§3.7), however, prefixes are common: the portion sizes *ko-mori* 'small' ~ *nami-mori* 'medium' ~ *oo-mori* 'large' ~ *toku-mori* 'supersize', where *mori* is the deverbal noun of *mor-u* 'heap on'.

Reduplication as a derivational strategy occurs with nouns, adjectives, verbs and adverbs, and we also note its use with mimetics in §5.2. It has three functions: indicating plurality, intensity or repetition. With nouns, reduplication is largely restricted to indicating plurality and is now largely unproductive: *yama+yama* 'mountains'. With foreign nouns, however, reduplication may signal intensity, as in *rabu+rabu* 'lovey-dovey'. This is also the case with adjectives and deverbal nouns, where reduplication of the stem typically yields adverbs signalling intensity: *aka+aka* 'very bright (lit. bright+bright)', *ari+ari* 'vivid (lit. being+being)'. Some of these adverbs can be turned into adjectives by means of the suffix *-ši-i*: *naga+naga-ši-i* 'long-winded'. Reduplication is rare with verbs and occurs with the full nonpast, or dictionary, form (§3.3). Here, it yields adverbs signalling repetition: *kawaru+gawaru* 'in turn (lit. change+change)'. Reduplicative compounds are also used in baby-talk (*o-te+te* 'handy-wandy'), where it serves the more prosaic function of enhancing language acquisition.

5.4 Compounding

Compounding is a frequently found word building strategy in Japanese. The components of which compounds are comprised are termed elements and, throughout this volume, an element boundary is indicated by means of a plus sign. In principle, the number of elements that may appear in a Japanese compound is infinite: while *tookyoo+toQkyo+kyoka+kyoku+čoo* 'Tokyo Patent Approval Office Director' is a longer example (and also a well-known tongue twister), it is not difficult to construct an even lengthier one. In the examples cited in this unit, compounds will be restricted to the most commonly found type, those consisting of two elements.

Elements can be from any major part of speech (§3.1). A given compound may consist of elements from only one (verb+verb: *mi+okur-u* 'see off') or be a hybrid of several (noun+adjective: *kazu+sukuna-i* 'scarce'). The rightmost element, known as the head, signals the part of speech of the compound as a whole. Elements may also be from any vocabulary stratum (§5.1). Again, a given compound may consist of elements from only one vocabulary stratum (native+native: *koi+bito* 'girlfriend/boyfriend') or be a hybrid of several (foreign + Sino-Japanese (SJ: §7.1) + native: *toraNpu+daitooryoo+girai* 'Trump-hater (lit. Trump-President-hater)'). See Table 5.1 for further examples.

Cross-linguistically, compounds are typically divided into three types. Endocentric compounds are those where the initial element modifies the head. Examples include *ie+neko* 'house cat' (a cat that lives in a house) or *suna+yama* 'dune' (a mountain made from sand). Exocentric compounds, on the other hand, are those where there is no such hierarchical relationship and where the overall meaning of the compound is difficult to ascertain from its component elements. Examples include *futoQ+para* 'generous (lit. fat belly)' or *ate+kom-u* 'rely on (lit.

5.4 Compounding

direct at and cram in)'. Copulative compounds are those where, semantically, either element is analysable as the head. Examples include *yomi+kaki* 'reading and writing' or *mono+goto* 'things in general, a matter (lit. physical things and abstract things)'. Sub-categories of copulative compounds include reduplicative compounds, where the same element is repeated (§5.3), and also appositional and oppositional compounds. In appositional compounds, both elements describe the same actor or thing (*kura+yami* 'darkness (lit. dark+darkness)'); in oppositional compounds they consist of two opposite extremes which together express a measurable concept (*tate+yoko* 'aspect, dimensions (lit. vertical+horizontal)'). Appositional and oppositional compounds were especially common in the history of Chinese and thus appear frequently in SJ words (although, formally, such words are not always considered compounds, since the individual components do not usually exist as independent words: see §7.1 for further discussion). To cite but a few examples, SJ words formed in Chinese through apposition include *sei+zoo* 'manufacture (lit. make+create)' or *tei+ši* 'stop (lit. halt+stop)'; those formed through opposition include *koo+tei* 'modulation, pitch (lit. high+low)' or *teN+či* 'the universe (lit. heaven+earth)'.

Compounds can be classified in yet other ways, one of these being a semantic classification applicable only to verb- or verbal adjective-final compounds. Here, compounds are labelled syntactic or lexical. In the former the final element carries the grammar of the verb itself. Syntactic compounding is highly productive and the meaning of an individual compound is predictable from its component elements—furthermore, there exists only a finite number of final elements, many of which are aspectual in nature: *yom-i+hajime-ru* 'begin to read', *kazoe+sokona-u* 'miscount', *i-i+zura-i* 'difficult to say'. The final elements of such compounds are commonly referred to as auxiliaries and covered in detail in §3.9. Lexical compounds, on the other hand, are unproductive and the meaning of an individual compound is not predictable from its component elements. Such compounds are stored individually in a speaker's mental lexicon. Examples of lexical compounds include *daš-i+nuk-u* 'outwit (lit. take out and pull out)' or *omo-i+agar-u* 'be arrogant (lit. think and rise)'.

Whether a sequence of words is just that, a sequence of words, or whether a sequence of words is in fact a compound may be signalled in three ways, neatly encapsulated in the compound *i+zaka+ya* 'pub, bar', where the middle element is an allomorph of *sake* 'alcohol'. The first marker is suprasegmental: in a sequence of words each individual word may have an accent, while in a compound there can be at most only one accent (*i+zaka+ya* is accented on its penultimate mora, as *i+zaka+ya*, or may also be unaccented). This marker of compoundedness is compulsory and its details complex: see §2.7 for a thoroughgoing discussion. The remaining two markers are optional: both, or neither, may occur in a given compound. The first of these, rendaku (*i+zaka+ya*), where the initial *s* of *sake* is voiced to *z*, is covered in detail in §5.5. The last, apophony (*i+zaka+ya*), manifests itself as a vowel alternation occurring at the end of non-final elements. There exist three pairs of alternations, *e~a*, *i~o*, *i~u*, the first by far the most common and the last rare. The first vowel in each pair is known as the 'exposed' form and the second as the 'covered'. Examples include *ame* 'rain' ~ *ama+ai* 'let-up in the rain', *ki* 'tree' ~ *ko+dači* 'thicket', and *cuki* 'moon, month' ~ *cuku+yo* 'moonlight'. Apophony is believed to be unproductive in the modern language and is restricted to a closed set of native nouns, some of which have low frequency (*suge* 'sedge' ~ *sugawara* 'Sugawara (family name)', *ine* 'rice plant' ~ *inasaku* 'rice cultivation'). Those nouns that do undergo apophony do so optionally—and can usually be attested as far back as Old Japanese (§1.3). This is evident from the following apophony-free compounds which contain the same three initial elements as the examples above: *ame+furi* 'rainfall', *ki+cucuki* 'woodpecker', *cuki+barai* 'monthly payment'. Research has shown that some nouns which undergo apophony do so at very high rates (*fune~funa* 'boat', *ue~uwa* 'above'), while others (*mi~mu* 'body', *te~ta* 'hand') do so very infrequently.

5.5 Rendaku

Rendaku, or sequential voicing, occurs in Japanese compounds (§5.4) and is a pervasive phenomenon straddling the domains of both phonology and morphology. Defined at its simplest, rendaku causes the initial voiceless consonant of a non-initial element in a compound to voice. These initial voiceless consonants are *c~č~f~h~k~s~š~t*, as illustrated in (1). For various historical reasons (§2.9), voicing may in fact be accompanied by other changes: *f~h* surface as *b* under rendaku (1c, 1d), while *č~š* are realized as *j* (1b, 1g).

(1) a. *mika* 'three days' + *cuki* 'moon' → *mika+zuki* 'crescent moon'
    b. *soko* 'bottom' + *čikara* 'power' → *soko+jikara* 'latent strength'
    c. *ča* 'tea' + *fukuro* 'bag' → *ča+bukuro* 'teabag'
    d. *hana* 'flower' + *hi* 'fire' → *hana+bi* 'fireworks'
    e. *seto* 'straits' + *kiwa* 'brink' → *seto+giwa* 'eleventh hour'
    f. *ire* 'insert' + *sumi* 'ink' → *ire+zumi* 'tattoo'
    g. *oso* 'late' + *šimo* 'frost' → *oso+jimo* 'late frost'
    h. *atari* 'hit' + *toši* 'year' → *atari+doši* 'bumper year'

Rendaku may occur not only with the final element in a compound but with any non-initial element. It may thus occur multiple times:

(2) *haki* 'sweep' + *tame* 'pile up' + *hako* 'box' → *haki+dame+bako* 'dustbin'

A number of different factors are known to block or constrain rendaku. The most well-known is Lyman's Law (named after the 19th century American Japanologist Benjamin Lyman: §8.13), which states that rendaku is blocked in

5.5 Rendaku

elements containing a voiced obstruent (*b~d~g~j~z*). This is illustrated in (3)–(4). Another factor is what is known as the 'right branch condition': a compound fails to undergo rendaku when it is itself the head (§5.4) of a 'nested' compound. In (5), although *te* 'hand' is a non-initial element and begins in a voiceless consonant, because it itself is the head of another compound, *teate* 'allowance', rendaku is blocked. The part of speech (§3.1) to which the non-initial element belongs also has an important role to play in triggering rendaku. Rendaku is infrequent when the non-initial element is a verb and extremely infrequent when both elements are verbs. Examples (6)–(7) are thus unusual in exhibiting rendaku, with compounds such as (8)–(9) by far and away more frequent. When the non-initial element is a verbal noun (§3.7), argument type compounds—those where the initial element is the internal argument of the verb—show low levels of rendaku (10). Rendaku never occurs after the native bare number *hito* 'one' (11), but does so frequently (12)–(13) after the native count numbers (§5.8). Certain prefixes (§5.3), such as (14) *kata-* 'one-sided' and (15) *hacu-* 'first', appear to dampen rendaku, while rendaku is blocked in coordinate (double-headed) compounds (16).

(3) haN 'half' + sode 'sleeve' → haN+sode 'short sleeves'
(4) ko 'child' + hicuji 'sheep' → ko+hicuji 'lamb'
(5) fuyoo 'family' + te 'hand' + ate 'prospect' → fuyoo+te+ate 'family allowance'
(6) šimo 'frost' + kare-ru 'wither' → šimo+gare-ru 'killed by frost'
(7) ik-u 'go' + cumar-u 'be blocked' → ik-i+zumar-u 'get bogged down'
(8) toši 'year' + tor-u 'take' → toši+tor-u 'grow old'
(9) nom-u 'drink' + hos-u 'dry' → nom-i+hos-u 'drink down'
(10) mono 'thing' + širi 'knowing' → mono+širi 'erudite'
(11) hito 'one' + koto 'word' → hito+koto 'a word'
(12) hitocu 'one' + ha 'leaf' → hitocu+ba 'species of fern'
(13) icucu 'five' + hoši 'star' → icucu+boši 'five-star'
(14) kata 'one-sided' + koi 'love' → kata+koi 'unrequited love'
(15) hacu 'first' + fuyu 'winter' → hacu+fuyu 'first winter'
(16) suki 'like' + kirai 'dislike' → suki+kirai 'likes and dislikes'

Vocabulary stratum (§5.1) also has a role to play. It is fair to say that rendaku is overarchingly a native stratum phenomenon (examples (1)–(16) are all taken from this stratum), since it occurs only sporadically in Sino-Japanese (§7.1) elements, typically those whose frequency is high (17)–(18). Elements from the foreign stratum (§7.2) eschew rendaku completely (19), except for a few very rare loanwords borrowed many centuries ago (20).

(17) saru 'monkey' + čie 'wisdom' → saru+jie 'thinking you're smart when you're not'
(18) take 'bamboo' + saiku 'craftwork' → take+zaiku 'bamboowork'
(19) šii 'sea' + čikiN 'chicken' → šii+čikiN 'tinned tuna'

(20) *uta* 'song'   +   *karuta* 'karuta'   →   *uta+garuta* 'tanka karuta'

It is not difficult to find exceptions to all the rules and constraints in (3)–(20), albeit to varying degrees. What is perhaps more interesting, however, is the fact that even in cases where no rule or constraint is applicable, rendaku may still fail to occur. A word, such as *suki* 'like', which exhibits rendaku in nearly all compounds in which it appears as a non-initial element, may fail to do so: *dai+suki* 'love'. Such examples can be multiplied almost *ad infinitum*. Although the majority of words show, like *suki*, a strong predilection towards rendaku, others show a strong antipathy towards it. Yet other words appear 'rendaku immune': they never undergo rendaku. For L2 learners of Japanese, these words are worth memorizing. The more frequent include *šio* 'tide', *saki* 'tip, point', *ko* 'powder', *hama* 'beach', *šita* 'bottom' and *cuyu* 'dew'.

Although there are a small number of compounds which show rendaku and non-rendaku variants in dictionary headwords (*curi+haši* ~ *curi+baši* 'rope bridge'), such variation is more frequent both across dialects (§7.7–§7.11) and individual speakers (see §6.1 for an age-based example). This sociolinguistic aspect of rendaku is, however, much understudied and juicy fodder for post-graduate theses.

Semantics also appear to play some, albeit comparatively minor, role in triggering rendaku. Homophones (§5.9) may show significantly different 'rendaku rates', illustrated by (21) *su* 'nest' (never) and (22) 'vinegar' (almost always). The same can be said for polysemes (§5.9). For instance, (23) *kawa* 'living cover on an animate object = skin, bark' never undergoes rendaku, whereas (24) *kawa* 'removed and processed cover of an animate object = leather, hide' may do so; (25) *kuči* 'taste' is rendaku immune, while *kuči* 'mouth' and (26) *kuči* 'portal' frequently undergo rendaku.

(21) *furu* 'old'   +   *su* 'nest'   →   *furu+su* 'former haunt'
(22) *yone* 'rice'   +   *su* 'vinegar'   →   *yone+zu* 'rice vinegar'
(23) *usu* 'thin'   +   *kawa* 'skin'   →   *usu+kawa* 'film'
(24) *šika* 'deer'   +   *kawa* 'leather'   →   *šika+gawa* 'buckskin'
(25) *ato* 'afterwards'   +   *kuči* 'taste'   →   *ato+kuči* 'aftertaste'
(26) *de* 'leave'   +   *kuči* 'portal'   →   *de+guči* 'exit'

The origins of rendaku are bound up in the complex history of the *sei-daku* distinction found in Japanese consonants (§2.9): the simplest explanation is that rendaku derives, via prenasalization, from a truncation (§5.6) of the particle *no* (§3.12, §3.13). Rendaku in verbs and adjectives cannot be explained in this way, however, so analogy across different parts of speech (§3.1) must also have played a role. Ultimately, it is analogy with other compounds in a native speaker's lexicon that drive rendaku's productivity, as can be seen from the example of Paul the Psychic Octopus, famous for picking the correct results at the 2010 football World Cup, and coined in Japanese the *yogeN+dako* (since *tako* 'octopus' invariably undergoes rendaku).

5.6 Truncation

Cross-linguistically, truncation—the erasure of parts of a word or compound to make it shorter—is almost universal. With Japanese, truncation is most conspicuous within the foreign stratum (§7.2) and it is by means of examples taken from English loanwords (§7.3) that the major processes involved in truncation will be illustrated. Truncation in other Japanese vocabulary strata (§5.1) will be considered briefly at the end of this unit.

Truncation can be broadly divided into two types: mora-clipping and compound reduction. These may in turn be divided into a number of subgroups, as illustrated in Table 5.6. Compound reduction, as its name implies, occurs only in compounds (§5.4); mora-clipping occurs overwhelmingly in non-compounds, though may occur in compounds too. For this reason a compound, *koNbinieNsu+sutoa* 'convenience store', has been chosen as the 'input', with a sample 'output' of the various truncation processes shown in the rightmost column. In practice, if a word undergoes truncation at all, it is typically found in one truncated form only or, if multiple truncated forms do exist, then usage is heavily skewed towards only one of them. In the case of *koNbinieNsusutoa*, for example, the back-clipped form *koNbini* is found with overwhelming frequency: other possible outputs are marked with an asterisk. Truncation processes are extremely fluid and the truncations themselves frequently highly transient and often confined to jargon, slang (§5.10) and dialects (§7.7–§7.11).

Mora-clipping can be subdivided into three categories. Back-clipping is, by a considerable margin, the dominant process. Here, the latter portion of a word is clipped and a number of initial moras (μ: §2.4) retained. Retention of the first two moras is preferred: *čokoreeto* → *čoko* 'chocolate'. Single mora back-clippings are, with very few exceptions, illicit. Linguistic analyses have demonstrated that the

	truncation type	input	output
mora-clipping	back-clipping	*koNbinieNsusutoa*	*koNbini*
	fore-clipping	*koNbinieNsusutoa*	**toa*
	mid-clipping	*koNbinieNsusutoa*	**koNnisu*
compound reduction	compound clipping	*koNbinieNsu+sutoa*	**koNsuto*
	ellipsis	*koNbinieNsu+sutoa*	**sutoa*
	morpho-orthographic	convenience store	**šiiesu* (CS)

Table 5.6: *Truncation types*

number of moras retained is governed by patterns of light and heavy syllables (§2.4), but these analyses are complex and will not be explored further here. Fore-clipping is the opposite of back-clipping and is considerably less common: between 2μ to 4μ are retained (*arubaito* → *baito* 'part-time job'). Mid-clipping is the rarest of the three types of mora-clipping. Here, moras from anywhere in the full form are clipped, typically including one or more word-final moras: *moruhine* → *mohi* 'morphine'.

Compound reduction too can be subdivided into three categories. In compound clipping, a compound is reduced to between 2μ and 6μ by means of clipping at least one mora from at least one element, usually from the rear. The compound clipping process thus produces a wide range of possible outputs. One output, the 2μ+2μ type, is overwhelmingly dominant: ***yuniiku***+***kuroojiɴgu*** 'unique clothing' → *yunikuro* 'Uniqlo' (name of a clothing retailer), ***kosučuumu***+***puree*** 'costume play' → *kosupure* 'cosplay'. The only other type to occur to any significant extent is the 2μ+1μ type: ***sumaato***+***hoɴ*** → *sumaho* 'smart phone'. Some compound clippings have even been borrowed back into English, 'cosplay' and 'Uniqlo' above being cases in point (§7.6).

In ellipsis, an entire element, either the final or the initial, is deleted. The former (***serufu***+*saabisu* 'self-service' → *serufu*) is considerably more common than the latter (*sukuryuu*+***doraibaa*** → *doraibaa* 'screwdriver'). There are also a few rare cases where the middle element in a three-element English loanword is deleted: ***masuto***+*habu*+***aitemu*** → *masutoaitemu* 'must-have'.

In morpho-orthographic truncation, a compound has its Japanese orthography transposed to its original Roman script and all but the initial letters of each element deleted. Thus, *ofisu*+*redii*, composed of two elements, is transposed into its English etymon 'office+lady' and the non-initial letters of each element then deleted to yield *OL* 'female office worker'. In this example, the result is pronounced according to the Japanese pronunciation of the letters of the alphabet in question: as *ooeru*. Occasionally, non-initial letters of an element may be retained or an initial letter deleted. Such compounds have become more common in recent years: *super urban intelligent card* → *SUICA* (a public transport smart card).

Although most conspicuous in the loanword stratum, truncation does occur in other strata. Mora-clipping is, however, relatively rare and usually found in slang: native Japanese *kemuri* → *kemu* 'smoke(screen)', Sino-Japanese (SJ: §7.1) *keimušo* 'prison' → *mušo* 'slammer, clink'. Examples of ellipsis outside the loanword stratum include SJ ***keitai***+*deɴwa* → *keitai* 'mobile (phone)'. Compound clipping is found frequently in SJ: ***tookyoo***+***daigaku*** 'Tokyo University' → *toodai*. Throughout all strata, processes broadly similar to morpho-orthographic truncation occur, particularly in slang: *joši*+*koosei* → *JK* 'high school girl', *kuuki=ga yom-e-na-i* → *KY* 'out of touch with reality (lit. can't read the air)'. Indeed, this type of non-loan morpho-orthographic truncation is colloquially known as *keewaišiki nihoɴgo* 'KY-style Japanese', after the second example cited.

5.7 Personal Pronouns

Japanese personal pronouns are an open class: there are no limits on what can be, or become, one. Historically, new personal pronouns have continually entered the language, while others have died. This is in contrast to most Western languages where membership of the personal pronoun class is closed and the personal pronouns themselves have been stable (ignoring sound change) for hundreds, if not thousands, of years. Further, personal pronouns are often optional in Japanese: for more detail see §3.1.

A selection of the most frequent Japanese personal pronouns currently in use is shown in Table 5.7, sorted by person and then by register (§6.2): ★★★★★ = highly formal, ★ = highly informal, ✖ = slightly derogatory, ✖✖✖✖✖ = hostile. They are marked in addition for gender (● = used, ○ = used occasionally), which is that of the speaker in the first and second persons, but that of the referent in the third. Personal pronouns may also mark the age of the speaker or addressee, the relationship between the two, or be restricted to certain media. In such cases, the relevant information is given in the rightmost column. The table, for the most part, ignores dialect (§7.8–§7.11) and obsolete forms, but includes a number of such forms still used in idioms and role language (§6.2). Obsolete personal pronouns are marked with a dagger †, those with strong role language tendencies with a double dagger ‡.

First person pronouns exhibit the greatest variation, running the gamut from highly formal to highly informal, with subtle gradations in between. Further complexity is introduced by the fact that, within each register, first person pronouns can be heavily skewed to specific media, restricted to certain social classes, or imbued with a particular flavour. To take the highest registers as an example, *watakuši* is neutral; *ware, yo* and *šoosei* are overwhelmingly literary, with *ware* generally only used in idioms; *čiN* is used only by the emperor (though no longer); *wagahai* and *seQša* were used by the aristocratic and samurai classes, respectively, but now only remain in role language; and *ware, yo, waga, wagahai* and *seQša* all have an archaic flavour. First person pronouns may be employed by either gender, something found most commonly in the highest registers; be used by one gender only, by females typically in the lower registers (*ataši, atakuši, atai, ačiki, wačiki*), by males typically in the higher registers (*wagahai, čiN, yo, šoosei, seQša*); or show a gender bias (*jibuN, boku, uči*), something found only in the mid-registers. That male exclusivity is a high, and female exclusivity a low, register phenomenon is sociolinguistically extremely interesting: for more on gender see §6.1. When the addressee is a young boy, *boku* can be used also as a second person pronoun, while *uči*, until quite recently, was only used as a pronoun in Western Japanese (§7.9). The pronoun *jibuN* has appeared relatively recently and *waši* is used by elderly males. The new kid on the block is *wai*, currently used by all genders. The pronouns *atakuši,*

	person	register	M	F	plural -tači	plural -ra	plural -domo	plural -gata	comments
čiN†‡	1	★★★★★	●						used by emperors or kings
temae	1	★★★★★	●	○			●		business-speak; humble
watakuši	1	★★★★★	●	●	●	○	●		'lit. private, self'
kočira	1	★★★★	●	●					'lit. here' (§3.2)
seǫša†‡	1	★★★★	●						samurai talk; humble
šoosei	1	★★★★	●						literary, humble; 'lit. young pupil'
wagahai†‡	1	★★★★	●						used by kings or nobility
yo†‡	1	★★★★	●						used by feudal lords; humble
atakuši	1	★★★		●	●	○	●		very feminine
jibuN	1	★★★	●	○	●	●			'lit. self'
waga	1	★★★	●	●					idiomatic, possessive (*waga kuni* 'our (beloved) country')
ware†	1	★★★	●	●			●		idiomatic (*ware=ni kaer-u* 'return to one's senses')
waši‡	1	★★★	●				●		used by elderly men
wataši	1	★★★	●	●	●	●	●		default first person pronoun
ataši	1	★★		●	●	●	○		very feminine
boku	1	★★	●	○	●	●			young boys and men; until recently also used by 'tomboy-ish' young girls
uči	1	★★	○	●		●			until recently, use as a personal pronoun restricted to Western Japanese (§7.9)
atai‡	1	★		●	●	●			rough city dweller
ačiki†‡	1	★		●	○	○			17th–19th century prostitute talk
wačiki†‡	1	★		●	○	○			17th–19th century prostitute talk
oira‡	1	★	●		●				country bumpkin talk
ora‡	1	★	●		●				country bumpkin talk
ore	1	★	●		●	●			very masculine
wai	1	★	●	●					popular among the young in recent years

Table 5.7: Personal pronouns

wataši, ataši, waši, atai and *wai* are all truncations of *watakuši*, informality increasing as the form becomes shorter, with deletion of initial *w-* marking femininity.

	person	register	M	F	plural -tači	-ra	-domo	-gata	comments
otaku	2	★★★★	•	•	•	•		○	may also be used when expressing anger or exasperation; 'lit. your home'
sočira	2	★★★★	•	•	•				'lit. there' (§3.2)
anata	2	★★★	•	•	•	○			overuse offensive
aNta	2	★★	○	•	•	•		○	contracted form of above
boku	2	★★	•		•	•			to young boys
kimi	2	★★	•	•	•	•			to subordinates
omae[*1]	2	★~✖✖	•	○	•	•	○		'lit. front'
omee[*1]	2	★~✖✖✖	•	○	•	•	○		alternative form of *omae*
temae	2	✖✖✖✖	•	○	•	•	○		from the identical 1st person pronoun
temee	2	✖✖✖✖✖	•	○	•	•	○		★★★★★ until 18th century
kisama	2	✖✖✖✖✖	•	○	○	•	○		alternative form of *temae*
seNpoo	3	★★★★★	•	•					literary
kanojo	3	★★★		•	•	•			also 'girlfriend'
kare	3	★★★	•		•	•			also 'boyfriend'
yacu	3	★~✖	•	•		•			offensive in many contexts
aicu[*1]	3	★~✖✖	•	•	○	•			distal (§3.2)
koicu[*1]	3	★~✖✖✖	•	•	○	•			proximal (§3.2)
soicu[*1]	3	★~✖✖✖	•	•	○	•			medial (§3.2)

[*1] offensive in some contexts; may be used for bonding

Table 5.7 (continued)

Second person pronouns exhibit the least gender variation but express the widest range of register, from formal (*otaku*, *sočira*) to derogatory (*omae*, *omee*, *temae*) or even hostile (*temee*, *kisama*): see §6.4 for more on derogatory language. They may also express the relative social status (§6.1) of the speaker and addressee: *kimi*, for example, is often used to subordinates. Although typically very polite, *otaku* can be used when expressing anger or exasperation. Perhaps the most complex second person pronoun is *anata*: if overused it can be offensive, and it possesses an additional meaning, restricted to female speakers, of 'lover' or 'partner'. Third person pronouns show the least variation, being typically either robustly neutral (*kare*, *kanojo*; both also used for boyfriends and girlfriends) or derogatory, with *aicu*, *koicu*, *soicu* exhibiting spatial deixis (§3.2). Formality can only be expressed via *seNpoo* or phrases such as *ano kata* 'that lady/gentleman'. The third person pronouns *aicu~koicu~soicu*, along with the second person pronouns *omae~omee*, are not always derogatory and may also be employed for bonding.

More common than the use of second and third person pronouns is their replacement by a name (§6.9) and honorific title (*nakamura-sama*), job and honorific title (*untenšu-san* 'Mr Driver'), relationship marker with (*onee-san* 'elder sister') or without (*imooto* 'younger sister') honorific title (see §1.2 for a discussion on the difference), status marker and honorific title (*o-kyaku-sama* 'customer') or, for professors, doctors, teachers, martial arts instructors, judges, lawyers, authors, composers, manga artists and politicians, just *sensei*. It is impolite to address a customer as *anata* or refer to someone's mother as *kanojo*. While *sensei* and many relationship markers may be used, under certain sociolinguistic circumstances, in place of a first person pronoun, one's own name sounds childish.

With the exception of some higher register first person pronouns, all pronouns have plural forms (● = used, ○ = used occasionally, both with considerable inter-speaker variation), as indicated in Table 5.7. These come in five different derivational types (§5.3): reduplication and the four suffixes *-tači* ~ *-ra* ~ *-domo* ~ *-gata*. Reduplication is found in one form only (*wareware* 'we'), not indicated in the table. Of the four suffixes, *-tači* and *-ra* do the most duty, with *-domo* restricted to first and second, and *-gata* to high register second, person pronouns.

Some pronouns, such as *wataši*, *otaku*, *anata* or *anta*, have three different plural forms. The suffixes *-ra* and *-domo* can also be used in a derogatory or self-humbling sense (*omee-ra* 'you assholes!'). When used in such a sense, *-domo* does not necessarily indicate plurality: *watakuši-domo* can mean both 'we' or 'I (humble)'. The four plural suffixes can also be used after nouns expressing the names of lifeforms, especially *-tači* (*neko-tači* 'cats'). When used after lifeforms, *-domo* does, and *-ra* may, express contempt (*kono gaki-domo* 'you little brats!'). The suffix *-gata* may be used after polite titles as well to express plurality (*sensei-gata* 'teachers'). See also §3.2 for a discussion on pluralizer suffixes.

With the exception of the archaic *waga*, which is possessive to begin with, pronouns are made possessive by the simple addition of the particle *no* (§3.12): *kimi=no* 'your', *kanojo=no* 'her'. Additionally, the prefix *mai-* (← English *my*) can be used in certain compounds to express the idea of '(one's) own': *mai-kaa* 'one's own (not a company) car', *mai-hoomu* 'privately owned (not rented) home'.

5.8 Numerals and Classifiers

Japanese is unusual cross-linguistically in possessing three different series of numerals, each from a different vocabulary stratum (§5.1): native, Sino-Japanese (SJ: §7.1) and foreign (§7.2). The last is the most recent and borrowed mostly from English (1–3: *wan~cuu~surii*), though there exist a few numbers loaned from other languages (o *zero* from French, 1 *ii* from Mandarin).

The native series is defective—there exist gaps in the series. The numbers 1–10 appear as both bare numbers (*hito, futa, mi, yo(n), icu, mu, nana, ya, kokono, too*) and

5.8 Numerals and Classifiers

as count numbers (*hitocu, futacu, mi(Q)cu, yo(Q)cu, icucu, mu(Q)cu, nanacu, ya(Q)cu, kokonocu, too=no*). The former are combined with classifiers (see below), while the latter, as the name implies, are used for counting and, with the exception of *too* 'ten', composed of a bare number plus the suffix *-(Q)cu*. Native numerals higher than 10 are never used for counting. They are unproductive fossils mostly confined to personal and place names (§6.9), as well as poetry: 20 *hacu~hata* (*hacuka* '20th day of the month', *hatači* '20 years old'); 30 *miso* (*oomisoka* 'New Year's Eve (lit. great 30th day)'); 40 *yoso* (*yosoji* '40 years old'); 80 *yaso* (*yasoji* '80 years old'); 100 *momo* (*momotose* '100 years'); 1,000 *či* (personal and place names, such as Chiaki or Chitose); and 10,000 *yorozu* (*yorozuya* 'general store'). The last of these is typically used in the sense of 'multitudinous, all things'.

The SJ series is, by contrast, complete, consisting of the core numbers 0–10 (*rei, iči, ni, saN, ši, go, roku, šiči, hači, kyuu~ku, juu*), 100 (*hyaku*), 1000 (*seN*), 10,000 (*maN~baN*) and powers of the latter: 10,000^2 (*oku*), 10,000^3 (*čoo*) and still greater powers, seldom used (§4.8). Non-core SJ numbers are formed by creating simple strings without the need for conjunctions (§3.11) or particles (§3.12, §3.13): 555 is *gohyaku+gojuu+go* (=(5×100)+(5×10)+5). The SJ series can be combined with classifiers or used for counting. When counting out loud, there is a tendency for single-mora (§2.4) SJ numerals to be lengthened to two moras: *ni* → *nii*, *ši* → *šii*, *go* → *goo*.

When a number from the native or SJ series (but not the foreign) is used to count something in particular, it must be used with a classifier, which come in two types: endocentric and exocentric. Endocentric classifiers are also known as measure words or quantifiers. A numeral together with an endocentric classifier forms a single compound (§5.4), with the classifier as its own referent. Examples of endocentric classifiers include *meetoru* 'metre', *jikaN* 'hour' or *kai* 'occasion, time'. When combined with a numeral, these yield compounds such as *iči+meetoru* '1 metre', *hači+jikaN* '8 hours' or *go+kai* '5th time'. Exocentric classifiers, on the other hand, refer to a 'third-party' noun and cannot typically be used as independent words. Examples include *dai* 'large machine', *-seki* 'ship' or *-ki* 'flying machine'. When combined with a numeral, these yield forms such as (*takušii*) *saN-dai* '3 (taxis)', (*rainaa*) *go-seki* '5 (ocean liners)' or (*heri*) *ni-ki* '2 (helicopters)'. Here we treat exocentric classifiers as affixes, while treating the majority of endocentric classifiers as words, although with classifiers, the boundary between word and affix is not always clearly defined.

Semantically, endocentric classifiers are fairly straightforward, certainly for the speaker of a European language. Exocentric classifiers are less so. A single classifier can be used to enumerate a range of different objects: *-dai*, for example, can be applied not only to taxis, but to cars, computers or refrigerators. Conversely, a single object can be counted using a range of different exocentric classifiers. A shrimp, when alive and moving around in its natural habitat, is counted using *-hiki*, the classifier for small animals; when uncooked at a market stall and destined for the dinner table, it is *-bi*; when put on top of rice and served on a plate in a sushi restaurant it is *-kaN*; when served as part of an individual course in a restaurant, it is *-hiN*. There exist many hundreds of endocentric classifiers, some of which are comparatively infrequent: *-kuči* for bank accounts or *-furi* for swords. Many L2 learners will opt for the default classifier *-ko*, which can be used with just about anything, or for a native count number. Thus, two pairs of chopsticks is *haši ni-zeN* if you want to sound intelligent, but *haši ni-ko* or *haši futacu* otherwise.

The number used with a given classifier is generally from the SJ numeral series, as illustrated in the examples in the previous paragraphs. This is usually the case even when the classifier itself is not SJ (*iči+kiro* '1 kilo', where *kiro* is a borrowing from French). The exceptions are the numbers 4 and 7, where the native numbers *yoN* and *nana* prevail (*yoN+kiro* ~ *nana+kiro*, not **ši+kiro* ~ **šiči+kiro*). There are, however, classifiers where 1 and 2 are native numbers and 3 fluctuates: *hito+eki, futa+eki, saN+eki* ~ *mi+eki* '1~2~3 stations/stops'. There exist also two suppletive classifier series which must be memorized. Here, not only the numeral series, but the classifier changes during counting: *-niN* ~ *-ri* for people (*hito-ri* ~ *futa-ri* ~ *saN-niN* ~ *yo-niN* '1~2~3~4 people') and *-ka* ~ *-niči* ~ *(-jicu)* for days (*miQ-ka* '3 days' ~ *juuiči-niči* '11 days' ~ *iči-ryoo-jicu* 'a day or two').

Another hurdle for the L2 learner is the allomorphic variation found with the initial consonant of certain classifiers. This variation is similar to rendaku (§5.5), though differs in subtle ways. Gemination (§2.2), too, occurs when the final mora of a numeral is *-či* or *-ku*. Space prohibits a full description but, at its simplest, classifiers beginning with *t~c~č~k~s~š~p* or *h~f* (→ *p*: further below) induce gemination at the morpheme boundary: almost always with 1 *iči* and 10 *juu*, and to a limited extent with 6 *roku*, 8 *hači*, 100 *hyaku* and 100,000,000 *oku* (*iQ+kai, roQ+kai, hači+kai* ~ *haQ+kai, jiQ+kai* ~ *juQ+kai, hyaQ+kai, (iči)oku+kai* ~ *(iči)oQ+kai* '1~6~8~10~100~ 100,000,000 times'). Meanwhile, an initial *h~f* in a classifier becomes *p* when gemination occurs (*iQ-paku* '1-night stay'), as well as after *saN* (*saN-paku* '3-night stay'), but not *yoN* (*yoN-haku* '4-night stay'). There exist many exceptions and quirks (*saN+kai* '3 times' but *saN+gai* '3rd floor', where *kai* is both 'time' and 'floor'), as well as considerable inter-speaker variation (*jiQ+puN* ~ *juQ+puN* '10 minutes').

Finally, there exist numeral affixes (§5.3), either ordinal, indefinite or definite. The ordinals *dai-, -baN, -goo, dai-...-baN, dai-...-goo* and *-baN-me* are used with the SJ series (*dai-iči* ~ *iči-baN* ~ *iči-goo* ~ *dai-iči-baN* ~ *dai-iči-goo* ~ *iči-baN-me* 'first'), while *-me* is used with the native count series (*hitocu-me* 'first'). Indefinite affixes can be used with either a numeral or a classifier and are highly productive: *suu-* ~ *-suu* 'several' (*suu-juu* 'scores, dozens (lit. many tens)', *juu-suu* 'a dozen or so (lit. ten and several)'). They can also be used together with an emphatic particle (§3.12): *naN-...=mo* ~ *naN-...=ka* 'many~some' (*naN-neN=mo* 'many years' ~ *naN-neN=ka* 'a few years'). Definite affixes, on the other hand, can only be combined with a noun and are less productive: *kata-* 'one of a pair' (*kata-te* 'single-handed'), *ryoo-* 'both' (*ryoo-gawa* 'both sides').

5.9 Homonymy, Polysemy and Heteronomy

Homonyms are words or phrases pronounced the same but with different meanings: identical phonology but differing semantics. English examples are the words *bear~bare* or the phrases *ice cream ~ I scream*. When orthography is taken into account, two further terms are employed: homographs and homophones. Although there are varying definitions, here we define a homograph as a homonym with identical orthography, while defining a homophone as a homonym which has differing orthography. English examples here include the homographs *bay* ('body of water' ~ 'animal noise') and the homophones *write~rite~right~wright*. Polysemes are homonyms where the meaning is related and which typically appear in dictionaries under a single headword. They often occur in groups with one polyseme considered the 'core' meaning. An example of an English polyseme group is 'watch', where the core sense of 'observe closely' has been widened to the senses of 'period of duty', 'group of people on duty', 'caution', 'timepiece' or, most recently, 'movie or TV show'. The line between a polyseme and homonym can often be difficult to draw. English polysemes are nearly always homographs, though British spelling tends to preserve different orthographies (*programme~program*, *cheque~check*), while US spelling tends to level them (*program* only, *check* only). Heteronyms are words with an identical orthography, but different phonology and semantics. English examples include *buffet* ('all-you-can-eat' ~ 'pound, beat') or *bow* ('ribbon' ~ 'front of a ship'). Homonyms, polysemes and heteronyms are summarized in Table 5.9, where ≈ indicates relatedness.

The level of homonymy in Japanese differs by vocabulary stratum (§5.1) although, outside the foreign vocabulary stratum (§7.2), there are few homographs, provided kanji are employed where convention dictates (§4.1). In other words, nearly all Japanese homonyms are differentiated in writing and are thus also homophones. What appear to be homonyms may in fact be distinguished suprasegmentally: by a different accent pattern. This is examined in greater detail in §2.6.

	phonology	semantics	orthography
homonym	=	≠	
homograph	=	≠	=
homophone	=	≠	≠
polyseme	=	≈	= / ≠
heteronym	≠	≠	=

Table 5.9: *Homonyms, polysemes and heteronyms*

In the native stratum, homonyms such as *fur-u* 'shake' ~ *fur-u* 'fall (of rain)' can be written identically in kana as ふる, but in practice are distinguished by being written in kanji as 振る ~ 降る. The same can be said for many other homonym groups, such as *sum-u* (住む 'live' ~ 済む 'conclude' ~ 澄む 'be clear') or *hači* (八 'eight' ~ 鉢 'bowl' ~ 蜂 'bee').

Homonym groups are far more prevalent in the Sino-Japanese (SJ) stratum, a result of the relatively small pool of potential kanji readings (§4.4, §7.1). SJ words are typically binoms (written with two kanji) and, when especially common readings such as *koo* or *ši* are paired, mass homonymy results: *kooši* may be 講師 'instructor' ~ 格子 'lattice' ~ 行使 'use' ~ 孔子 'Confucius' ~ 公私 'public and private' ~ 光子 'photon' and many others, while *šikoo* may be 思考 'thought' ~ 志向 'intention' ~ 施行 'enforcement' ~ 試行 'trial' ~ 嗜好 'penchant' ~ 至高 'supremacy' ~ 歯垢 'plaque' and more. In the small number of cases where SJ homophony is pernicious, one kanji, generally the first, may purposely be 'misread' as native Japanese to avoid confusion: *ičiricu* 市立 'municipal' ~ *watakuširicu* 私立 'private' (both properly *širicu*), *šinagaku* 科学 'science' ~ *bakegaku* 化学 'chemistry' (both properly *kagaku*).

Homonymy is perhaps least prevalent in the foreign stratum. One example is the reduction to an identical form, as a result of truncation (§5.6), of many English loanwords (§7.3) appearing as the second element in a compound. This has yielded forms such as *misukoN* 'beauty contest' ~ *rajikoN* 'radio-controlled' ~ *cuakoN* 'tour conductor' ~ *bodikoN* 'body conscious' ~ *mazakoN* 'mother complex' and many others, where the *koN* element is a truncation of English *contest~controlled ~conductor~conscious~complex*. While fairly similar English words such as *coat~court* both become *kooto* in Japanese, what to the English ear are totally dissimilar pronunciations from two different languages may also conflate in Japanese: *Louvre~rouble* → *ruuburu*.

Japanese polysemes may or may not be distinguished by orthography. Examples where they are include *kawa* (革 'leather' ~ 皮 'skin') or *šio* (塩 'salt' ~ 潮 'tide'); examples where they are not *ki* (木 'tree' ~ 'wood'), *hi* (日 'day' ~ 'sun'), or *kuči* (口 'mouth' ~ 'portal'). Polysemes are especially apparent among verbs. Apart from the more obvious polysemes 見る 'look, watch' ~ 診る 'look at (examine by doctor)', the verb *mi-ru* can also be written 観る 'watch (a show or movie)' ~ 視る 'look cautiously' ~ 看る 'look after, take care of'. The semantic differences are subtle and not always clear to the native speaker. Indeed, it can be argued that these polysemes are artificial, having been 'forced' upon Japanese through the influence of kanji orthography. A similar example of 'forced polysemy' is *aši* 足 'foot' ~ *aši* 脚 'leg'. In some cases, one or more of these meanings may be borrowed from Chinese (see §7.1 for an example).

Though rare cross-linguistically, heteronomy is widespread in Japanese. Since most kanji have multiple readings, the kanji script is heteronymous by default. On the other hand, heteronomy in kana script is arguably absent, although see §4.6 for a discussion of the few exceptions.

5.10 Slang and Jargon

Before setting out to describe slang and jargon, we must define what is meant by the terms. Definitions of slang and jargon vary greatly among researchers and the two terms are not always exclusive. Here, we will adopt the quasi-standard definitions most commonly found in linguistics reference works.

- **Slang:** A set of continuously changing words and phrases, absent from (or possessing a significantly different meaning in) the standard language, that are used among a specific social group to establish a sense of communal identity or exclusiveness. While not always rude or offensive *per se*, slang words more often than not have a low or vulgar image and are thus avoided in formal conversation or conversation with members outside the in-group.
- **Jargon:** A set of technical vocabulary, expressions or shorthand forms, not easily understood by the general public, used among members of a specific trade or profession to facilitate communication and the exchange of knowledge in their field. Unlike slang, jargon is not typically associated with rudeness or vulgarity, but is nonetheless avoided in conversation with members outside one's field to avoid misunderstandings.

Slang is often broken down into primary slang and secondary slang. The former refers to the specialized vocabulary of a specific subculture, usually incomprehensible to members outside the in-group, while the latter refers to a broader category of expressions used within, or at least understood by, society at large as a stylistic preference rather than for communal identity. In Japanese, gamer slang, high school girl slang or drag queen slang can all be defined as primary slang. On the other hand, words such as *yaba-i* 'dangerous' used in the sense of 'awesome, badass', or as an adverb expressing emphasis (*yabai omoširo-i* 'interesting as hell!'), can be defined as secondary slang. Japanese slang, for the most part, follows the same word formation principles as standard vocabulary. That is, derivation (§5.3), compounding (§5.4), rendaku (§5.5) and truncation (§5.6) are all frequently employed. When undergoing truncation, newly coined words tend to follow the canonical 2 mora + 2 mora (2μ+2μ) pattern: in gamer slang, for example, the terms *kamigee* 'legendary game (lit. god game)', *ryoogee* 'great game', *kusogee* 'shitty game', *bakagee* 'stupid game' and *murigee* 'impossible game' are all 2μ+2μ compounds with the second element *gee*, a back-clipping of *geemu* 'game'.

Perhaps the most well-known innovators of new slang in Japan are high school girls, commonly referred to as *JK* (an abbreviation of *jošikoosei*: §5.6). In fact, *JK* slang is so famous, that a popular morning television show conducted a survey each year from 2014 to 2017 ranking the top ten *JK* slang words. In 2017, *iɴsutabae*, a compound formed from a back-clipping of *iɴsutaguramu* 'Instagram' and the rendaku form of *hae* 'shining, flashy', was awarded first place. Meaning a sight or photo worth posting to the photo-sharing application Instagram, *iɴsutabae* is roughly synonymous with English 'instagrammable', coined at around the same time. In 2016, first place went to *maɴji* 'swastika', a term initially used to express a swastika-like pose girls made with their arms when taking selfies, but later expanded to cover a plethora of meanings including 'crazy, hip, in the zone' (in Japan, swastikas do not bear the negative connotation that they do in Western culture and can be frequently observed as religious symbols at temples: §4.14). The mortality rate of *JK* slang is extremely high, with the typical word falling out of use along with the departure of the graduating class that coined it. Words such as *ičikita* 'temporary stop home' (a truncation of *ičiji+kitaku*) and *gaɴnae* 'totally lame' (a combination of the prefix *gaɴ-*'very' and a back-clipping of *nae-ru* 'grow weak'), both of which once basked in the glory of the 2014 top ten *JK* slang awards, are now nothing more than shadows of their former glory, long forgotten relics of a departed graduating class. One could argue, however, that it is the short longevity of these words that make them so appealing to their users in the first place, their very exclusiveness creating a sense of identity.

Examples of jargon include used bookseller jargon, linguistics jargon or computer jargon. Jargon is largely constructed using Sino-Japanese (SJ: §7.1) morphemes, similar to the use of Latin and Greek morphemes when constructing technical vocabulary in English and other Western languages. Depending on the field, loanwords (§7.2, §7.3) may do duty too, sometimes at an even higher rate than SJ coinages, but there has been a recent tendency towards replacing lengthy or obscure loanwords with SJ coinages (§8.3). Native morphemes may be employed as well, particularly in more traditional disciplines, such as archery jargon (*ikomi* 'shoot multiple arrows into a single target', *curune* 'the sound a bow makes when releasing an arrow') and equestrian jargon (*namiaši* 'walk', *hayaaši* 'trot'), but are overall less common in modern technical vocabulary. Like slang, jargon too may undergo truncation. Some examples familiar to linguists in Japan include *koqkeɴ* for *kokuricu kokugo keɴkyuujo* 'National Institute for Japanese Language and Linguistics (NINJAL)' (§8.12) or *niqkoku* for *nihon* (also read *niqpoɴ*) *kokugo daijiteɴ* 'Great Dictionary of the Japanese Language' (§8.10). While short life expectancy and exclusivity are defining characteristics of slang, the main purpose of jargon is to facilitate communication among members of the same trade or field, and thus mortality rates here are overall much lower. Needless to say, as old technologies are abandoned and new ones adopted, jargon too may go in and out of usage in a relatively short span of time.

5.11 Discriminatory Vocabulary

Despite its reputation as a language with many layers of politeness (§6.3), spoken by a people for whom politeness is an important element in their culture, like any other language Japanese has its fair share of impolite terms. While it is fair to say that swearwords *per se* are far rarer than in, for example, European languages or in Chinese (although see §6.4), Japanese is not lacking in discriminatory vocabulary.

Perhaps the best way of forming an overview of discriminatory vocabulary is through the well-documented list of words and phrases avoided in public television and radio broadcasting. Before embarking on such an analysis, however, it should be mentioned that there exist no laws in Japan banning either discriminatory vocabulary or swearwords in broadcasting or other media, nor in daily life. Television channels and radio stations police themselves, while making allowances for the time of day and the presumed age and background of the audience. The list in question, widely available on the internet, does not exist in any formal form and carries no legal force. For ease of reading, all words appearing on the broadcasting list are marked in this unit by ⁂, while non-discriminatory alternatives are marked by ♥. It should also be borne in mind that the English translations offered for the various terms cited in this unit may not lie in the same 'discomfort zone' as the Japanese originals—in some cases the English translation may be too strong, in others a derogatory English term is wholly lacking. Observe that many derogatory terms end in the suffixes *-bo*, *-boo* or *-ko*.

Discriminatory terms designated as 'harming the individual and human rights' have perhaps been the most contentious in recent Japanese history. The vast majority concern themselves with the group of people now known as ♥*doowakaNkeiša*, formerly called *eta*, *hiniN* (lit. 'nonhuman'), ⁂*burakumiN* or ⁂*tokušuburakumiN* (these terms get longer with time). Generally known in English as *burakumin*, these were the untouchable class of feudal Japan whose occupations —undertakers, tanners, slaughterers—were considered polluting under Buddhist doctrine. Their descendants suffered widespread discrimination until the mid-20th century and even later in the Kansai area. Among the discriminatory terms cited above, the first two words, *eta* and *hiniN*, are considered so taboo that they do not even appear on the broadcasting list. There are obvious linguistic and historical similarities here with derogatory terms in US English for a person now referred to as an *African American*, which itself replaced *black*, which in turn replaced the now very uncomfortable *negro*, which in its turn replaced the now taboo *nigger*.

'Physical and mental discriminatory terms' include ⁂*cuNbo* 'deaf', ⁂*katawa* 'cripple', ⁂*mekura* 'blind', ⁂*oši* 'dumb' and ⁂*raibyoo* 'leprosy'. Many of these words are replaced by terms such as ♥*mimi=no fujiyuu* 'aurally impaired' or ♥*me=no fujiyuu* 'visually impaired'. The inclusion of ⁂*raibyoo* 'leprosy' (and its now almost universal replacement by ♥*haNseNbyoo* 'Hansen's disease') is a legacy of previous longstanding social discrimination. Not on the list, presumably because obviously taboo, are *biᴏko* 'lame (lit. limper)' and *fugu* 'deformity (lit. defective)'. Some examples of discriminatory terms connected to 'occupation' are *⁎ooeru* 'office lady' (§5.6), *⁎oɴboo* 'cemetery worker', *⁎genaɴ*~*⁎gejo* '(male~female) servant', *⁎hyakušoo* 'peasant' and *⁎jokoo* 'factory girl'. Not a few of the words listed in this section would probably only be considered marginally derogatory by many native speakers, while the compositional pattern of suggested replacements mirrors closely English terms such as 'sanitation worker' (♥*seisooiɴ*) for 'dustman' (*⁎gomiya*).

It is no surprise that discriminatory terms for 'nationality and ethnic group' are concentrated on neighbouring countries: *⁎seɴjiɴ* 'Korean', *⁎čaɴkoro*~*⁎šinajiɴ* 'Chink', *⁎dojiɴ* 'native, aborigine', *⁎ainoko* 'half-caste, mutt', *⁎haafu* 'lit half', *⁎ketoo*~*⁎ketoojiɴ* 'honkey' and *⁎kuroɴbo* 'nigger'. Once again we find words missing from the list which are now taboo, such as *asačaɴ*~*asako*~*čoɴ[ko]* for Koreans, while here, too, many of the words listed would probably only be considered marginally, or not at all, derogatory by many native speakers. One word not on the list is taboo for many foreigners living in Japan: *gaijiɴ* '(non East Asian) foreigner'. 'Slang and jargon' (§5.10) include *⁎butabako* 'nick, clink, slammer', *⁎gaki* 'brat', *⁎himo* 'pimp', *⁎iɴbai* 'whore', *⁎sacu* 'pigs (=police)', *⁎seɴzuri* 'wanking, jerking off' and, most oddly, the ubiquitous *⁎yaba-i* 'dangerous' (§5.10). The final section in the list is headed 'unpleasant terms' and includes *⁎uɴko* 'shit' and *⁎očikobore* 'student with low grades (lit. dropped and broken)'.

It is noticeable that there are no sections devoted to derogatory terms for women (*miboojiɴ* 'widow', *kurisumasukeeki* 'unmarried woman over 25 (lit Christmas cake: nobody wants to buy one after the 25th of December)'), the elderly (*kusojijii* 'old fart (lit. shit old man)', *kusobabaa* 'old bag (lit. shit old woman)') or LGBT people (*okama* 'queer (lit. pot, itself slang for 'anus')', *onabe* 'dyke (lit. pan)'). Also conspicuous in their absence from the broadcasting list are terms such as *maɴjuu* 'bean jam bun' ~ *maɴko* 'baby bean jam bun' ~ *zakuro* 'pomegranate' for the female sex organ, *čiɴko* ~ *čiɴpo* (both etymology unclear) ~ *nakaaši* 'middle leg' for the male sex organ and *kiɴtama* 'balls (lit. golden balls)' for the testicles.

As anywhere else, there has been a backlash in some quarters of Japanese society against overzealous political correctness, known in Japanese as *kotobagari* 'lit. word hunting'. One example is *⁎šina*, a derogatory term for someone or something Chinese. The fact that, while *⁎šinasoba* 'Chinese noodles' and *⁎šinačiku* 'pickled bamboo shoots' are frowned upon, *minamišinakai* 'South China Sea' has been deemed perfectly respectable, is seen as hypocritical by some. Moreover, the replacement for *⁎šina*, ♥*čuugoku*, can itself be regarded as discriminatory since, written as 中国 ('lit. middle country') it carries the nuance that China is the centre of the world and, by implication, that everyone and everywhere else is second-rate.

Chapter 6 Language and Society

6.1 Gender, Age and Social Class

Cross-linguistically, females speak at a higher pitch—for biological reasons—than males, and in Japan there is perhaps a tendency for this to be exaggerated, especially in announcements on public transport or in advertising. Such a biological difference is determined by a speaker's sex: a speaker's gender, on the other hand, is defined psychologically. For most people, sex and gender are identical. As is well known, however, not all people who are biologically male, for example, feel themselves to be so and for these people sex and gender do not match. When it comes to language, the utterances produced by such people tend to conform to their gender, not their sex.

Japanese is often said to be a language where differences between utterances produced by the two genders are comparatively pronounced. Such differences can be gender preferential, meaning an utterance type is skewed heavily towards one gender, or they can be gender exclusive, meaning an utterance is employed solely by one gender. Table 6.1 shows some examples—out of many—of gender differences which occur in the lexicon, morphosyntax and phonology of Standard Japanese. The examples are divided into five columns, running from male exclusive ♂♂ leftmost, through male preferential ♂, gender neutral ◎ and female preferential ♀, to female exclusive ♀♀ rightmost. Rather than 'real life situations', some of the forms cited in the table are more often encountered in certain media where they are used for stylistic effect (so-called 'role language': §6.2). These are marked with a double dagger ‡.

Probably the most obvious gender differences to an L2 learner of Japanese are lexical, and those they likely encounter first are the first person pronouns. Although the mother tongue of many readers will possess gender-differentiated third person pronouns, this is probably not the case for the first person. These run the gamut from female exclusive *ataši* and female preferential (and, until recently, mostly Western Japanese) *uči*, through gender neutral *wataši*, to male preferential *boku* (also used, until fairly recently, by young 'tomboyish' girls) and male exclusive *ore* (although, as *ora* and *oira* also, this can be used by females in many dialects). Personal pronouns are covered in more detail in §5.7. Subtle differences can be found elsewhere in the lexicon, with nouns (*meši*~*gohaN* 'meal') for example, though such differences are generally only weakly preferential.

	Japanese					English
	♂♂	♂	◎	♀	♀♀	
personal pronouns	ore, waši‡	boku, aicu	wataši, kare	uči	ataši	see Table 5.7
nouns		meši	gohaN			meal
particles		ka*³, ze, zo, sa	yo, ne, no, wa↘	kašira‡	wa↗‡, koto*¹, mono*²	see §3.12
copula deletion			da=yo, da=ne		~~da~~=yo, ~~da~~=ne	see §3.6
beautification prefixes			o-ča	o-hana		tea, flower
imperatives	ki+tama-e‡	ko-i	ki-te, ki+na	ku-ru=no		come!
prohibitives		ku-runa	ko-naide	ko-na-i=no		don't come!
interjections		oi		ara		hey! oh my!
phonology	trilled r‡	sugee	sugo-i			fantastic

*¹ exclamative usage only (not imperative)
*² after polite predicates (§6.3), otherwise ◎
*³ but ◎ after polite predicates (§6.3)

Table 6.1: Examples of gender differences

Discourse particles (§3.12) are another salient gender difference: *kašira* is female preferential, while *mono* after polite predicates (§6.3) and exclamative *koto* are female exclusive. The particle *wa* has two variants, differing only in intonation: emphatic *wa*↗ is female exclusive, whereas *wa*↘ can be used by either gender. The question particle *ka* too evinces gender differences: when used with a non-polite predicate (§6.3), usage is male preferential (*aQ-ta=ka* 'was it there?'). The female strategies are either to employ the question particle *no*, or to eschew any particle while using a rising intonation: *aQ-ta=no* or *aQ-ta*↗. Both these strategies are also employed by males. As well as being used by males of all ages, the emphatic particles *zo* and *ze* are also used by younger female speakers; *sa* appears to be slowly drifting from male preferential to gender neutral.

Tied in with discourse particles is the non-polite form of the copula, *da* (§3.6). When followed by the particles *yo* or *ne*, this can be dropped by females, but rarely by males: *kirei=ne* ~ *kirei=da=ne* 'beautiful, isn't it?'. However, when absolute sentence-final and thus not followed by a particle, *da* can be dropped by either gender in casual speech and certain writing styles (§4.13). Female speakers, but never males, may also delete *da* when it appears after the nominalizer *no*. In hyperpolite female speech, this *no* has been reanalysed as an exclamative discourse particle and may appear after the polite form of the verb: *sore=ga itadak-e-mase-N=no* 'I can't accept that'. The use of beautification prefixes (§6.3) is a marker of 'refined' speech, especially in females (*o-hana* 'flower'), though still employed by males in polite situations and with specific words where the prefixed form is the default regardless of gender (*o-ča* 'tea').

6.1 Gender, Age and Social Class

With forms employed to mark the imperative and prohibitive (§3.7), a wide variety of gender-differentiated forms are evident in Table 6.1. Yet another major morphosyntactic difference between the two genders can be seen in interjections: those such as *oi* 'UK oi!, US hey!' are preferentially male, while interjections such as *ara* 'oh!' are preferentially female. Differences in phonology are slight. The most widely documented is the preferentially male anti-honorific (§6.4) usage of the long vowel *ee* for the vowel combinations *oi, ai* and *ae* (*sugee* for *sugo-i* 'fantastic') and the long vowel *ii* for the vowel combination *ui* (*samii* for *samu-i* 'cold'). In recent decades, however, these long vowels have also come to be employed by younger females. Another phonological difference is the trilled *r* used exclusively by males when wanting to appear threatening (§2.2, §6.4).

While age differences are apparent in Japanese, they are less salient than gender differences. The most frequently cited example is the first person pronoun *waši*, used exclusively by elderly males, but this is also used by younger speakers in certain dialects. Older speakers are more likely to use *ošibaraku desu* for 'it's been a while', while younger speakers prefer *ohisašiburi desu*. Many greetings also differ according to age cohort (§6.6). Age differences in sociolinguistic studies generally manifest themselves in the data gleaned from surveying particular variables. Older speakers of Tokyo Japanese, for example, show significantly higher rates for the word-internal velar nasal [ŋ] variable, signifying their increased likelihood of pronouncing a word like *kagi* 'key' as *ka*[ŋ]*i* rather than *ka*[g]*i* (§2.2). As the exact opposite is the case for younger speakers, we can deduce two things from this age-grading: either that we are witnessing an ongoing linguistic change whereby word-internal /g/ is shifting from a velar nasal [ŋ] to a velar stop [g]; or that a majority of speakers change linguistic behaviour with age. To ascertain which is the case, a longitudinal study must be conducted. In this particular instance, the former is the case.

Many other sociolinguistic studies have revealed age-grading in Japanese. Variables include rendaku (§5.5): older speakers show higher rates of rendaku in compounds such as *waka+jiraga ~ waka+širaga* 'prematurely grey hair', but lower rates in those such as *cumi+cukuri ~ cumi+zukuri* 'cruel'. Other such variables include so-called *ra-nuki* rates (older speakers are less likely to use *ra*-dropping potential verb forms such as *tabe-re-ru* 'can eat' ~ *ko-re-ru* 'can come' in place of *tabe-rare-ru ~ ko-rare-ru*: §3.8) and *sa-ire* rates (older speakers are less likely to use *sa*-inserted causative verb forms such as *yasum-asase-ru* 'let rest' in place of *yasum-ase-ru*: §3.8).

Despite some of the pioneering work in Western sociolinguistics having had its focus on language differences apparent across socioeconomic groups, or social classes, such studies have not been to the fore in post-war Japan. The rise in living standards apparent across all socio-economic groups brought about by the post-war economic boom, combined with increased social mobility generated by efficient mass public transport and a relatively inexpensive, readily accessible education system, has caused a widespread levelling in both socioeconomic and class terms. Most Japanese, when asked in public surveys, now describe themselves as 'middle-class'. One of the few studies surveying socioeconomic-grading —examining honorific variables in Toyama Prefecture in the 1970s—found them to have been largely levelled when the study was replicated in the 1990s.

6.2 Register and Role Language

Register, in its linguistic sense, has a narrow and a broad definition. The narrow definition limits the use of the term to jargon, the use of technical or specialist vocabulary, or what can sometimes be called 'talk'. Examples include a pilot talking to the control tower, a conversation between a doctor and nurse or a speaker delivering a lecture at an academic conference. All languages possess this 'narrow' register, and Japanese is no exception. The reader is referred to §5.10, where the topic is dealt with in greater detail.

The broad definition of register—the definition we will be looking at in this unit —also encompasses issues of style (for written style, see §3.14). These are governed by the social context in which a discourse is taking place and the relative status of the interlocutors involved, both of which dictate the levels of formality employed. Formality may be expressed through morphosyntax or lexicon and, to a far lesser extent, through phonology (see Table 6.1 for an example). The Japanese language offers speakers a rich choice of honorifics (§6.3) and anti-honorifics (§6.4), slang (§5.10), discriminatory vocabulary (§5.11) and an array of pronouns (§5.7) and discourse particles (§3.12). Non-verbal communication (§6.7) also plays its part. In Japanese, to a considerably greater extent than in many other languages, social context and status dictate not only the formality encoded in an utterance, but the gender- and age-specific language (§6.1) encoded too. It is these added factors which make Japanese register especially rich, indeed so rich that it is possible for a multi-person conversation appearing in a novel to run for many pages without the author having to indicate directly which character is saying what.

A concrete example of register is offered in Table 6.2, where the rightmost column indicates relative status ('A' means A is higher than B and vice versa). Conversations 1–6 are ranked in terms of formality from low to high, although reflect only the tip of the iceberg: hundreds of other fine gradations are possible, not illustrated here. Gender- and age-specific language, as well as jargon, are also ignored. Regardless of whether such a dialogue would take place or not, the conversation in question can, in all cases, be translated into English as: *A: Have you eaten (lunch), (Mr/Ms Yano)? B: Yes, I had a good lunch.* Generally speaking, status differences become less transparent as the level of formality increases, as evident by the question mark for Conversations 5 and 6. These could be between two relatively unacquainted equals, or two equals keeping a judicious distance; or it could

6.2 Register and Role Language   163

	conversation	formality	relative status
1	A: kuq-ta=ka, omee B: ume-e meši kuq-ta=zo	A: rough B: rough	=
2	A: yano-kuɴ, kuq-ta=ka B: oiši-i hirugohaɴ tabe-ta=yo	A: rough B: casual	A?
3	A: yano-saɴ, hirugohaɴ tabe-ta=no B: hai, oiši-i hirugohaɴ tabe-maši-ta	A: casual B: polite	A
4	A: yano-saɴ, hirugohaɴ tabe-maši-ta=ka B: uɴ, oiši-i meši tabe-ta=yo	A: polite B: casual	B
5	A: yano-saɴ, hirugohaɴ tabe-maši-ta=ka B: hai, oiši-i hirugohaɴ itadak-imaši-ta	A: polite B: humble	?
6	A: yano-sama, o-hirugohaɴ=o mešiagar-imaši-ta=deš-oo=ka B: hai, oiši-i hirugohaɴ=o itadak-imaši-ta	A: respectful B: humble	?

Table 6.2: Register in conversation

just as easily be the case that one or other of the two has higher status, but is just being polite due to the setting. The verb 'eat' is one of a small set of verbs in Japanese that possess individual respectful (*mešiagar-u*), humble (*itadak-u*) and anti-honorific (*ku-u*) forms: their use, combined with polite or non-polite verb forms (§6.3), signals the relative status of both the speakers. Titles are a highly salient marker of relative status, with -*saɴ* being the default title indicating politeness, -*sama* indicating respect and -*kuɴ* indicating the addressee is of equal or lower status (or age) than that of the speaker. Finally, phonology can signal register, as shown by the diphthongs *ae* in *omae* 'you' and *ai* in *uma-i* 'delicious' both becoming *ee* in Conversation 1 (§6.1, §6.4).

Although register is expressed by means of style, it can also be employed for effect. Interlocutors can be rendered overtly feminine, elderly, intellectual, country bumpkin, dishonest, childlike, aristocratic, camp, foreign or many other things, by the intentional overuse or exaggeration of register. This phenomenon is known as 'role language' (*yakuwarigo*) and is especially visible in manga, anime and video games (§6.5); on terrestrial television, where non-Japanese speech is almost always dubbed rather than subtitled; or in Japanese translations of foreign novels. Across all these media, there is a strong tendency to exaggerate a speaker's gender, age and social status.

Commonly encountered role language patterns (Japanese research generally anthropomorphizes these as *kyara* 'characters') include 'female talk' and 'old timer' talk. Female characters are accorded liberal use of the discourse particles *wa* ✔ and *kašira* (§6.1), copula deletion (§6.1) and, in media with sound, unnaturally high-pitched voices. Old-timer characters, mostly elderly males, use *ja* ~ *or-u* ~ *-(a)ɴ*, these being the Western (§7.9) forms of the copula *da* (§3.6), the perfect-progressive auxiliary *i-ru* (§3.9) and the negative verb suffix *-(a)na-i* (§3.8). In this kind of talk,

Fig. 6.2.1: Ramu-chan's use of the made-up particle qča (高橋 2017)

Fig. 6.2.2: Funasshi's use of the made-up particle naqšii (twitter.com/funassyi/status/1077573066576650241)

characters are made to use the first person pronoun *waši* and, in media with sound, are frequently made to speak slowly and enunciate clearly. These two language patterns possess more finely-tuned subcategories, such as 'housewife (*okusama*) talk', 'princess (*ojoosama*) talk', 'delinquent girl (*sukebaɴ*) talk', 'boss (*jooši*) talk' or 'nutty professor (*hakase*) talk'.

Particular professions have spawned their own role language. In 'gangster (*yakuza*) talk' or 'teenage rebel (*yaɴkii*) talk', characters use exaggerated anti-honorifics, derogatory vocabulary and trilled *r* (§2.2); in 'squaddie (*guɴtai*) talk', characters use the first person pronoun *jibuɴ* and the copula *de ar-imas-u*; while in 'old-fashioned prostitute (*yuujo*) talk' characters use the first person pronouns *wačiki~ačiki* and the copula *de ar-iɴs-u*. Role language can be used to give characters classical or samurai colour through, for example, liberal use of the first person pronoun *seqša* or the copula *de gozar-u*; or country bumpkin colour through the pronouns *ora~oira* and the use of the copula *da* after the nonpast form of verbs, where it would normally be ungrammatical (**su-ru=da*).

Role language can be extended to imaginary beings or non-humans. The dialogue in §6.5, taken from video games, is but one example. Another is alien or robot speech, such as the space alien Ramu-chan from the manga *Urusei Yatsura* who ends her sentences in *qča* (Fig. 6.2.1). This discourse particle does not exist in any dialect or register of Japanese (at least in the sense and syntactic environment in which we find it used here) and such novel morphology or grammar may be found elsewhere. Examples include the persistent, and frequently grammatically illicit, use of sentence-final *desuu* (← *des-u*) by the character Tara-chan in the anime *Sazae-san*, even following other copulas (**iya=da=desuu*) and verbs (**tabe-ru=desuu*); or the pear-shaped mascot character Funasshii who ends its sentences in *naǫšii*, a wordplay on *naši* 'pear'. The latter even has a Twitter account, where the use of sentence-final *naǫšii* runs rampant (Fig. 6.2.2). Role language can also be employed superficially through script choice (§4.12): robots, aliens and foreigners 'speak' only in katakana in manga, while females have their subtitles in pink with liberal use of heart emoji on television variety shows.

6.3 Honorifics

Japanese honorifics can be divided into four main categories: (I) polite language, which does not explicitly express respect or humility *per se*, but is a social prerequisite when speaking with superiors or in formal situations; (II) respectful language, which expresses respect towards another; (III) humble language, which expresses humility; and (IV) beautification language, which is not directly related to politeness but instead makes words sound more refined. In addition to these four categories of honorifics, we can add a fifth anti-honorific category: (V) derogatory language, which makes one's speech sound rough and unrefined and often expresses contempt. We will cover (I)–(IV) in this unit, reserving discussion of (V) to §6.4.

Polite language is the most straightforward category of honorific speech as it typically only involves modifying the end of a clause or sentence. Polite forms of noun, verb and verbal adjective predicates can all be obtained through the use of polite copulas or verbal suffixes:

- For noun predicates, the polite copula *des-u* or super-polite copula *de gozar-u* (usually in the form *de goza-imas-u*) are employed (§3.6): *ašita=des-u* ~ *ašita=de goza-imas-u* 'it's tomorrow'.
- Verb predicates take the polite verb suffix *-(i)mas-u* (§3.8): *omo-imas-u* 'think'.
- While there is no polite adjective suffix, the polite form of a verbal adjective can be obtained by adding *des-u* to the end of the nonpast or past form (§3.7): *tanoši-i=des-u* 'is fun', *tanoši-kaǫta=des-u* 'was fun'.

Until the mid-20th century, the polite form of verbal adjective predicates was obtained by adding *gozar-u* to the Western Japanese adverbial form (§7.9):

- Stems ending in *ši* → *šuu*: *oiši-i* → *oišuu goza-imas-u* 'is delicious'.
- Stems ending in *i* → *yuu*: *ooki-i* → *ookyuu goza-imas-u* 'is big'.
- Stems ending in *u* → *uu*: *samu-i* → *samuu goza-imas-u* 'is cold'.

- Stems ending in *a* → *oo*: *aka-i* → *akoo goza-imas-u* 'is red'.
  When the adjective stem ends in *wa* (*kowa-i* 'is scary'), many speakers pronounce the polite forms as *woo* (*kowoo goza-imas-u*), despite modern kana usage (§8.2) dictating a spelling of こおう <ko.o.u>.
- Stems ending in *o* → *oo*: *kuro-i* → *kuroo goza-imas-u* 'is black'.
  An *ooo* string is reduced to *oo*: *too-i* → *too goza-imas-u* 'is far', not *tooo goza-imas-u*.

Such verbal adjective + *gozar-u* forms are now regarded as super-polite and restricted to the most formal of registers or to role language (§6.2). They may also be encountered in such set expressions as *ohayoo gozaimasu* 'good morning (lit. is early: §6.6)' and *arigatoo gozaimasu* 'thank you (lit. existence is difficult)'. In addition to the analytic polite forms listed above, there are numerous lexically distinct polite forms used in place of their more casual counterparts in formal speech and writing: *keredo[mo]* (formal) ~ *kedo[mo]* (casual) 'but', *taiheN* (formal) ~ *to[Q]temo* (casual) 'very', *nočihodo* (formal) ~ *atode* (casual) 'later'. See §4.13 for a discussion on formal and casual writing styles.

Moving on to respectful and humble language, many nouns (as well as adjectives and verbs: see further below) can be made polite by adding the prefixes *o-* ~ *go-* (both written in kanji as 御). The prefix *o-* is typically used with native vocabulary (*o-kaNgae* 'thoughts', *o-toiawase* 'inquiries'), while *go-* is used predominantly with Sino-Japanese (SJ: §7.1) (*go-keNtoo* 'consideration', *go-šidoo* 'guidance'). There are, however, a number of notable exceptions, such as *o-deNwa* 'telephone' or *o-keiko* 'practice, training' (both SJ). Whether *o-* ~ *go-* express respect or humility is largely a matter of context. The SJ noun (and also nominal verb) *reNraku* 'contact' → *go-reNraku*, for example, expresses respect when used to refer to the addressee's action, but humility when referring to the actions of the speaker. Furthermore, *o-* ~ *go-* may simply express politeness when used in a formal setting. Thus, the terms *o-toiawase* 'inquiries' or *go-aNnai* 'information', often found on company websites, do not necessarily indicate respect or humility. Such honorific prefixes also play a major role in beautification language (see below).

In addition to *o-* ~ *go-*, the prefixes *oN-* and *mi-* (both also written as 御) are also encountered before certain nouns, but are no longer productive in the modern language. Both of these prefixes are used to express respect, with the latter common in Shintō and Christian vocabulary: *oN-čuu* 'Messrs', *oN-ši* 'mentor', *mi-ki* 'sacred saké', *mi-te* 'holy hands', *mi-kotoba* 'holy scripture'. Also encountered, but no longer productive, are the humble SJ prefixes *gu-* (愚) 'lit. foolish' and *secu-* ~ *seQ-* (拙) 'lit. unskilled, inferior', used to demean oneself or one's family members: *gu-sai* 'my idiot wife', *gu-soku* 'my foolish son', *securoN* 'my inferior theory/paper', *seQčo* 'my inferior book'.

Similar to polite language, a number of words possess lexically distinct respectful or humble forms. With nouns, such forms are most common in kinship terminology (*ani* 'my older brother (humble)' ~ *aniki* 'my older brother (respectful)') and personal pronouns (*temae* 'I (humble)', *otaku* 'you (respectful)'): see §1.2 and §5.7 for further discussion. Respectful and humble counterparts are especially common in verbs, with many possessing neutral, respectful and humble forms: *tabe-ru* 'eat (neutral)' ~ *mešiagar-u* 'eat (respectful)' ~ *itadak-u* 'eat (humble)'. A list of the most common such verbs is given in Table 6.4. When used sentence-finally, respectful and humble verb forms nearly always appear in their polite form together with *-(i)mas-u*.

For verbs not possessing respectful or humble forms, these are rendered via the following grammatical modifications:

- The respectful form of a native verb is yielded by adding the honorific prefix *o-* to the nominalized form (§3.7: hereafter, the 'honorific stem'), followed by the particle *ni* (§3.12) plus the verb *nar-u* 'become', or by the auxiliary verb *nasar-u* (§3.9): *kake-ru* 'dial, sit' → *o-kake=ni nar-u* ~ *o-kake+nasar-u*.
- The respectful form of an SJ nominal verb is yielded by adding *go-* to the nominal base of the verb (hereafter, the 'honorific base') followed by *ni nar-u* ~ *nasar-u*: *jooša+su-ru* 'get on, ride' → *go-jooša=ni nar-u* ~ *go-jooša+nasa.ru*.
- The humble form of a native verb is yielded by adding *su-ru* 'do' ~ *itas-u* 'do (humble)' ~ *moošiage-ru* 'speak, do (super-humble)' to the honorific stem: *okur-u* 'send' → *o-okur-i+su-ru* ~ *o-okur-i+itas-u* ~ *o-okur-i+moošiage-ru*.
- The humble form of an SJ nominal verb is yielded by either (i) adding *itas-u* to the unmodified base, or (ii) adding *su-ru* ~ *itas-u* ~ *moošiage-ru* to the honorific base: *reNraku+su-ru* 'contact' → *reNraku+itas-u* ~ *go-reNraku+su-ru* ~ *go-reNraku+itas-u* ~ *go-reNraku+moošiage-ru*.
- Respect can be expressed through the use of a verb's passive form (§3.8): *okur-u* → *okur-arer-u* 'lit. be sent', *saNka+su-ru* 'join' → *saNka+s-are-ru* 'lit. be joined'. Such honorific meaning arises due to defocalization of the actor.
- Humility can be expressed via the causative form of a verb (§3.8) followed by *-te* (§3.7) and the benefactives (§3.10) *mora-u* 'receive' ~ *itadak-u* 'receive (humble)': *deNwa+su-ru* 'call' → *o-deNwa+s-ase-te itadak-u* 'lit. receive the privilege of you allowing me to call you'.
- Various other constructions using benefactives may be employed to express respect or humility: *šiNpai+su-ru* 'worry' → *go-šiNpai+kudasar-u* 'worry about me (respectful)', *šihara-u* → *o-šihara-i+itadak-u* 'pay me (humble)'.

Unlike verbs, adjectives do not possess respectful or humble counterparts. Instead, they may express respect by taking the prefixes *o-* ~ *go-*, the former with native verbal and nominal adjectives and the latter with SJ nominal adjectives: *o-ucukuši-i* 'beautiful' (native), *o-šizuka* 'quiet' (native), *go-keNkoo* 'healthy' (SJ). Similar to nouns, however, there are a number of exceptions: *o-geNki* 'in good spirits', *o-daiji* 'important' (both SJ), *go-moQtomo* 'reasonable' (native), *go-iriyoo* 'necessary' (hybrid). Also, again as with nouns, such *o-* ~ *go-* adjectives may simply express politeness in certain contexts.

In addition to the standard respectful forms, there are a number of super-respectful forms reserved for the emperor and the imperial family. The super-respectful form of the verb, illustrated in (1)–(2), is formed by the same rules as the respectful form, but with *asobas-u* ~ *ar-ase-rare-ru* used in place of *ni nar-u* ~ *nasar-u*. The former is the passive of the verb *asobas-u* 'lit. play (respectful)', the latter the causative passive of the verb *ar-u* 'be'. The SJ honorific prefixes *ei-* (叡) and *gyo-* (御) are also found before emperor- or imperial family-related vocabulary: *ei-ryo* 'emperor's thoughts (lit. wise considerations)', *ei-daN* 'decision made by the emperor (lit. wise decision)', *gyo-i* 'imperial garment', *gyo-eN* 'imperial banquet'. Such expressions are rarely used by the general public and are mostly limited to extreme right wing publications and blog posts. There are a few examples of super-respectful expressions still in general use, however: *gyookoo* 'imperial outing taken by the emperor', *gyookei* 'imperial outing taken by the empress, empress dowager, crown prince or crown princess', their collective form *gyookookei* 'imperial outing taken by the emperor and empress', *hoogyo* 'death of the emperor, empress or empress dowager', *kookyo* 'death of another member of the imperial family'. These last two forms are also occasionally used by the mass media to respectfully reference the death of foreign royalty.

(1) teNnooheika=ga   buji   go-toočaku+asobas-are-maši-ta
    His.Majesty.the.Emperor=NOM   safely   HPFX-arrive+play.RESP-PASS-POL-PST
    'His Majesty the Emperor has arrived safely.'

(2) teNnooheika=ga   hoNjicu   gozeN   roku-ji   saNjuusaN+puN
    His.Majesty.the.Emperor=NOM   today   AM   6-o'clock   33+minute

    hoogyo+ar-ase-rare-maši-ta
    die.RESP+be-CAUS-PASS-POL-PST
    'His Majesty the Emperor passed away at 6:33 this morning.'
    (from an NHK news report on the death of Emperor Hirohito in 1989)

Beautification language is formed by adding the prefix *o-* or, less commonly, *go-*, to the beginning of a word—as with other honorific language—but with the proviso that the prefixed form does not necessarily indicate respect, humility or politeness. In some cases, the polite prefix is lexically fused, or mandatory: *okazu* 'side dish', *omucu* 'nappy, diaper', *gohaN* 'meal'. In others, the prefix is not mandatory, though rarely omitted: *o-ča* 'tea', *o-kaši* 'sweets'. There are cases where the addition of a polite prefix narrows, or specificizes, the meaning of the modified word: *kane* 'metal, gold, money' ~ *o-kane* 'money', *širu* 'juice, sap' ~ *o-širu* 'soup'. In other cases, it can expand the meaning: *yu* 'hot springs' ~ *o-yu* 'hot springs, hot (drinking) water'. Other words take on a complete change of meaning: *tama* 'ball, jewel' ~ *o-tama* 'ladle', *kama* 'cauldron' ~ *o-kama* 'homosexual, transvestite' (§5.11), kaɴmuri 'crown' ~ o-kaɴmuri 'bad temper'. Yet others, such as *tegami* 'letter' or *sakana* 'fish', are used with or without *o-*, with little difference other than the beautified form sounding more elegant. A small number of words possess etymologically distinct beautified counterparts: *o-hiya* 'lit. coldness' is used in place of *mizu* 'water' at restaurants, while *o-tearai* 'lit. hand washing' is found in place of *beɴjo~toire* 'bathroom' in polite or formal speech and signage (neither *hiya* or *tearai* are used in these senses). The line between beautification language and the other honorific categories is not always clear: *o-tegami* could be beautificatory if referring to letters in general, respectful if referring to the letter of a social superior or polite if used in a formal setting at the workplace.

6.4 Anti-Honorifics

The polar opposite of honorifics (§6.3)—what we will term here anti-honorifics, but also known as deprecatives or pejoratives—are generally given short shrift in grammars. Indeed, it is widely believed that it is not possible to swear in Japanese. Although Japanese possesses no multi-purpose form employable across all parts of speech akin to English 'fuck' ('Fuck! The fucking fucker's fucking fucked!'), Japanese anti-honorifics do manifest themselves across many domains: in the syntax, lexicon, phonology and morphology. Anti-honorifics are not derogatory in all contexts—as with derogative personal pronouns (§5.7), many of the anti-honorific forms introduced in this unit may be used in rough speech in general or to reinforce bonding, especially between young male speakers. The reader is also urged to consult unit §5.11 on discriminatory vocabulary.

A small number of verbs possess anti-honorific forms—these are listed in Table 6.4. The best known of these is *yar-u* 'do', which is used in place of *su-ru* in informal or derogatory situations (1). In slang speech, *yar-u* also takes on the meanings 'fuck (have sex with)' and 'whack (kill)'. Depending on context, *yar-u* may be used in place of *su-ru* without any deprecative connotation as well: *yaq-te mir-u* 'I'll give it a try', *yaq-ta* 'I did it!'. In addition, as illustrated in (2), *yar-u* may be used in place of the benefactive *age-ru* 'give' in casual speech towards a social equal or inferior, or to express contempt towards the recipient (§3.10). Other verbs possessing anti-honorific forms are *tabe-ru* 'eat', *i-u* 'say' and *šin-u* 'die', whose anti-honorific forms are *ku-u* 'chow', *hozak-u* ~ *nukas-u* ~ *kok-u* 'crap on about' and *kutabar-u* 'croak'. While the subject of these verbs is typically the target of deprecation, this is not necessarily the case with *ku-u*. When a 19-year old male asks a male friend of a similar age, *meši kuq-ta=ka* 'Have you chowed down yet?', this does not usually imply contempt towards the addressee.

neutral	respectful	humble	anti-honorific	gloss
a-u		o-me=ni kakar-u		'meet'
age-ru		sašiage-ru	yar-u*¹, komas-u*²*³	'give' (centrifugal: §3.10)
ar-u		gozar-u		'exist'
ir-u	iraQšar-u, o-ide=ni nar-u	or-u	kecukar-u*²*³	'be'
i-u	oQšar-u	moos-u, mooš iage-ru	hozak-u, nukas-u, kok-u, kamas-u*³	'say'
ik-u	iraQšar-u, o-ide=ni nar-u	mair-u, ukaga-u		'go'
kari-ru		haišaku+su-ru		'borrow'
ki-ru	o-meš-i=ni nar-u			'wear'
kik-u		ukaga-u, haičoo+su-ru, uketamawar-u		'hear'
ku-ru	iraQšar-u, o-ide=ni nar-u, mie-ru, o-mie=ni nar-u	mair-u		
kure-ru	kudasar-u			'give' (centripetal: §3.10)
mi-ru	go-raɴ=ni nar-u, go-kooraɴ=ni nar-u	haikeɴ+su-ru, haikaɴ+su-ru		'see'
mora-u		itadak-u, tamawar-u, čoodai+su-ru		'receive'
ne-ru	o-yasum-i=ni nar-u		nekusar-u, dobusar-u*³	'sleep'
nom-u	mešiagar-u	itadak-u		'drink'
omo-u ~ šir-u	go-zoɴji=ni nar-u, obošimes-u	zoɴ+ji-ru, zoɴjiager-u		'think, know'
šin-u	nakunar-u, takai+s-are-ru, eimiɴ+su-ru		kutabar-u, ik-u*¹	'die'
su-ru	nasar-u	itas-u	yar-u*¹, saras-u*³	'do'
tabe-ru	mešiagar-u	itadak-u	ku-u*¹	'eat'
uke-ru		uketamawar-u, haiju+su-ru		'accept'
wakar-u		kašikomar-u, šooči+su-ru, uketamawar-u		'assent'
yom-u		haidoku+su-ru		'read'

*¹ not always derogatory depending on context
*² restricted to auxiliary usage (§3.9)
*³ Kansai dialect (§7.9)

Table 6.4: Verbs with separate honorific and anti-honorific counterparts

(1) nani **yaQ-te**=ɴ=da   (← yaQ-te i-ru=ɴ=da)
    what do.AHON-CVB=NMNLZ=COP.NPST (← do.AHON-CVB PROG-NPST=NMNLZ=COP.NPST)
    'What the hell are you doing!?'

(2) aicu=ni=wa   kas-u=kedo   omee=ni=wa   kaši-te
    he.AHON=DAT=TOP   lend-NPST=AVS   you.AHON=DAT=TOP   lend-CVB

    yaN-nee=zo   (← yar-ana-i=zo)
    give.AHON-NEG.NPST=EXCL   (← give.AHON-NEG-NPST=EXCL)
    'I'll lend it to him, but no fucking way will I lend it to you!'

(3) nani   ši-te   kecukaN=neN   (← kecukar-u=neN)
    what   do-CVB   PROG.AHON.NPST=CONF   (← PROG.AHON-NPST=CONF)
    'What the fuck are you doing?'

(4) i-te   komaši-taro=ka   (← komaši-te yar-oo=ka)
    go-CVB   give.AHON-CVB.CJT=Q   (← give.AHON-CVB do.AHON-CJT=Q)
    'You want me to go beat the shit out of you!?'

(5) name-ta   mane   ši+kusaQ-te   šibai-taro=ka
    disparage-PST   behaviour   do.ADV+AHON-CVB   beat-CVB.CJT=Q
    'I oughta beat you to a pulp for pulling that shit!' (see (4) for the underlying
    form of -taro)

(6) zamaa   mi+saras-e
    condition.AHON   look+AHON-IMP
    'That'll fucking show you!'

In Kansai, *saras-u* 'lit. expose' may be used as an anti-honorific form of *su-ru* (but never with a nominal verb: **beNkyoo+saras-u* 'fucking study'), *kecukar-u* (3) used as an anti-honorific of the perfect-progressive auxiliary *-te i-ru* (§3.9) and *-te komas-u* as an anti-honorific of the benefactive auxiliary *-te age-ru* (4). The verbs *saras-u* and *kusar-u* may also directly follow the adverbial, acting as anti-honorific auxiliaries similar to *-(i)yagar-u* in the Standard (§3.8). Their use, illustrated in (5)–(6), is considered extremely impolite and typically limited to only the coarsest of speech. In addition, *docuk-u ~ dozuk-u ~ kačiwar-u ~ šibak-u* (5) *~ iwas-u ~ kamas-u* are all anti-honorific verbs roughly equivalent to *nagur-u* 'punch' or *yaQcuke-ru* 'beat up' in Kansai dialect, but are rarely heard outside stereotypical role language (§6.2): for example, delinquent or gangster speech in anime and other media. As is apparent in (1)–(5), strings of verbal suffixes and particles undergo various types of reduction in rough speech. Similar to *ku-u* above, such reduced forms are not always derogatory.

Anti-honorifics can also be created using affixes (§5.3). The most frequent of these is the verbal prefix *buQ-* (*buN-* before nasals), a reduced form of the verb *buc-u* 'beat'. Thus, the anti-honorific forms of *koros-u* 'kill', *kowas-u* 'break', *nagur-u* 'strike' and *tob-u* 'come flying' are *buQ-koros-u* 'waste, whack', *buQ-kowas-u* 'trash, bust up', *buN-nagur-u* 'beat to shit' and *buQ-tob-u* 'be gobsmacked, freak out'. The nominal suffix *-me* served an analogous function, but such examples are now mostly relegated to role language: *namakemono-me* 'lazy bastard', *hyakušoo-me* 'dumb hick', *usocuki-me* 'fucking liar'. This suffix *-me* should not be confused with the identical adjective (§3.5) and ordinal suffixes (§5.8), neither of which carry any anti-honorific connotation. The pluralizer suffix *-domo* may also bear anti-honorific connotations in some scenarios: see §5.7 for an example.

In terms of phonology, the realization of the phoneme /r/ (§2.1) may act as an anti-honorific. Usually articulated as a tap [ɾ], when articulated as a trill [r] with a pronunciation similar to that found in Spanish *burro*, an utterance may take on a threatening tone deprecating the addressee. Since *rVrV* strings frequently occur in verb suffixes (§3.7), this trilled articulation is most apparent with verbs, and in consequence particularly salient sentence-finally. This 'anti-honorific phonology' is especially marked in the speech of yakuza, but may be employed for effect by any speaker. For the reader interested in studying the phenomenon in greater depth, the movie series *Otoko wa tsurai yo* 'It's Tough Being a Man!' offers excellent material: the *r*-trilling (when he wants to) hero Tora is an itinerant peddler (*tekiya*), a social group whose history is inextricably linked with the yakuza.

The vowel combinations *ai~ae~oi* all possess the anti-honorific long vowel form *ee* (*nee* ← *na-i* 'not', *omee* ← *omae* 'you', *omoširee* ← *omoširo-i* 'funny'), while *ui* possesses the anti-honorific long vowel *ii* (*warii* ← *waru-i* 'bad'). It should be cautioned, however, that the long vowels are not necessarily derogatory but, as with *ku-u* and the reduced forms mentioned above, are often employed for bonding purposes. The frequently encountered *sugee* (for *sugo-i* 'great') is rarely derogatory, for example. Moreover, anti-honorific long vowels are not universally available: *kee* for *koi* 'love' is probably impossible. These long vowels are also features of Tōhoku (§7.10) and Kyūshū (§7.11) dialects, where they do not typically carry any anti-honorific connotations.

6.5 Language in Subculture

There is no shortage of traditional culture in Japan, with Buddhist temples and Shinto shrines on what can seem like every street corner and sumo wrestling matches broadcast regularly on national television. There is no denying, though, that it is the subculture that attracts millions of visitors to Japan each year. While subculture remains a major motivation for studying Japanese, beginners in the language may be surprised to discover that the language in their textbook and that used in manga, anime and gaming are quite different. In this unit, we will focus on the language of one aspect of subculture, gaming—in particular, text-heavy role-playing games (RPGs). We have chosen this medium as its trends are representative for other realms of subculture as well.

6.5 Language in Subculture

One feature which is common across games, manga and anime in general is heavy use of role language (§6.2). Example (1) is an excerpt from a scene in *Final Fantasy IX*, an RPG released by Square (modern day Square Enix) in 2000, in which the main character Zidane is greeted by a pack of dwarves. We place the amusing English localization below.

(1) Male villager: *rarihoQ*
     Zidane: *na, naN=da=yo*
     Male villager: *rariho=wa seinaru aisacu=da=do*
     Female villager: *rariho=mo iw-anee moN=wa kono dowaafu=no sato koNdeya pata=ni=waire-nee=do*

     Male villager: Rally-ho!
     Zidane: Oh, come on…
     Male villager: Rally-ho's oor sacred greetin'!
     Female villager: If ye dinnae say Rally-Ho, then ye cannae enter Conde Petie, hametoon o' the dwarves!

In the Japanese version, these dwarves speak in what looks to be some sort of dialect (§7.7–§7.11), placing the particle *do* at the end of their sentences, using the negative *-(a)nee* instead of the more proper *-(a)na-i* (§3.7) and *moN* in place of *mono* 'thing, person'. All of these traits are characteristic of certain dialects—the discourse particle *do* is found in a number of Tōhoku (§7.10) and Chūbu dialects and the long vowel *ee* for *ai* is observed across many dialects and is common in coarse speech in general (§6.1, §6.4)—but the dwarf speech does not represent any dialect in particular. It simply portrays an image of what one would expect an unsophisticated country bumpkin character to talk like. In other words, the dwarf speech is a form of role language, or what is sometimes referred to as a 'virtual dialect'.

While the dwarf speech in (1) is based on features from actual dialects, there are numerous examples of characters whose speech is not representative of any living language form. For example, the Gorons, a race of mountain dwelling, rock-eating humanoids in *The Legend of Zelda* series by Nintendo, end their sentences with the pseudo-particle *goro*, likely derived from the mimetic (§5.2) *gorogoro* 'rolling around' (as is the name *goroN* itself). Meanwhile, the Moogles, a race of flying feline-like creatures in the *Final Fantasy* series, end their sentences with the pseudo-particle *kupo*, a phonomime of the chirping sound they make in the games. Obviously, neither *goro* nor *kupo* exist in actual speech but are used as an artificial way to bring out the characteristics of these two races. Interestingly, in *The Legend of Zelda: Breath of the Wild* (2017), there is a young, rather timid, Goron by the name of Yunbō (Yunobo in the English localization) who uses *koro* at the end of his sentences instead of *goro*. This variant is a product of sound symbolism, as it is common for the unvoiced variant of a mimetic word to indicate something lighter than its voiced counterpart (cf. *korokoro* 'rolling gently' ~ *gorogoro* 'rolling around heavily'). Another point of interest is how role language is reproduced in English localizations of Japanese games. In (1), for example, the dwarves of Conde Petie use Scots English. On the other hand, the pseudo-particles *kupo* and *goro* are borrowed wholesale into the English localizations. Interestingly, Yunbō's *koro* is rendered as *goro* in the English localization, undoubtedly because the nuanced sound symbolism from the Japanese does not carry over into English.

A phenomenon similar to role language is the use of pseudo-Classical Japanese (§8.7) to portray medieval settings, especially in high fantasy settings and in prophecies. The original *Final Fantasy* (1987), for example, opens with the prophecy given in (2) which contains a number of archaic elements, such as the omission of nominative case marker particles (§3.12)—in Classical Japanese the nominative was typically not marked—and the use of the now extinct verb suffixes *-(i)ši* (empirical past) and *-(a)n* (← *-(a)m-u*: conjectural) (§3.15, Table 3.15.3). The conjectural suffix *-(a)n* happens to be homonymous with the Western Japanese negative suffix *-(a)n* (§3.7, §7.9) and there is a joke among fans that when children from Kansai first played *Final Fantasy* in the late 1980s, they threw their Famicom cassettes at the wall in despair lamenting that their dear heroes would not come forth to save the world.

(2) kono   yo   aNkoku=ni   somar-iši   toki   yo-niN=no
    this   world   darkness=DAT   be.dyed-EPST.ADN   time   4-people=ADNLZ

    hikari=no   seNši   araware-N
    light=ADNLZ   warrior   appear-CJT

    'When the world is veiled in darkness, four warriors of the light shall appear.'

Games also provide an ideal environment for neologisms. These range from the pseudo-Germanic toponyms given to towns and regions in RPGs, such as *arefugarudo* 'Alefgard' (*Dragon Quest*, 1986) or *miQdogaru* 'Midgar' (*Final Fantasy VII*, 1997), to the lengthy names of attack moves strung together using loanword (§7.2) and Sino-Japanese (SJ: §7.1) morphemes in fighting games: *saiko+kuraQšaa+ataQku* 'psycho-crusher-attack' (*Street Fighter II: Champion Edition*, 1992), 前壁加横架推掌 *zeNhekikaookasuišoo* 'front-wall-adding-side-hanging-thrusting-fist' (*Tekken 3*, 1997; translated as 'fortune cookie' in the English localization). The mixing of vocabulary strata (§5.1) is also common (below, SJ morphemes are bolded and loanword morphemes underlined). Examples of two-way hybrids include *hagure+<u>metaru</u>* 'stray metal (slime)' (*Dragon Quest IV*, 1990; 'metal babble' in the English localization) or *kuro+**majucuši*** 'black mage' (*Final Fantasy*), while an example of a three-way hybrid is <u>suupaa</u>+**hyaQkaN**+*otoši* 'super 100 kan smash' (*Street Fighter II Turbo: Hyper Fighting*, 1992; 'sumo smash' in the English localization).

Fig. 6.5: Katakana in graphics pattern table of Dragon Quest
(Borders added by authors)

One point of especial interest is the creation of spell names in the *Dragon Quest* series. While it is common for games to use English loanwords as spell names (*faia* 'fire', *burizaado* 'blizzard', *saNdaa* 'thunder' from the *Final Fantasy* series), *Dragon Quest* famously took an alternate approach by mixing a combination of mimetic elements together with wordplay. For example, the basic healing spell *hoimi* is said to be a combination of the SJ morpheme 保 *ho* 'keep, protect' and the native morpheme *mi* 'body', while the fire attack spells *mera* and *gira* are said to come from the mimetics *meramera* 'burst into flames' and *giraQ(=to)* 'flash quickly and intensely'. Other spells, such as *medapani*, which causes confusion, and *mahotora*, which steals enemy magic, are formed through truncation (§5.6), the former being a back-clipping of ***medama+pani***Qku 'eye+panic', the latter a back-clipping of ***mahoo+torae***-ru 'magic+steal'. Notice how in each of these examples the spell names follow the canonical 2-mora + 2-mora truncation pattern (§5.6).

It is a well-known anecdote amongst fans that the spell names in the first *Dragon Quest* game were constructed using just 20 katakana (31 if we are to include *dakuon* and *handakuon* kana: §4.6) due to memory restrictions, a limitation without which we may have never witnessed the sharp linguistic intuition of the series' creators. Fig. 6.5 shows the numerals and letters section of the *Dragon Quest* graphics pattern table with katakana encircled. Observe how り <ri> and ヘ <he> double as both hiragana and katakana since the corresponding graphs in each syllabary are virtually indistinguishable at such a low resolution.

6.6 Greetings and Partings

Similar to English and many other languages, Standard Japanese has a three-tier system of greeting expressions, consisting of morning, afternoon and evening varieties, with the morning form alone possessing a polite variant. These are illustrated in Table 6.6. The exact chronological boundary between each expression is somewhat vague, with *ohayoo* in use until around 10–11am, *koNničiwa* until around 5pm and *koNbaNwa* any time after that. The morning greeting *ohayoo* is the Western

	morning	afternoon	evening
casual/neutral	ohayoo	koɴničiwa	koɴbaɴwa
polite	ohayoo gozaimasu		

Table 6.6: Japanese greetings

Japanese adverbial form (§7.9) of the adjective *haya-i* 'early' (for the derivation of its polite form, see §6.3) and literally means 'be early'. An example of its polite form *o-hayoo gozar-imas-u* (→ *ohayoo gozaimasu*) being used in this literal sense from the 1802 novel *Tōkaidō-chū hizakurige* 'Travels on the Eastern Seaboard Highway' is shown in (1).

(1) šitaku+su-ru   uči   baɴtoo   ide-te   kore=wa
    preparation+do-NPST   within   inn.keeper   come.out-CVB   this=TOP

    o-hayoo   gozar-imas-u.   kyoo=wa   doQči=e=zo
    HPFX-early.ADV   exist.POL-POL-NPST   today=TOP   where=ALL=Q

    okoši=de   gozar-imas-u=kai=na
    going.POL=CVBLZ   exist.POL-POL-NPST=Q=CONF

    'While the men were making preparations, the innkeeper came out and said, "You sure are up early. Where are you gentlemen planning to go today?"'

This connotation of earliness has been mostly lost in the modern language, with expressions such as *ohayoo gozaimasu, kyoo=mo oso-i=des-u=ne* 'Good morning. You're late as always' being perfectly licit—after its inception, *ohayoo [gozaimasu]* underwent semantic bleaching and formulation into a greeting expression. Meanwhile, *koɴničiwa* and *koɴbaɴwa* are derived from the Sino-Japanese *koɴniči* 'this day' and *koɴbaɴ* 'this night'. Both are observed from Late Middle Japanese (§1.3), but did not undergo formulization until approximately the late 18th century.

In recent years, there has been a trend among the younger generation to use *ohayoo gozaimasu* when greeting superiors regardless of time of day. This development can be attributed to a type of paradigm optimization in which younger cohorts compensate for the lack of polite afternoon and evening greetings by expanding the use of *ohayoo gozaimasu* to cover all times of day. We see a similar development in the rise of the expression *ocukare* as a greeting. This expression, along with its polite counterpart *ocukaresama desu*, literally means 'tiredness'. Examples are attested from the early 20th century which express sympathy towards someone who has completed a difficult task or day of work, similar to American English 'good job'—*ocukare* is still commonly used in this sense today. Over the past two decades, however, the expression has taken on new life as a greeting similar to *ohayoo* or *koɴničiwa* among younger cohorts. The rise of *ocukare* as an all-day greeting expression can also be attributed to paradigm optimization —since it possesses both casual and polite variants, it is ideal for expressing the social relationship between speaker and listener. At the same time, *ocukare* has also come to be used as a parting expression at school or the workplace, in which case it still retains to a degree its lexical meaning.

It is not only younger cohorts who have found a way around the lack of polite afternoon and evening greetings—a number of dialects possess both casual and polite forms for them. Most Tōhoku dialects, for example, use the expressions *obaɴ desu* (polite) and *obaɴ de gozaimasu* (super-polite), both 'lit. it is evening', as evening greetings, while many rural dialects reject formulized greeting expressions altogether, opting for small talk instead, such as *dogo=sa ig-u=no=ša* (Miyagi) or *doke iQkyaQ=to gowas-u=ka* (southern Kyūshū), both 'where are you going?'. Opting to use small talk instead of formulized expressions may be attributable to the convenience of being able to switch between casual and polite forms depending on situation. Finally, when answering the telephone, the greeting *mošimoši*, a truncation of *mooš-i+mooš-i* 'lit. speak, speak', is used regardless of social rank or time of day.

There is perhaps less standardization when it comes to parting expressions. The standard expression is *sayoonara* (also *sayonara*), highly iconic in the West partly due to John Belushi's famous catchphrase 'Sayonara sucker!' in the movie *1941*. One will find after spending some time in Japan, however, that *sayoonara* is actually one of the least used parting expressions. Similar to 'farewell' in English, *sayoonara* bears the connotation that the two parties will not be meeting again for an extended period of time (or ever) and is thus avoided in casual speech in favour of more cordial expressions such as *jaane~matane* 'catch you later', *baibai* 'bye bye', *mata ašita* 'see you tomorrow' or *mata raišuu* 'see you next week'. This is not to say that *sayoonara* is never used, but its use has declined considerably in recent years, especially among younger cohorts. At school or in the workplace, the expressions *ocukaresama desu* (also used in the past tense, *ocukaresama dešita*)—see discussion above—and *osakini šicurei šimasu* 'pardon me for leaving first' are commonly used. Both greetings and partings are typically accompanied by gestures, most commonly a nod of the head or a bow known as an *ojigi*. The degree and length of an *ojigi* varies depending on the social relationship of the greeter and addressee. See §6.7 for further discussion. When greeting equals or inferiors it is common to give a quick wave of the hand and, when parting with family or friends, waving is just as common as it is in the West.

6.7 Non-Verbal Communication

Non-verbal communication (NVC) as exhibited by Japanese acculturated people (and thus the overwhelming majority of Japanese native language speakers) may differ markedly from that employed by the non-Japanese acculturated. NVC may

178   Chapter 6   Language and Society

Fig. 6.7.1: 'Female lover' gesture

Fig. 6.7.2: 'Come here' gesture

be divided into three major types: gestures, facial expressions and greetings (bowing). In this unit, 'Japanese gestures' should be understood to mean 'gestures used by the Japanese acculturated'.

While some gestures are identical for both Japanese and English speakers (nodding and shaking the head to indicate agreement and disagreement, or placing the index finger vertically in front of the lips to indicate silence), many are different. These include pointing to the nose, instead of the middle of the chest, to indicate oneself; raising the little finger to indicate a female lover (Fig. 6.7.1); and waving the hand in front of the face, or crossing the arms into an *X* in front of the body, to indicate 'no good'. Some Japanese gestures run the risk of being misinterpreted by English speakers: a downward beckoning hand to indicate 'come here' (Fig. 6.7.2) may be misconstrued as 'go away'; a circle made by the thumb and index finger to mean money may be misunderstood as 'OK'; and, when the palm faces inwards towards the signer, the so-called 'peace sign' used in photographs, can easily be misinterpreted by English speakers from the British Isles as 'fuck off'. A few gestures used by English speakers have recently started to be used by younger Japanese, as they are now widely taught in school English lessons. These include shrugging the shoulders to show a lack of knowledge and the 'so-so gesture' (making a seesaw movement with the hand at waist level) to show neutral sentiment or mild dissatisfaction.

Differences in facial expression must be viewed not just in terms of their physical manifestation but also in terms of their abstract idealization. These idealizations are apparent in the verbal idioms in which they appear. When it comes to physical manifestation, the smile is probably the most notable point of difference —in Japan the smile is often used as an indicator of embarrassment or inability to express oneself. An example of abstract idealization is narrowing of the eyes: in English distrust, in Japanese happiness. Eye contact is another area in which the English speaking world differs from the Japanese—many Japanese, especially the older generation, find prolonged eye contact difficult. This can be misconstrued by

Fig. 6.7.3: Apology gesture

Fig. 6.7.4: Tegatana *gesture*

an English speaker as a sign of embarrassment, weakness, disinterest or even rudeness.

The use of the bow (*ojigi*) instead of the handshake is perhaps the type of NVC most widely known outside of Japan. As bowing in the West was common among the upper classes until the 19th century and indeed is still employed in certain situations (the stage), it is important to bear in mind that bowing is not a uniquely Japanese phenomenon. That said, it is equally true that, viewed cross-culturally, the bow is at its most alive and well in modern Japan. To sum up in a few lines a subject on which much research has been carried out, we can say the following. Respect can be indexed both by the length of the bow (the number of seconds at which the head is held stationary at its lowest position) and the angle at which the back is bent (the lower the angle, the more the respect). A woman bows with her hands held one over the other in front of her stomach, a man with his hands at his side. Importantly, the bow in Japan is not just a greeting (§6.6), it is also used in religious worship and as an apology (Fig. 6.7.3). Combined with a one-handed chopping gesture while walking, repeated bowing indicates an advance apology for cutting or pushing through. Illustrated in Fig. 6.7.4, this gesture is known as the *tegatana* 'hand sword'.

Beyond the three major divisions discussed above, further differences exist in spatial awareness (the distance between speakers is generally a little greater than for English speakers), physical contact (Japanese culture eschews public kissing and hugging) and in the use and acceptance of silence.

6.8 Attitudes to Language

In the last 150 years or so, attitudes towards Japanese have focused largely on three areas: what to call the Japanese language itself; attitudes towards dialects (§7.8–

§7.11); and, inextricably connected with both of these, the 'spirit', 'purity' and 'uniqueness' of Japanese.

In 2003, one of the most revered academic societies in Japan, the *Kokugo gakkai* (The Society for *Kokugo*—'National Language'—Linguistics) voted to change its name to the *Nihongo gakkai* (The Society for *Nihongo*—'Japanese'—Linguistics). Famous as a bastion of reactionary academia, many of whose membership adhere to the widely criticized notion of 'school grammar' (§8.6), few of whose membership are non-Japanese citizens, the name change marked a seismic shift in language attitudes within higher education. Both 日本語 *nihoNgo* and 国語 *kokugo* (in its current sense) are relatively new words, rarely attested before the early 19th century. Historically, 国語, as used in China and the sinosphere, had the meaning of 'local vernacular' (while now largely obsolete, this meaning is still listed first in most dictionaries). It gradually came to mean the vernacular of a foreign (non-Chinese) state then, in Japan (and also Korea), the vernacular of a particular foreign state, namely Japan (or Korea) itself. As the written standard in Japan moved from Classical Chinese (§1.3, §4.10) to a written form of the Japanese vernacular (§1.3), and as *kokugo* came to designate standard written Japanese as studied and used by speakers of this Japanese vernacular (§8.5), *nihongo* came to be employed for the Japanese language as studied by non-native speakers (§8.8). This dual designation for the same language was bound up with undertones of nationalism and, as we shall see below, was not unrelated to attitudes towards dialects and to notions of 'purity' and 'uniqueness'. Although the 'in-group' *kokugo* is still used in compulsory education to designate Japanese classes, its general demise from academia means that what many view as a divisive term may soon disappear from the schoolroom too.

One of the principal drivers behind the 'national language' notion of *kokugo* was Ueda Kazutoshi (§8.1, §8.12, §8.13), professor at Tokyo Imperial University from 1894 to 1927, whose overtly political agenda also included the creation of a national 'standard language' (*hyōjungo*: §7.7) and, in consequence, the eradication of dialects. From the turn of the 20th century, *hōgenfuda* 'dialect tags' (Fig. 6.8) were put to use in the school system, wooden tags hung as punishment around the necks of children caught speaking dialect. Also employed were 'oral calisthenics', where children gathered *en masse* to enunciate in 'standard' pronunciation, while signs reading 方言撲滅 *hoogeNbokumecu* 'exterminate dialects' were hung in public spaces. Decades of such government policy led to what came to be known as a nationwide 'dialect complex'. During and prior to WWII, the *Kokutai no hongi* 'Cardinal Principles of the National Body', a pamphlet

Fig. 6.8: A dialect tag

containing the official teachings of the Japanese state, including the notion of *kotodama* 'spirit of the language', circulated in large numbers. At the same time, local governments sought to purge English and English loanwords (§8.4).

By the 1970s, when the country had recovered from post-war reconstruction, attitudes of eradication had given way to notions of purity and uniqueness, finding voice in the linguistic subdivision of a genre of literature known as *nihonjinron*. It can perhaps be epitomized by one notorious work, written for the layman by a prominent academic, in which it is claimed repeatedly that Japanese is vague, that much of its vocabulary is untranslatable, and that its culture-related vocabulary is unique. Despite the dubious nature and factual inaccuracies of much of its content, it cannot be denied that *nihonjinron* literature resonates deeply with the general Japanese public, presumably reflecting accurately its attitudes towards language. Such books sell in large quantities and the royalties accrued by their authors provide a lucrative side line.

The retreat of insularity witnessed in recent decades has led to the disappearance of the 'dialect complex' and the retreat of *nihonjinron*. Mass-market books on Japanese have concentrated recently on notions of beauty and, if the content of regular surveys conducted by the Agency for Cultural Affairs is to be believed, the focus of public attitudes towards the Japanese language has shifted to the use of polite language (§6.3) and the influx of loanwords (§7.2, §7.3). In the Agency's most recent survey, more than half of the language-related questions surveyed attitudes towards polite language. These ranged from the specific (*In what situations should junior high school students use polite language towards a teacher?*) to the vague (*How do you see polite language in the future?*). Other questions provide valuable data on ongoing linguistic change, in this case greetings (§6.6): *What is the appropriate way to address a delivery person?* – *ocukaresama* 11% (+4% on 10 years previously); *gokuroosama* 37% (−13%); *arigatoo* 48% (+13%); *doomo* 2% (−2%). Others still are woolly and of dubious academic worth (*Is Japanese important to you?*), or pander to recent publishing trends (*Do you think such a thing as 'beautiful Japanese' exists?*).

6.9 Names

The linguistic study of names is known as onomastics, and can be broadly divided into place names (toponyms) and personal names (anthroponyms). The latter can be further subdivided—in the case of modern Japanese—into family names and given names.

Cross-linguistically, toponyms show a strong tendency to describe their locale. Japanese toponyms largely conform to this trend: Ōsaka 'big slope', Yamagata 'mountain shapes', Tochigi 'chestnut trees'. With very few exceptions (the city, but not the prefecture, of Saitama is one), Japanese toponyms are written in kanji. They are generally two characters long, due in the main to an ancient imperial edict dating from 713 CE. In line with the extremely varied topography of a highly mountainous archipelago, toponyms frequently contain kanji describing common features of the terrain. Exceptions to descriptively derived toponyms include 'capitals' (Tokyo 'eastern capital', Kyoto 'capital city', formerly Saikyō 'western capital' or Kyō 'capital') and, in the extreme north and south of the islands, names of Ainu (Sapporo, Wakkanai) and Ryūkyūan (Naha, Nago) etymology (§7.5). In these last two cases, kanji are used phonographically (so-called *ateji* §4.4).

Nowadays, only those foreign toponyms located within the sinosphere are written in kanji: all others are written in katakana (§4.1). Until the first half of the 20th century, however, many non-sinosphere toponyms were also written in kanji: 智利 *čiri* 'Chile', 巴里 *pari* 'Paris'. Such spellings can still occasionally be encountered today, generally for aesthetic reasons in shop, restaurant, business or brand names. Kanji abbreviations for foreign countries are still employed widely: see §4.1 for examples. Chinese toponyms are generally pronounced according to the Japanese reading of the kanji with which they are written: *koošuu* for 広州 Guangzhou, *bukaɴ* for 武漢 Wuhan. Korean toponyms, on the other hand, tend to be read according to an adaptation of the Korean reading of the kanji: 平壌 *pyoɴyaɴ* 'Pyongyang', 釜山 *pusaɴ* 'Pusan'. More recently, however, some Chinese toponyms have also come to be read this way, as attested by 台北 *taipei* 'Taipei' or 上海 *šaɴhai* 'Shanghai' (§4.4).

Unlike most Western anthroponyms, but in line with the rest of East Asia, Japanese personal names are ordered surname first, given name second. This order may be reversed when overseas or in a Western milieu. In modern Japanese society, middle names are virtually unknown. There are believed to be approximately 130,000 different surnames used in Japan today. The total number cited varies depending on whether orthographic variants are included—some surnames, for example Saitō or Watanabe (§4.3), are notorious for their wide range of alternative spellings—and on whether non-Japanese names are included (on whether the data source is drawn from records of Japanese citizenship or Japanese residency). This large number of surnames is roughly comparable to the UK (considering the two countries' relative populations), but vastly greater than neighbouring countries such as China or the Koreas. While the five most common surnames nationally are Satō, Suzuki, Takahashi, Tanaka and Itō, all with over one million holders each, strong regional variation is apparent. In Metropolitan Ōsaka, for example, the three most common surnames are Tanaka, Yamamoto and Nakamura; while in Miyazaki Prefecture they are Kuroki, Kawano and Kai. As an indication of the geographical source of historical emigration, the most common Japanese surnames in Hawaii are Nakamura and Ōshiro.

There is no reliable data on the number of given names, though a glance at any roster, roll or name list makes the richness apparent. Here, generational variation is starker than regional variation, an example being the huge decline, evident in recent decades, in female names ending in *-ko* 子 'child' and male names ending in *-roo* 郎 'man'. In 2018 the three most common male names registered for babies were Ren, Minato and Hiroto; the three most common female baby names Yuzuki, Yua and Yuina/Yuna. Male given names frequently use the *on-yomi* kanji reading, female names the *kun-yomi* (§4.4), making long vowels more frequent in male names, rarer in female. Male names tend to be written with kanji evoking images of strength, steadfastness, loyalty and study; female names in hiragana or in kanji evoking beauty, nature, jewels and fragrance.

Although surnames are now known as *myōji* or *sei*, formerly these two were distinguished while, in addition, other types of naming device were employed, such as *uji* or *kabane* (both a type of clan name) and *kakibe* (a name indicating feudal servitude, roughly equivalent to the English Jones 'of John' or Roberts 'of Robert'). Until 1870, the formal use of surnames was forbidden for ordinary Japanese, with only the nobility and the samurai classes permitted them. Shortly thereafter, the government ordered all Japanese to adopt a surname. Many people who did not already have an informal one sought help from priests at the local temple or made one up themselves, often describing the location in which they lived. For this reason, the majority of Japanese surnames are toponyms, 'locality labels' or, since most toponyms also have a descriptive etymology, very often both. Locality label kanji such as those in (1) occur in different combinations across many thousands of surnames. Many Japanese who already possessed a formal surname held one connected to the 藤原 Fujiwara clan, hence the prominence of the kanji 藤 'wisteria', usually pronounced *too~doo*, and less commonly *fuji*, in many surnames: 佐藤 Satō, 近藤 Kondō, 加藤 Katō, 藤田 Fujita. Such names constitute the major exception to the 'toponym or locality label' surname norm.

(1) 田 'rice paddy'   竹 'bamboo'   小 'small'
   野~原 'field'   森 'forest'   大 'large'
   川~河~沢 'river~stream'   林 'woods'   高 'high'
   池 'pond'   坂 'slope'   中 'middle'
   石 'stone'   岡 'hill'   内 'inside'
   水 'water'   山 'mountain' 前 'in front of'
   土 'earth'   谷 'valley'   上 'upper'
   木 'tree'   島 'island'   下 'lower'
   松 'pine'   村 'village' 本 'main'
   杉 'cedar'   寺 'temple'

The Japanese emperor and the imperial family have no surname. Formerly, it was considered discourteous or even taboo to call a person by their given name: this is still the case with the emperor. Although known by his given name overseas (Akihito, Hirohito), within Japan an emperor is simply called *teNnooheika~kiNjooteNnoo* 'His Majesty the Emperor' while on the throne and, after death, identified by his reign name (Heisei, Shōwa). Currently, an individual emperor has only one reign name throughout his time on the throne, but prior to Emperor Meiji (reigned 1867–1912) it was common for a given emperor to have several.

Most surnames are written with two kanji, although those with a single kanji (林 Hayashi, 辻 Tsuji) and those written with three kanji (佐々木 Sasaki, 小野寺 Onodera) are not uncommon. Surnames with four or more kanji (日根野谷 Hinenoya, 左衛門三郎 Saemonsaburō) are unusual. Exactly the same comments apply to given names, although the proportion of 2-kanji female names is probably higher than 2-kanji male names. The kanji that can be used in a new given name are restricted by law, not only by limiting them to the 2,136 currently in the *jōyōkanjihyō* and the 863 in the *jinmeiyō* kanji lists (§8.2), but also by banning certain words and kanji combinations, such as 悪魔 *akuma* 'devil'.

As well as a name's traditional kanji/kana spelling, Japanese names must also be written in the Roman alphabet for use overseas, or for use in Japan with credit cards and passports, something which has created a host of privacy and security issues (§4.7). As noted already, many surnames have multiple kanji spellings: the same applies, though even more so, to given names, especially male (see §4.4 for an example). The opposite is also true: many spellings have multiple pronunciations. A particularly egregious example is the surname 東海林, which can be Shōji~Shōshi~Tōkairin. There is also a strong tendency for rendaku (§5.5) to apply to surnames in eastern Japan, but not in the West: 山崎, for example, is generally Yamazaki in Tokyo, but Yamasaki in Kyoto. Since it is never obvious how a person's name is to be pronounced—even an everyday name such as 山本俊介 could in theory be read as something other than Yamamoto Shunsuke—it is standard practice in Japan to employ *furigana* (§4.10) in application forms, registration documents and records. Until relatively recently, those naturalizing to Japanese citizenship were legally required to adopt a Japanese name. Although this is no longer the case, many still do so to ease assimilation or avoid discrimination.

CHAPTER 7 Language Contact and Dialects

7.1 Sino-Japanese

Over the past two millennia, the Japanese have borrowed a wealth of vocabulary from Classical Chinese (CC) and, in addition, coined countless words of their own using 'morphemes' borrowed from CC. This vocabulary stratum (§5.1), consisting of both borrowed and coined words, is collectively referred to as Sino-Japanese (hereafter SJ) or, in Japanese, *kango* 'CC words'. SJ vocabulary makes up a significant percentage of the Japanese lexical inventory, with a 2 million token survey of 70 magazines published in 1994 placing the type ratio of SJ at 34% of all vocabulary. SJ vocabulary permeates nearly every semantic sphere of the language, from the cultural vocabulary listed in §5.1, through numerals (一 *iči* 'one', 二 *ni* 'two': §5.8) and greetings (今日は *koNničiwa* 'good afternoon', 今晩は *koNbaNwa* 'good evening': §6.6), to names (§6.9), both family (佐藤 *satoo* 'Satō') and given (大 *dai* 'Dai'). Chinese characters are generally said to have been introduced to Japan some time between the 1st and 4th century CE (§4.2) and, while there do exist a number of loans predating their adoption (*uma* 'horse' ← Old Chinese (OC) 馬 **mˤraʔ*, *ume* 'plum' ← OC 梅 **C.mˤə*), such preliterate loans are far outnumbered by 'learned borrowings'—loans absorbed through the medium of Classical Chinese (CC). Due to their high degree of assimilation, preliterate borrowings are typically treated as part of the native stratum (§5.1).

The use of the term 'morpheme'—in this unit and elsewhere in this book—to describe the unit of language expressed by a single kanji is in several ways problematic. Not all 'SJ morphemes' are capable of expressing meaning on their own—at least in the traditional sense. Take, for example, the 'morphemes' 経 *kei* and 営 *ei* which make up 経営 *keiei* 'management'. The character 経 possesses the meanings 'pass through, elapse, manage' and occurs elsewhere in SJ words such as 経済 *keizai* 'economy'. Meanwhile, 営 has the meanings 'carry out, operate' and occurs elsewhere in, for example, 営業 *eigyoo* 'business'. Divorced from their kanji notation, however, the utterances *kei* or *ei* are at best ambiguous, at worst unintelligible. When referring to SJ morphemes, we refer thus not to the traditional morpheme (discussed in §3.1), but a bundled unit of sound, meaning and notation.

The majority of SJ words are 'binoms', written with two kanji: 天国 *teNgoku* 'heaven', 地獄 *jigoku* 'hell'. Mononoms—single-kanji morphemes—also exist (癌 *gaN* 'cancer', 五 *go* 'five'), as do trinoms, although these often consist of a binom+affix (無責任 *mu-sekinin* 'irresponsibility', 責任者 *sekinin-ša* '**person** responsible': §5.3). These binoms and mononoms can then be compounded (§5.4), 4-character binom+binom compounds being particularly common (刑事責任 *keiji+sekinin* 'criminal liability', 責任問題 *sekinin+mondai* 'question of who is to blame'), especially so in idioms borrowed from CC (温故知新 *on+ko+či+šin* 'learning from the past') or coined in Japan (順風満帆 *junpuu+manpan* 'smooth sailing').

As with other foreign borrowings (§7.2), SJ vocabulary is typically limited to nouns, nominal adjectives and nominal verbs (勉強 *benkyoo+su-ru* 'study': §3.3). There also exist a number of SJ adverbs (突然 *tocuzen* 'suddenly', 随分 *zuibun* 'significantly') and conjunctions (乃至 *naiši* 'or', 一方 *ippoo* 'on the other hand'). SJ is also commonly employed in affixes: the prefixes 不 *fu*, 非 *hi* 'non-', 御 *go~gyo* 'honorific' (§6.3); the suffixes 的 *teki* '-like, -wise', 性 *sei* '-ness', 風 *fuu* '-style'. While such affixes most commonly attach to SJ nouns, there is no lack of examples of them being used with the native and foreign lexicon as well: *fu-barai* '**un**paid', *hi-ion-sei* '**non**-ionic', *furansu-fuu* 'French-**style**'.

Examples of SJ are sparse in Old Japanese (§1.3), though this is largely due to a lack of sources—by Middle Japanese (§1.3) examples are plentiful in the native literature. These increase even more by Modern Japanese, increasing exponentially from the mid-19th century when numerous new SJ words were coined to express novel scientific and cultural concepts from the West: 哲学 *tecugaku* 'philosophy', 大学院 *daigakuin* 'graduate school'. These made-in-Japan SJ words make up a substantial portion of the modern SJ lexicon, with new coinages being added to the arsenal every day. Known in Japanese as *waseikango* 'made-in-Japan CC words', they are referred to here as 'pseudo-sinicisms'. In many cases, Japanese pseudo-sinicisms have been 'reimported' into Chinese topolects or borrowed into Korean (§7.6). Likewise, neologisms from Chinese topolects have also been borrowed into Japanese in modern times. Usually, these are given traditional Japanese kanji readings (§4.4). There are, however, examples of pronunciations from Chinese topolects being borrowed in Japanese with 'contemporary' pronunciations. Such modern renderings are typically treated as loanwords and distinguished from SJ proper (§6.9, §7.2). The abundance of pseudo-sinicisms can be attributed to the high word-building potential of SJ morphemes. Take the term 相対性理論 *sootaiseiriron* 'theory of relativity (lit. mutually-opposing-attribute theory)', for example. The same compound using native morphemes only would run something like **ai+muka-u sama=no kotowari* 'theory of the attribute of facing one another', which is both lengthy and ambiguous compared to the SJ alternative. Another reason for the high prevalence of pseudo-sinicisms stems from the general academic prestige attributed to such vocabulary, similar to that of Ancient Greek or Latin vocabulary in English and other European languages. Thus, just as classical morphemes play a crucial role the formation of novel scientific terms in European languages, SJ morphemes play a similar role in Japanese.

In addition to being a major source of vocabulary in itself, CC also acted as a vessel for the introduction of Sanskrit loanwords through the transmission of Buddhist texts. The majority of Sanskrit loanwords are limited to Buddhist contexts: 菩提 *bodai* 'enlightenment' ← *bodhi*, 阿羅漢 *arakaN* 'worthy one' ← nominative of *arhat*, *arhan*. Nevertheless, a number of words have worked their way into common speech: 旦那 *daNna* 'husband' (a truncation (§5.6) of *dānapati*, originally 'almsgiver'), 刹那 *secuna* 'instant' (← *kṣaṇa*), 魔羅 *mara* 'penis' (← *māra*, originally 'demon of temptation'). There are also a small number of loans seemingly borrowed directly from Sanskrit (*ama* 'nun' ← *ambā*, *kawara* 'clay tile' ← *kapāla*) although, similar to preliterate Chinese borrowings, such loans are few and far between. Perhaps more numerous than actual Sanskrit loans are Chinese calques (or loan translations) modelled after Sanskrit vocabulary and subsequently borrowed into Japanese. In many cases, there even exist both a transliteration and calque for the same term: 陀羅尼 *darani* ~ 総持 *sooji* 'all+hold', a transliteration and calque, respectively, of *dhāraṇī* 'incantation (lit. holding)'.

Also important are so-called 'imitations': reproductions of foreign words and grammatical structures using native morphemes. For SJ, these include (1)–(4). Such imitations are particularly numerous in academic writing, as this register (§6.2) draws heavily from the *kanbun kundoku* tradition (§1.3, §4.4). Such tactics were also employed during WWII and the loanword prohibition period (§8.4).

(1) LOAN TRANSLATIONS. A Chinese word is reproduced morpheme by morpheme using native morphemes: CC 光耀 'shine+glisten' → *hikar-i+kagayak-u* 'shine and glisten'.

(2) LOAN MEANINGS. A novel sense is carried over into a native word based on a Chinese model: *ucus-u* 'transfer' used in the sense 'transcribe', after CC 写 'transfer, transcribe'.

(3) LOAN DERIVATIONS. A native Japanese word undergoes a functional extension through derivation based on a Chinese model: *oyobi* 'and' (the nominalized form (§3.7) of *oyob-u* 'reach'), used as a conjunction based on CC 及 'reach, and' (§3.11).

(4) LOAN SYNTAX. A Chinese syntactic construction is replicated in Japanese: a shift from SOV to SVO word order in translations of CC (*ši iw-aku* 'Confucius says', where *iw-aku* is the nominalized form of *i-u* 'say': see §8.7 for an example).

SJ lexemes possess distinct phonotactics (§2.5) that set them apart from other vocabulary strata. These are complex and summarized in Table 7.1. An SJ morpheme consists of either one or two moras (μ: §2.4). Or, put another way, the SJ reading (§4.4) assigned a kanji must be 1μ~2μ, never longer. This results in a large number of homophones, some pernicious, leading to comprehension issues (§5.9). An SJ morpheme may begin, amongst others, in a voiced obstruent (§2.2) or in *r*, both of which are illicit or quasi-illicit in the native stratum (Table 2.5.2); and it may

first mora	second mora
• checked cells in Table 2.5.1, though some accidental gaps • h~f → p when preceded by SJ morpheme ending in N~Q	• ø (no second mora): 車 ša, 外 ge, 胃 i, 無 mu, 魚 gyo • V: 中 čuu, 某 boo, 例 rei, 賄 wai, 追 cui • CV: 百 hyaku, 罰 bacu, 駅 eki, 一 iči (may → Q when followed by SJ morpheme beginning in t~c~č~k~s~š or h~f (→ p)) • N: 感 kaN, 貪 doN, 品 hiN, 雲 uN, 元 geN

Table 7.1: Phonotactics of SJ morphemes

contain a *y*-glide (§2.4), mora consonant (§2.4), long vowel or diphthong (§2.3), all of which were historically illicit in the native stratum (§2.9). Its initial mora displays accidental gaps (§2.5): the 1μ-morphemes *mya* and *re*, for example, are not found; the same applies to *byu* or *myu*, which are not found as the initial mora of a 2μ-morpheme either. The second mora of an SJ morpheme, where it exists, may be (with a tiny number of exceptions) a single vowel *i~u~o* (V in Table 7.1), *ki~ku~či~cu* (CV in Table 7.1) or the mora nasal *N* (§2.4). When word-internal and followed by another SJ morpheme beginning in *t~c~č~k~s~š*, a CV second mora may, under certain conditions which space precludes us from detailing, become the mora obstruent *Q* (§2.4), as in (1)–(2). When word-internal and preceded by another SJ morpheme ending in a mora nasal *N*, an initial mora beginning in *h~f* becomes *p*, as in (3)–(4). When a CV second mora is followed by an initial mora beginning in *h~f*, both these processes may combine, as in (5)–(6). When compound-, rather than word-internal, both these processes typically fail to occur, however, as illustrated in (7)–(8).

(1) 白米 hakumai 'polished rice' ~ 白金 haQkiN 'platinum'
(2) 日常 ničijoo 'daily' ~ 日産 niQsaN 'Nissan'
(3) 整髪 seihacu 'hairdressing' ~ 金髪 kiNpacu 'blonde'
(4) 台風 taifuu 'typhoon' ~ 旋風 seNpuu 'whirlwind'
(5) 鉄道 tecudoo 'railway' ~ 甲板 koohaN 'deck' ~ 鉄板 teQpaN 'griddle'
(6) 切断 secudaN 'amputation' ~ 開腹 kaifuku 'laparotomy' ~ 切腹 seQpuku 'disembowelment'
(7) 地下鉄工事 čikatecu+kooji, not *čikateQ+kooji 'subway construction work'
(8) 人件費 jiNkeN+hi, not *jiNkeN+pi 'personnel costs'

7.2 Foreign Borrowings

Foreign borrowings, known as *gairaigo* in Japanese, can be defined in many ways. The definition we will use here is: a word borrowed into Japanese after the mid-16th century which has undergone adaptation to Japanese phonology. Words

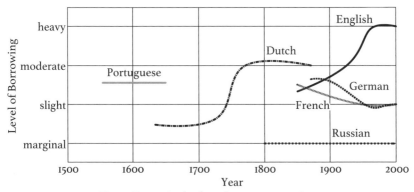

Fig. 7.2: *Borrowing by donor language across time*

borrowed before the mid-16th century are almost all from Chinese and these we deem Sino-Japanese (SJ: §7.1). Those not adapted to Japanese phonology must be considered *gaikokugo*, or 'foreign words'.

The mid-16th century has been chosen as a cut-off point for our definition because this was the date of Japan's first regular contact with the Western world: in 1543 Portuguese sailors landed on the small island of Tanegashima, now part of Kagoshima Prefecture. This marks the first of the three broad streams into which Japanese loanword history can be divided. This first phase, the Iberian, runs from the mid-16th to mid-17th century and was initiated by Portuguese-speaking Jesuits (§1.3, §8.13), followed by Spanish-speaking missionaries and other foreign merchants. The bulk of the loans in this period are from Portuguese: *paN* 'communion wafer (later bread)' ← *pão*, *botaN* 'button' ← *botão*. After the *sakoku* laws (the isolationist policies of the Tokugawa Shogunate enacted in 1633, lifted in 1853), the Dutch merchants permitted to remain in Nagasaki drove the second loanword phase: *biiru* 'beer' ← *bier*, *gomu* 'rubber' ← *gom*. During its two centuries, the Japanese absorbed contemporary European scientific learning via Dutch texts, a practice known in the Japanese tradition as *rangaku* 'Dutch learning'. Running from the mid-19th century to the present day, the most recent 'Western' phase refers initially to the languages of the 19th century European Great Powers— Russian (*seeuči* 'sea lion' ← сивуч (*sivuch*), *kačuuša* 'hairband' ← катюша (*katyusha*), French (*puči* 'small' ← *petit*, *biniiru* 'plastic' ← *vinyle*), German (*genomu* 'genome' ← *Genom*, *gereNde* 'piste' ← *Gelände*) and English (*keesu* 'case', *orieNteešoN* 'orientation') —but more recently, with the rise of American economic and political power, almost exclusively to American English (§7.3). Fig. 7.2 is a rough schematization of the level of borrowing from the main donor languages during these three phases. Not shown are borrowings from other Western languages, such as Spanish (*gerira* 'guerrilla' ← *guerrilla*) or Italian (*esupureqso* 'espresso' ← *espresso*), as well as from modern Chinese topolects (*raiči* 'lychee' ← Cantonese 荔枝 *lai⁶zi¹*, *čaahaN* ←

Mandarin 炒飯 *chǎofàn*: §4.4), Korean (*haNguru* 'Korean alphabet, Korean language' ← *hangeul*), Arabic (*jihaado* 'jihad' ← [dʒihaːd]) or Ainu (*šišamo* 'smelt' ← *susam*).

Since the second loanword phase, foreign words have, in most cases, been borrowed into Japanese via writing. These 'orthographic borrowings' have been, and still are, adapted to Japanese phonology by means of dictionary traditions, whose rules were established and standardized by Japanese scholars of foreign languages, then perpetuated through their pedagogical practices and foreign language textbooks. The two main adaptation strategies are phonic substitution and epenthesis. In phonic substitution a Japanese speaker attempts to replace a sound in a donor language with one in her native language: *raibu* 'live concert' ← English 'live' (Japanese has no *l* or *v*). Epenthesis, meanwhile, is the insertion of additional phonemes (§2.1) by the borrowing language. Since the Japanese syllable (§2.4) must either end in a vowel or mora consonant (N~Q: §2.4), the closed syllables and consonant clusters found frequently in donor words are dealt with by means of inserting a vowel: *kurisumasu* 'Christmas'.

Once borrowed, the vast majority of foreign borrowings function as nouns, although a few function as verbs, adjectives or adverbs. Verbs generally take the verbalizer *su-ru* 'do' (*aQpu+su-ru* 'increase' ← Eng. 'up'), though a small number take the suffix *-ru* (*memo-ru* 'jot down' ← Eng. 'memo': see §3.3 for further discussion). Adjectives, meanwhile, take the particle *na* to form nominal adjectives (*furii=na jikaN* 'free time': §3.5) and adverbs the particle *ni* (*haado=ni* 'in a hard way': §3.5). Affixes (§5.3) may be attached to foreign borrowings (*surimu-ka* 'downsizing' ← Eng. 'slim' + SJ *-ka* '-ization'), while foreign borrowings may themselves function as affixes (*mai-beya* 'My Room (name of real estate company)' ← Eng. *my* + native *heya* 'room'). With English borrowings especially, loanwords may be compounded (§5.4), these compounds then frequently truncated in various ways (§5.6).

While previously there was more variation, foreign borrowings are now generally written in katakana, though there do exist a small number of exceptions (珈琲 *koohii* 'coffee' ← Dutch *koffie*, 倶楽部 *kurabu* 'club' ← Eng. *club*), especially those borrowed from modern Chinese topolects (麻雀 *maajaN* 'mahjong' ← Mandarin *májiàng*, 飲茶 *yamuča* 'dimsum' ← Cantonese *yam²cha⁴*). Recently, the Roman alphabet (§4.7) is being used more and more for writing foreign borrowings, especially with initialisms, some borrowed directly (*UFO*, *pH*), others created in Japan (*1LDK* 'apartment with 1 bedroom, living room, dining room and kitchen', *IC* 'motorway interchange').

7.3 English Borrowings

The English had a trading post at Hirado (modern Nagasaki Prefecture) between 1613 and 1623, from which time dates the oldest English loanword, *gereborotaN* (now *gureetoburiteN*) 'Great Britain'. However, English loans did not begin to appear in any significant number until the mid-19th century, along with sailors' pidgins (*hoteru* 'hotel', *hausu* 'greenhouse, glasshouse') in Nagasaki and Yokohama (§7.4) and the arrival in 1853 of US Commodore Perry and his Black Ships. An influx of loanwords related to American trends in sports (*faN* 'fan', *riigu* 'league'), fashion (*suucu* 'suit', *burausu* 'blouse') and music (*jazu* 'jazz', *metoronoomu* 'metronome') in the early 20th century ushered in a shift from UK to US English. This influx of borrowings was punctuated by government propaganda campaigns against the English language from 1941, with English branded a 'hostile language' (§8.4). With the post-war US occupation, borrowing intensified (*saNgurasu* 'sunglasses', *puraibašii* 'privacy') and has continued to do so with globalization (*fasutofuudo* 'fast food', *rejaa* 'leisure') and current Japanese government education policy which, until the early 21st century, ignored all varieties of English other than General American.

In the late 19th and very early 20th century, English donor words accounted for just over half of all loans, though this proportion had grown to around 75% by the 1950s (Fig. 7.2). Since the 1960s, it has hovered virtually unchanged at around 85%, while at the same time the share of other donor languages has plummeted, often drastically. Now, it is no exaggeration to say that any English word or phrase is fair game for borrowing. Not unconnected is the rise of what are referred to in Japanese as *waseieigo* 'pseudo-anglicisms' (cf. pseudo-sinicisms, §7.1): *bebii+saakuru* 'playpen' ← 'baby+circle', *beQdo+tauN* 'commuter town' ← 'bed+town'. These describe a number of morphosyntactic phenomena, including truncation (§5.6), compounding (§5.4) and semantic shift (*komiQšoN* 'kickback' ← Eng. 'commission', *kureemu* 'complaint' ← Eng. 'claim'). As there exists a strong tendency for any loanword to be viewed as having an English source, the term *waseieigo* may be erroneously used to describe words whose components have been borrowed from German, French or wherever.

One mark of the power of English loanwords is that they are not, as with other donor languages, overwhelmingly borrowed from nouns and verbs, but also from adjectives and adverbs (*riizunaburu* 'reasonable', *haQpii* 'happy'), greetings and interjections (*baibai* 'bye', *ookee~oQkee* 'OK'), prepositions (*aQpu* 'up', *auto* 'out'), numbers (*cuu* 'two', *faasuto* 'first'), pronouns (*mai* 'my', *ooru* 'all'), affixes (*iNtaa* 'inter-', *izumu* '-ism'), and even articles (*za~ji* 'the') or conjunctions (*aNdooa* 'and/or'). They have permeated the language to such an extent that they constitute some of the first words children acquire (*mama* 'mummy', *papa* 'daddy'). English loanwords have also exerted their power in the recent rise of the Roman alphabet (based on English spelling conventions: §4.7) and, even more recently, abbreviations written in this script. Now commonplace are what may be termed 'pseudo-English initialisms', formed through a process whereby a pseudo-anglicism is converted into Roman spelling and then abbreviated: ゴールデンウィーク *gooruden+wiiku* 'golden week (series of national holidays in early May)' → <Golden

Week> → <GW> (neither *golden week* nor *GW* exist in English in a sense similar to the Japanese).

Much has been written about how Japanese has, since WWII, succumbed to a 'deluge' of English loans. While such a deluge is quite possibly an illusion created by the comparatively short lifespan of the average loan, a range of surveys, many conducted by government agencies, has returned a low level of positive responses to loanwords in general. By 2002, this had spurred the government to establish a Loanword Committee whose brief was to submit loanword replacements (§8.3). Very few of these have found their way into everyday use and the number of English loans continues to grow, spurred on ironically by politicians and government agencies who greatly value their powers of obfuscation and ambiguity (*nookomeNto* 'no comment').

Just as imitation played a major role in Sino-Japanese borrowings (SJ: §7.1), similar tactics have been employed for English. Loan translation (both direct and approximate) and semantic borrowing in particular were common tactics in the late 20th century for coining novel terms related to Western culture and science. Examples of direct (morpheme-by-morpheme) loan translations from English include 幹線 *kaNseN* 'trunk line' ← 幹 'trunk' + 線 'line' (also in 新幹線 *šiNkaNseN* 'bullet train (lit. new trunk line)') and 外野 *gaiya* 'outfield (baseball)' ← 外 'outside' + 野 'field'. Approximate loan translations include 摩天楼 *mateNroo* 'skyscraper' ← 摩 'scraping' + 天 'heavens, sky' + 楼 'tower' and 燕尾服 *eNbifuku* 'swallow-tailed coat' ← 燕 'swallow' + 尾 'tail' + 服 'clothes'. A well-known example of semantic borrowing is 愛 *ai*, which originally expressed 'affection' or 'lust', but borrowed the meaning 'love' (in the sense of ancient Greek *agape* or *eros*) from English. These imitation examples all employ SJ morphemes. While fewer in number, native morphemes (§5.1) may also be found: *uwagaki* 'overwrite (a file)' ← *uwa* 'above' + *gaki* 'writing' is an example of a loan translation, while the computer jargon (§5.10) *war-u* 'crack', in the sense of 'manipulating a piece of software', is an example of a loan meaning. Government language policy (§8.3, §8.4) is also a common driving force for such imitational borrowing tactics.

7.4 Japanese Pidgins and Creoles

In some areas of the world, where people have no shared native language, a 'third-party' language is employed as a means of communication. This language, known as a lingua franca, may not be indigenous to the region in question and instead learned via formal education (English in India); or it may be indigenous to some (usually a small part) of the region and have gained its status as lingua franca through trade (Swahili in East Africa), cultural prestige (Latin in Europe until recently) or political dominance (Mandarin in non-Mandarin speaking areas of China). In all such cases, there exists a competence continuum running from native speaker (where available) through native-like competence, to 'working knowledge', and finally to 'extremely rough and ready'. Although social and educational factors may also play a role, native-like competence is generally found in areas geographically most proximate to the lingua franca.

When speakers in the last, least competent, category are required to speak the lingua franca they will subject a 'foreigner-talk' version (the version in which they are typically addressed by a more competent speaker) to radical simplification: verbs and nouns are shorn of endings, word order is distorted and pronunciation approximates the speaker's mother tongue. This process of radical simplification is known as pidginization. When such a radically simplified language stabilizes and comes to be learnt itself as a lingua franca, it is known as a pidgin. Pidgins thus have no native speakers. When, however, children grow up acquiring the pidgin language around them, it complexifies into what is known as a creole, which does have native speakers. While many pidgins were based on English, French, Spanish or Portuguese, colonies of foreigners living in designated trading ports in Japan, as well as Japanese colonization in East Asia from the late 19th century, have produced Japanese-based pidgins and creoles. Pidgins were also used by English-speaking soldiers garrisoned in Japan during the post-WWII occupation period, and pidgins are still spoken today by some migrant workers.

The earliest recorded pidgin spoken on Japanese soil is the Nagasaki Pidgin, spoken by Portuguese and Spanish missionaries, and later Dutch traders, from the late 16th century. Later, after Japan opened to the West in 1859, non-Japanese nationals could lease land, build and trade in an area of Yokohama known as the *gaikokujin kyoryūchi* 'foreign concession'. By 1893, it is estimated that just under 5,000 foreign nationals resided in the area, the majority Chinese, with much of the remainder English-speaking British or Americans. The area was formally closed in 1899. The Japanese-based pidgin that was spawned in this milieu was known as Yokohama Pidgin Japanese (YPJ), with most available data reliant on a pamphlet published in 1879. Since YPJ is written using English spelling conventions, and real English words where extant, it is difficult to know how it was pronounced: presumably, however, with an English phonology. The local Japanese dialect feature of vowel devoicing (§2.3, §7.9) can be seen from words such as *shto* 'person' (← *hito*) or *stoats* 'one' (← *hitocu*). Simplification was commonplace: case marker particles (§3.12) were dropped; tense and aspect (§3.4) were generally lacking; *die-job* (← *daijoobui* 'OK') was used for any word or phrase meaning 'good'. Compounds (§5.4) were right-headed, as in Japanese, and appear without rendaku (§5.5) or apophony (§5.4): *ah-kye kimono shto* (← *aka-i kimono hito*) 'soldier (lit. red-clothes-person)'. Word order was, as in Japanese, SOV (§3.1), with the negative markers *nigh~arimasen* following the verb: *oh-my nangeye tokey high-kin nigh* (← *omae naga-i toki haikeɴ na-i*) 'haven't seen you in ages'. Finally, not all vocabulary was from Japanese: *bynebai* (← English *bye and bye*), for example, was used as a future marker, while *come-here* (borrowed into Japanese as *kame[ya]*) was the word for 'dog'.

On a somewhat smaller scale than YPJ was Bamboo English, a pidgin spoken by the, predominantly, American military stationed in Japan during the 1945–1952 occupation. Much of the vocabulary recorded for this pidgin is related to entertainment and nightlife (for which read alcohol and prostitution), the focus of linguistic contact between local Japanese and their English-speaking occupiers: *anone* 'hey!', *dai jobu* 'OK', *hayaku* 'quick!', *ichiban* 'best', *josan* 'girl', *morskosh* 'soon' (← *moo sukoši* 'a little more'), *mus* 'girlfriend' (← *musume* 'girl') and *skoshi* 'small' (← *sukoši* 'a little'). How much of this pidgin survives today in the US bases still dotted around Japan is unknown.

Moving outside Japan, Yilan Creole first appeared in the 1930s in Yilan county in north-eastern Taiwan, whose local inhabitants are mostly speakers of Atayal. It is pronounced with a mainly Atayal phonology, its vocabulary estimated to be around 65% Japanese (*anta* 'you', *oru* 'be', *ski* 'like', *taru* 'suffice', *wasi* 'I'). The negative marker is *cigo* (← *čiga-u* 'be mistaken').

In contrast to the Japanese-based pidgins examined above, Bonin Creole English with Japanese input, is spoken on the Ogasawara Islands. Japanese vocabulary found in this creole includes *morokoshi* 'corn', *muguru* 'dive' and *hibo* 'rope', all borrowed from dialects but *toomorokoši*, *mogur-u* and *himo* in the Standard. Another, better known, English-based creole with large-scale Japanese input appeared in the last quarter of the 19th and first quarter of the 20th centuries, when an estimated 100,000 or more Japanese, mainly from Hiroshima and Yamaguchi Prefectures, emigrated to Hawaii as agricultural labourers. It is assumed, due to the relatively low socio-economic status of most emigrants worldwide at this time, that most were speakers of local dialects (§7.8–§7.11), rather than Standard Japanese. Japanese were not only the source of immigrant labour to Hawaii, which also included Chinese, Koreans and Filipinos, but the Chūgoku dialects (of which Hiroshima and Yamaguchi form a part) made a major contribution to the Hawaii Creole English that grew out of this multi-ethnic multilingual immigrant pool. Sometimes also known as Hawaiian Japanese, conspicuously Japanese lexical items include *boroboros* 'dirty clothes, rags' (← *boroboro* 'dirty, ragged'), *hanakuso* 'snot', *hashi* 'chopsticks', *shishi* 'pee', *skebe* 'horny' (← *sukebe* 'lecher'), *skosh* 'just a little' (← *sukoši* 'a little') and *zori* 'flip-flops'. Words from local Chūgoku dialects include *bobora* 'pumpkin, Japanese hick straight off the boat' (← *boobura~bobura~bobora*), *girigiri* 'cowlick', *habuts* 'pout' (← *habute-ru*), *hoito* 'selfish person' (← *hoito* 'beggar') and *menpachi* 'squirrelfish, person with big round eyes'.

7.5 Language Murder

Language death, though in all probability having picked up speed in the last couple of centuries, is not a new phenomenon. It has occurred throughout recorded history—we know, for example, that Latin wiped out several languages on the Italian peninsula and elsewhere—and throughout the world. Death may be gradual or sudden. Languages may die through persecution, genocide, population collapse, forced resettlement, rapid economic, cultural or climatic change, or for many other reasons. In cases where an outside language is largely responsible for a language's demise, the process may be referred to as 'language murder'. Although some linguists reserve this term only for cases of persecution leading to death, here we will use a broader definition, employing the term when the cause of death is economic or cultural also. Unlike the murder of human beings, the murder of languages is not, and has never been, treated as a crime. Languages such as English, French, Latin, Mandarin and Spanish, responsible together for the deaths of hundreds of languages over the centuries, have never been held accountable in a court of law.

Japanese committed attempted murder on Korean during the colonial period in the 1930s and 1940s, though failed through lack of time (had the Japanese not lost the war, the Japanese Empire remained intact and policies towards Korea left unchanged until the present day, it is likely the Korean language would now be in a precarious position). Currently, Japanese is responsible for the ongoing murder of several languages on the archipelago, the roots going back many years: Ainu and the Ryūkyūan languages.

Ainu was formerly spoken in Sakhalin, the Kurile Islands, Hokkaidō and northeast Honshū. From toponym evidence (§6.9) it is possible the language was also spoken further south on Honshū and perhaps also in southern Kamchatka. Ainu is what is known as a language isolate (§1.1), although, similar to both Japanese and Korean, its word order is SOV (§3.1) and it has no noun inflection, instead possessing case marker particles (§3.12).

Although Japanese colonization of Hokkaidō, known at the time as Ezo, goes back to at least the 12th century, it did not gather pace until the establishment of the Matsumae domain in the southwestern corner of the island in 1604. Driven by the establishment of trade and fishing posts, and combined with fear of the encroaching Russian Empire, the government subsequently pursued a policy of Japanization, despite the fact that, following the Chinese tradition, Ainu were viewed by the Japanese as barbarians. Their otherness was frequently objectified pictorially in the form of a bearded hairy man and a woman with a tattooed upper lip. As the 1960s postcard shown in Fig. 7.5 illustrates, this objectification persisted well into modern times. The famous British explorer Isabella Bird was told in 1878 that the Ainu were 'dogs' (the similarity to the Japanese *inu* 'dog' is unfortunate) and it was widely believed they were unable to count.

The Ainu language began to die in the late 19th century: the Ainu people were designated Japanese citizens and their forced resettlement caused the collapse of speech communities. This was followed by the enactment of the Ainu Education System, under which compulsory education was conducted in Japanese only. Children were taught they were from an inferior race, resulting in negative attitudes towards their own culture and ethnicity. The Ainu people were only recognized by the Japanese government as an indigenous people in early 2019 and few, if any, monolingual native speakers of Ainu remain alive on Japanese territory. This state, where the only speakers remaining are elderly and bilingual, is termed 'moribund'. The Japanese government policy of murder is evident not only in the lack of even vague speaker numbers, but in the non-existence of any official programme of language revitalization.

Fig. 7.5: Objectification of the Ainu

The Ryūkyūan languages, spoken mainly in the Amami archipelago and Okinawa, are conventionally divided into northern and southern groups, each of which is further subdivided into a number of mutually unintelligible languages, the most widely-spoken being Uchināguchi (Okinawan: §1.1). Despite this, they are still frequently referred to as 'dialects of Japanese' (§7.7) in the Japanese popular media and the vast majority of Japanese linguistics textbooks and research encyclopaedias published in Japan. The Ryūkyūan languages and Japanese are generally held to be descended from the same proto-language, known as Proto-Japonic (§1.1). Due to this, the morphosyntax and phonology of Ryūkyūan languages are very similar to Japanese, and many vocabulary items are cognates.

Ryūkyū was an independent kingdom until 1609, when it was invaded by the Satsuma clan and made a vassal. The Japanese state annexed the territory in 1879 and the king was exiled to Tokyo. Despite contemporary research concluding that Luchuan (as it was then called) and Japanese were as far apart as Spanish and Italian, government administration and the prevailing academic zeitgeist of national linguistics (§8.1) saw to it that Ryūkyūan languages were branded dialects. Dialect tags were used in schools in the first half of the 20th century (Fig. 6.8). These were small wooden placards forcibly hung around a pupil's neck when caught speaking a Ryūkyūan language. The pupil could pass it on to someone else when they were heard to speak 'dialect', thus reinforcing peer pressure towards the 'standard' (§7.7). Today, it is unknown how many monolingual speakers of Ryūkyūan languages, if any, are alive. Although, like Ainu, many are elderly and bilingual, unlike Ainu, there exist more grassroots programmes aimed at keeping the languages and culture alive. At the time of writing, six of the Ryūkyūan languages were on the UNESCO endangered list.

7.6 Japanese Words in Foreign Languages

Borrowings from Japanese can be found in many languages across the world. In this unit, we will examine these borrowings by considering whether the loan process has been non-orthographic or orthographic. The non-orthographic pathway is that taken by the majority of the borrowing languages: these do not share a writing system with Japanese and borrowing was initially by word of mouth. Subsequently, once written down in the borrowing language's orthography, it would have spread further by means of the written word also. As a representative example of this kind of language, we will consider English. The orthographic pathway, on the other hand, has been employed by only those small number of languages within the sinosphere: Korean, Vietnamese (formerly) and the Chinese topolects. As representative examples of these kinds of language, we will consider Mandarin and Korean. As we shall see, however, even these languages have at times resorted to non-orthographic borrowing.

Older Japanese borrowings into English can be distinguished from the more recent by their spelling. While newer borrowings tend to be written according to the Hepburn transcription system (§4.7), this was often not the case for older borrowings, whose etyma may be somewhat opaque. Such examples include (with approximate date of first attestation in brackets): moxa (17th century; ← †*mogusa*, now *kyuu*), soy (17th; ← *šooyu*), adzuki (18th), ginkgo (18th; ← †*ginkyoo*, now *ičoo*), tycoon (19th; ← *taikuɴ* 'great ruler', a term for the shogun used by and to foreigners) and rickshaw (19th; ← truncation of *jiɴrikiša*). There are, however, many older borrowings which do conform to Hepburn, generally due to the lack of any orthographic alternative: katana, shogun (both 17th century), Shinto (18th), geisha, kimono, futon (all 19th).

Broadly speaking, Japanese borrowings into English can be divided into a number of semantic groups. Cuisine-related vocabulary (1) is probably the largest and, at present, continues to expand. Many borrowings are very recent, having come into English from the late 20th century. Terms taken from specific aspects of Japanese 'highbrow' culture (2) are also relatively numerous. Few, however, are recent. Recent cultural borrowings have centred on the 'lowbrow' everyday cultures (3) of gaming and tech and what can be loosely termed 'subculture'. Martial arts and bushido-related terms (4) are another obvious category. Borrowings related to Japanese flora and fauna (5) are surprisingly few, while miscellaneous loans include tsunami, harakiri, zaibatsu and WWII terms, such as kamikaze and the derogatory Nip (← *niqpoɴ* 'Japan').

(1) bento, daikon, fugu, gyoza, miso, ramen, saké, sashimi, shiitake, sukiyaki, sushi, tempura, teriyaki, tofu, umami, wasabi
(2) bonsai, futon, haiku, ikebana, kabuki, kimono, koto, no(h), obi, origami, shamisen, shiatsu, tanka, tatami, waka, yukata, zen
(3) anime, cosplay, Digimon, emoji, gacha, hentai, karaoke, kawaii, manga, moe, otaku, Pokémon, sudoku, Tamagotchi, waifu, yuri
(4) aikido, dojo, judo, jujutsu, karate, kendo, ninja, samurai, sensei, sumo, yakuza
(5) akita, ayu, koi, kudzu

Borrowings from Japanese into Mandarin are, with very few exceptions, orthographic, the vast majority Sino-Japanese (SJ: §7.1) coinages dating from the late 19th century. These include both true neologisms (系統 *keitoo* 'system', 国会 *koɴkai* 'parliament', 内容 *naiyoo* 'content', 科学 *kagaku* 'science'; pronounced in Mandarin as *xìtǒng, guóhuì, nèiróng, kēxué*) and obsolete words from Classical Chinese resurrected and given new meanings (文化 *buɴka* 'culture', 世界 *sekai* 'world', 社会 *šakai* 'society', -主義 -*šugi* '-ism'; pronounced in Mandarin as *wénhuà, shìjiè, shèhuì, -zhǔyì*). Recent borrowings into Mandarin are also orthographic: 数独 *suudoku* is *shùdú*, 山葵 *wasabi* is *shānkuí*, 絵文字 *emoji* is *huìwénzì*, *yakuza* is *jídào* from the more formal term 極道 *gokudoo*. Two exceptions to the above, and notable non-orthographic borrowings, are the Mandarin for karaoke and the cartoon character Doraemon, written 卡拉 OK (pronounced *kǎlāōké*) and 哆啦 A 夢 (pronounced *duōlāēīmèng*). Here, both Chinese characters and Roman letters are employed for their phonetic values.

Unlike Mandarin, Japanese borrowings into Korean are both orthographic and non-orthographic, nearly all dating from the late 19th century. Due, however, to the often fraught and bitter relationship wrought by the Japanese colonial legacy on the Korean peninsula, there are cases where Japanese loans have been replaced (sometimes via government directives) by native Korean or Sino-Korean coinages. These loans may nevertheless still be used by older speakers, or be generally understood: they are marked below with an asterisk. What follows is applicable only to South Korea: research for North Korea (DPRK) is lacking. Examples of orthographic borrowings include *suhyeong (← 手形 *tegata* 'bank draft') or *harin* (← 割引 *waribiki* 'discount'), where Japanese native readings are replaced by Sino-Korean readings; and *banjanggo* 'Band-Aid' (← 絆創膏 *baɴsookoo*), *maekju* 'beer' (← †麦酒 *bakušu*), *sinmun* 'newspaper' (← 新聞 *šiɴbuɴ*) or *japji* 'magazine' (← 雑誌 *zaqši*), where SJ is substituted by Sino-Korean. Non-orthographic borrowings include *jeumekkiri 'nail clippers' (← *cumekiri*), *gabang* 'bag' (← *kabaɴ*), *guruma* 'wheelbarrow' (← *kuruma*), *gudu* 'shoe' (← *kucu*) or *uwagi* 'jacket' (← *uwagi*), as well as many loans which Japanese itself borrowed, or created, from Western languages (§7.2), such as *apateu* 'apartment' (← *apaato*), *jeubong 'trousers' (← *zuboɴ*), *ppang* 'bread' (← paN), *saelleorimaen* 'office worker' (← *sarariimaN*), *dambae* 'cigarette, tobacco' (← *tabako*) or *terebi* 'TV' (← *terebi*).

7.7 Japanese Dialects and Dialect Divisions

When speaking of Japanese dialects, the following three Japanese technical terms are commonly used: *kyōtsūgo* 'common language', *hyōjungo* 'standard language' and *hōgen* 'dialect'. *Kyōtsūgo* can be defined as the common tongue spoken and understood throughout Japan between individuals from all different regions (what this book terms 'Standard Japanese' or 'the Standard'), while *hyōjungo* can be defined as a government-promoted variety of this common tongue used in the bureaucracy, education and the media. *Hōgen* can be defined as a regional variant of the common tongue, whose divergence from it may range from slight to extreme, but is intelligible, at least to some extent, to speakers from other regions. These three terms are not mutually exclusive. *Kyōtsūgo* is based on Tokyo Japanese and is thus a dialect itself, albeit one that just happens to have acquired national status. Likewise, *hyōjungo* could be said to be the 'official dialect' for use in public discourse. Until now, *kyōtsūgo* has been the primary focus of this book. A description of the Japanese language, however, would not be complete without a discussion of the great variety of dialects spoken throughout the country. In this unit, we will provide a brief overview of Japanese dialects, first by setting out to define the term 'dialect', and then examining a number of different Japanese dialect divisions put forward by a number of scholars. In subsequent units, we will examine dialect diffusion (§7.8), differences between Eastern and Western dialects (§7.9) and, finally, the dialects of Tōhoku (§7.10) and Kyūshū (§7.11). We do not include the Ryūkyūan languages or Hachijō (§1.1, §7.5) in our analysis, all of which are Japonic languages and not dialects of Japanese.

There exists a great deal of debate concerning the definition of dialect versus language. One major criterion used when distinguishing the two is the concept of mutual intelligibility. Two varieties of speech that are mutually intelligible are said to be dialects of a larger language, while two incomprehensible varieties are said to be separate languages. This definition is not without its problems, though. First and foremost, for socio-political reasons, two mutually unintelligible variants of a language may be defined as the same language, while two mutually intelligible variants may be defined as separate ones. For example, the Japanese government views the Ryūkyūan languages and Hachijō as dialects of Japanese (a view unfortunately held by many linguists in Japan as well), even though Japanese and Amami (the northernmost Ryūkyūan language), for example, are almost entirely mutually unintelligible. On the other hand, Dutch and Afrikaans are generally defined as separate languages despite being mutually intelligible to a large degree.

Even when we exclude the Ryūkyūan languages and Hachijō, many Japanese dialects still display a large degree of mutual unintelligibility. For instance, Tsugaru, spoken in the west of Aomori Prefecture, and Tokara, spoken in the Tokara Islands south of Kagoshima Prefecture, are almost mutually unintelligible. Why then should we classify Tokara as a dialect, but Amami as an independent language? We can answer this question by looking at Japanese dialects as a dialect continuum—a group of connected regions in which speech varies only slightly between each adjacent region but becomes increasingly less intelligible with distance. Speakers of the Kagoshima mainland dialect, for example, would have only moderate difficulty understanding Tokara, but as we go further north the level of comprehension drops. On the other hand, speakers of Tokara would be unable to comprehend Amami, even though the Amami islands, where it is spoken, are located just 90 kilometres to the south. Thus, even though Japanese and Amami have shared affinity and belong to the same Japonic language family, they cannot be considered to be part of a dialect continuum.

It is impossible to state exactly how many dialects there are in Japan, as nearly every proposed dialect could be broken down into smaller dialects or merged with others to form a larger one. Dialects are usually divided across prefectural or municipal boundaries and given titles such as Yamagata-ben or Sendai-ben, with -ben 'lit. speech' denoting a dialect. They may also be divided according to former province borders (Mikawa-ben in eastern Aichi prefecture) or across larger regions which share similar features (Kansai-ben, comprising all the dialects spoken throughout Kansai, or Zūzū-ben, comprising all dialects spoken throughout Tōhoku). None of these divisions are without their flaws, however. It is not uncommon for two adjacent municipalities or even two adjacent neighbourhoods within the same municipality to display dialect differences, even if only minor. The *Linguistic Atlas of Japan* (§8.12), which collects data from dialect surveys conducted in the 1950s and 1960s, records 482 dialect forms for the word for 'tadpole', many of which are limited to a single town or village on the map: the form *moqkenoko*, for example, is observed only in the Jūsan neighbourhood of Shiura village (now part of Goshogawara, Aomori Prefecture), but not in the Aiuchi neighbourhood, less than five kilometres away.

Over the past century, Japanese linguists have proposed a number of different schemata for dividing dialects based on more objective linguistic features. The largest and most commonly used division is the East-West division, which divides Japanese into Eastern and Western macro-dialects (§7.8, §7.9). Another more precise schema, proposed by the dialectologist Tōjō Misao (§8.12), separates mainland dialects (Tōjō recognizes Ryūkyūan and Hachijō as dialects, while we treat them as independent languages) into Eastern, Western and Kyūshū dialects, each of which is then further subdivided along prefecture or former province boundaries. As illustrated in Fig. 7.7, this yields a total of 12 dialect divisions, based on a mix of the phonological and morphological traits of the different regions. Other proposed

Fig. 7.7: *Tōjō's dialect divisions*

schemata divide dialects based on their phoneme inventory (§2.1), accent (§2.6), grammar, lexicon or honorific usage (§6.3). One recent proposal even attempts to divide dialects based on language-thought processes, such as overall verbosity, rigidity of set expressions or consideration towards the addressee. Each of these schemata have their own merits depending on what aspect of the language one wishes to examine: there is no single definitive model.

7.8 Dialect Diffusion

Dialects do not typically exist in a vacuum. As different groups of speakers come into contact, they often borrow new elements from each other, enriching, and in some cases replacing, their native tongue. In the words of the 18th century philologist Motoori Norinaga (§8.12), 'It is common for old words to survive in the countryside. Especially in the speech of folk from far away provinces we find many words of interest [...] In busy settlements where travellers from other provinces and the capital pass through regularly, the people acquire words from here and there and begin to choose their words more carefully, trying to sound refined and modern.'

Chapter 7 Language Contact and Dialects

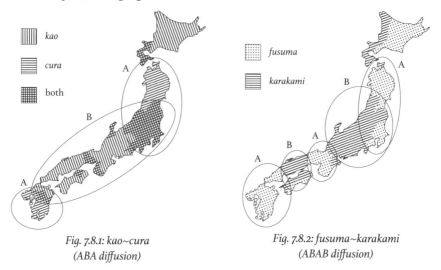

Fig. 7.8.1: kao~cura
(ABA diffusion)

Fig. 7.8.2: fusuma~karakami
(ABAB diffusion)

While these words were written over 200 years ago, they paint an accurate picture of how dialects are spread to this day: as people travel from one place to another and their dialects come into contact, new expressions are adopted and old ones abandoned. Dialect diffusion is, in its essence, a reflection of the travels and interactions of people from different regions (or, in some cases, the lack thereof) throughout history.

Modern research shows us that there are two major diffusion patterns for Japanese dialects. The first is known as ABA diffusion in the Japanese tradition, contagious diffusion or the wave model in the Western. ABA diffusion describes a state in which words are dispersed outwards from the cultural centre to peripheral regions in a wave-like pattern. In other words, when a new form A is coined in the cultural centre of Japan, it is gradually dispersed outwards until it reaches the edge of the Japanese archipelago. Eventually, A is replaced with a newer form B, which in turn works its way out into the peripheral regions, followed by C, D and so on, forming a ripple-like pattern outward from the centre. ABA diffusion was originally proposed by the early 20th century ethnologist Yanagita Kunio (§8.12) when surveying the dialect forms for 'snail'. He found that the dialect forms for snail formed a five-tier system starting with *deNdeNmuši*, the newest form, in the Kinki region, followed by *maimai* in Chūgoku and Chūbu, *katacumuri* in Kantō and Shikoku, *cuburi* in most of Kyūshū and Tōhoku and finally *namekuji*, the oldest form, in the southernmost regions of Kyūshū and northernmost regions of Tōhoku. Yanagita gave the name *hōgenshūkenron* 'peripheral zone theory' to the phenomenon. A less complex example of ABA diffusion can be observed in the dialect forms for 'face' (Fig. 7.8.1), where the form *kao* is observed in central regions and *cura* in peripheral regions (excluding Hokkaidō, which was not colonized until

7.8 Dialect Diffusion

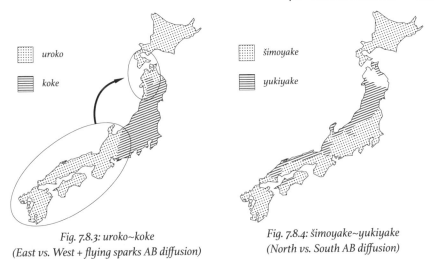

Fig. 7.8.3: uroko~koke
(East vs. West + flying sparks AB diffusion)

Fig. 7.8.4: šimoyake~yukiyake
(North vs. South AB diffusion)

relatively recently: §7.5). Both forms are used together in Kantō, southern Tōhoku and northern Kyūshū. A less common variant of ABA diffusion is ABAB diffusion in which, after the forms A and B have been dispersed to peripheral regions, A is 'resurrected' in the centre, forming a stripe-like pattern of distribution. An example of ABAB diffusion is the dialect forms for 'fusuma', a type of sliding door in traditional architecture. The form *fusuma* is used in Kyūshū, Kinki, Kantō and Tōhoku, with *karakami* used in Chūgoku, Shikoku, Chūbu and Hokuriku (Fig. 7.8.2).

The second major pattern is AB diffusion. This describes a state in which one form is dispersed to one side and another form to the other side of some type of natural or man-made boundary. By far the most common example of AB diffusion is East vs. West. Prior to the advent of modern day transportation networks, a number of natural barriers impeded transportation between regions. Naturally, oceans and other waterways form one of the largest barriers and are responsible for the many dialect differences observed between Honshū, Shikoku, Kyūshū (§7.11) and their outlying islands. Mountain ranges form another major barrier and historically one mountain range in particular, the Japan Alps, running from the southwestern edge of Niigata Prefecture in the north, down through Nagano Prefecture and into Shizuoka Prefecture in the south, served as a barrier separating Eastern (E) and Western (W) dialects. In Japanese dialectology, this boundary is known as the Itoigawa-Hamanako line, after its northernmost and southernmost points. Multiple isoglosses distinguishing E and W dialect features can be drawn along it (Fig. 7.9.1). Some examples of words displaying AB diffusion roughly along the Itoigawa-Hamanako line are the dialect forms for 'fish scale', which is *uroko* in W, but *koke* in most E dialects (Fig. 7.8.3); or 'salty', which is *kara-i* in W and *šoqpa-i* in E dialects. Another less common example of AB diffusion is North vs. South, in which variant forms of a word are dispersed along the Pacific and Sea of Japan coastlines. The dialect forms for 'frostbite' show such a distribution with *šimoyake* used along the Pacific and *yukiyake* along the Sea of Japan coastline (Fig. 7.8.4).

Of course, dialect diffusion is not always straightforward and a number of other factors may come into play. In the case of *uroko~koke*, for example, the W form *uroko* is also observed along the western and northern coastlines of Tōhoku (Fig. 7.8.3). Given its prevalence along coastal regions, we can speculate that the W form was carried directly to these coastal regions by sea. This type of diffusion, in which a form is carried directly to a remote region, bypassing the region in between, is referred to as *tobihi* 'flying sparks' diffusion in the Japanese tradition and is similar to what is known as hierarchical diffusion in the Western tradition (although in the latter, instead of jumping from region to region, the form jumps from urban conurbation to urban conurbation and may even cross language barriers). At the same time, there is an older form *iroko*, attested in written sources dating back to the 10th century: *uroko* is not attested until the 15th century. It is equally plausible that the form *uroko* in northern Tōhoku developed from *iroko* independently of the W form. When the same form develops in two regions independently of each other, the form is said to have 'pluralistic origins'. Another example of a phenomenon with pluralistic origins is the shift of vowel-stem verbs to a consonant-stem-like pattern (especially in the imperative: *mi-ro* → *mi-re* (or *mir-e*) 'look!', *oki-ro* → *oki-re* (or *okir-e*) 'wake up!') observed in Kyūshū and Tōhoku dialects (§7.10, §7.11). Here, we observe a 'reverse ABA' (or BAB) pattern of distribution in which the newer consonant-stem variants are used in peripheral regions and the older vowel-stem variants preserved in the cultural centre. It is not uncommon for a certain development to be rejected in cultural centres where norm-consciousness towards the Standard is strong, while being promoted in peripheral regions, where the same norms are not as rigidly adhered to.

Starting in the 20th century, with the rigorous promotion of *hyōjungo* (§7.7) by the government, many dialects have been undergoing a process of standardization, gradually approaching Standard Japanese. With the advent of public education (§8.5) and, more recently, the public broadcasting organization NHK, whose announcers follow strict guidelines concerning choice of vocabulary and use of pitch accent (§2.6), nearly all speakers of dialects are 'bilingual' in their native dialect and Standard Japanese. Few 'monolingual' speakers of dialects remain and the majority of minor dialects are, or will soon be, endangered. This does not mean that all is lost, however. Kansai dialect, the variety spoken in and around the greater Ōsaka region (§7.9), for example, remains an active source of innovations into other dialects, due to its domination of the television comedy scene (*owarai bangumi*). Likewise, there has been a recent trend among the young to incorporate elements of different dialects regarded as hip or cute into their parlance, a phenomenon sometimes referred to as 'dialect accessorization' (§7.11).

7.9 Eastern and Western Dialects

Japanese dialects are typically divided into Eastern (E) and Western (W) according to whether they lie east or west of the Itoigawa-Hamanako line (§7.8). While on maps the Itoigawa-Hamanako line is drawn as a single physical entity running north to south, there is no single line at which E dialect features magically cease to exist and W features take over. Instead, the Itoigawa-Hamanako line can be better interpreted as the median point along which a number of different isoglosses—an isogloss bundle—between E and W features can be drawn (Fig. 7.9.1 shows five). Likewise, just because a specific feature is defined as E or W does not mean all regions east of the line will display such a feature and vice versa. Factors such as geography, topography, dialect contact or the propagation of Standard Japanese all influence the diffusion of dialects as well (§7.8). Furthermore, Tōhoku dialects and Kyūshū dialects display a number of features absent from central, eastern or western Honshū and can be better placed into categories of their own. We therefore assign these peripheral dialects their own units, §7.10 and §7.11.

From a phonological standpoint, E and W dialects are quite similar, apart from the pronunciation of the vowel /u/, which is generally more rounded in W dialects (close to [u]) than in E ones (where it is typically unrounded [ɯ]). As a general trend, vowels are pronounced more prominently and consonants less prominently

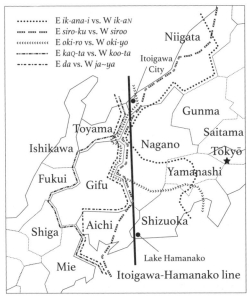

Fig. 7.9.1: Isoglosses along the Itoigawa-Hamanako line

in W dialects. Thus, lengthening of vowels, especially in single-mora words (§2.4), is a common feature in W dialects, while vowel devoicing (§2.3) is common in E ones. In addition, W dialects prefer vocalic *onbin* (§2.9) in the -*te* and -*ta* forms of verbs (§3.7), while E dialects display mora obstruent *onbin* (W *koo-ta* ~ E *kaQ-ta* 'bought'). With adjectives, *onbin* is productive in W dialects, where the initial *k*- of the adverbial suffix disappears, while in E dialects (apart from the highly formal *gozar-u* forms: §6.3) *onbin* does not surface and the suffix consonant is retained: W *široo nar-u* ~ E *široku nar-u* 'turn white'.

One area in which E and W dialects do display a large degree of divergence is pitch accent (§2.6). Pitch accent across dialects can be grouped into three types: *n*+1 type, *n*-type and 0-type. The *n*+1 type exhibits *n*+1 possible pitch patterns for a word with *n* moras. It is further subdivided into Tokyo (which includes Standard Japanese analysed in §2.6) and Keihan (Kyoto and Osaka). The *n*-type possesses a fixed number *n* of patterns, the value of *n* being one or two depending on dialect. This type is rare, all known examples being from southern Kyūshū dialects. The 0-type, meanwhile, has no set patterns at all and is also termed 'accentless'. These 0-types are comparatively uncommon, widely dispersed and found only in southeastern Tōhoku, northern Kantō and central Kyūshū. Apart from the areas just mentioned where 0-type is found, all E dialects follow the Tokyo *n*+1 type accent or a variant thereof (with the sole exception of Sado dialect (Sado Island, Niigata), which follows Keihan *n*+1 type). W dialects are far more varied, containing all three pitch accent types and both *n*+1 variants. The Keihan *n*+1 type is distributed throughout the Kinki area, Hokuriku and Shikoku, although Chūgoku notably falls under Tokyo *n*+1 type. Meanwhile, Kyūshū displays all three accent types, though only the Tokyo variant of *n*+1. The geographical distribution of accent types across dialects is illustrated in Fig. 7.9.2.

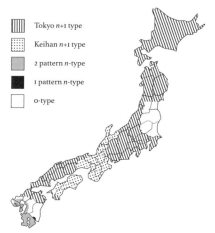

Tokyo *n*+1 type
Keihan *n*+1 type
2 pattern *n*-type
1 pattern *n*-type
0-type

Fig. 7.9.2: *Accent types across dialects*

The two *n*+1 variants, Tokyo and Keihan, are in many ways the exact opposite of each other, as illustrated in Table 7.9. Tokyo displays three patterns for 2-mora nouns while Keihan displays four and, of these four, B and C are accentuated in exactly the opposite manner from Tokyo. This leads to a reversal in the meaning of several homonyms (§5.9) only distinguishable by pitch accent: *haši* (LH) is 'edge' or 'bridge' in Tokyo, while it is 'chopsticks' in Keihan. Keihan also possesses what is known as a falling pitch: the pitch drops from H to L within a single mora.

	Tokyo	Keihan	examples
A	LH(H)	HH(H)	*ame* 'candy', *kaze* 'wind', *haši* 'edge', *hana* 'nose', *mizu* 'water'
B	LH(L)	HL(L)	*aši* 'foot', *kawa* 'river', *cuki* 'moon', *haši* 'bridge', *hana* 'flower'
C	HL(L)	LH/LL(H)	*iki* 'breath', *kata* 'shoulder', *sora* 'sky', *haši* 'chopsticks', *mugi* 'wheat'
D		LF(L)	*ame* 'rain', *kage* 'shadow', *saru* 'monkey', *curu* 'crane', *mado* 'window'

L = low, H = high, F = falling pitch, ( ) = particle: see §2.6 for further discussion.
Table 7.9: *Accent patterns of 2-mora nouns in Tokyo and Keihan n+1 type dialects*

Perhaps the most noticeable difference between E and W dialects lies in grammar. Here we list just a few of the more prominent differences:

- The negative verb suffix *-(a)na-i* (§3.8) is used in E, with *-(a)N ~ -(a)heN ~ -hiN* used in W. The final two of these three forms display complementary distribution, with *-hiN* occurring after vowel-stem verbs ending in *i* (*oki-hiN* 'don't wake up') and *-(a)heN* occurring after all other verbs (*ik-aheN* 'don't go', *tabe-heN* 'don't eat', *koo-heN* 'don't come'). The negative of S-irregular verbs can be either *šii-hiN* or *see-heN* (see §3.3 for a summary of verb classes).
- The copula *da* is used in E, while *ja~ya* is used in W (all three deriving from *de ar-u*: §3.6).
- The existential verb *i-ru* 'be' is used in E, *or-u* in W. This applies to the perfect-progressive auxiliary (§3.9) as well: E *yaQ-te i-ru ~ yaQ-te-ru* vs. W *yaQ-te or-u ~ yaQ-tor-u* 'be doing, have done'.
- The imperative *-ro* is used in E, *-yo* in W: E *oki-ro* vs. W *oki-yo* 'wake up!' (§3.7).

Of course, there is no lack of lexical differences between E and W dialects. Some well-known examples include E *kusuriyubi ~* W *benisašiyubi* 'ring finger', E *hikiniku ~* W *minči* 'minced meat', E *sute-ru ~* W *hoor-u* 'throw away', E *kari-ru ~* W *kar-u* 'borrow', E *kusuguQta-i ~* W *kosobayu-i* 'ticklish' and E *maQku ~* W *makudo* 'McDonalds'. Broader differences in speech styles are observed as well, such as a more complex system of (anti-)honorific verbal morphology (§6.3, §6.4) in W dialects (in Kyoto dialect, *iw-ahar-u ~ i-i+nahar-u ~ o-i+yas-u* are all respectful forms, while *i-iyor-u ~ yuu-te kecukar-u* are both anti-honorific forms of the verb *i-u ~ yu-u* 'say') or the ubiquitous use of *doomo* as a greeting, parting (§6.6), apology or expression of gratitude in E dialects, especially in Tōhoku.

7.10 Tōhoku Dialects

In this unit, as well as §7.11, we take a look at two well-known peripheral dialect clusters: the Tōhoku dialects in the far north of Honshū and the dialects of Kyūshū, the southernmost of Japan's four main islands. As the spread of *hyōjungo* (§7.7, §7.8) is murdering (§7.5) dialects at an unprecedented rate, the following descriptions, while still representative of the speech of older cohorts, may appear in free variation and in many cases not apply to younger cohorts or in higher register social situations. We hope, nevertheless, they provide a snapshot of the huge variety of speech found throughout the main islands of Japan.

Tōhoku dialects are divided into Northern (N: Kita Ōu ~ Hokuō) and Southern (S: Minami Ōu ~ Nan'ō): Fig. 7.10.1. N dialects consist of those spoken in Aomori, Akita, central and northern Iwate, the coastal regions of Yamagata (Shōnai) and the far northern regions of Niigata. The dialects of the Oshima peninsula and southern coast of Hokkaidō also share a large degree of similarity with N dialects. S dialects are composed of those spoken in southern Iwate, inland Yamagata, Miyagi and the northern half of Fukushima. Some scholars also include the remainder of Fukushima, as well as the Tochigi and Ibaraki dialects of northern Kantō in this grouping (Fig. 7.7).

Fig. 7.10.1: Tōhoku dialects

We turn first to phonology where, henceforth, we indicate Standard Japanese forms by means of a dotted underline. Perhaps the most salient feature of nearly all Tōhoku dialects is the intervocalic voicing (§2.2) of t~č~c~k to d~j~z~g and the concomitant prenasalization of intervocalic b~d~z~j~g to ᵐb~ⁿd~ⁿz~ⁿj~ⁿg. For example, ake-ru 'open' is age-ru, while age-ru 'raise' is aⁿge-ru. While prenasalized ⁿg is still commonly found, in many dialects ᵐb~ⁿd~ⁿz have been lost, or simply reduced to nasalization of the previous vowel: aᵐbu → ābu 'horsefly'. Intervocalic voicing is typically suppressed after devoiced vowels: kita not *kida 'north', fuke not *fuge 'dandruff'. In the examples below, we will represent intervocalically voiced t~č~c~k as d~j~z~g and prenasalized b~d~z~j~g as ᵐb~ⁿd~ⁿz~ⁿj~ⁿg.

Nearly all Tōhoku dialects are held to have six vowel phonemes, in contrast to the five found in the Standard (§2.3). These consist of a~i~u~e~o and a sixth phoneme æ, which lies between [a] and [ɛ] (Fig. 2.3). This sixth phoneme corresponds to the vowel sequences ai, ae and, to a lesser extent, oi: hai 'ash' and hae 'housefly', for example, are both pronounced hææ.

The high vowels i~u are centralized in many Tōhoku dialects and indeed merge as a high central vowel after c~č~s~š~z~j and, less commonly, n~m~k~g~r. This vowel is realized somewhat forward of [i] in N, but somewhat back of it in S dialects: for simplicity's sake, it is represented as Y below. In most of these dialects, čY~šY~jY are depalatalized to cY~sY~zY. This, together with the Y merger, results in a number of homonyms (§5.9) not found in the Standard: suši 'sushi' ~ susu 'soot' ~ šiši 'lion' are all sYsY while, combined with intervocalic voicing, čiči 'breasts' ~ cuči 'dirt' ~ *cucu* 'tube' are all levelled to *cYzY*. Meanwhile, *juusaN* '13' and *jiisaN* 'old man, grandfather' are both *zYYsaN*. It is from this that Tōhoku dialect gets its common nickname of *zuuzuubeN* or, in Tōhoku, *zYYzYYbeN*.

The mid front vowel *e* is raised in most regions to a phone roughly halfway between [i] and [e]. When word-initial or post-vocalic it is raised further and merges with *i*, resulting in a number of homonyms not found in the Standard: *eki* 'station' ~ *iki* 'breath' are pronounced identically, as are *koe* 'voice' ~ *koi* 'carp'. While some dialects do distinguish between word-initial and post-vocalic *i*~*e* to a degree, any such distinction does not necessarily correspond to forms found in the Standard. Hereafter, we represent this vowel as *E*. Note that *Y* and *E* are not phonemes, but merely representations of mergers with varying realizations from dialect to dialect. Long vowels (including *ææ*) are commonly shortened in Tōhoku dialects: *zaigoo* 'countryside' may be *zææ^{ŋ}go*~*zæ^{ŋ}go*, while *ie* 'house' may be *EE*~*E*.

In contrast to the depalatalization mentioned above, in some dialects *s*~*z* may be palatalized before *e*~*æ*: *sensei* 'teacher' is *šeNšee*~*šeNše*, while *zæ^{ŋ}go* is *jææ^{ŋ}go*~*jæ^{ŋ}go* in these dialects. In recent years, however, this type of pronunciation has shown a tendency to be avoided due to dialect stigmatization (§6.8). With some speakers, this stigmatization has resulted in hypercorrection: *jeeaaru* 'JR (Japan Railways)' may be *zeeaaru*. Less prominent features of Tōhoku dialects include the palatalization of *ky* to *č* (*kyoo* 'today' is *čoo*~*čo*) and *ki* to *či*~*cY* (*kiNko* 'safe' is *čiNko*~*cYNko*), the retention of Sino-Japanese post-consonantal *w*-glides after *k*~*g* (*kwazY* for *kaji* 'fire': §2.9) and, less commonly, the realization of *h* as *f* (*fi* for *hi* 'sun', *febi* for *hebi* 'snake'). The latter two of these features, as well as the intervocalic voicing of obstruents and prenasalization of voiced obstruents, are all features from earlier stages of Japanese in general (§2.9).

Pitch accent (§2.6), for the most part, follows Tokyo *n*+1 type accent (and variants thereof), though is 0-type—accentless—in the southeast (§7.9, Fig. 7.9.2). A number of N dialects are syllable- rather than mora-timed (§2.4): here, the locus of the pitch accent is assigned syllabically rather than moraically. Thus, *ga.Q.ko.o.ši.N.bu.N* 'school newspaper', which a speaker of the Standard will perceive as having eight moras, is perceived as having four syllables, *gaQ-ko-sYN-buN*. Such dialects are referred to as syllabeme (syllable-timed) dialects in Japanese dialectology—as opposed to mora-timed dialects—and are observed to an extent in southern Kyūshū as well.

Tōhoku dialects also display a number of interesting grammatical features, one of the most characteristic being the use of the verbal suffix/discourse particle (§3.12) *be* (and its many reflexes: *besY* ~ *beoN* ~ *byoN* ~ -*pe* ~ -*pesY*), derived from Middle Japanese -(*u*)*be-si* (§3.15), to express conjecture, probability or invitation: *yaQ-pe*, *sYQ-pe*, *odoQ-pe* 'let's do it, let's do it, let's dance!' (lyrics from *Yappe Taisō*, a television exercise song on NHK Sendai: Fig. 7.10.2). Following the 2011 Tōhoku earthquake and tsunami, dialect was used as a form of moral support in earthquake relief slogans, with *gaNbaQ-pe* 'keep up the fight!' (*gaNbaQ-pe miya^{ŋ}gi*: Fig. 7.10.3) being a

Fig. 7.10.2: Yappe Taisō on NHK Sendai (www.nhk.or.jp/sendai/yappetaisou/link.html)

Fig. 7.10.3: T-shirt with gaNbaQ-pe miya^{n}gi slogan

common slogan. Equally characteristic is the use of the case marker particle (CMP: §3.12) *sa* in place of <u>ni</u>. Unlike <u>ni</u>, *sa* typically only marks the allative (*dogo=sa* EQ-*ta=be* 'where could he have gone?') or dative (*kare=sa a^{n}ge-ru* 'give to him') case. Examples of *sa* replacing other usages of <u>ni</u>, such as the locative (*asogo=sa ar-u* 'it's over there'), or even being used in place of the purposive converb <u>-(i)ni</u> (*mi-sa ig-u* 'go to see': §3.7) are observed in some dialects, though. Other unique particles include the accusative CMPs *godo* (Aomori, Fukushima, Niigata, Tochigi, Ibaraki), *dogo* (Akita, Yamagata, Fukushima) and *ba* (Aomori, Iwate, Yamagata, Miyagi), the last of which is also observed in Kyūshū dialects. In many Tōhoku dialects, the use of these accusative CMPs is restricted to animate objects and not typically found after inanimate ones: Okitama dialect in Yamagata, for example, has *ore=[N]dogo* CYQ-*če gee* 'take me with you!' (animate object), but *sage nom-u* 'drink saké' (inanimate object). This phenomenon, known as 'differential object marking', is observed cross-linguistically and also found to an extent in Kyūshū dialects.

Verbal morphology and suffixes in Tōhoku dialects are, for the most part, identical to the Standard. There have been a number of unique developments, however, such as a distinction between 'abilitative' potential (that which one can do ability-wise) and circumstantial potential (that which one can do due to circumstances): *-e-ru* ~ *-(r)are-ru* expresses the former, while *-(r)u=ni* E-E ~ *-(r)uEE* ~ *-(r)uE* indicates the latter (*kag-e-ru* 'have the ability to write' ~ *kag-u=ni* E-E 'can write due to circumstances'). For consonant-stem verbs, the negative abilitative and circumstantial potential can also be distinguished through the use of *-e-na-i* and *-are-na-i*, respectively (usually in coalesced form: *kag-e-næ[æ]* ~ *kag-are-næ[æ]*). Another unique feature is the use of the past tense suffix *-ta* (§3.7) after the existential verb E-*ru* 'be' (Standard <u>i-ru</u>) to express present tense: E=*sa* E-*da* 'be at home', not 'was at home'. This has led to the development of novel past forms such as E-*de aQ-ta* (Akita), E-*deda* (Aomori) and E-*deQta* (Iwate). Many Tōhoku dialects also possess what is known as an 'anti-causative' verb suffix (*-(r)asar-u* in N, *-(r)ar-u* in S dialects), which changes a transitive verb into an intransitive one: *kowas-y* 'break' → *kowas-asar-u* ~ *kowas-ar-u* 'be broken'. While causativization (intransitive → transitive) is a productive process in the Standard through the use of the causative suffix *-(s)ase-ru* (§3.7), anti-causitivization (intransitive → transitive) is only productive in Tōhoku dialects. A shift from a vowel-stem to consonant-stem-like pattern in verbs, especially in the imperative (see §7.8 for examples) is also observed in several Tōhoku dialects. This is of particular interest, as the same phenomenon is observed to a larger degree in Kyūshū dialects.

Naturally, there is a great deal of unique dialect vocabulary in Tōhoku, as anywhere. Some notable examples include *me^{n}go-E* ~ *meNko-E* ~ *meNgo-E* (also with *o-E* as *æ[œ]*) 'cute' (all regions), *E^{n}zy-E* ~ *ENzy-E* 'an itchy or uncomfortable feeling' (Aomori, Iwate, Miyagi), *gaor-u* 'grow weak' (all regions), *ošoosyna~ošoosynaqsy* 'thanks ~ thank you' (Okitama, Yamagata), *moqkedano* 'thank you' (Shōnai, Yamagata), *wa* 'I' and *na* 'you' (both Aomori). Dialect honorific forms are also numerous, with slight variation from region to region. Polite forms of the imperative include *-te kero=ja* in Aomori, *-te kere=dæ[œ]* in Akita), *-(r)aiN* ~ *-te keraiN* ~ *-te kesaiN* (also with *ai* as *æ[œ]*) in Miyagi, *-te keNda* in Iwate, *-te kero=haa* ~ *-te keraqšai* ~ *-te kudai* (also with *ai* as *æ[œ]*) in Yamagata, *-te kuNnasæ[œ]* in northern Niigata and *-(r)aNšo* ~ *-te kuNce* ~ *-te kunaNšo* in northern Fukushima.

7.11 Kyūshū Dialects

Kyūshū dialects can be divided into three groups: Hichiku, made up of the dialects spoken in Nagasaki, Saga, Kumamoto, southwestern Ōita and the western and central regions of Fukuoka; Hōnichi, comprised of the dialects spoken in eastern Fukuoka, the remainder of Ōita and most of Miyazaki; and Satsugū, composed of the dialects spoken in southwestern Miyazaki and in Kagoshima (Fig. 7.11.1). In addition to the mainland, there are numerous islands surrounding Kyūshū, each with their own dialects. These include the Gotō Islands, Tsushima and Iki off Nagasaki, and the Koshiki (Kami- and Shimo-) Islands, Tokara Islands, Tanegashima and Yakushima off Kagoshima. While typically assigned to one of the three divisions above, the dialects spoken on many of these islands possess unique features distancing them from their mainland siblings.

We turn first to phonology, where we indicate Standard Japanese forms by means of a dotted underline. As is common in Western Japanese (§7.9), the vowel *u* is generally more rounded (§2.3). In certain environments—see below for examples—the mid vowels *e* and *o* are raised to *i* and *u*, while *u* may be fronted to *i*. Throughout Kyūshū, it is common for vowel sequences or diphthongs to coalesce as long or, in the Satsugū dialects, short vowels: *ai* can be *ee~e~aa~yaa* (*taka-i* 'high, expensive' is *takee~take~takaa~takyaa*); *ei* can be *ee~ii* (*rei* 'manners' is *ree~rii*); *oi* can be *ii~i~ee~e* (*oso-i* 'late' may be *ošii~oši~osee~ose*); and *ui* can be *ii~i* (*samu-i* 'cold'

Fig. 7.11.1: Kyūshū dialects

is *samii~sami*). While several of these mergers occur in the Standard as well, they are generally male-preferential (§6.1) and restricted to anti-honorific registers (§6.4). In some Kyūshū dialects, such as the Shiiba dialect of Miyazaki, word-initial or post-vocalic *e* is realized as *ye* (*eda* 'branch' is *yeda*, *hae* 'housefly' is *haye*).

Most Kyūshū dialects retain a Late Middle Japanese (LMJ) feature known as the *kai-gō* 'lit. open-closed' distinction (§2.9), where there were two variants of long *o*: an 'open' variant pronounced *åå* [ɔː] and a 'closed' variant *oo*. Both of these have merged as *oo* in Modern Japanese, but are still separate in Kyūshū: LMJ *åå* is now realized as *oo~o*, while LMJ *oo* has been raised to *uu~u*: LMJ *kyåådai* → Kyūshū *kyoodee~kyode* 'siblings'; LMJ *kyoo* → Kyūshū *kyuu~kyu* 'today'. Other, seemingly more sporadic, examples of *o* being raised to *u* are observed as well: *asob-u* → *asub-u* 'play' (all regions), *onaji* → *unaši* 'same' (Tsushima and Iki islands).

Across most Kyūshū dialects, the high vowels *i~u* are devoiced, or even elided entirely, when word-final: *aki* 'autumn' is *aki̥~ak*, *saku* 'fence' is *saku̥~sak*. Consonant codas other than N~Q are thus phonotactically licit in these dialects, unlike in the Standard (§2.5). In Satsugū dialects in particular, the final consonant surfaces as a mora nasal (§2.4) when elision of the final vowel exposes a nasal, or as a mora obstruent (realized as a glottal stop [ʔ]: §2.2) when it exposes an obstruent: *kani* 'crab' ~ *kami* 'paper' are both *kaN*, while *aki* 'fall' ~ *aji* 'taste' ~ *abu* 'horsefly' ~ *aku* 'lye' are all *aQ*. Should *i~u* follow *r* in Satsugū dialects, the *r* elides and *u* is fronted to *i*: m̲a̲c̲u̲r̲i̲ 'festival' is *macui*, while h̲i̲r̲u̲ 'afternoon' is *hii*. This pattern can also be observed word-medially or before *e* in some Satsugū and Gotō Island dialects: k̲o̲r̲e̲ 'this' is *koi*, k̲u̲r̲u̲m̲a̲ 'car' is *kuima*. Mora obstruents also frequently appear before voiced obstruents (k̲o̲k̲u̲g̲o̲ 'Japanese (lit. national language)' is *ko*Q*go*, t̲e̲c̲u̲d̲o̲o̲ 'railway' is *te*Q*doo*) across most Kyūshū dialects, making Q + voiced obstruent strings licit in all vocabulary strata (whereas in the Standard they are licit only in the mimetic and foreign strata: Table 2.5.2).

Moving on to consonants in general, we find that Kyūshū dialects share a number of features with Tōhoku dialects (§7.10), as well as displaying many unique features of their own. Those shared with Tōhoku dialects include preservation of Sino-Japanese post-consonantal *w*-glides (§2.9) after *k*~*g*, depalatalization of š̲~̲j̲ to *s*~*z* before *u* (also before *a*~*o* in Satsugū dialects: j̲a̲m̲a̲ 'obstruction' is *zama*) and palatalization of s̲~̲z̲ before *e*. Intervocalic voicing of t̲~̲č̲~̲c̲~̲k̲ as *d*~*j*~*z*~*g*, prenasalization of *g* as *ᵑg* and palatalization of k̲y̲ as *č* have all been reported in island dialects and those on the southern tip of the Satsuma Peninsula, but are nowhere as widespread as they are in Tōhoku.

On the other hand, there are many consonant-related features unique to Kyūshū dialects. In Hōnichi dialects, t̲~̲d̲ are palatalized before *e* (t̲e̲ 'hand' is *če*, s̲o̲d̲e̲ 'sleeve' is *soje*), while in southern Satsugū dialects n̲ is palatalized before *e* (f̲u̲n̲e̲ 'boat' is *funye*). Particularly prominent in Hakata and outlying island dialects is the lenition of d̲ to an apical consonant [d̥], which to the untrained ear sounds identical to r̲: k̲a̲d̲o̲ 'corner' sounds like *karo*. A number of Kyūshū dialects preserve a four-way *zi*~*di*~*zu*~*du* distinction (realizations varying across dialects), despite these moras having merged as j̲i̲~̲z̲u̲ in the Standard and as *zy* in Tōhoku dialects. These four moras and their mergers are referred to as the *yotsugana* 'four kanas' in Japanese linguistics, as they each possess unique kana and were pronounced differently in earlier stages of the language. In some dialects, mergers have resulted in *w*-glides appearing in native stratum (§7.2) words: in Kumamoto k̲u̲-̲e̲ 'eat!' is *kwee* and e̲g̲u̲-̲i̲ 'pungent' is *egwii*. The moras *wi*~*we*~*wo*~*fa*~*fi*~*fe*~*fo* can be found in native stratum words in certain Kyūshū dialects: in Sato dialect (Kamikoshiki Island) f̲u̲i̲-̲t̲e̲ 'blow, and' is *fii-te* and t̲o̲o̲f̲u̲=̲w̲a̲ 'as regards tofu' is *toofaa*, while in Kumamoto a̲o̲-̲i̲ 'blue' is *awee*. Such moras are rarely found in the native stratum in the Standard. Most interesting, however, is *wya*, illicit in the Standard (Table 2.5.1), but found in Kumamoto: w̲a̲i̲-̲t̲a̲ 'boiled' is *wyaa-ta*.

Pitch accent (§2.6, §7.9, Table 7.9.2) tends to follow Tokyo *n*+1 type in northeastern dialects (Ōita, most of Fukuoka) and a two-pattern *n*-type in southwestern dialects (most of Nagasaki and Kagoshima, parts of Saga and Kumamoto). The remaining dialects either follow 0-type (parts of Nagasaki, Saga, Fukuoka and Kumamoto; most of Miyazaki) or a single-pattern *n*-type (Miyakonojō, Miyazaki; Shibushi, Kagoshima). A number of Satsugū dialects are also syllabeme dialects similar to those found in Aomori (§7.10).

case	tooki 'time'	aaku 'lye'	ike 'pond'	koko 'here'	ika 'squid'
nominative	tooki=ga	aaku=ga	ike=ga	koko=ga	ika=ga
accusative	tooki=ba	aaku=ba	ike=ba	koko=ba	ika=ba
genitive	tooki=N	aaku=N	ike=N	koko=N	ika=N
dative	tookii	aakii	ikee	kokee	ikyaa
topic	tookyaa	aakaa	ikyaa	kokaa	ikaa

Table 7.11.1: Sato dialect case/topic marking system

Moving on to grammar and syntax, one of the most striking differences between Kyūshū dialects and the Standard is perhaps the system of case and topic marking (§3.12, §3.14) and, in particular, the lack of morphological transparency therein. The case/topic marking system from Sato dialect, illustrated in Table 7.11.1, is an example. We see that the dative case marker particle and topic particle fuse with the noun creating multiple inflectional forms depending on the final vowel. This is a classic example of agglutinative morphology developing into fusional morphology (§1.2), a common pattern in linguistic change. Kumamoto dialect and Sato dialect have also been reported to exhibit what is known as 'split intransitivity', in which the subject of an intransitive verb is marked differently according to whether it is the agent or patient of a verb: *otooto=ga ik-u=doo* 'my younger brother will go' (agentive), but *mago=no Nmare-ta=na* 'my grandchild was born'. Such split intransitive case marking systems are extremely rare cross-linguistically.

Kyūshū dialects also display a number of unique verb classes and verbal suffixes (§3.7, §3.8). Two particularly interesting features are the retention of dual vowel-stem verbs (§3.15) and the shift from a vowel-stem to consonant-stem-like pattern in single vowel-stem verbs. This latter feature is also observed, albeit to a lesser degree, in Tōhoku dialects. Table 7.11.2 shows three verb classes from Sato dialect that are not observed in the Standard.

class	dual vowel-stem I	dual vowel-stem II	hybrid vowel-stem
stem	tome- ~ tomu- 'stop'	ne- ~ nu- 'sleep'	mi- ~ mir- 'see'
-te form	tome-te	ne-te	mi-te
provisional conditional	tomu-reba	nu-reba	mi-reba
nonpast	tomu-i	nu-i	mi-ru
conjectural-hortative	tomu-u	nu-u	mir-oo
imperative	tome-e	ne-e	mir-e
negative	tome-n-	ner-an-	mir-an-
negative -te form	tome-jiN	ner-ajiN	mir-ajiN

Table 7.11.2: Sato dialect verb classes not found in Standard Japanese

(a) (b) (c) (d)

(a) *yo-ka yo-ka* (b) *bari sui-too=yo* (c) *ryookai=bai* (d) *ureši-kaa*
'good, good'   'I love you!'   'roger that'   'I'm so happy!'

Fig. 7.11.2: *Kyūshū dialect stickers found on LINE*
(store.line.me/stickershop/product/1228126/)

Just as with Tōhoku dialects, it is possible in Hichiku and Hōnichi dialects to distinguish between abilitative potential and circumstantial potential (§7.11) by using the suffixes *-(i)kir-u* and *-(r)are-ru*: *kak-ikir-u* 'have the ability to write' ~ *kak-are-ru* 'can write due to circumstances'. A distinction between the perfect/stative and progressive aspect, both expressed by *(-te) i-ru* in the Standard, also exists in Kyūshū dialects, the former expressed by *-tor-u ~ -čor-u* (with the allomorphs *-dor-u ~ -jor-u* occuring in the relevant *onbin* environment: Table 3.7.2) and the latter by *-(i)yor-u ~ -(i)or-u*: *ame=ga fur-iyor-u ~ ame=ga fur-ior-u* 'it's raining' vs. *ame=ga fuQ-tor-u* 'it's rained'. Adjectives take the suffix *-ka* to express the nonpast (*yo-ka* 'good', *futo-ka* 'fat') in Hichiku and Satsugū dialects. This suffix is highly productive, also attaching to nominal adjectives in some dialects: *geNki-ka* 'in good spirits', *nigiyaka-ka* 'lively'.

Some examples of dialect vocabulary include *bari* 'very' (Hakata), *dogai* (usually in coalesced forms, such as *dogee~doge~dogaa~dogyaa*: see above) 'how' (all regions), *iQčoN* 'not at all' (Ōita), *mijo-ka* 'cute' (all regions), *čaare-ru* 'fall, drop' (western Kyūshū), *cuu~too* 'scab' (all regions), *gi* 'backchat' (Kagoshima) and *bobura~boobura* 'pumpkin' (Fukuoka, Saga, Nagasaki, Ōita, Kumamoto). This last form is also found in Hawaii Creole English (§7.4). The word *bari* is especially well-known outside Kyūshū: it is found on the menus of Hakata-style ramen shops across Japan in the compounds *barikata* 'al dente (lit. very hard)' and *bariyowa* 'overcooked (lit. very soft)', denoting the hardness of noodles. Recently, Kyūshū dialects have often been perceived in pop culture as 'cute' due to the increasing number of female teen pop stars from the region who have popularized them. Kyūshū dialect stickers from the popular SNS software LINE are illustrated in Fig. 7.11.2. In (a) and (d) we see the adjective suffix *-ka*, in (b) the adverb *bari* 'very' and the suffix *-too* (a reduction of *-tor-u*) and in (c) the discourse particle (§3.12) *bai*, expressing affirmation.

Chapter 8 Education, Research and Policy

8.1 Government Language Policy

It is not uncommon for governments to issue legislation concerning language use within a state. The most common type of legislation is the designation of an official language to be used as the main vehicle of communication. For example, the US has one designated official language, English, while Switzerland has four, German, French, Italian and Romansh. Some countries go further by restricting the ways in which official languages can be used. Some examples are the Official Languages Act of Ireland which requires public bodies to keep official documents and display public signage in both Irish and English, or the German Orthographic Reform of 1996, which outlines a number of modifications to German spelling and punctuation to be adhered to in public education and administration throughout all German-speaking countries. Japan is no exception and over the past century and a half, as Japan has moved forward as a major world power, a number of regulations have been put into place in order to facilitate the use and acquisition of Japanese for both native and non-native speakers.

The earliest example of a government issued regulation on language in Japan is an edict from Emperor Kanmu in 792 CE that ordered students of the Confucian classics to study the more recently adopted *kan-on* reading of kanji in place of the antiquated *go-on* (§4.4). Throughout the early Heian period a number of similar edicts were issued, although these only targeted specific groups of scholars and were by no means comprehensive. The true beginning of government language policy in Japan can be traced back to the Meiji Restoration of 1868 and more specifically, the establishment of the National Language Investigation Committee (NLIC) by the Ministry of Education, Science and Culture (modern day MEXT; hereafter, 'the Ministry') in 1902. Headed by political scientist Katō Hiroyuki (1836–1916) and made up of a number of reputable linguists including Ueda Kazutoshi (§6.8, §8.12, §8.13), Ōtsuki Fumihiko (§8.10) and Yamada Yoshio (§8.12), the NLIC's main goals were to: (1) adopt a phonographic writing system for the Japanese language and conduct surveys concerning the merits and demerits of such a system; (2) adopt *genbun itchi* (§1.3) as the official style for writing and conduct surveys thereon; (3) conduct surveys on Japanese phonology; and (4) conduct surveys on dialects (§7.8–§7.11) and establish a 'standard language' (§7.7). Although the NLIC was eventually dissolved in 1913 without ever passing any actual legislation, it did publish a number of reports based on the findings of its surveys. These remain valuable linguistic resources to this day.

The next committee to be founded for regulating language policy was the Interim NLIC, founded by the Ministry in 1921 and headed by the renowned author Mori Ōgai (1862–1922), who was quickly succeeded by Ueda Kazutoshi upon his untimely death in 1922. The Interim NLIC presented multiple proposals for regulations on kanji and kana usage, but due to a number of obstacles, such as the Great Kantō Earthquake of 1923 and criticism from renowned linguists and authors of the time such as Yamada Yoshio and Akutagawa Ryūnosuke (1892–1927), none of these propositions ever saw the light of day. The Interim NLIC was dissolved in 1934 to be replaced with the National Language Council (NLC).

The NLC was the longest standing and most influential government body in the history of Japanese language policy. It was initially headed by Minister of Communications, Minami Hiroshi (1869–1946), and included prominent linguists of the time, such as Shinmura Izuru (§1.1) and Andō Masatsugu (1878–1952). During the years leading up to WWII, the NLC proposed numerous kanji and kana reforms, as well as a regulation calling for vertical text to be written from left to right instead of from right to left. Due to the political climate of the time, however, none of these proposals were ever officially put into place. True action came after WWII, when Andō Masatsugu was promoted to NLC chairman and, under his leadership, the *tōyōkanjihyō* 'list of kanji for general use' and *gendai kanazukai* 'modern kana usage' orthographic reforms were officially promulgated by the government. The *tōyōkanjihyō* limited the number of kanji to be used in official and public publications, as well as prescribing simplified forms for a number of kanji, while *gendai kanazukai* reformed kana usage to match the phonology of the modern language. The NLC also issued a list of rules concerning the use of *okurigana* (§4.10) in 1959. Kanji and kana reforms are covered in greater detail in §8.2.

In addition to reforming kanji and kana usage, the NLC was responsible for the spread of *kunrei-shiki* (§4.7), which was made the official system of romanization through the *rōmaji no tsuzurikata* 'Roman alphabet spelling guide' proclamation issued in 1954. However, as the proclamation did not forbid the use of other romanization systems, a large amount of confusion in romanization remains to this day. In 1981, the NLC issued a revised version of the *tōyōkanjihyō*, entitled *jōyōkanjihyō* 'list of kanji for daily use'; in 1986 a revised version of *gendai kanazukai*; in 1973 a revised version of *okurigana* rules; and in 1991 a list of spelling rules for foreign loanwords (§7.2, §7.3). This was to be the final piece of legislation promulgated by the NLC. It was dissolved in 2000 and replaced by the Council for Cultural Affairs Subdivision on National Language (SNL), which consists of a number of subcommittees each dedicated to specific topics such as kanji reform (§8.2), *kokugo* education (§8.5), Japanese as a second language education (§8.8) and the use of honorifics (§6.3). The most significant piece of legislation concerning language policy to be issued by the SNL since its inception is the 2010 revision of the *jōyōkanjihyō*, which lists a total of 2,136 kanji for daily use. In addition to the SNL, a short-lived Loanword Committee (§8.3) was established by the government between 2002 and 2006 to devise replacements for loanwords with low levels of comprehension among the general public.

8.2 Kanji and Kana Reform

In December 1866, Maejima Hisoka (1835–1919), a scholar at the Edo Kaiseijo (School of Western Studies) presented a petition to Shogun Tokugawa Yoshinobu calling for the abolishment of kanji, triggering the beginning of the kanji abolishment movement. Maejima argued that Japan could not keep up with Western nations if schools were to continue devoting so much time to teaching kanji. Maejima was not the first scholar to criticize kanji. Nationalist scholars as far as back as the 17th and 18th centuries, including Kamo no Mabuchi (§8.13) and Motoori Norinaga (§8.12), also lamented the difficulty of learning kanji in comparison to kana or the Roman alphabet. In the words of Motoori, 'What a foolish notion it is that now, even with the existence of kana, with which we can write freely, people still strive to write in cumbersome *kanbun* [Classical Chinese: §8.7].' While a total abolishment of kanji never saw the light of day, from the early 20th century up until the modern day the Japanese government has issued a number of restrictions on how many kanji should be taught in school or used in publications. The earliest of these restrictions appeared in the *shōgakkōrei* 'primary school ordinance' of 1900 (§8.5). This ordinance limited the number of kanji taught in primary schools to 1,200 and stipulated they were to be written either solely in regular script or in a combination of regular and semi-cursive script (§4.2, §4.3).

The first major restriction on kanji to affect not only schools, but also publications in general was the *tōyōkanjihyō* 'list of kanji for general use' issued by the National Language Council (NLC) in 1946 (§8.1). The *tōyōkanjihyō* listed 1,850 characters for use in 'legal and government documents, newspapers, magazines and in society in general'. In addition to restrictions on the number of characters to be used, the *tōyōkanjihyō* also listed simplified forms for 132 of the more difficult characters in order to facilitate writing. It was replaced by the *jōyōkanjihyō* 'list of kanji for daily use' in 1981, containing 1,945 characters, later increased to 2,136 in a revised version issued in 2010. The *jōyōkanjihyō* also significantly increased the number of simplified characters from 132 to 364, although many of the additional simplified forms were already in use at the time the list was issued (this holds true for the *tōyōkanjihyō* as well). In addition to the *jōyōkanjihyō*, the government issued a list of 92 supplementary characters for use in personal names (*jinmeiyō* kanji: §6.9) in 1951. Over the years, this list has been gradually expanded, its 2017 revision consisting of 863 characters, of which 212 are *jōyōkanjihyō* kanji variants, predominantly traditional forms.

Writing system reforms were not limited to kanji: a number of reforms have been promulgated for kana usage as well. Debates over kana usage are by no means a product of modern times. A long tradition of prescriptive kana usage, commonly referred to as *rekishiteki kanazukai* 'historical kana usage' exists in Japan, said to originate with the calligrapher Fujiwara no Teika (1162–1241). Fujiwara originally set out to create a list of prescriptive kana spellings in an attempt to reduce 'confusion' among scribes and, after undergoing several revisions, by the turn of the 17th century a standardized system of historical spellings had been established. This remained in use up until the end of WWII: see §1.3 and §8.7 for further detail.

The first, and by far most important, government reform on kana usage was issued by the NLC in 1946, alongside the *tōyōkanjihyō*. In this proclamation, known as *gendai kanazukai* 'modern kana usage', the NLC called for an end to *rekishiteki kanazukai*, laying out a set of mostly descriptive rules for spelling Japanese words. These included the abolishment of the obsolete kana ゑ~ヱ <we>, ゐ~ヰ <wi> and ゎ~ヮ <[wa]> (w-glides: §2.9), the use of miniscule to express y-glides and the mora obstruent Q (§2.4, §4.6) and the repeal of a number of archaic spelling rules for the remaining letters (Table 8.7). *Gendai kanazukai* is not entirely descriptive and a number of exceptions do exist—namely the retention of は~ハ <ha>, へ~ヘ <he> and を~ヲ <wo> for the particles *wa*, *e*, and *o* (§3.12)—but compared to *rekishiteki kanazukai*, it is much more in line with the spoken language. Moreover, until WWII, many hiragana could be written with more than one variant: see §4.6 for examples. The promulgation of *gendai kanazukai* officially brought this to an end by providing a definitive list of graphs to adhere to. Although a revised version of *gendai kanazukai* was issued in 1986, its contents were by and large the same as its predecessor.

In addition to *gendai kanazukai*, the NLC issued a list of rules concerning the use of *okurigana* (§4.10) entitled *okurigana no tsukekata* '*okurigana* spelling guide' in 1959, as well as a revised version of the same rules in 1973. *Okurigana no tsukekata* presents a total of seven rules (each with numerous exceptions) outlining which parts of words possessing kanji notation are to be written in kana. For example, Rule 1 states that 'conjugational endings' (§8.6) of verbs and adjectives are to be written in kana, while Rule 3 states that, apart from a few exceptions such as 辺り *atari* 'area' and 後ろ *uširo* 'behind', *okurigana* should never be used with nouns. The final kana reform to be passed by the NLC was a set of rules for spelling foreign loanwords (§7.2, §7.3) using katakana, entitled *gairaigo no hyōki* 'notation of loanwords', and promulgated in 1991. The proposal presents a chart of what could be referred to as 'kana digraphs'—combinations of full-height and miniscule kana such as フ ァ <[fu.a]> *fa* or ト ゥ <[to.u]> *tu*—for expressing non-core moras (grey in Table 2.5.1; see §4.6 for details) not native to Japanese. It also offered examples of when to use such digraphs, as well as a number of other spelling rules. The proposal is by no means comprehensive, stating that for sounds not representable by digraphs in the chart, writers are free to devise new spellings as seen fit. It does, however, present a firm set of guidelines for the majority of cases.

8.3 Loanword Reform

Loanword reform—a government backed or controlled effort at eradicating or reducing the number of loanwords in a language—has been attempted on numerous occasions worldwide. We have already briefly discussed Japanese speaker attitudes to loanwords in §7.3. In 1989, in an attempt to take such public opinion into account—or perhaps on a personal crusade—then Minister of Health and Welfare, Koizumi Jun'ichirō, set up a committee to look into the overuse of loanwords in government. Shortly after he became prime minister in 2001, the National Institute for Japanese Language and Linguistics in Tokyo set up a Loanword Committee (LC) with responsibility for creating loanword replacements. Between 2002 and 2004, the LC carried out four public surveys to gauge levels of awareness, comprehension and usage of nearly 400 loanwords. Those most widely understood were removed from further analysis. Replacements for the remainder became the focus of the LC's deliberations, the results of which were published in a series of four reports.

As examples of the LC's work, Table 8.3 lists the 20 least comprehended loanwords, along with their main recommended replacements. All are from English etyma, shown in the third column. The fourth and fifth columns show the degree of comprehension (information the LC garnered from their surveys), both overall and restricted to the oldest over-60 age cohort. In all cases, average comprehension rates among the elderly were lower than those of the general population. In most instances, the LC recommended only one replacement, shown in the rightmost column, although two are put forward for both (n) *eNpawaameNto* 'empowerment' and (q) *riterašii* 'literacy', corresponding to different English meanings. In all cases, the replacements are drawn wholly or partly from Sino-Japanese (SJ: §7.1). Hybrids drawn only partly from SJ are typically mixed with native Japanese words: *riyoo+<u>šiyasusa</u>* 'lit. use + <u>ease of doing</u>' for (g) *akusešibiritii* 'accessibility' (the native Japanese element is underlined). Two suggested replacements still contain loanwords: (f) *geNširyokuboosai+<u>seNtaa</u>* 'lit. nuclear power disaster prevention + <u>centre</u>' and (t) *haišucu+<u>zero</u>* 'lit. emission+<u>zero</u>' (loanwords underlined).

Loanwords are often regarded by native speakers as being overly long. In only one case does the recommended replacement consist of more characters than the loan: *yomikaki+nooryoku* 'lit. reading and writing ability' for (q) *riterašii* 'literacy'. Overall, therefore, loanword replacements offer significant economies for the printed word: the average replacement is composed of 4.3 characters, as opposed to 7.7 characters for the average loan. In some cases a recommended replacement fails

8.3 Loanword Reform

	loan	English etymon	degree of comprehension (%)		recommended replacement
			all	over-60s	
a	roodo+puraišiNgu	road pricing	3.0	1.1	doorokakiN 道路課金
b	paburiQku+iNborubumeNto	public involvement	3.3	1.4	juumiNsaNkaku 住民参画
c	iNkyubeešoN	incubation	3.3	3.3	kigyoošieN 起業支援
d	eNfoosumeNto	enforcement	3.4	1.1	hoošiQkoo 法執行
e	koNsoošiamu	consortium	4.1	2.2	kyoodookigyootai 共同事業体
f	ofusaito+seNtaa	off-site centre	4.2	3.9	geNširyokuboosai+seNtaa 原子力防災センター
g	akusešibiritii	accessibility	4.4	2.1	riyoo+šiyasusa 利用しやすさ
h	akauNtabiritii	accountability	4.4	3.4	secumeisekiniN 説明責任
i	ajeNda	agenda	4.7	3.2	keNtookadai 検討課題
j	rešipieNto	recipient	4.9	2.7	išokukaNja 移植患者
k	tasuku+foosu	task force	4.9	3.7	tokubecusagyoohaN 特別作業班
l	kauNtaapaato	counterpart	5.3	4.1	taiooaite 対応相手
m	koNpuraiaNsu	compliance	5.7	1.6	hooreijuNšu 法令遵守
n	eNpawaameNto	empowerment	5.7	2.3	nooryokukaika 能力開化 keNgeNfuyo 権限付与
o	haamonaizeešoN	harmonization	5.8	3.0	kyoočoo 協調
p	toreesabiritii	traceability	6.1	0.6	rirekikaNri 履歴管理
q	riterašii	literacy	6.3	1.1	yomikaki+nooryoku 読み書き能力 kacuyoonooryoku 活用能力
r	saabeeraNsu	surveillance	6.4	3.8	čoosakaNši 調査監視
s	sapurai+saido	supply side	6.6	4.8	kyookyuugawa 供給側
t	zero+emiQšoN	zero emissions	6.7	3.0	haišucu+zero 排出ゼロ

Table 8.3: The 20 least comprehended loanwords

to convey the full meaning of the loan. The LC admitted it received considerable criticism for its recommendation of naQtokušiNsacu 'lit. consented medical examination' for iNfoomudo+koNseNto 'informed consent'. No notion of any 'informing' on the part of the physician is contained in the SJ replacement.

While local government bodies' reaction to the LC's replacement recommendations was generally favourable, some academics saw them as a waste of time. One found it difficult to imagine anyone leafing through any future 'loanword replacement manual' while penning an essay or newspaper article. The reaction of the general public appears to have been mixed, with many of the recommended replacements regarded as difficult to understand. More than a decade later, few seem to have captured the public imagination outside of the government sector. Those that have caught on, such as (b) *juumiɴsaɴkaku* 'lit. resident participation' for *paburiǪku+iɴborubumeɴto* 'public involvement', were already observed before the formation of the LC.

8.4 Loanword Prohibition

Official prohibition of a language can take on many forms. Worldwide, prohibitions have been implemented within education systems, legal systems and the mass media, or have been limited to public places or specific scripts. The severity of a given prohibition may vary from linguicidal (premeditated language murder: §7.5) through to ordinances whose ultimate sanction is weak while, in some cases, only 'part' of a language may be prohibited. In such instances, loanwords are generally the victims. In Japan, between 1940 and 1945, English was officially declared a *tekiseigo* 'combatant language' and a concerted attempt was made to remove it from public life. This was in stark contrast to the US, where during this time, on the basis of 'know thy enemy', the study of Japanese was actively promoted. The US War Department even issued a number of education manuals on Japanese including *Spoken Japanese* (1945), authored by leading linguists of the time Bernard Bloch and Eleanor Harz Jorden (§8.13).

Calls had been made to ban English classes in Japanese schools as far back as the mid-1920s as a response to the Asian Exclusion Act, signed into US Federal Law in 1924. The previous year, the Anglo-Japanese Alliance, dating back to 1902, had been terminated. A series of events then conspired to cause further deterioration in relations between Japan and the two major English-speaking countries, contributing to strong anti-British and anti-American sentiment. These included the Japanese invasion of Manchuria and the establishment of the Manchukuo state in 1932, which caused Japan to quit the League of Nations in 1933; the termination of the Washington Naval Treaty the following year; the provision by the British of materiel and support for China after the beginning of the Sino-Japanese War in 1937; a US embargo on the export of aviation fuel and scrap metal to Japan in 1940; and, finally, later the same year, Japan's signing of the Tripartite Pact with Germany and Italy, both of whom were already at war with Britain.

By 1940, schools operating under the auspices of the Ministry of War had removed English from their entrance examinations and by 1943 foreign language education (effectively English) had become an elective in all secondary schools. Immediately after the Pacific War broke out in December 1941, American and British movies were banned in cinemas and all 'enemy music' forbidden, with the exception of *Hotaru no hikari* 'Firefly Glow', whose melody is that of *Auld Lang Syne*.

In the vast majority of cases, what were banned after 1940 were not English words, but English borrowings (§7.3). In the 1940s, the overwhelming majority of

Fig. 8.4: De-anglicization of cigarette brands
Left: Golden Bat (1906–1939), Right: Golden Kite (1940–1949)

loanwords were written in katakana while, unlike the modern convention, katakana was also employed in additional domains which employ hiragana today (Table 4.1). Katakana loanwords were thus frequently underlined, conferring on them a high level of saliency on a page of printed matter and further heightening their loan status in the mind of the Japanese reader. This made loanwords (though, of course, not necessarily English loanwords) easy targets for bowdlerizers and censors, as easy as words written in Roman script: in other words, English proper. This, coupled with linguistic ignorance and propagandistic zeal on the part of the prohibitors, offers a compelling explanation for the blurring of English with English loans.

Prohibitions on English loans originated from a variety of different sources. The most important were those emanating from government ministries. These began in the spring of 1940 and included a promulgation by the Ministry of Railways which removed English signage from over 4,000 stations nationwide. Erected in the preceding decades for the convenience of overseas visitors, signs such as *ENTRANCE, WC* or *STATION MASTER* were taken down, while Japanese signs containing English loanwords were 'cleansed': the loan *puraqtofoomu* 'platform' was altered to *joošaroo* 'boarding passage' (for a modern multilingual station sign see Fig. 4.14.3). The Ministry of Education, Science and Culture ordered educational institutes containing English personal names, or even the kanji 英 'English, UK', to change their names. The Ministry of Finance, meanwhile, banned cigarette brands with English names. *Golden Bat*, one of the leading tobacco brands, for example, was renamed 金鵄 *kinši* 'golden kite' (Fig. 8.4), the name of a military decoration possessing strong mythical-imperial associations.

Other sources of prohibitions were police departments (the Tokyo Metropolitan Police Department banned the use of English loanwords in table tennis matches); sports societies (the All Japan Physical Education Society prohibited sports names, such as *ragubii* 'rugby', *gorufu* 'golf' and *hoqkee* 'hockey', replacing them with *tookyuu* 'fight ball', *dakyuu* 'strike ball' and *jookyuu* 'stick ball'); local and municipal bodies (Kyoto Botanical Gardens banned English loanword plant names: *kosumosu* 'cosmos', for example, was changed to *akizakura* 'autumn cherry'); and NHK, which stopped using *rajio* 'radio' and *suteetomeNto* 'communiqué' and then banned the use of *anauNsaa* 'announcer'. The final source for prohibitions were self-regulatory. Here, independent corporations or private bodies took it upon themselves to fall in line: *burijisutoNtaiya* 'Bridgestone Corporation' changed their name to *niQpoNtaiya* 'Japan Tyres' in 1942.

One common strategy encountered in the coining of *tekiseigo* replacements was imitation (§7.1, §7.3), namely through the creation of loan meanings and loan translations based on the pre-prohibition English loans. An example of a loan meaning, as a replacement for the English borrowing *seefu*, is the additional application to Japanese *aNzeN* 'safe' of the sense 'reaching a base without being put out' (baseball). Another example, this time as a replacement for *hooruiNwaN,* is the application of the sense 'hole in one' (golf) to Japanese *hoo* 'phoenix', an extension of the English series 'birdie, eagle, albatross'. An example of a loan translation, on the other hand, can be seen in the replacement of the loan *iNfiirudofurai* 'in-field fly' (baseball) by Sino-Japanese morphemes (§7.1) to form the novel compound 内野飛球 *naiyahikyuu* 'lit. inside field + fly ball'. Loan translations were not always direct and in many cases only part of the original loanword was rendered into Japanese, as in 金鵄 *kiNši* 'golden kite' for *Golden Bat* (Fig. 8.4), or in the replacement *niQpoNtaimuzu* 'Nippon Times' for *japaNtaimuzu* 'Japan Times', the name of a newspaper. In other cases, additional elements were added to a loan translation: *kurowaši* 'Black Eagles' for *iiguruzu* 'Eagles', the name of a Tokyo baseball team.

Perhaps the most common strategy, however, was to create neologisms not deducible from their English counterparts, a strategy sometimes referred to as 'loan creation'. The replacements 球童 *kyuudoo* 'ball-child' for *kyadi* 'caddy', 正球 *seikyuu* 'correct-ball' for *sutoraiku* 'strike' (baseball) and 音盤 *oNbaN* 'sound-disk' for *rekoodo* '(musical) record' all fall under this category. An English loan was not unfrequently replaced with an unrelated Japanese term carrying heavy undertones of government propaganda. The magazine *modaNniQpoN* 'Modern Japan' was renamed *šiNtaiyoo* 'New Sun', while Singapore, occupied by Japan from 1942–1945, was renamed *šoowatoo* 'Shōwa Island', after the reign name (§6.9) of Emperor Hirohito.

8.5 The *Kokugo* Curriculum

Japanese, or *kokugo* (§6.8), is a required subject in Japanese schools from the first grade of elementary school (six years old). The modern Japanese educational system can be traced back to the *gakusei* 'educational system order' (hereafter, 'the Order') of 1872. Issued by the Ministry of Education, Science and Culture (modern day MEXT; hereafter, 'the Ministry'), established the previous year in 1871, the Order established eight school districts across Japan (reduced to seven the next year) consisting of primary schools (ages six to 14), secondary schools (ages 14 to 19) and institutes of higher education (ages 20 and above), with primary schools being compulsory. Primary schools were divided into ordinary primary schools for children aged six to 10 and higher primary schools for children aged 10 to 14. The Order listed spelling, calligraphy, vocabulary, conversation, book reading, ethics, letter writing, grammar, arithmetic, health, geography, science, physical education and music as required subjects for ordinary primary schools, with the addition of history, geography and cartography, natural history and chemistry to the higher primary school curriculum. It did not, however, define *kokugo* as an independent subject. This did not happen until the third revision of the *shōgakkōrei* 'primary school ordinance' issued by the Ministry in 1900, in which *kokugo* was listed along with ethics, arithmetic and physical education as a required subject for ordinary primary schools; and along with ethics, arithmetic, Japanese history, geology, science, drawing, singing, physical education and, for girls, sewing as a required subject for higher primary schools. From 1903, government-issued textbooks were prescribed to primary schools and the propagation of the 'standard language', or *hyōjungo* (§7.7), became a top priority throughout the country.

Starting in 1946, after the end of WWII and the occupation of Japan by the Allied forces, the Order underwent a major reform in which it was remodelled to resemble the educational system of the US. This included the reestablishment of ordinary primary schools as elementary schools (six years) and higher primary schools as junior high schools (three years)—both of which had been renamed 'National People's Schools' during the war—as well as the creation of non-compulsory high school education (three years). Government-issued textbooks were also abandoned and a system of authorization for privately published textbooks was set up by the Ministry.

A new set of educational guidelines, known as the *gakushū shidō yōryō* 'guidelines for school teaching' (hereafter, 'the Guidelines') were compiled by the Ministry in 1947, under the guidance of the Allied General Headquarters (GHQ). These were heavily centred on the 'education through experience' model promoted by American educational theorist John Dewey (1859-1952). This meant the focus of *kokugo* education shifted from the memorization of vocabulary and reading of texts to its practical use in society. This is nowhere more apparent than in the preface to the *kokugo* section of the Guidelines which sets the following four goals: (1) to help students function better in society by enriching their expressive willpower; (2) to develop student speaking and writing skills as a tool for self-expression and influencing others; (3) to encourage students to read books to increase their knowledge, for enjoyment and to experience the richness of literature; and (4) to help students improve their social lives through the use of proper and refined language. While idealist from a Western educational standpoint, the experience-based curriculum of the first Guidelines was met with heavy criticism in Japan and eventually replaced in a 1958–1960 revision with a more systematic approach based on acquisition of knowledge.

This revision was, in many ways, the foundation of the modern approach to elementary and secondary education in Japan. *Kokugo* was listed as a required subject for elementary and junior high school students and, for high schools, it was separated into the two required subjects of Modern Japanese and Classical Japanese, the latter including the study of *kanbun* 'Classical Chinese' (§8.7). One major development in the revised Guidelines was the addition to the elementary school curriculum of *kyōiku kanji* 'educational kanji', a list of kanji to be taught each year, beginning in the 1st grade. The 1958 Guidelines listed 881 characters, which were increased to 996 in 1968 and finally to 1,006 in 1989. The 881 characters of the 1958 Guidelines were originally issued as a supplement to the *tōyōkanjihyō* in 1948 (§8.2), with a preamble stating that the kanji listed in the supplement were to be taught during compulsory education. That said, the 1958 Guidelines were the first attempt to arrange the kanji into groups for each specific school year. In its current incarnation, the educational kanji lists 80 characters for 1st grade, 160 for 2nd, 200 each for 3rd and 4th, 185 for 5th and 181 for 6th grade. There are plans to add 20 new characters from the names of prefectures (岐 and 阜 from 岐阜 Gifu, 沖 and 縄 from 沖縄 Okinawa) to the list in the next major revision in 2020. While there is no official number of kanji required to be taught in junior high and high schools, in a 2010 memorandum MEXT suggested that the bulk of the remainder of the characters in the *jōyōkanjihyō* (§8.2) be taught by the end of the 3rd grade of junior high school. Interestingly, the same memorandum states that, due to the widespread use of computers and smart devices, it is no longer crucial for students to be able to write every character in the *jōyōkanjihyō* and that in many cases reading comprehension alone is adequate.

The latest incarnation of the Guidelines, issued in 2008–2010, lists detailed curricula for *kokugo* classes from the 1st grade of elementary school through to high school graduation. Approximately 225 hours, or 1/3 of the curriculum, are allotted to *kokugo* in the 1st and 2nd grades of elementary school. This number is gradually decreased in each subsequent grade, with 131 being allotted for the 6th grade. The number is decreased still further in junior high school with 117 hours allotted in the 1st and 2nd grades and 88 in the 3rd. High school *kokugo* classes are divided into General Skills (117 hours), Expression Skills (88 hours), Modern Literature A and B (175 hours) and Classical Japanese A and B (175 hours), these being the total number of hours over three years. Classes are distributed across school years as seen fit by each individual school or school district.

8.6 Prescriptive Grammar in Education

In §8.5, we presented an overview of the development of the modern day *kokugo* curriculum. Here, and in §8.7, we will take a deeper look at two specific aspects of this curriculum: prescriptive grammar and Classical Japanese education.

A highly prescriptive system of grammar, known as *gakkō bunpō* 'school grammar' (SG), is taught in Japanese schools from elementary school to high school. SG is based, with a few minor modifications, on the grammatical analysis of the early 20th century linguist Hashimoto Shinkichi (§8.12). The first textbook to adopt SG was *Chūtō bunpō* 'Intermediate Grammar', published by the Ministry of Education, Science and Culture in 1943. A revised edition was issued in 1947, which went on to become the foundation of the SG taught in schools today. SG classifies words into free forms and bound forms (§3.1), each of which are then separated into words which inflect and words which do not. This classification is schematicized in Fig. 8.6.1. Inflecting free forms are broken down into predicates, or verbals, which consist of verbs (§3.3, §3.4), adjectives (what we call 'verbal adjectives': §3.5) and adjectival verbs (what we call 'nominal adjectives': §3.5); while non-inflecting free forms are broken down into subjects, or nominals (nouns and pronouns: §3.2), modifiers (adverbs and adnouns: §3.5), conjunctives (conjunctions: §3.11) and independents (interjections: §3.1). Bound forms, meanwhile, consist of auxiliary verbs (a misnomer for verbal suffixes: see §3.7, §3.8 and below), which are inflecting, and particles (§3.12, §3.13), which are not.

Predicates are grouped into seven conjugational classes: *godan* 'quinquagrade' (consonant-stem), *kami ichidan* 'upper monograde' (vowel-stem ending in *i*), *shimo ichidan* 'lower monograde' (vowel-stem ending in *e*), *kagyō henkaku* 'K-irregular', *sagyō henkaku* 'S-irregular', *keiyōshi-gata* 'adjective-type' and *keiyōdōshi-gata*

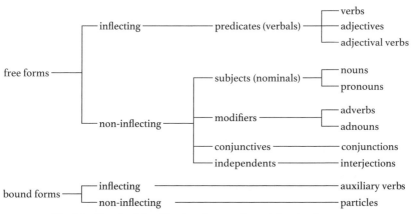

Fig. 8.6.1: Standard classification of parts of speech in school grammar

'adjectival verb-type'. Each class is then given six conjugational forms: irrealis, adverbial, conclusive, adnominal, conditional and imperative. See Table 8.6 for a summary. Each of these conjugational forms is then said to take various suffixes—or 'auxiliary verbs'—to express grammatical meaning. For example, the suffix *-nai* attaches to the irrealis from of a verb to express the negative (*noma-nai* 'don't drink' or *oki-nai* 'don't wake up'), while *-tai* attaches to the adverbial to express desideration (*nomi-tai* 'want to drink', *oki-tai* 'want to wake up').

At first glance, SG appears to be not so different from the descriptive analysis given in Chapter 3 of this volume, apart from some disagreements in terminology and the place of segmentation between elements in a verbal suffix string. In our analysis, *nomanai* consists of the stem *nom-*, followed by the union vowel *a* and the suffix *-na-i* (Fig. 3.7), while in SG the stem is *no-*, followed by the irrealis ending *ma* and the suffix *-nai*. On further inspection, however, some major problems quickly become apparent. First and foremost, the stem of the quinquagrade verb *nomu* is said to be *no-*, but each of the conjugational endings, *ma~mo, mi, mu, mu, me, me*, contain the same initial consonant *m*. If a verb stem is to be defined as the part of a verb that stays constant across all inflections, then why is *m* not included in the stem? The same can be said for the *ki* found in all the conjugational endings of *okiru*, or the *be* found in all the conjugational endings of *taberu*. And why do *kuru* and *suru* have no stem at all?

The answers to these questions lie in the fact that the six conjugational forms posited by SG are not based on a phonemic analysis (§2.1), but instead on a flawed kana-based analysis of Japanese dating back to the 18th century. Since kana are moraic and cannot represent individual consonants (with the exception of the mora consonants: §2.4), there is no concept of a consonant-stem verb in SG. Instead, segmentation of verbs and suffixes takes place not on the morpheme (§3.1), but on the mora (or kana) level. Thus, *nom-u* 'drink' (nonpast) is interpreted as

verb class	example	stem	irrealis	adverbial
quinquagrade	*nomu* 'drink'	*no*	*noma~ nomo*	*nomi*
upper monograde	*okiru* 'wake up'	*o*	*oki*	*oki*
lower monograde	*taberu* 'eat'	*ta*	*tabe*	*tabe*
K-irregular	*kuru* 'come'	—	*ko*	*ki*
S-irregular	*suru* 'do'	—	*sa~ši~se*	*ši*
adjective-type	*akai* 'red'	*aka*	*akakaro*	*akaku~ akakaQ*
adjectival verb-type	*šizuka* 'quiet'	*šizuka*	*šizukadaro*	*šizukani~ šizukade~ šizukadaQ*

Table 8.6: Conjugational classes and forms in school grammar

no.mu (with periods indicating mora boundaries), while *nom-e* 'drink' (imperative) is interpreted as *no.me*. Here, *no* is treated as the stem and *mu* and *me* are deemed 'conjugational endings'—in reality *m* is part of the stem *nom-*, with *u* and *e* being verbal suffixes. Just as there was no concept of the phoneme in the 18th century, there was also no concept of the morpheme, let alone the idea that a morpheme could be null: in SG, conjugational endings were posited in all cases, even when it would make more sense to have no ending at all. Thus, despite the fact that *ki* and *be* appear in all inflections of *okiru* and *taberu*, they are not included in the stems of these verbs as this would yield forms such as *oki-ø-nai* or *tabe-ø-nai*, where the conjugational ending is null. The same can be said for *suru* and *kuru*, which lose their stems entirely in SG.

The names of the conjugational classes are also based on a non-descriptive pre-modern analysis, with the terms *godan* 'quinquagrade (lit. five rows)' and *ichidan* 'monograde (lit. one row)' originating in the *gojūonzu* '50-sounds table'. The *gojūonzu* is a chart of the 47 original kana, dating back to at least the 11th century, with the letters arranged across five rows for the vowels, *a~i~u~e~o*, and ten columns for the consonants *k~s~t~n~h~m~y~r~w* and ø (no consonant). Since *nom-u* is interpreted as possessing the five forms *no.ma ~ no.mi ~ no.mu ~ no.me ~ no.mo* (the conjectural-hortative *nom-oo* 'will probably drink ~ let's drink ~ I think I'll drink' is interpreted as *nomo-o* in SG), it is said to conjugate across five rows of the table, hence the name *godan*. Likewise, the vowel-stem verbs *oki-ru* and *tabe-ru* only conjugate across one row of the table (*o.ki ~ o.ki.ru ~ o.ki.re ~ o.ki.ro, ta.be ~ ta.be.ru ~ ta.be.re ~ ta.be.ro*), giving rise to the name *ichidan* 'monograde'. When the 50-sounds table is presented vertically in the traditional fashion (Fig. 8.6.2), kana ending in *i* come in the upper half of the table, while those ending in *e* come in the lower half, giving rise to the terms *kami* 'upper' and *shimo* 'lower'.

(verb class)	conclusive	adnominal	conditional	imperative
quinquagrade	*nomu*	*nomu*	*nome*	*nome*
upper monograde	*okiru*	*okiru*	*okire*	*okiro*
lower monograde	*taberu*	*taberu*	*tabere*	*tabero*
K-irregular	*kuru*	*kuru*	*kure*	*koi*
S-irregular	*suru*	*suru*	*sure*	*širo~seyo*
adjective-type	*akai*	*akai*	*akakere*	—
adjectival verb-type	*šizukada*	*šizukana*	*šizukanara*	—

Table 8.6 (continued)

	consonants									
w	r	y	m	h	n	t	s	k	ø	
わ	ら	や	ま	は	な	た	さ	か	あ	a
ゐ	り		み	ひ	に	ち	し	き	い	i
	る	ゆ	む	ふ	ぬ	つ	す	く	う	u
ゑ	れ		め	へ	ね	て	せ	け	え	e
を	ろ	よ	も	ほ	の	と	そ	こ	お	o

☐ *godan* (all five rows)

☐ *kami ichidan* (one row, upper half)

☐ *shimo ichidan* (one row, lower half)

Fig. 8.6.2: Role of the 50-sounds table in conjugational class names

Another major problem with SG is that much of its terminology is based on Classical Japanese and thus does not accurately describe the morphology of the modern language. For example, SG posits a conclusive and adnominal form for all verbals, but the conclusive and adnominal merged in Late Middle Japanese (§1.3), leaving only a distinction between nonpast and past (§3.7, §3.15). It is thus inappropriate to distinguish between these two forms in a synchronic analysis. Perhaps most jarring, though, is the use of the term 'auxiliary verb' to describe verbal suffixes. Though it is true that there is semantic overlap between Japanese verbal suffixes and what we call auxiliary verbs in English and other languages (*can* and *-e-ru* ~ *-(r)are-ru* both express the potential, while *want* and *-(i)ta-i* both express the desiderative), Japanese verbal suffixes are morphologically bound to their stems, while auxiliary verbs possess a degree of morphological freedom, capable of being separated from the main verb in a sentence: 'I *can* most likely not *go* there'. Further complicating the issue is the fact that the distinction between verbal suffixes and particles is often not clear in SG, which defines verbal suffixes as inflecting and particles as non-inflecting. This means bound forms, such as *-te* (*-te* form) and *-cucu* (iterative), treated as final suffixes in §3.7, end up being treated as particles in SG. This would be forgivable if SG was consistent in its distinction: this is far from the case, however. While *-te* and *-cucu* become particles in SG, *-ta* (past tense) is treated as a verbal suffix, the reasoning being that *-ta* is derived from Middle Japanese *-tari* (or *-(i)tar-i* in our analysis: §3.15), which was an inflecting form. Similar to the conclusive/adnominal distinction discussed above, such a classification bears little meaning from a synchronic perspective.

These are just a few of the many issues surrounding SG and a full analysis of its deficiencies is well beyond the scope of this volume. Although most linguists are aware of such issues, SG is still regarded as a practical system in Japan for pedagogical reasons—its kana-level analysis makes it easy for schoolchildren to comprehend. The true problem lies with the many linguists in Japan who choose to turn a blind eye to its inadequacies and adhere to SG even in academic analyses.

8.7 Classical Japanese and *Kanbun* Education

Apart from the modern language, schoolchildren in Japan are also required to study Classical Japanese (CJ) and Classical Chinese (CC), or *kanbun*, from junior high school. Both are also required subjects in the National Centre Test for University Admissions (*sentā shiken*). While in the West, the term 'Classical Japanese' is typically used to refer to Middle Japanese—specifically, the language of the mid-late Heian period (10th–12th century)—CJ education in Japan focuses not only on Middle Japanese, but Old Japanese (OJ) and Early Modern Japanese (EMJ) as well (§1.3). A major focus is put on not only being able to comprehend CJ, but on being able to translate classical texts into Modern Japanese (MoJ), word-by-word. In fact, it is not uncommon for natural sounding translations to receive lower marks than artificial direct translations. While this style of teaching is useful for helping students to remember the meaning of each individual grammatical form, criticisms have been voiced that it impedes student comprehension of the text as a whole, leaving them with only a superficial knowledge of the language.

Similar to Ancient Greek or Latin taught in the West, there exists a traditional style for reading CJ which does not accurately reflect the actual pronunciation of the time in which the texts were written. Although CJ is written in *rekishiteki kanazukai* 'historical kana usage' (§1.3, §8.2), a prescriptive system of orthography based on the pronunciation of the 9th–10th century (§2.9), each word is pronounced as it would be in MoJ. For example, the EMJ words *opoki* 'big' and *apugi* 'fan' are written おほき <ohoki> and あふぎ <afugi>, but pronounced *ooki* and *oogi*, as they are in MoJ. See Table 8.7 for a selection of some of the more common 'reading rules', along with examples.

The study of *kanbun* has played a major role in education since the earliest days of the literate period (7th–8th century). In fact, the first educational institution to be established in Japan, the Daigakuryō, or Imperial University, centred its education on the Chinese classics, while most education before the late 19th century was focused around the study of such classics as well. What is unique about *kanbun*, and the reason why we explicitly use the word *kanbun* here instead of 'Classical Chinese', is that *kanbun* entails not only the study of CC literature, but a specific

reading rule	examples
word-internal <ha> read as *wa*	あは <aha> *awa*, かは <kaha> *kawa*
all other word-internal <h~f> dropped	かひ <kahi> *kai*, さへ <sahe> *sae*
<au> (or <afu>) read as *oo*	たう <tau> *too*, あふ <afu> *oo*
<iu> (or <ifu>) read as *yuu*	きう <kiu> *kyuu*, いふ <ifu> *yuu*
<eu> (or <efu>) read as *yoo*	れう <reu> *ryoo*, えふ <efu> *yoo*

Table 8.7: *Spelling versus pronunciation in historical kana usage*

method of reading CC in Japanese known as *kanbun kundoku* (§1.3, §4.4). In *kanbun kundoku*, a CC text is translated—more appropriately, 'transposed'—into Japanese word-by-word in a prescribed manner by means of reading marks, or glosses. These include lexical glosses providing *kun-yomi* and *on-yomi* for kanji (§4.4); morphosyntactic glosses providing grammatical morphemes, such as particles (§3.12, §3.13) and verbal suffixes (§3.7, §3.8), not in the original Chinese; and word order inversion marks for converting the passage to Japanese word order. The first passage of the *The Analects*, for example, given in the original CC in (1a), emerges as (1b) when read in Japanese using the *kanbun kundoku* method.

(1a) Chinese text:

子	曰	学	而	時	習ㇾ	之
Confucius	say	study	and.then	in.time	learn	this

不㆓	亦	説㆒	乎
NEG	EXCL	delightful	Q

(1b) Prescribed reading:

子	曰はく	学びて	時に	之を	習ふ
ši	iw-aku	manab-ite	toki=ni	kore=o	nara-u
Confucius	say-NMNLZ	study-CVB	time=DAT	this=ACC	learn-CCL

亦	説ばしからずや
mata	yorokobaši-kar-azu=ya
EXCL	delightful-VBLZ-NEG.CCL=Q

'Confucius says, "Study, and in time, you shall learn. How can one not be delighted (by such acquisitions of new knowledge)?"'

For the Japanese student, this sentence is not read in Sino-Japanese or Mandarin, but in a prescribed Japanese rendering that is a direct word-by-word translation of the original CC. A certain amount of what one might call 'translational acrobatics' are performed in order to attain this. For example, the verb 曰 'say' is rendered *iw-aku*, a nominalized form of *i-u* 'say' dating back to OJ, allowing it to precede the quotation (normally in Japanese, being an SOV language, the verb would need to come at the end of the sentence: §1.2, §3.1). Further, the final two words of the first sentence, 習之 'learn this', and the first three words of the second sentence, 不亦説 'not also delightful', are reordered to match Japanese word order. In the case of 習之, an inversion gloss ㇾ (known as *re-ten* in Japanese due to its similarity to the katakana レ) is appended to the first character to show that it is to be inverted with the second one; in the case of 不亦説, the kanji numerals 一 'one' and 二 'two' are placed next to the characters showing the appropriate Japanese word order. Such Japanese renderings of *kanbun* are always given in CJ (not in MoJ), although in a register of the language heavily influenced by CC lexicon and grammar (see §7.1 for further discussion).

8.8 Japanese as a Second Language Education

Presumably, some form of Japanese as a second language (JSL) education has existed since the dawn of Japan's foreign relations. The earliest record of L2 learners studying Japanese is from the 8th century, when scholars from the Korean kingdom of Silla came to Japan to study the language. Centuries later, in 1414, the Joseon dynasty Bureau of Interpreters would establish Japanese as an official language of study, publishing *Iropa*, the world's first JSL textbook in 1492. The Jesuits arrived in Japan around the same time, becoming the first Westerners to study the language (§1.3, §8.13) and, over the next three centuries, the works of the Jesuits, written mainly in Portuguese, would be translated into Spanish and French, bringing the language to a larger audience. Following the opening of Japan's ports in the mid-19th century (§7.2), studies in Japanese took on a new life in the West, bringing the first bilingual dictionaries (§8.10) and grammars (§8.13) of the language. JSL education became prominent in the US and UK in the years leading up to and during WWII, under the premise of 'know thy enemy' (§8.4). At the same time, Japanese was heavily promoted or, under less favourable conditions, mandated throughout the Japanese colonial empire, consisting of Korea, Taiwan, parts of China and the South Pacific.

The modern field of JSL education can largely be attributed to the Japanese educator, Naganuma Naoe (1894–1973). Trained in the 'oral method' by the British applied linguist, Harold Palmer (1877–1949), Naganuma devoted his life to creating a system of JSL education which focused on learning Japanese through actual conversation. His original series of texts, *The Standard Japanese Readers*, first published in the early 1930s, became a staple for JSL classrooms both in and outside Japan. Naganuma was hired by the US Embassy in Tokyo prior to WWII to teach Japanese to embassy staff and military attachés and, following the war, appointed chief instructor of the Army Area and Language Course of the Allied forces. Shortly afterwards, in 1948, he founded the Tokyo School of Japanese Language (now the Naganuma School), the first school in Japan devoted solely to JSL education.

JSL institutions began to increase in the 1950s and 1960s with the initiation of the Japanese Government Scholarship programme for international students in 1954. JSL departments were established at many universities, increasing exponentially in the 1980s and 1990s following the promulgation in 1984 of the 'Plan to Accept 100,000 International Students' by Prime Minister Nakasone Yasuhiro. The number of JSL institutions in Japan peaked in 2011 at 451 institutions, but decreased significantly following the 2011 Tōhoku earthquake and tsunami, with just 258 institutes reported in 2018. This number does not include JSL programs in universities, however, and the actual number of international students in Japan has been steadily increasing since 2014, with a total of just under 300,000 students reported in 2018. The number of JSL programs outside Japan is significantly larger. In 2015, over 16,000 JSL institutions in 137 countries and territories offered JSL education to over 3.6 million students. This number has been on the rise since 1979, when 1,145 institutions and just over 127,000 students were reported.

Currently, JSL education in Japan adheres very closely to the direct method, in which instructors use only Japanese in the classroom and avoid using the learner's native language. The benefits of the direct method are that it allows instructors to teach Japanese to groups of students from various backgrounds, with no common language, while promoting immersion in the spoken language. It is not without its issues, however. Most notable is that it hinders proper instruction in grammar, for which many elements can only be correctly explained through the use of an intermediary language. Many instructors thus supplement the direct method with texts, in English or the learner's native language, on grammar, vocabulary and, in the case of non-sinolingual students, kanji.

The most widely used series of JSL textbooks in Japan is the *Minna no nihongo* series, first published in 1998 by 3A Corporation. *Minna no nihongo* has a long history, being the spiritual successor of the *Nihongo no kiso* (1972–) and *Shin nihongo no kiso* (1990–) series, designed by the Association for Overseas Technical Scholarship. Other commonly used textbooks include the *Genki* series (1999–), which is currently the best-selling JSL textbook series in the West, and the more recent *Marugoto: Japanese Language and Culture* series (2013–). Each of these series are similar in their approach, using sample conversations to teach grammar and vocabulary, starting out with simple structures such as noun-predicate sentences (*wataši=wa amerikajiN=des-u* 'I am an American') and working their way up to the more complex. Grammatical explanations are usually quick and to the point, avoiding presenting the learner with too much information at once. Information on pitch accent (§2.6, §2.7) and on dialects (§7.7–§7.11) is generally conspicuous in its absence. While effective in equipping learners with a repertoire of useful expressions in a short period of time, these textbooks have a tendency to grossly oversimplify (and as a consequence, ironically, complicate) grammar. For example, nearly all JSL textbooks start out by teaching the polite form of copulas and verbs (§6.3), which from a practical standpoint makes sense: better safe than sorry. Many textbooks, however, take this method too far, not even acknowledging the existence of neutral forms until far into the course. *Minna no Nihongo*, a major culprit of this practice, does not cover neutral, or 'dictionary forms', until Lesson 18, whereupon it enters into a bizarre explanation of 'how to make the dictionary form' of a verb from its polite form, as if the neutral form is some kind of back-formation. Given the transparency and simplicity of Japanese verbal morphology (§3.3, §3.7, §3.8), this method leaves students at a major disadvantage once they encounter more complex structures, a problem which is all too common in direct-method-heavy JSL education.

8.9 Language Tests and Examinations

A useful way of viewing Japanese language tests and examinations is to broadly divide them according to the type of examinee for whom the test is designed: the native or non-native speaker. The latter type of test has been the subject of more research, and more criticism, than the former. Non-native speaker orientated tests are used, for example, as selection criteria in university entry examinations for overseas students, or must be passed in order to obtain a vocational licence, such as that of a nurse or caregiver. Japanese language tests geared towards the native speaker, on the other hand, tend to be taken for fun or as a personal challenge and studied towards as a hobby. Since a native speaker is not particularly challenged by a test seeking to establish levels of reading or listening comprehension, native speaker tests tend to focus on difficult vocabulary and grammar, correct usage of honorifics (§6.3) and, biggest of all, 'kanji power'.

The most widely taken non-native speaker Japanese language test is the Japanese-Language Proficiency Test (*nihongo nōryoku shiken*; JLPT). The test was first held in 1984 in 15 countries and 21 cities and sat by just over 7,000 examinees. By 2017, it was typically being held twice a year in 80 countries and 239 cities and was taken by just over 887,000 examinees: an 11-fold increase in test cities and 127-fold increase in examinees. The JLPT currently has five levels, N1–N5, with the linguistic competence required to pass N1 described as 'the ability to understand Japanese used in a variety of circumstances' and N5 as 'the ability to understand some basic Japanese'. All JLPT levels test kanji (reading and usage), vocabulary, grammar, reading comprehension and listening. Depending on level, test times run from 105 minutes (N5) to 170 minutes (N1), while estimated study times range from 250 (N5) to 2,600 hours (N1) for sinosphere students, and 325 (N5) to 4,800 (N1) hours for non-sinosphere students. Scaled scores are used for passing and candidates must pass all individual sections, as well as achieving an overall pass score. In 2016, N2 was the most popular level, while just under a quarter of candidates sat N1. A little under half of all candidates across all levels were higher education students.

While the adoption of scaled scores when the examination was redesigned in 2010 has undoubtedly succeeded in more accurate measurement of a candidate's Japanese ability, the JLPT has been a target of criticism on several fronts. One gripe is its multiple-choice format throughout. More serious is the fact that the JLPT fails to examine either writing or speaking ability, this despite the organizers' claim that the 'JLPT places importance on [...] [the] ability to use the knowledge [of vocabulary and grammar] in actual communication'. A pass mark in the JLPT is no guarantee the person concerned possesses interpersonal speaking, or writing, skills. The test also places a disproportionately large emphasis on kanji which puts sinosphere students at a major advantage as they can solve many of the kanji questions without knowing the Japanese readings or connotations. Not to mention that kanji knowledge is not a reliable indicator of communicative ability.

In recent years, the Examination for Japanese University Admission for International Students (*nihon ryūgaku shiken*; EJU) has become the test of choice for Japanese university admissions departments. First held in 2002, the EJU can now be sat twice a year in Japan and selected Asian countries. Just over 51,000 students took the test across both 2017 sessions, of whom more than half were Chinese nationals. Covering writing, listening and reading, the EJU, though still not testing speaking ability, also tests candidates' Japanese knowledge of specific subject areas, such as physics, mathematics or, for liberal arts, 'Japan and the world'.

Three other non-native speaker Japanese language tests deserve mention. The first is the Test of Practical Japanese (*jitsuyō nihongo kentei*; J.TEST). Established in 1991, the J.TEST has six levels, testing reading, writing and listening, and is held six times a year in Japan and selected East Asian countries. The J.TEST markets itself towards businesses looking to ascertain the Japanese level of non-native speaker jobseekers or promotion-material employees. The second, the Business Japanese Proficiency Test (*bijinesu nihongo nōryoku tesuto*; BJT), was established somewhat later in 1996. The BJT is geared specifically towards attaining the 'communicative proficiency required in business settings'. Held in Japan and selected centres worldwide, in 2016 there were approximately 6,500 applicants. It is entirely computer-based, with examinees placed in booths with individual headphones. Finally, the Japanese Computerized Adaptive Test (*nihongo konpyūtā tekiōgata tesuto*; J-CAT), in development since 2004, is a free web-based test, sittable anytime anywhere. While still not a replacement for the JLPT or EJU, an increasing number of universities and organizations have introduced the test for level placement purposes.

The number of language tests for native speakers is far fewer, with only two main players: the Japan Kanji Aptitude Test (*nihon kanji nōryoku kentei*, or *kanken*) and the *nihongo kentei* 'Japanese Test'. Established in 1992, the *kanken* is currently held three times a year at 124 test centres in Japan and 13 test centres abroad. Several levels of the test are also available in a computer-based format more regularly. The number of examinees peaked in 2008 at around 2.9 million annually, but plunged to 2.1 million the following year due to a string of scandals. These numbers have never recovered. The test offers 12 levels, with the easier levels generally sat by young children. The easiest, Level 10, for example, tests the 80 *jōyōkanjihyō* kanji (§8.5) studied in the first year of elementary school. Level 1, on the other hand, is formidably difficult. Candidates must be able to read and write 6,535 kanji and answer questions dealing with their meanings, synonyms, antonyms and homonyms (§5.9); on *ateji* (§4.4) and *kokuji* (§4.5); on traditional and simplified character forms (§4.3); Sino-Japanese vocabulary (§7.1); classical proverbs; complex radicals (§4.2); and rare or unusual readings. Fig. 8.9.1 shows some of the notoriously difficult kanji reading questions from Level 1. The readings for the

嶮路を辿り開敞せる海水に達した。
講師は異国の禽獣を裝養した。
眞夏の如き溽暑が續く。
矯めつ眇めつして品騭する。
疆界の内側は外國人居留地である。
寰中塞外ともに万歳を謳う。
過去の罪咎を教え立てる。
両者の間に罅隙を生じた。
羈軛を脱して別世界の人となる。

【介】

一、〔　〕の漢字を使った①〜④の言葉の中に、その漢字が、他の三つとは異なった意味で使われているものが一つあります。その言葉をそれぞれ番号で答えてください。

① 介在　② 介助　③ 紹介　④ 仲介

Fig. 8.9.1: *Notoriously difficult questions from the Level 1* kanken *(2009 examination)*

Fig. 8.9.2: *More practical questions from the Level 1 JT*

Sino-Japanese words given in order are: 1. *kaišoo* 'unobstructed', 2. *kaɴyoo* 'raise livestock', 3. *koodoo* 'school', 4. *jokušo* 'hot and humid', 5. *hinšicu* 'appraise', 6. *kaɴčuu* 'jurisdiction of the emperor', 7. *kyookai* 'border', 8. *zaikyuu* 'sins and faults', 9. *kiɴgeki* 'discord', 10. *kiyaku* 'bindings'. All of these words are obsolete fossils from *kanbun* (§8.7) and would never be encountered in everyday life. They can be looked at as a type of trivia, rather than practical knowledge.

The Japanese Test (JT) was established more recently, in 2007. It consists of seven levels which test kanji (usage and reading), orthography, honorifics, semantics, vocabulary and grammar. Levels 7 to 4 are aimed at elementary school and junior high school students, with Levels 3 to 1 aimed at high school graduates and above. The JT is held twice a year, with 88 test centres and 76,640 examinees in 2017, most of whom were high school and university students. While the *kanken* tends to focus on 'kanji trivia', the JT focuses on prescriptive—or in the words of its organizers, 'proper'—language usage and critical thinking. The question in Fig. 8.9.2, for example, asks the examinee to pick one out of four kanji compounds containing the character 介 *kai* 'mediate, help', in which 介 is used in a different sense from the others: 1. 介在 *kaizai* 'intervene', 2. 介助 *kaijo* 'assist' (correct answer), 3. 紹介 *šookai* 'introduce' and 4. 仲介 *čuukai* 'mediate'.

8.10 Dictionaries and Lexicography

The Japanese have a long history of lexicography, the earliest dictionaries dating back to roughly the beginning of the literate period (7th–8th century). Most early dictionaries were Chinese character dictionaries and provided definitions in Classical Chinese, with little or no Japanese. By the 9th century, it had become common practice to add Japanese readings to headwords, starting with

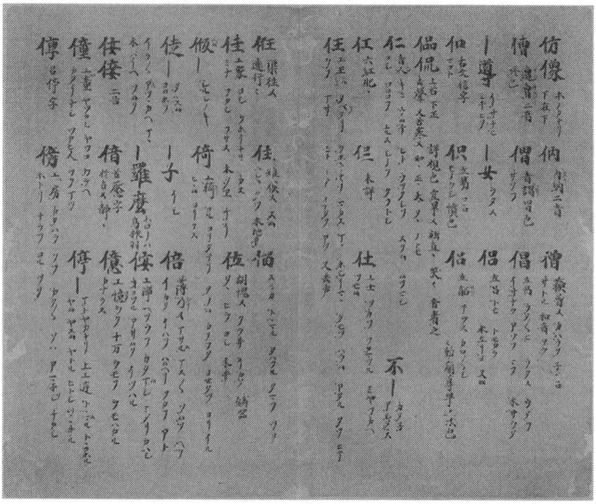

Fig. 8.10: Ruijumyōgishō, *Kanchiin manuscript (山田 1937)*

dictionaries such as *Shinsenjikyō* 'Compiled Mirror of Chinese Characters' (892–901), which provided approximately 3,700 Japanese readings, and *Wamyōruijushō* 'Dictionary of Japanese Terms in Topical Order' (931–938), which provided approximately 2,200.

As time progressed, the number of Japanese readings increased as well, with the 12th century *Ruijumyōgishō* 'Dictionary of Terms and Meanings in Topical Order' providing an impressive 35,585 Japanese readings in its Kanchiin manuscript (Fig. 8.10). The first dictionary to list as headwords Japanese lexemes, rather than Chinese characters, was the 12th century *Irohajiruishō* 'Dictionary of Chinese Characters in *Iroha* Order', the *iroha* order being an early ordering of kana based on a Buddhist poem originating in the *gojūonzu* '50-sounds table' (§8.6). Later dictionaries would adopt *aiueo* order—*Onkochishinsho* 'Book of New Discoveries Through Scrutiny of the Past' (1484) was the first dictionary to do so—but such ordering did not become commonplace until the 19th century.

Most early Japanese dictionaries did not contain detailed definitions, but simply lists of characters with which to write each word. Interestingly, the first dictionary to provide detailed definitions of words was not compiled by a Japanese, but by Portuguese missionaries in Nagasaki at the turn of the 17th century (§1.3, §7.2, §8.13). *Vocabulario da Lingoa de Iapam* (1603–1604), commonly referred to as *Nippo jisho* 'Japanese-Portuguese Dictionary', contained roughly 32,000 headwords with definitions in Portuguese.

The first Japanese-compiled dictionary in the modern sense of the word—a volume of headwords with definitions—was *Wakun no shiori* 'Guide to Japanese Readings', complied by Tanikawa Kotosuga (1709–1776), begun in 1777 and completed posthumously in 1877. Comprising roughly 20,000 entries, Tanikawa's dictionary was the first to adopt *aiueo* order down to the second mora of each lexeme (*a.ka* precedes *a.ki*, but the words in between such as *a.ka.ru* ~ *a.ka.me* ~ *a.ka.ne* come in no particular order). Tanikawa's dictionary was succeeded by dictionaries such as Ōtsuki Fumihiko's (1847–1928) *Genkai* 'Sea of Words' (1889–1891) and Yamada Bimyō's (1868–1910) *Daijiten* 'Great Dictionary' (1912). The first comprehensive multi-volume dictionary was Heibonsha's *Daijiten* (not to be confused with Yamada's work), published in 26 volumes between 1934 and 1936 and comprising 720,000 entries.

The current major Japanese dictionaries are *Kōjien* 'Wide Garden of Words' (1955–), *Daijirin* 'Great Forest of Words' (1988–) and *Daijisen* 'Great Fountain of Words' (1995–). Roughly comparable in size and scope to *Merriam-Webster's Collegiate Dictionary* in the US or the *Concise Oxford English Dictionary* in the UK, each have undergone multiple revisions since their first editions. The gold-standard of modern Japanese lexicography is *Nihon kokugo daijiten* 'Shogakukan's Unabridged Dictionary of the Japanese Language', first published in 1972–1976, with a second edition in 2000–2002. This dictionary is Japan's equivalent of the multi-volume *Oxford English Dictionary*, and comprises 14 volumes with roughly 500,000 entries and 1,000,000 quotations. While an indispensable source of knowledge for any researcher of the language, it is not without its criticisms, in particular its lack of proper etymologies and its failure, in many instances, to include the earliest known attestation of a word.

The gold-standard of kanji lexicography is *Daikanwajiten* 'Great Classical Chinese-Japanese Dictionary', sometimes referred to as 'the Morohashi' in the West after its head editor, Morohashi Tetsuji (1883–1982). First completed in 1960, the most recent revision, published in 1989, boasts 15 volumes with over 51,000 characters and 560,000 compounds and idioms. Japanese kanji dictionaries arrange characters by radicals (§4.2), of which there are traditionally 214, following the system of the authoritative *Kangxi Dictionary*, compiled in China at the order of the Kangxi Emperor in 1716. Most kanji dictionaries for Japanese native speakers focus on Classical Chinese, or *kanbun*, and in many cases do not include modern terms. In addition to the above, various smaller dictionaries can be found in bookstores and there is an extensive market for electronic dictionaries (§8.11).

A wealth of Japanese-English and English-Japanese dictionaries have also been compiled over the past 150 years, starting with James Hepburn's (§8.13) landmark *A Japanese and English Dictionary: With an English and Japanese Index* in 1867. Most modern bilingual dictionaries are designed with Japanese native speakers in mind and do not provide readings of kanji in the definitions, limiting their accessibility for L2 learners. The most expansive Japanese-English dictionary is *Kenkyusha's New Japanese-English Dictionary* (5th edition, 2003), which boasts a total of roughly 230,000 entries including headwords, compounds and idioms. English-Japanese dictionaries are much more numerous than their Japanese-English counterparts, with no less than four large-scale dictionaries boasting over 250,000 entries on the

lexeme	English translation
bunnagur-u	give *sb* a good whaling; dust [thrash] *sb's* jacket (= *nagur-u*)
koibito	(male) a boyfriend; (lit. arch.) a sweetheart; (col.) a boy; a man; *a steady; "a bloke; (female) a girlfriend; (lit. arch.) a sweetheart; (col.) a girl; *a steady
koicu	(towards males) this man [(col.) guy, "fellow, "chap, "bloke]; he (towards females) this woman (lady); she (towards objects) this; this one; this thing *koicu sonna itazura=o ši-te* What do you think you're doing, you naughty boy (girl)?; What do you think you're up to, you little villain?
yaroo	(curse word) a fellow; *(col.) a guy; "(col.) a chap *futo-i yaroo=da* You shameless scoundrel! *namaiki=na yaroo=da* You smart-alecky jerk

Abbreviations: * Americanism; " Briticism; col. = colloquial; lit. = literary; arch. = archaic

Table 8.10: Antiquated slang expressions from a Japanese-English dictionary

market, as well as dozens of smaller ones. The quality of English-Japanese dictionaries is generally high, given the heavy focus on English learning in Japan. Unfortunately, the same cannot be said for Japanese-English dictionaries, many of which contain antiquated translations and recurring errors. Take the list of entries in Table 8.10 from *Kenkyusha's New Japanese-English Dictionary*, where such antiquated slang expressions as 'a steady' or 'dust *sb's* jacket' are given as English translations for *koibito* 'significant other' and *bunnagur-u* 'beat to shit'. This trend is even more pronounced in smaller non-academic dictionaries, where it is not uncommon to have few, or even no, native English speakers on the editorial board.

All these bilingual dictionaries published in Japan, as well as those for other languages, such as Japanese-French or Korean-Japanese, are oriented towards the native speaker of Japanese—bilingual dictionaries for L2 learners are much less numerous. In the English market, there are only two major contenders: *Kodansha's Furigana Japanese Dictionary* (1995–1996) and *Random House Japanese-English English-Japanese Dictionary* (1996). With just 30,000 and 50,000 entries, respectively, and two decades since their publication, neither are recommendable to serious learners. Fortunately, a number of online bilingual dictionaries have been developed in recent years to make up for the lack of published material: see §8.11 for an in-depth review.

Kanji-English dictionaries, on the other hand, are more numerous, with three large-scale dictionaries readily available to learners: *The Kanji Dictionary* (1996), *The New Nelson Japanese-English Character Dictionary* (1997) and *The Kodansha Kanji Dictionary* (2013). The last of these also has a more affordable abridged version available, *The Kodansha Kanji Learner's Dictionary: Revised and Expanded* (2013). The Kodansha kanji dictionaries use a unique system referred to as SKIP (System of Kanji Indexing by Patterns) to index characters. SKIP assigns three numbers to a character based on the location of division points in the overall structure of the character, and then on stroke count. For example, the character 明 'bright' is first divided vertically across its centre (pattern #1), yielding 日 and 月, and then the strokes of each division are counted. This results in a SKIP number of 1-4-4. From a pedagogical stance, the SKIP system is much more practical for non-sinolingual L2 learners than the traditional Kangxi system, which is highly arbitrary in its designation of radicals.

8.11 Language Software

Since their widespread adoption in the 1980s, computers have played an indispensable role in how we deal with language on a daily basis. The case could not be stronger for Japanese, a language in which no less than four scripts are regularly intermixed (§4.1, §4.10) and an extensive knowledge of at least 2,000 kanji is required for reading and writing fluently (§4.4). The advent of the computer—or more specifically word processing software—has greatly facilitated Japanese writing, and it is now possible to conjure up even the most difficult kanji simply by inputting its reading into your computer or device. With this ease of use, though, comes a number of pitfalls, the most apparent being a phenomenon known as *waapuro baka* 'word processor idiocy', in which one forgets how to write kanji due to an overreliance on word processing software. Other pitfalls include an increase in typos, as the large number of homophones (§5.9), especially Sino-Japanese (§7.1), inevitably leads to mistaken conversions when typing with the Roman alphabet or kana (see further below).

Japanese typing is typically carried out by means of an input method editor (IME). On computers and computer-like interfaces, users will type a Japanese word or phrase on their keyboard either in the Roman alphabet using the standard QWERTY layout (usually in *kunrei* or *hebon* style: §4.7), or through the use of a kana layout unique to Japanese keyboards. When using the Roman alphabet, the IME will automatically convert the text into hiragana as the user types. Next, the user will press the conversion key (which is usually the spacebar) to convert the hiragana text into kanji, katakana or a mix of scripts. The IME presents a number of different possible conversions between which the user can switch by pressing the conversion key again, and once the user finds their desired outcome they press the enter key to lock down the conversion and continue on with the rest of the text. Recently, more simplified versions of such interfaces have been developed for handheld devices, such as mobile phones, smart phones and tablets.

Given the large number of kanji, character codesets developed for European languages, such as ASCII which can only encode up to 128 characters, are inadequate for processing Japanese text. This has led to the development of codesets specifically designed for Japanese text, such as Shift JIS, EUC-JP, or the more universal Unicode, which has code points for nearly every letter and character in modern human languages. Even with robust codesets such as Unicode, which encodes an impressive 87,887 Chinese characters in its latest version (12.0), there are still instances in which specific variants or obsolete characters (§4.3) are unavailable. A number of software solutions have thus been developed solely for the purpose of displaying non-standard characters. The most well-known of these solutions is the program *Konjaku mojikyō* (Fig. 4.3.3), which is a frontend for a collection of fonts that replace specific character code points in the JIS-Shift code set with alternative characters. While the frontend is propriety software, the individual fonts can be downloaded free of charge from the Mojikyo Institute's website. At the time of writing, the latest version of this software allows for the input of roughly 160,000 Chinese characters, or about twice the number of characters registered in Unicode. Other solutions include Microsoft Window's built-in Private Character Editor, which allows users to add their own characters to empty code points in Shift JIS or Unicode, and *Chō kanji*, an entire operating system designed around imputing and displaying non-standard kanji.

L2 learners of Japanese will be pleased to hear that a large variety of language learner software has been developed for the language. These range from online and offline dictionaries (§8.10), through kanji/kana recognition software, to memorization software. By far the oldest and most comprehensive online Japanese-English dictionary is WWWJDIC, which is a frontend for EDICT and a number of other dictionaries developed by the Electronic Dictionary Research and Development Group. EDICT is a plain text file originally developed in the early 1990s that contains a comprehensive list of Japanese headwords with English definitions. Over the years, EDICT has been complemented with ENAMDICT for looking up Japanese names (§6.9), KANJIDIC for looking up kanji and a large number of technical dictionaries covering a variety of fields, such as engineering, science, linguistics and Buddhism. EDICT is available free of charge under a Creative Commons licence and is integrated into a number of different websites and applications for handheld devices. Dictionaries from Japanese publishers are often available for use on computers and handheld devices in a common format known as EPWING, developed by Fujitsu Ltd. A number of free dictionaries (including the aforementioned EDICT) are also available in EPWING format, allowing users to access their contents even when they are offline. Another popular Japanese-English dictionary is *Eijirō*, originally designed as part of a collaboration among translators to pool knowledge for more accurate translations, but now available online through ALC Press free of charge or as an offline application for Windows, Mac OS and handheld devices for a nominal fee.

Kanji recognition software has been available as a feature in major IMEs and electronic dictionaries since the 1990s. Recently, a number of iOS and Android applications have also taken advantage of such software as a device for studying new characters. One notable example is Kanji Recognizer which, in addition to allowing users to look up characters by drawing them on the screen of their smartphone or tablet, also adds numbers to each stroke of the character in real time as the user writes it, allowing them to compare their stroke order with the correct one.

While memorization software is by no means unique to Japanese or to language learning in general, the application Anki deserves mention here. Named after the Japanese word for 'memorization' and originally created with the study of Japanese (and English) in mind, Anki functions by using a memorization method known as spaced repetition. Once users have created decks of flashcards containing words, kanji or concepts which they wish to memorize, an algorithm then presents the same cards at pre-defined and auto-adjusted intervals until they can be correctly and consistently identified. Recent versions have even added kanji recognition functionality, greatly increasing productivity.

8.12   Japanese Research on the Japanese Language

The study of the Japanese language in Japan can be traced back to approximately the 13th century—even further if we are to include comments on Japanese in studies of Classical Chinese (CC) and Sanskrit. Just as classical languages, such as Latin and Greek, were the focus of linguistic study in medieval Europe, the first endeavours into linguistics by Japanese were to better understand CC and Sanskrit. By the 17th century, scholars such as Fujitani Nariakira (1738–1779), Motoori Norinaga (1730–1801) and his son Motoori Haruniwa (1763–1828) had laid down what came to be the foundations of Japanese linguistics with their studies on parts of speech (§3.1) and conjugation (§3.3, §8.6). Most early studies on Japanese, however, were impeded by a lack of understanding of basic linguistic principles, such as the phoneme (§2.1) and morpheme (§3.1) and, in many cases, a nationalistic agenda. For example, Norinaga, in a treatise on Sino-Japanese (§7.1), described the native Japanese sound system as 'pure, proper and elegant', while likening all 'foreign sounds' (those used in Sino-Japanese) to 'the cries of birds and beasts'. Ironically, Norinaga's understanding of what was native and what was not was flawed to begin with, rendering his argument meaningless.

While the scholarship described above laid a firm footing for further research, the modern field of Japanese linguistics can be said to have undergone its key formational period during the first half of the 20th century. It was during these years that Yamada Yoshio (1873–1958), Matsushita Daizaburō (1878–1935), Hashimoto Shinkichi (1882–1945) and Tokieda Motoki (1900–1967) each published what would go on to be known collectively as the 'Four Great Grammars of Japan'. Yamada's grammar was the first of the Four Greats and is most renowned for its theory of predication (*chinjutsuron*: §3.6) and classification of parts of speech into 'concept words' (*kannengo*: nominals §3.2, verbals §3.3–§3.5, adverbs §3.5) and 'relationship words' (*kankeigo*: particles §3.12, §3.13). His sub-classification of particles into case, adverbial, conjunctive, focus, sentence-final and interjectory was especially influential and is, for the most part, identical to the classification taught in schools (§8.6) and used in dictionaries to this day. Matsushita's grammar was unique in being the first Japanese grammar to define a unit of language equivalent to the modern-day morpheme; a unit referred to by Matsushita as a 'core unit' (*genji*). Matsushita is also credited with coining the term 'formal noun' (§3.2), although Yamada had earlier acknowledged the existence of such a group of nouns. Of the Four Greats, perhaps Hashimoto's grammar was the most influential, being incorporated into the *kokugo* curriculum (§8.5) early on and forming the basis of the school grammar taught today. Tokieda rebutted the earlier grammars, forming his own unique 'language-as-process theory' in which he viewed language as a mental process where speakers string so-called 'objective forms' (*shi*: nominals, verbals, adverbs, adnouns §3.5) and 'subjective forms' (*ji*: particles, verbal suffixes §3.7–§3.8, conjunctions §3.10, interjections §3.1) to form 'nested structures' of objective and subjective thought. These, he argued, then go on to form sentences and, in turn, entire discourses.

During this formative period, a great number of contributions to historical linguistics and dialectology were also made. In particular, numerous breakthroughs on the historical front greatly advanced knowledge of earlier stages of the language, while the establishment of the short-lived (1902–1913) National Language Investigation Committee (§8.1) gave rise to the first government-sponsored language surveys on a national level. Perhaps the most famous historical discovery of this period was that of the so-called *kō-otsu* kana distinction in Old Japanese (OJ: §2.9) by Hashimoto Shinkichi (actually a rediscovery: the distinction had been observed earlier by Motoori Norinaga and Ishizuka Tatsumaro (1764–1823) but largely ignored). Other major findings of the time included the discovery by Ueda Kazutoshi (1867–1937: §6.8, §8.1, §8.13) that Modern Japanese /h/ was pronounced as a bilabial [p] in OJ, and of vowel harmony in OJ by Arisaka Hideyo (1908–1952). The period also witnessed the founding of the field of *kuntengo* studies (the study of glossing practices of CC texts, the lexicon therein and *kanbun kundoku* at large: §1.3, §4.4) by scholars such as Ōya Tōru (1851–1928), Yoshizawa Yoshinori (1867–1954) and Kasuga Masaji (1878–1962), which greatly expanded our knowledge of Middle Japanese (§1.3) through analysis of lexical and morphosyntactic glosses in CC texts. Much progress was also made in the field of textual criticism by Ikeda Kikan (1896–1956), Yamada Yoshio and others, making available reliable editions of many classical texts for the first time.

It was also during this formative period that Yanagita Kunio (1875–1962) published his famous essay on the dialect forms for the word *katacumuri* 'snail', giving rise to the fundamental 'peripheral zone theory' (§7.8). Meanwhile, Hattori Shirō (1908–1995) published a number of studies on pitch accent (§2.6) in dialects, dividing accents into the modern-day Tokyo and Keihan type divisions (§7.9), while Tsuzuku Tsuneo (1920–1984) and Tōjō Misao (1884–1966) published their pioneering dialect divisions, separating mainland dialects into Eastern, Western and Kyūshū dialects (§7.8). Around the same time, Kobayashi Yoshiharu (1886–1948) conducted his massive dialect survey of roughly 2,000 locations throughout the Tōhoku region, helping to establish surveying methods used to this day. The Society for Japanese Linguistics (1944–present), the largest academic society devoted solely to the study of the Japanese language (§6.8), and the National Institute for Japanese Language and Linguistics (NINJAL) (1948–present) were also founded towards the end of this period. The latter has been responsible for national level dialect surveys, large-scale surveys on lexical strata (§5.1) and, in recent years, the development of contemporary and historical corpora of Japanese as well as documentation of minority dialects and the Ryūkyūan languages.

With much of the foundations now laid down, the latter half of the 20th century brought a surge of studies in all fields of Japanese linguistics, both modern and pre-modern. On the grammatical front, Mikami Akira (1903–1971) fiercely attacked the notion that Japanese sentences have grammatical subjects, advocating the notion of topic (§3.14) instead; Kindaichi Haruhiko (1913–2004) presented his famous four-tier classification of Japanese verbs based on aspect (§3.4); and Kiyose Gisaburō Norikura (1931–2017) proposed his system of derivational grammar. This is a structuralist approach to the language, explaining the morphology of verbs and adjectives through simple agglutination (§1.2) instead of through 'meaningless conjugational forms' (in the words of Kiyose) dating back to an 18th century analysis of the language (§8.6). Noam Chomsky's (1928–) theory of generative grammar also caught on firmly among Japanese linguists, with Kuroda S.-Y. (Sige-Yuki) (1934–2009), Inoue Kazuko (1919–2017) and Kuno Susumu (1933–) publishing the first generative grammars of Japanese and introducing the field to a new generation of scholars.

Historical studies took a huge leap forward with the establishment of the Society for Research in Kunten Language (1953), which created a surge of interest in the previously under-researched field of *kuntengo* studies. Nakada Norio (1915–2010), Tsukishima Hiroshi (1925–2011), Kobayashi Yoshinori (1929–) and Ōtsubo Heiji (1910–) not only elucidated the language of Middle Japanese through their research on glosses but facilitated further research on the topic through the transcription and publication of much previously unavailable material. Perhaps most noteworthy is the discovery by Tsukishima that two separate registers (§6.2) of Japanese, one for writing native literature and the other for glossing CC texts, were in concurrent use in Early Middle Japanese (§1.3). At the same time, studies on 14th–16th century *shōmono* (vernacular commentaries on CC texts) and Jesuit texts (§1.3, §8.13) helped shed light on the phonology and spoken language of Late Middle Japanese (§1.3).

The two largest contributions to dialectology during the late 20th century were the *Linguistic Atlas of Japan* (1966–1974) and the *Grammar Atlas of Japanese Dialects* (1989–2006), both of which were spearheaded by NINJAL. The former collected dialect forms of 285 words and expressions from 2,400 locations, while the latter collected dialect forms of 287 grammatical structures from 807 locations throughout Japan. NINJAL also undertook some of the earliest, and longest-running, longitudinal dialect surveys in the world, surveying the same communities of speakers in Tsuruoka (Yamagata Prefecture) and Okazaki (Aichi Prefecture) numerous times between the 1950s and early 2000s. One other work that deserves mention is the *Linguistic Atlas of Itoigawa* (1988–1995), compiled by Sibata Takesi (1918–2007) and Willem Grootaers (1911–1999). The atlas collected dialect forms of 500 words and expressions from 186 locations in the Itoigawa region of Niigata Prefecture, the northern limit of the Itoigawa-Hamanako dialect division line (§7.9).

Countless more contributions have been made by Japanese scholars in recent years and for a more in-depth discussion the reader is urged to consult Further Reading at the end of this volume.

8.13 Non-Japanese Research on the Japanese Language

In addition to Japanese scholars (§8.12), non-Japanese have also made major contributions to the study of the Japanese language. In fact, Western scholars got a head start on the linguistic analysis of Japanese: Jesuits and other Christian missionaries (§1.3, §8.13), such as João Rodrigues (1561–1633) and Diego Collado (1589–1641), published the first descriptive grammars of Japanese in the early 17th century. Both Rodrigues and Collado adhere to a rather antiquated Latin grammatical framework and, from a modern structural perspective, their descriptions of the language are not always accurate. Nonetheless, both works provide crucial insight into the language of the late 16th to early 17th centuries, including many notes on honorifics (§6.3) and dialects (§7.8–§7.11) and serve as ideal examples of early European missionary grammars. Unfortunately, with the establishment of the Tokugawa shogunate (1600–1868) and the subsequent ban on Christianity and Christian missionaries (§7.2), Rodrigues and Collado's works would not be surpassed for another two and a half centuries when Japan once again opened her ports in the mid-19th century.

Western pioneers of the modern field of Japanese linguistics in the 19th century include the Americans, James Hepburn (1815–1911) and Benjamin Lyman (1835–1920), and the Britons, William Aston (1841–1911), Ernest Satow (1843–1929) and Basil Hall Chamberlain (1850–1935). Hepburn was a Christian missionary and physician who travelled to Japan in the mid-19th century. He is known for authoring the first comprehensive Japanese-English dictionary (§8.10) and establishing the 'Hepburn-style' (*hebon-shiki*) of romanization still in use (although with minor modifications) to this day (§4.7). Lyman was a 'foreign employee' hired by the Japanese government to conduct geological surveys. Being an amateur linguist, Lyman made ground-breaking discoveries on rendaku (§5.5), proposing what would later come to be called 'Lyman's Law'. It is now known that the Japanese scholars Kamo no Mabuchi (1697–1769) and Motoori Norinaga (§8.12) had made identical discoveries a century earlier, but Lyman was the first to conduct in-depth research on the phenomenon. Chamberlain was also a foreign employee, hired by the government to teach Japanese language and literature at the Imperial University (modern Tokyo University). Satow and Aston were both diplomats to Japan with a keen interest in Japanology. Chamberlain, Satow and Aston all published grammars on the spoken language, with Aston and Chamberlain publishing grammars on the written language as well. Of the three British Japanologists, Chamberlain had a particularly long-lasting impact on the field, publishing well over a dozen works not only on Japanese language and literature, but also on Ryūkyūan languages and Ainu (§1.1, §7.5). Chamberlain also mentored Ueda Kazutoshi (§6.8, §8.1, §8.12), one of the founding fathers of modern Japanese linguistics, during his tenure at the Imperial University and is said to have left a heavy impression on him.

Western interest in Japanese declined during the first half of the 20th century with the end of the foreign employee policy in 1899 and the rise of Japanese militarism, but was quick to take off again after WWII. One milestone was Bernard Bloch's (1907–1965) series of four papers on the phonology, morphology and syntax of Japanese, published in the academic journal *Language* from 1946–1950. Bloch's work is widely regarded as the first modern descriptive analysis of Japanese and heavily influenced other Western scholars of the time, such as Eleanor Harz Jorden (1920–2009) and Samuel Martin (1924–2009), both of whom were Bloch's students. Unfortunately, Bloch's work was not available to Japanese scholars for many years because of a bizarre decision by the Allied forces to block publication in Japan—it did not adhere to the Hepburn system of romanization they had declared the standard (§4.7). While overlooked for many years by scholars both inside and outside Japan, the German linguist Günther Wenck (1916–1992) also made a number of revolutionary breakthroughs in historical Japanese phonology and syntax which have helped shape our understanding of Old Japanese (§2.9). These appeared in his four-book series, *Japanische Phonetik* (1954–1959).

Later in the 20th century, Martin, Roy Andrew Miller (1924–2014) and others would go on to publish a number of influential volumes on both the history of Japanese and on the modern language. Miller's *The Japanese Language* (1967) and Martin's *The Japanese Language Through Time* (1987) and *A Reference Grammar of Japanese* (1988) stand out particularly as pioneering works, offering indispensable insights to this day. Miller was also known for his strict, but fair, criticism of *nihonjinron* (§6.8) and of contemporary Japanese linguists. Miller and Martin were both strong proponents of the Japanese-Altaic hypothesis (§1.1), with Miller focusing on the Altaic hypothesis at large and Martin focusing on the relationship between Japanese and Korean. Although research on the Altaic languages was at its zenith in the mid-20th century, with the Finnish scholar Gustaf Ramstedt

(1873–1950) in particular advocating the affinity of Japanese with the Altaic languages, it was the works of Miller and Martin that introduced the topic to an English-speaking audience. The Altaic hypothesis was the predominant theory concerning the origin of the Japan language for most of the 20th century, even making its way into Japanese textbooks. In recent years, however, the theory has lost a large number of supporters and is now only adhered to by a marginal number of linguists (§1.1).

With Japan's continuing economic growth in the late 20th century, interest in the Japanese language has increased exponentially. For a list of more recent studies by non-Japanese scholars on Japanese, the reader should consult Further Reading at the end of this volume.

Further Reading

With the exception of cases where the only good sources are in Japanese, suggestions for further reading are limited to works written in the English language.

§1.1 For an overview of the languages spoken in Japan, see Shibatani (1990); for the Ryūkyūan languages in particular, Shimoji & Pellard (2010) or Heinrich et al. (2015). See Wang & Ogura (1999) for a summary of the major Japanese language origin theories; Unger (2009, 2014), Whitman (2011) or Vovin (2017) for more recent research. For an overview of research conducted over the past two centuries on the Altaic hypothesis, see Robbeets (2005). Whitman (1985, 2012), Martin (1987) and Francis-Ratte (2016) provide the most convincing arguments for the Japanese-Korean hypothesis; see Vovin (2010) for a rebuttal. See Beckwith (2004) for an in-depth analysis of the Japanese-Koguryoic hypothesis, although caution is advised with regard to the Middle Chinese data. For the reconstruction of Proto-Japonic, try Thorpe (1983), Martin (1987) or Frellesvig & Whitman (2008). Fig. 1.1 is adapted from Pellard (2015); the Koguryo phonetic reconstructions in Table 1.1 are from Vovin (2017). **§1.2** For an overview on the typology of Japanese, see Shibatani (1990), Iwasaki (2013) or Horie (2018); see the papers in Pardeshi & Kageyama (2018) for further discussion. Data on the average number of consonants and vowels in world languages is from Maddieson (2010), while data on Rotokas is from Firchow & Firchow (1969) and on Taa from Traill (1994). See Ramus et al. (1999) or Peppé (2012) for a discussion of prosodic units. For Greenberg's linguistic universals, see Greenberg (1963). For a statistical survey of trends concerning head-directionality, see Liu (2010); for word order alignment Murray & Ruhlen (2011) or Hammarström (2016). The canonical work on the evolution of colour terms is Berlin & Kay (1969), although this has been largely superseded by Kay et al. (2009). For a cross-linguistic overview of counting systems, see Ifrah (2000); for kinship terms Murdock (1970). Middle Chinese examples in this unit and others are based on the transcription system of Baxter & Sagart (2014). **§1.3** For a comprehensive analysis of the history of the Japanese language, see Frellesvig (2010, 2018). Individual chapters on Old, Early Middle and Late Middle Japanese can be found in Tranter (2012a). Book-length descriptive analyses of Old Japanese prose can be found in Bentley (2001), of Old Japanese poetry in Vovin (2005–2009) and of Early Middle Japanese prose in Vovin (2003). See Takayama (2015) for an overview of historical phonology; for Old Japanese phonology in particular, see Lange (1973) or Miyake (2003). For readers of German, Wenck (1954–1959) provides an excellent overview of historical phonology. **§1.4** For data on L2 learners, see the further reading for §8.8; figures for other major languages are from URL1. Bear in mind that in both these cases there exists no consensus on absolute figures and sources disagree. For an overview and history of Japanese as an L2 language worldwide, see 井上 (2000). For *nihonjinron* and 'allegations of uniqueness', see Miller (1982). Japanese population statistics are from URL2.

§2.1 For thorough overviews on Japanese phonology that cover nearly all the topics explored in this chapter, see Vance (1987, 2008) or Labrune (2012). For the International Phonetic Alphabet, see URL3. **§2.2** For more detail on *g*-allophones, see Hibiya (1995, 1996, 1999) or 斎藤 (1997, 2003). Conservative phonemic analyses have been put forward by, among others, Rothaug (1991), Rickmeyer (1995), Yamaguchi (2007) and Tsujimura (2014); for an innovative phonemic analysis, see Irwin (2011a). **§2.3** For discussion on vowel devoicing, see Kondo (2005), Maekawa & Kikuchi (2005) or Fujimoto (2015); for vowel sequences and diphthongs see Kubozono (2001b, 2015a) or Vance (2018); more on vowel epenthesis in loanwords can be found in Kubozono (2001a) or Irwin (2011a). **§2.4 & §2.5** For a more complex discussion than we have room for here on the mora and syllable, see Kubozono (1989, 1999), Labrune (2012), Otake (2015) or Vance (2018). The Western scholar who defined the mora as 'something of which a long syllable consists of two and a short syllable consists of one' was McCawley (1968). For a discussion of the foot, see Kubozono (1999). The frequency data for moras, consonants and vowels are adapted from Tamaoka & Makioka (2004). **§2.6 & §2.7** A good pitch accent dictionary is 文研 (1998). For more detailed accounts of standard Japanese accent than space permits in this volume, see McCawley (1977), Vance (1987, 2008), Haraguchi (1999), Labrune (2012), Tsujimura (2014), or Kawahara (2015). See Martin (1987), Shibatani (1990) or Kubozono (2012, 2015c, 2018) for detail on accent across Japanese dialects. For statistical analyses of accent placement and pitch patterns, see 柴田 (1994) or Kubozono (2006); for accent and homophony, consult Shibatani (1990). Thoroughgoing accounts of pitch accent in compounds are available in McCawley (1968), Poser (1990) or Vance (2018), as well as in Kubozono (1995, 1999, 2002, 2006, 2008, 2018). **§2.8** For an analysis of punning in Japanese, see Nagashima (2006); for number mnemonics Schourup (2000); for the *babibu* secret language Haraguchi (1991). For Japanese wordplay in general, try 荻生 (2007). **§2.9** See further reading for §1.3.

§3.1 Much of the analysis in this chapter is inspired by Kiyose (1995). There are many books which provide a comprehensive overview of Japanese grammar and syntax in English, including Kuno (1973), Hinds (1986), Shibatani (1990), Iwasaki (2013), Tsujimura (2014), Hasegawa (2015) and, what is widely considered to be the 'bible' of reference grammars, Martin (1975). More user-friendly grammars, geared towards the L2 learner rather than the linguist, include Alfonso (1966), Makino & Tsutsui (1986, 1995, 2008), Jorden & Noda (1987–1990), Johnson (2008), Kaiser et al. (2013) and Group Jammassy (2015). The foregoing provide rich detail on many of the topics covered below and will henceforth be referenced by name only (in SMALL CAPS). For readers of German, Rickmeyer (1995) provides one of the best structural grammars of Japanese available in any language: see Narrog (2009a) for an overview in English. For what constitutes a part of speech in Japanese, see Uehara (1998) or Kishimoto & Uehara (2016); for word order, Nemoto (1999) or Shimojo (2018); for Japanese sentence types, Bloch (1946b) or Nitta (2017). **§3.2** A morphological treatment of Japanese nominals can be found in KIYOSE, an overview of nouns in KAISER ET AL. and a summary of noun phrase types in IWASAKI. See KAISER ET AL. for an overview of Japanese demonstratives, interrogatives and pronouns in general; Shimoyama (2008) for a look at indefinite pronouns. For discussion on discourse deixis through demonstratives, see ALFONSO, KUDO, MARTIN or Hoji et al. (2003); for discussion on how mutual knowledge relates to demonstratives, see Takubo & Kinsui (1997). For a discussion of formal nouns, see ALFONSO or MARTIN; for evidentials, Narrog (2009a). **§3.3** The morphological analysis of verbs presented here broadly follows KIYOSE and Bloch (1946a): see MARTIN, IWASAKI or HASEGAWA for alternate analyses. Takezawa (2016) and SHIBATANI provide useful overviews of the various analyses adopted by both Japanese and non-Japanese scholars in the 20th century. **§3.4** See Jacobsen (1992, 2017), ALFONSO or KIYOSE for more on intransitive-transitive pairs. Kageyama & Jacobsen (2016) is a useful collection of papers on transitivity and valency in Japanese and other languages. Table 3.4 draws its examples from KIYOSE and Kageyama & Jacobsen (2016). Kindaichi's classification of verbs can be found in 金田一 (1950): English summaries appear in IWASAKI and TSUJIMURA. For Kudo's classification, see 工藤 (1995). For an analysis of the various aspectual meanings of the auxiliary -te i-ru, see Shirai (2000). **§3.5** See IWASAKI for a general overview of adjectives, adverbs and adnouns; Takezawa (2016) for a syntactic overview of verbal and nominal adjectives; KIYOSE for an analysis of Japanese verbal adjectives as qualitative verbs; KUDO for a discussion on the semantic similarities between verbs and adjectives. For propositional speech acts, see Searle (1969) or Croft (1991). Haspelmath (2012) is a good cross-linguistic analysis of reference, predication and attribution. **§3.6** For the Japanese copula, consult Nakahara (2002) or Wenck (1973) for an overview of its morphology and history; Nishiyama (1999) for its use with adjectives; and KIYOSE for a more general treatment. For an overview of early works on *chinjutsu* in English, see Larm (2008); for a discussion on how *chinjutsu* relates to the more modern notion of modality, see Narrog (2009a, 2009b). **§3.7 & §3.8** For a structural analysis of verbal suffixes in line with this volume, see Bloch (1946a, 1946c) or KIYOSE. See Crystal (2008) for the standard definitions of inflection and derivation; Haspelmath (1996) for a definition that includes word-class changing inflection. For a cross-linguistic look at converbs, see Haspelmath & König (1995); for converbs in Japanese in particular, see KIYOSE or Alpatov & Podlesskaya (1995). The notion of cosubordination was first introduced by Olsen (1981), that of coordinate-dependent by Foley (1986). For subordination and cosubordination using -te, see Hasegawa (1996). See ALFONSO, KUDO, JOHNSON or Fujii (2018) for discussion on the different types of conditionals. Try any of SHIBATANI, IWASAKI, Tsujimura (1999, 2014), Miyagawa & Saito (2008), Hasegawa (2015, 2018b) or Shibatani et al. (2017) for causatives and passives. The irrealis analysis for *sa-ire* is based on Sasaki (2013). For a list of verbal and nominal adjectives which take the emotive verbalizer -*garu*, see MARTIN. Frellesvig (1995) provides a history of *onbin*. **§3.9** See MARTIN for a comprehensive list of auxiliaries. Lists of auxiliaries are also available in any of the L2 grammars listed in §3.1. See IWASAKI for aspectual auxiliaries in particular and IWASAKI or HASEGAWA for a comparison between -*te i-ru* and -*te ar-u*. For an in-depth discussion of auxiliaries following the -*te* form of verbs, see Hasegawa (1996) or Nakatani (2013, 2016); for verb-compounding Kageyama (2016b); for complex predicates in general Matsumoto (1996). **§3.10** See KUDO, JOHNSON or HASEGAWA for an overview of giving and receiving verbs and their usage as benefactive auxiliaries. For discussion of benefactives in particular, consult KAISER ET AL., Nakatani (2013) or Hasegawa (2018a). **§3.11** See KAISER ET AL. for an overview of conjunctions and conjunctive forms. For discussion on why conjunctions do not form a valid word class in Japanese, see 森岡 (1973) or 石黒 (2018); for an overview of the various approaches to conjunctions in the previous literature, see 井手 (1973). **§3.12 & §3.13** Particles are given ample coverage in any of the general grammars listed in §3.1. See KIYOSE for an analysis similar to the one in this chapter. For the definition of particle, try 服部 (1950), Vance (1993) or Kageyama (2016a). An English translation of 服部 (1950) by Zisk is currently complete and will be available from NINJAL in 2019. For thoroughgoing discussion on all types of particles, see MARTIN, ALFONSO or KAISER ET AL; for case maker particles in particular, consult also KUDO and JOHNSON; for case and case marking in general, try Kishimoto (2018) or Nakamura (2018); for discourse particles, see also Maynard (1993), Ogi (2017) or Morita (2018). For studies on *wa*, see the further reading for §3.14; for *mo*, see Shudo (2002). See MARTIN for discussion on the different types of *no*; SHIBATANI, Maki & Uchibori (2008) or Ochi (2018) for *ga/no* conversion; MARTIN or ALFONSO for *no* before copulas. See MAKINO & TSUTSUI, GROUP JAMMASSY, Kawashima (1999) or Chino (2001) for particle dictionaries aimed towards L2 learners. **§3.14** The issue of *wa* vs. *ga* is given ample coverage in most general grammars: see KUDO, IWASAKI, TSUJIMURA or

HASEGAWA, for example. See Hinds et al. (1987), Tateishi (1994) or Hasegawa (2018c) for more in-depth discussion. For contrastivity and exhaustivity, see Heycock (2008) or Tomioka (2016); for a look at previous research on subject and topic, see Fujii (1991) or Masuoka (2018); for a cross-linguistic approach to subject and topic, see Li (1976). §3.15 See further reading for §1.3.

§4.1 For the history of writing in Japan, see Seeley (1984, 1991), Frellesvig (2010) or Lurie (2011); for writing in Modern Japan, see Coulmas (1989, 2003, 2018), Shibamoto-Smith (1996), Talyor & Taylor (2014) or Sampson (2015). DeFrancis (1989) and Tranter (2012b, forthcoming) offer a typological discussion of Japanese writing. Table 4.1 is adapted from Irwin (2011a). §4.2 For an overview on the origin and development of Chinese characters, see Dong (2000), Qiu (2000), Boltz (2003) or Sampson (2015). See Kennedy (1964a, 1964b), DeFrancis (1984) or Unger (2004) for analyses of how Chinese characters represent sound and meaning. Miller (1967), Seeley (2000), Lurie (2011) and Inui (forthcoming) provide detailed accounts of the adoption of Chinese characters in Japan, as well as early sources. §4.3 See Gottlieb (2012) for discussion on smartphone dependency and its effect on kanji production; for script reform, see the further reading for §8.2. For an introduction to kanji variants and their history, see 杉本 (1978); for their use in Modern Japanese 笹原他 (2003); for their use in dialects 笹原 (2013). The koseki unification character database is available at URL4. For information on *Konjaku mojikyo*, see the further reading for §8.10. §4.4 See Miller (1967) or Frellesvig (2010) for the history of kanji readings; Tsukishima (1993) for *go-on* and *kan-on* in particular; Mair (2016) for a dictionary of kanji readings. For *tō-on*, see 湯沢 (1987, 2014); for *kanyō-on* 湯沢 (1996); for Sinoxenic readings Osterkamp (2017b). Consult Frellesvig (2010), Lurie (2011) or Zisk (2017, forthcoming) for discussion on *kanbun kundoku* and its influence on Japanese. §4.5 See 笹原 (2007) for a thoroughgoing analysis of the history and sociolinguistic background of *kokuji*. For a discussion on *kokuji* as a form of 'sinoform writing', along with similar developments in other Far East Asian languages, see Osterkamp (2017a). §4.6 See Seeley (1991), Frellesvig (2010) or Lurie (2011) for the historical development of kana. For spelling devices in loanwords, see Irwin (2011a); for kana reform see further reading for §8.2. Fukuzawa discusses his coining of the kana ヴ to render English *v* in the foreword to his collected works, 時事新報社 (1897). §4.7 A more detailed overview and history of the various romanization systems used for Japanese appears in Seeley (1991), Gottlieb (1995) or Unger (1996). Links between literacy and romanization are explored in Coulmas (2018). Transcription problems related to Japanese passports are discussed in DeChicchis (2009). For Japanese Passport Office romanization rules, which are more complex than space allows us to introduce in the main text, see URL5. §4.8 See Ifrah (2000) for the history of Chinese, Arabic and Roman numerals; Yamaguchi (2007) for an overview of numerals in Japanese. §4.9 See Twine (1984) for the history of punctuation in Japanese script; 伊坂 (1997) provides a summary of comma usage. §4.10 For a discussion on script mixing in Modern Japanese, try Backhouse (1984), Kess & Miyamoto (1999), Joyce et al. (2012), Joyce (2013), Taylor & Taylor (2014), Sampson (2015), Joyce & Masuda (2018) or Tranter (forthcoming). §4.11 The quote by Nitobe Inazō is from Takagi (1972). For an overview of Japanese braille, see Unger (1984) or 石川 (1984); for its historical development 大河原 (1937); for *kantenji* 川上 et al. (1999). §4.12 & §4.13 See 国研 (1983), Shibamoto-Smith & Schmidt (1996) or Tranter (2008) for issues of orthographic variation. For copula choice, see Maynard (1993). For more on the *genbun itchi* movement, see Twine (1991), Lee (2010) or Coulmas (2018); for orthographic play Gottleib (1995) or Coulmas (2013, 2018). See 笹原 (2012) for abundant examples of *ateji* and *ateyomi*;

荻生 (2007) for examples of orthographic play. *Ateji* and *ateyomi* examples are from 笹原 (2012). Kanji graphs from *Ono ga bakamura usojizukuši* and the *Sankei Shimbun* kanji creation contest, as well as the Gundam kanji graphs, are from URL6. **§4.14** For an introduction to semiotics, see Johansen (2002). The linguistic landscape of Japan is explored by Inoue (2005), Backhaus (2007, 2011), Heinrich (2011) or Wetzel (2011). For amusing mistranslations of signs (and more), see URL7.

§5.1 For more on Japanese vocabulary strata in general, see Shibatani (1990), Backhouse (1993), Irwin (2011a) or Kageyama & Saito (2016). Some scholars, for example Ito & Mester (1995) or Fukuzawa & Kitahara (2005), eschew the idea of strata and instead posit alternative models. The magazine survey data is taken from 国研 (1964, 2005). **§5.2** The standard English reference work on Japanese mimetics is Hamano (1998): see also Akita & Tsujimura (2016), Iwasaki et al. (2017) or Toratani (2018). Numerous Japanese-English mimetic dictionaries are also available for L2 learners, with Chang (1990) and Kakehi et al. (1996) highly recommended. **§5.3 & §5.4** For greater detail on derivation, affixation and compounding, try Shibatani (1990), Kageyama (1999), Yamaguchi (2007), Nishiyama (2008), Tsujimura (2014), the papers in Kageyama & Kishimoto (2016) and, for plurality and reduplication especially, Martin (1975). McClure (2000) is an excellent guide to affixation and compounding for the L2 learner. For apophony, see 有坂 (1934), 阪倉 (1966) or Frellesvig (2010). **§5.5** For a thorough account of all aspects of rendaku, see Vance (2015). Although of a more technical nature, the papers contained in Vance & Irwin (2016) are also important reading. For Lyman's Law, see Lyman (1894) for the original formulation, as well as Vance (1980a, 2007a) or Kawahara & Sano (2014); for the right-branch condition, see Otsu (1980) for the original formulation, as well as Vance (1980b, 1987), Ito & Mester (1986) or Kubozono (2005); for other constraints against rendaku, see Martin (1952), Rosen (2003), Takayama (2005), Vance (2007b) or Irwin (2012, 2014, 2016b). Rendaku predilection, antipathy and immunity are discussed in Irwin (2009, 2015, 2016c), while the link between rendaku and homophony is examined in Irwin & Lyddon (2016). The origins of rendaku are covered in greater detail than space allows here in Martin (1987) or Frellesvig (2010). **§5.6** General accounts of truncation appear in Irwin (2011a, 2016a). More technical analyses of particular types of truncation can be found in Ito (1990), Ito & Mester (1992), Kubozono (2002), Labrune (2002) or Irwin (2011b). For 'KY-style' Japanese, see 北原 (2008). **§5.7** For general discussions of Japanese pronouns, see Miller (1967), Martin (1975) or Shibatani (1990); for honorific, gender and other sociolinguistic differences, see Ide (1982), Kondo (1990), Wetzel (1994) or Barke & Uehara (2005). For the history of personal pronouns, see Yamaguchi (forthcoming). **§5.8** For a cross-linguistic discussion of classifiers, see Allan (1977) or Beckwith (2007). Japanese numerals and classifiers are discussed in greater detail than space allows here in Miller (1967), Martin (1975), Matsumoto (1993), Labrune (2012), Tranter & Kizu (2012) or Iwasaki (2013). For allomorphic variation, see Martin (1975) or Rickmeyer (1995). **§5.9** See Kaplan & Muratani (2015) for a phonological approach to homophony; Tamaoka (2005, 2007) for the interaction with literacy; Backhouse (1984) for homophony and writing. **§5.10 & §5.11** See Dumas & Lighter (1978) or Eble (2006) for the definition of slang; Allan (2006) for that of jargon. For academic overviews of discriminatory vocabulary, see Gottlieb (2005, 2006); for more light-hearted coverage extending into slang and underworld argot, try Kasschau & Eguchi (1995). For discussion of Japanese slang, jargon and discriminatory language from a sociolinguistic perspective, see Kunihiro et al. (1999). The JK slang awards are hosted by *Mezamashi terebi* on Fuji Television

254 Further Reading

Network. While the broadcasting list used for explicatory purposes is no longer available online, a largely similar list can be found at URL8.

§6.1 & §6.2 For more on gender variation cross-linguistically, try Romaine (1994), Trudgill (2000) or Cheshire (2002); for Japanese in particular, try any of Ide (1982), Ide et al. (1986), Ide & McGloin (1991), Takahara (1991), Ide & Yoshida (1999), Okamoto & Shibamoto-Smith (2004), Ogi & Lee (2013), Ogi (2017) or Okamoto (2018). For age variation cross-linguistically, see Bailey (2002); for longitudinal studies Sankoff (2013). For the velar nasal studies mentioned, refer to 金田一 (1942) and Hibiya (1995, 1996, 1999); for the rendaku studies 太田 (2010, 2011); and for both the *ra-nuki* and *sa-ire* studies the 2016 survey at URL9. For the pioneering social class related sociolinguistic research mentioned in the unit, see Labov (1963, 1966); the studies conducted in Toyama Prefecture appear in 真田 (1973, 1990). For a cross-linguistic overview of class-based variation, try Ash (2002) or Meyerhoff (2006). Role language in Japanese is discussed in Teshigawara & Kinsui (2011), Kinsui (2017) or Oki (forthcoming). For issues of intonation, on which this volume does not unfortunately touch, see Igarashi (2015, 2018). §6.3 & §6.4 Deprecatory and pejorative language are examined cross-linguistically in Allan & Burridge (2006). For a sociolinguistic look at politeness in Japanese, see Ide (1982), Ide & Yoshida (1999) or Kunihiro et al. (1999). The grammar and syntax of honorifics is covered in most of the grammars listed in further reading for §3.1. See Martin (1975), Shibatani (1990) or Hasegawa (2015) for a linguistic analysis; Jorden & Noda (1987–1990), Johnson (2008) or Kaiser et al. (2013) for a more L2 learner-geared discussion. For the historical development of honorifics, see Nagata (2006) or Mori (forthcoming). For the grammar and syntax of anti-honorifics, see Martin (1975). The history of the *yakuza* and *tekiya* is discussed in Kaplan & Dubro (2003). The complete *Otoko wa tsurai yo* movie series is available at URL10. §6.5 Unfortunately, there is little academic discourse on the Japanese language in subculture. See Kinsui (2017) for a discussion on role language and 'virtual Japanese'. For an entertaining look at the localization of Japanese video games and what is 'lost in translation', see Mandelin (2015, 2016) or the many articles at URL11. §6.6 For an in-depth overview of greetings in both the Standard and dialects, see Nakanishi (forthcoming). The discussion on recent changes in *ohayoo* and *ocukare* type greetings, as well as the choice to use small talk instead of formulized greeting expressions, largely follows Nakanishi (forthcoming). The *tōkaidōchū hizagurige* excerpt is transliterated from 麻生 (1958). §6.7 For bowing in particular, see De Mente (1993) or Ohashi (2013); while for a cross-linguistic look at gestures in general, see Church et al. (2017). See Aqui (2004) for an entertaining guide to Japanese gestures. For silence, see Saville-Troike (1985). §6.8 The theories associated with linguistic relativism and linguistic determinism were originally put forward in the works of Sapir (1931) and Whorf (1956): see Deutscher (2010) for a highly readable overview of the subject. For issues of *kokugo* and dialect eradication, see Ramsey (2004), Gottlieb (2005), Lee (2010) or Heinrich (2012). *Kotodama* is discussed in Miller (1977). See Kunihiro et al. (1999) for a discussion of language norm consciousness in Japanese. The 'notorious' *nihonjinron* work 'written for the layman by a prominent academic' is 金田一 (1988), available in English as Kindaichi (2010). Recent public surveys on the Japanese language can be found at URL9. §6.9 For a linguistic introduction to onomastics, try Nuessel (1992). O'Neill (1972) and 藤原 (2008) are useful Japanese personal name dictionaries; for Japanese place name dictionaries, see 角川 (1978–1991) or 吉田 (1981). The culture of names and naming in Japan is covered in Plutschow (1995). The truncation patterns found in the short forms of personal names were first analysed by Poser (1990). Rankings of Japanese surnames are taken from URL12; those for given names from

Meiji Yasuda Life Insurance rankings (ranked orthographically) at URL13. Details on Japanese surnames in Hawaii are from the Hawaii State Department of Health 2010 death certificate lists. The 713 edict concerning kanji in toponyms is found in part in 黒坂他 (1965) and 黒坂他 (1966a).

§7.1 See Kobayashi et al. (2016) for an analysis of Sino-Japanese morphology and word formation in Modern Japanese. For an overview of historical Sino-Japanese borrowing processes, see Frellesvig (2010); for semantic shifts in Chinese loanwords Narumi (forthcoming). Try Fogel (2015) for studies on Sino-Japanese coinages in the Meiji era. For the phonotactics of Sino-Japanese 'morphemes' and the morphological processes involved in their compounding, consult Wenck (1954–1959), Vance (1987), Rickmeyer (1995) or Ito & Mester (2015). See 野村 (1999) or 森岡 (2004) for a discussion on how Sino-Japanese 'morphemes' are inseparable from their kanji notation. For a thoroughgoing discussion of imitational borrowings from Classical Chinese, see Zisk (2017, forthcoming). Old Chinese reconstructions follow Baxter & Sagart (2014). §7.2 & §7.3 For an examination of loanwords in Japanese, see Irwin (2011a). For further detail on the history of loanwords in Japan, see 楳垣 (1963), 土井 (1971) or 石綿 (2001); for loanword phonology Lovins (1973) or Kubozono (2015d); for morphology Irwin (2016a). The most comprehensive loanword dictionary is あらかわ (1977). For English borrowings, see Irwin (2016a). For the Loanword Committee, English as a hostile language during World War II and borrowing strategies in general, see further reading for §8.3 and §8.4. §7.4 Holm (2000), Trudgill (2000), Holmes (2001), Thomason (2001) and Webb (2013) all provide useful overviews of the concepts of lingua franca and pidgin. Maher (2004) is a useful, though brief, history of pidgins and creoles in Japan. For analyses of Yokohama Pidgin Japanese, see Daniels (1948) and Inoue (2007); for the original pamphlet, see Atkinson (1879). Bamboo English is examined in Norman (1955) and Miller (1967). Yilan Creole is described in Chien & Sanada (2010), which the reader should consult for an explanation of the phonemicization cited in the unit. For Bonin Creole English, see Long (2007). Hawaii Creole English is discussed by Nagara (1972), St. Clair & Murai (1974), 比嘉 (1985) or Fukazawa & Hiramoto (2004). §7.5 For general accounts of language death and murder, see Dressler (1988), Crystal (2000), Thomason (2001) or Wolfram (2002). Japanese colonial language policy on the Korean peninsula is discussed in 李 (1975) or Gottlieb (1995). General descriptions of both Ainu and Ryūkyūan appear in Shibatani (1990), 亀井 et al. (1997) or Tranter (2012a). See the further reading for §1.3 for more on Ryūkyūan. Japanese government policy towards the Ainu is covered in meticulous detail in Siddle (1996); linguistic policy in particular is examined in Heinrich (2012); the current state of the language in DeChicchis (1995) or 佐藤 (2012). For the history of linguistic policy towards Ryūkyūan, see Heinrich (2012); for the language today Osumi (2001). The scholar who likened the relationship between 'Luchuan' and Japanese to that between Spanish and Italian was Chamberlain (1895). UNESCO endangered languages are listed in Moseley (2010). §7.6 See Evens (1997) and Hayakawa (2014) for an historical account, and dictionary, of Japanese loanwords in English. For Chinese borrowings from Japanese, see Tranter (2009), for Korean Lee & Ramsey (2000). First attestation dates for Japanese borrowings into English are taken from the *Oxford English Dictionary*. §7.7 & §7.8 For a general overview of Japanese dialects, see Shibatani (1990), Shimoji (2018) or Onishi (2018). For sketches of individual dialects arranged by prefecture, see 飯豊他 (1982–1986); for maps of dialect forms and features 国研 (1966–1974, 1989–2006); for the promotion of *hyōjungo* Kunihiro et al. (1999) and Lee (2010). For discussion of accent across dialects, see further reading for §2.6 & §2.7. Preston (1999) examines dialect divisions and dialect boundaries, while Kawaguchi & Inoue (2002) discuss dialect diffusion. See 小林・澤村 (2014) for language-thought processes in dialects. The dialect forms of 'tadpole', as well as Figs. 7.8.1–4, are from 国研 (1966–1974). Fig. 7.7 is based on 加藤 (1977): see 東条 (1954) for Tōjō's original proposal. For Yanigita's 'peripheral zone theory', see 柳田 (1930). For the shift of vowel-stem verbs to a consonant-stem-like pattern, see de Chene (2016). The Motoori quotation is taken from 大野・大久保 (1968). **§7.9** For a thoroughgoing summary of the historical development of the Eastern vs. Western division of dialects, see 小林 (2004) or 柳田 (2010); see Sibata (1960) or Shibatani (1990) for a brief overview of some Eastern vs. Western differences. For readers interested in Kansai Japanese, there are currently two Kansai-ben 'phrase books' available for L2 learners: Tse (1993) and Palter & Slotsve (2005). Fig. 7.9.1 is adapted from 牛山 (1953), Fig. 7.9.2 from 平山 (1957). **§7.10 & §7.11** For detailed sketches of Tōhoku and Kyūshū dialects, see 飯豊他 (1982–1986). Matsumori & Onishi (2012) provide a comparison of a Tōhoku dialect, Tsuruoka, and a Kyūshū dialect, Ei. Dialect forms cited are taken primarily from 国研 (1966–1974, 1989–2006) and 飯豊他 (1982–1986). Examples of vowel elision in Satsugū dialects are taken from 木部 (2001), as well as the above. All examples from Sato dialect, including the forms given in Tables 7.11.1 and 7.11.2, are taken from 窪薗他 (2015). In addition, a small number of forms were acquired through fieldwork on native Tōhoku and Kyūshū speakers. For anti-causativity in Tōhoku dialects, see Sasaki (2016). For differential object marking in Tōhoku and split intransitivity in Kyūshū dialects, see Shimoji (2018), from where the examples in the text are drawn. Fig. 7.10.1 and 7.11.1 are based on the dialect divisions outlined in 飯豊他 (1982–1986).

§8.1 & §8.2 For the history of government language policy in Japan during the pre- and postwar period, including script reform, see 大野 (1983) or 杉森 (1983). Much information, including the key legislation cited in these units, is available (in Japanese) at URL14 and URL15. See Carroll (2001) or Gottlieb (2005, 2008, 2012) for an overview of government language policy in English. For script reform in particular, see Seeley (1984, 1991), Twine (1991), Gottlieb (1995), Unger (1996) or Kaplan & Baldauf (2008). The Emperor Kanmu edict promoting *kan-on* can be found in 黒坂他 (1966b), while the Motoori quote is taken from 大野・大久保 (1968). See 高松 (1993) or 湯沢 (1996) for discussion on early edicts concerning kanji readings. **§8.3** For examples of loanword reform by the Académie Française, see URL16. The four reports containing the results of NINJAL's Loanword Committee recommendations are in 国研 (2006); local government body reaction to them appears in 国研 (2007), 山田 (2005) providing a good critical academic assessment thereof. **§8.4** For more detail on linguicide and linguistic prohibitions from a cross-linguistic angle, see Skutnabb-Kangas & Phillipson (1995). For the War Department Education Manual *Spoken Japanese*, see Bloch & Jorden (1945). For more on English as a *tekiseigo* 'combatant language' in Japan, see Irwin (forthcoming); for a deeper analysis on borrowing strategies in general, see Betz (1949, 1974), Haugen (1950) or Duckworth (1977). **§8.5** See Duke (2009) for an overview of the establishment of compulsory education in late 19th century Japan. For the history of compulsory education up to the late 20th century, including copies of key legislation, see 文部省 (1981a, 1981b, 1992). An abridged English translation of 文部省 (1981a) is available from URL17. Copies of all previous versions of the *gakushū shidō yōryō* dating back to 1947 can be found at URL18, with the latest version available at URL19. The 2010 memorandum on kanji education in junior high and high schools can be found at URL20; the 2020 *kyōiku kanji* revision at URL21. **§8.6** For Hashimoto's original system of Japanese grammar, see 橋本 (1948, 1963). For an up-to-date overview of the grammar currently taught in schools, consult 中山・飯田 (2013–2015). For a critique of Japanese school grammar, see 鈴木 (1972, 1996), Rickmeyer (1986) or 清瀬 (2013). §8.7 Textbooks on Classical Japanese in English include McCullough (1988), Komai & Rohlich (1991), Shirane (2005, 2007) and Wixted (2006), all of which rigidly adhere to Japanese school grammar. For a more linguistic approach, consult further reading for §1.3 and §3.15. As of early 2019, there were only two short textbooks on *kanbun* in English: Crawcour (1965) and Komai & Rohlich (1988). For the history of *kanbun kundoku*, consult further reading for §4.4; see Whitman (2010) or Moran & Whitman (forthcoming) for discussion on how *kanbun kundoku* relates to the medieval practice of adding glosses to Latin manuscripts in the West. §8.8 For a summary of recent work on Japanese applied linguistics, see the papers in Minami (2016). For the history of JSL education inside and outside of Japan, see 関 (1997) or 関・平高 (1997). See 保坂 (2000) for language studies in the 8th century and Song (2001) for language studies in the Joseon Dynasty in particular. For JSL education in colonial Taiwan, see Tsurumi (1977); for JSL education in Japan during the allied occupation, see Binkley (2011). Figures for JSL institutions in Japan are taken from URL22, those for L2 learners of Japanese in Japan from URL23, those for L2 learners abroad from URL24. §8.9 Information on the Japanese-Language Proficiency Test is available at URL25; for an overview and critique, see Kobayashi (2016). Information on the Examination for Japanese University Admission for International Students can be found at URL26; on the J-test at URL27; and on the Business Japanese Proficiency Test at URL28. Although information on the *kanken* is available at URL29, a better feel for it can be obtained by downloading any number of free smartphone apps: search your app store under 漢検. Information on the *nihongo kentei* is available at URL30. The sample questions in Fig. 8.9.2 are from URL31; those in Fig. 8.9.1 from URL32. Both are periodically updated. §8.10 For the history of Japanese lexicography up until the 16th century, see Bailey (1960); for the history of English-Japanese dictionaries, see Hayakawa (2001). Brief overviews of Japanese lexicography from the 9th century to modern times can be found in Tono (2006) or McCreary (2013), while Nagashima (1991) provides a history of bilingual dictionaries. See JACET (2006) for a collection of papers on English-Japanese and Japanese-English dictionaries; Kembō (1961) for an annotated bibliography of Japanese dictionaries published before the 1950s. §8.11 *Konjaku mojikyō* was developed and distributed by AI Corporation, but is no longer for sale. The final version of the fonts themselves (but not the frontend) is available at URL33. *Chō kanji* is developed and distributed by Personal Media Corp. at URL34. WWWJDIC can be accessed at URL35. *Eijirō* is available free of charge at URL36 or for purchase on DVD-ROM from Alc Press Inc. Kanji Recognizer is available for Android devices on Google Play: a similar app, Kanji Lookup, is available on the App Store for iOS devices. Anki is available as open source software at URL37. §8.12 For an overview and bibliography of Japanese linguistic research from the early 1900s to 1950s, see Yamagiwa (1961); for a more general overview covering a longer timespan, see 古田・築島 (1972); for a selection of key papers with English annotations, see Yamagiwa (1965). Grootaers (1982) or Onishi (2018) provide summaries of previous studies and methodologies in Japanese dialectology. For the history of language study in Japan, see Doi (1976). §8.13 For the history of early Portuguese missionary grammars in Japan and Asia, see Zwartjes (2011); for an English translation of Collado's grammar see Spear (2007). Many of the 19th century works on Japanese linguistics by Western scholars are reprinted in Kaiser (1994). See Ota (1998) for a biography of Chamberlain; 山本 (1975) or Okagaki (forthcoming) for Chamberlain's relationship with Ueda. See Miller (1970) for a discussion of Bloch's impact on Japanese linguistics.

Bibliography

Akita, Kimi & Tsujimura, Atsuko. 2016. Mimetics. In Kageyama & Kishimoto, 2016, pp. 133–160.
Alfonso, Anthony. 1966. *Japanese language patterns*, Vol. 1 & 2. Jesuit Center of Applied Linguistics.
Allan, Keith. 1977. Classifiers. *Language* 53:285–311.
Allan, Keith. 2006. Jargon. In *Encyclopedia of language & linguistics*, 2nd ed., ed. Keith Brown, Anne Anderson, Laurie Bauer, Margie Berns, Jim Miller & Graeme Hirst, pp. 109–112. Elsevier.
Allan, Keith & Burridge, Kate. 2006. *Forbidden words: Taboo and the censoring of language*. Cambridge University Press.
Alpatov, Vladimir & Podlesskaya, Vera. 1995. Converbs in Japanese. In *Converbs in cross-linguistic perspective: Structure and meaning of adverbial verb forms*, ed. Martin Haspelmath & Ekkehard König, pp. 465–485. De Gruyter Mouton.
Aqui, Hamiru (trans. Aileen Chang). 2004. *70 Japanese gestures: No language communication*. IBC Publishing.
Ash, Sharon. 2002. Social class. In Chambers et al., 2002, pp. 402–422.
Atkinson, Hoffman. 1879. *Revised and enlarged edition of exercises in the Yokohama dialect*. Japan Gazette Office.
Backhaus, Peter. 2007. *Linguistic landscapes: A comparative study of urban multilingualism in Tokyo*. Multilingual Matters.
Backhaus, Peter. 2011. Multilingualism in Japanese public space: Reading the signs. In *Language in public spaces in Japan*, ed. Nanette Gottlieb, pp. 39–50. Routledge.
Backhouse, A. E. 1984. Aspects of the graphological structure of Japanese. *Visible Language* 18.3:219–228.
Backhouse, A. E. 1993. *The Japanese language*. Oxford University Press.
Bailey, Don Clifford. 1960. Early Japanese lexicography. *Monumenta Nipponica* 16:1–52.
Bailey, Guy. 2002. Real and apparent time. In Chambers et al., 2002, pp. 312–332.
Barke, Andrew & Uehara, Satoshi. 2005. Japanese pronouns of address: Their behaviour and maintenance over time. In *Broadening the horizon of linguistic politeness*, ed. Robin Lakoff & Sachiko Ide, pp. 301–314. John Benjamins.
Baxter, William & Sagart, Laurent. 2014. Baxter-Sagart Old Chinese reconstruction, version 1.1 (20 September 2014). Available at URL38.
Beckwith, Christopher. 2004. *Koguryo, the language of Japan's continental relatives*. Brill.
Beckwith, Christopher. 2007. *Phoronyms: Classifiers, class nouns, and the pseudopartitive construction*. Peter Lang.
Bentley, John. 2001. *A descriptive grammar of Early Old Japanese prose*. Brill.
Berlin, Brent & Kay, Paul. 1969. *Basic color terms: Their universality and evolution*. University of California Press.
Betz, Werner. 1949. *Deutsch und Lateinisch: die Lehnbildungen der althochdeutschen Benediktinerregel*. Bouvier.
Betz, Werner. 1974. Lehnwörter und Lehnprägungen im Vor- und Frühdeutschen. In *Deutsche Wortgeschichte*, Band I, ed. Friedrich Maurer & Helmut Rupp. De Gruyter Mouton.
Binkley, Cameron. 2011. *The Defence Language Institute Foreign Language Center: A pictorial history*. Available at URL39.
Bloch, Bernard. 1946a. Studies in colloquial Japanese I: Inflection. *Journal of the American Oriental Society* 66.2:97–109.
Bloch, Bernard. 1946b. Studies in colloquial Japanese II: Syntax. *Language* 22.3:200–248.
Bloch, Bernard. 1946c. Studies in colloquial Japanese III: Derivation of inflected words. *Journal of the American Oriental Society* 66.4:304–315.
Bloch, Bernard & Jorden, Eleanor Harz. 1945. *War Department education manual for spoken Japanese*. Linguistic Society of America and the Intensive Language Program American Council of Learned Societies.
Boltz, William. 2003. *The origin and early development of the Chinese writing system*. American Oriental Society.
Carroll, Tessa. 2001. *Language planning and language change in Japan*. Curzon Press.
Chamberlain, Basil. 1895. *Essay in aid of a grammar and dictionary of the Luchuan language*. Yumani Shobo.

Bibliography

Chambers, J.K.; Trudgill, Peter & Schilling-Estes, Natalie (eds.). 2002. *The handbook of language variation and change*. Blackwell.
Chang, Andrew. 1990. *A thesaurus of Japanese mimesis and onomatopoeia*. Taishukan.
Cheshire, Jenny. 2002. Sex and gender in variationist research. In Chambers et al., 2002, pp. 423–443.
Chien, Yuehchen & Sanada, Shinji. 2010. Yilan Creole in Taiwan. *Journal of Pidgin and Creole Languages* 25:350–357.
Chino, Naoko. 2001. *All about particles: A handbook of Japanese function words*. Kodansha International.
Church, R. Breckinridge; Alibali, Martha & Kelly, Spencer. 2017. *Why gesture?* John Benjamins.
Coulmas, Florian. 1989. *The writing systems of the world*. Blackwell.
Coulmas, Florian. 2003. *Writing systems: An introduction to their linguistic analysis*. Cambridge University Press.
Coulmas, Florian. 2018. Writing and literacy in modern Japan. In Hasegawa, 2018b, pp. 144–132.
Crawcour, Sydney. 1965. *An introduction to kambun*. The University of Michigan.
Croft, William. 1991. *Syntactic categories and grammatical relations: The cognitive organization of information*. University of Chicago Press.
Crystal, David. 2000. *Language death*. Cambridge University Press.
Crystal, David. 2008. *A dictionary of linguistics and phonetics, 6th ed.* Blackwell.
Daniels, F. J. 1948. The vocabulary of the Japanese ports lingo. *Bulletin of the School of Oriental and African Studies* 12:805–823.
de Chene, Brent. 2016. Description and explanation in morphophonology: The case of Japanese verb inflection. *Journal of East Asian Linguistics* 25.1:37–80.
De Mente, Boye Lafayette. 1993. *Behind the Japanese bow*. Passport Books.
DeChicchis, Joseph. 1995. The current state of the Ainu language. *Journal of Multilingual and Multicultural Development* 16:103–124.
DeChicchis, Joseph. 2009. The transcription of personal names: The Japanese passport. In *Current issues in unity and diversity of languages*, ed. The Linguistic Society of Korea. Dongnam Publishing.
DeFrancis, John. 1984. *The Chinese language: Fact and fiction*. University of Hawaii Press.
DeFrancis, John. 1989. *Visible speech: The diverse oneness of writing systems*. University of Hawaii Press.
Deutscher, Guy. 2010. *Through the language glass: Why the world looks different in other languages*. Metropolitan Books.
Doi, Toshio. 1976. *The study of language in Japan: A historical survey*. Shinozaki Shorin.
Dong, Hongyuan. 2014. *A history of the Chinese language*. Routledge.
Dressler, Wolfgang. 1988. Language death. In *Linguistics: The Cambridge survey, Vol. IV, Language: The socio-cultural context*, ed. F.J. Newmeyer, pp. 184–192. Cambridge University Press.
Duckworth, David. 1977. Zur terminologischen und systematischen Grundlage der Forschung auf dem Gebiet der englisch-deutschen Interferenz. In *Sprachliche Interferenz: Festschrift für Werner Betz zum 65. Geburtstag*, ed. Herbert Kolb & Hartmut Lauffer. Max Niemeyer Verlag.
Duke, Benjamin. 2009. *The history of modern Japanese education: Constructing the national school system, 1872–1890*. Rutgers University Press.
Dumas, Bethany & Lighter, Jonathan. 1978. Is slang a word for linguistics? *American Speech* 53.1:5–17.
Eble, Connie. 2006. Slang, argot and ingroup codes. In *Encyclopedia of language & linguistics, 2nd ed.*, ed. Keith Brown, Anne Anderson, Laurie Bauer, Margie Berns, Jim Miller & Graeme Hirst, pp. 412–415. Elsevier.
Evens, Toshie. 1997. *A dictionary of Japanese loanwords*. Greenwood Press.
Firchow, Irwin & Firchow, Jacqueline. 1969. An abbreviated phoneme inventory. *Anthropological Linguistics* 11.9:271–276.
Fogel, Joshua (ed. & trans.). 2015. *The emergence of the modern Sino-Japanese lexicon: Seven studies*. Brill.
Foley, William. 1986. *The Papuan languages of New Guinea*. Cambridge University Press.
Francis-Ratte, Alexander. 2016. *Proto-Korean-Japanese: A new reconstruction of the common origins of the Japanese and Korean languages*. Doctoral dissertation, The Ohio State University.
Frellesvig, Bjarke. 1995. *A case study in diachronic phonology: The Japanese onbin sound changes*. Aarhus University Press.
Frellesvig, Bjarke. 2010. *A history of the Japanese language*. Oxford University Press.
Frellesvig, Bjarke. 2018. The history of the language. In Hasegawa, 2018b, pp. 15–39.
Frellesvig, Bjarke & Whitman, John (eds.). 2008. *Proto-Japanese: Issues and prospects*. John Benjamins.
Fujii, Noriko. 1991. *Historical discourse analysis: Grammatical subject in Japanese*. De Gruyter Mouton.
Fujii, Seiko. 2018. Conditionals. In Hasegawa, 2018b, pp. 557–584.
Fujimoto, Masako. 2015. Vowel devoicing. In Kubozono, 2015b, pp. 167–214.

Fukuzawa, Haruka & Kitahara, Mafuyu. 2005. Ranking paradoxes in consonant voicing in Japanese. In van de Weijer et al., 2005, pp. 105–121.
Gottlieb, Nanette. 1995. *Kanji politics: Language policy and Japanese script*. Kegan Paul International.
Gottlieb, Nanette. 2005. *Language and society in Japan*. Cambridge University Press.
Gottlieb, Nanette. 2006. *Linguistic stereotyping and minority groups in Japan*. Routledge.
Gottlieb, Nanette. 2008. Japan: Language planning and policy in transition. In *Language planning and policy in Asia, Vol. 1: Japan, Nepal, Taiwan and Chinese characters*, ed. Robert Kaplan & Richard Baldauf, pp. 102–169. Multilingual Matters.
Gottlieb, Nanette. 2012. *Language policy in Japan*. Cambridge University Press.
Greenberg, Joseph. 1963. Some universals of grammar with particular reference to the order of meaningful elements. In *Universals of human languages*, ed. Joseph H. Greenberg, pp. 73–113. MIT Press.
Grootaers, Willem. 1982. Dialectology and sociolinguistics: A general survey. *Lingua* 57:327–355.
Group Jammassy, (trans. Yuriko Sunakawa & Priscilla Ishida (supervising eds.)). 2015. *A handbook of Japanese grammar patterns for teachers and learners*. Kurosio.
Hamano, Shoko. 1998. *The sound-symbolic system of Japanese*. CSLI Publications.
Hammarström, Harald. 2016. Linguistic diversity and language evolution. *Journal of Language Evolution* 2016:19–29.
Haraguchi, Shosuke. 1991. *A theory of stress and accent*. De Gruyter Mouton.
Haraguchi, Shosuke. 1999. Accent. In Tsujimura, 1999, pp. 1–30.
Hasegawa, Nobuko. 2018a. Benefactives. In Hasegawa, 2018b, pp. 509–529.
Hasegawa, Yoko. 1996. *A study of Japanese clause linkage: The connective TE in Japanese*. CSLI Publication.
Hasegawa, Yoko. 2015. *Japanese: A linguistic introduction*. Cambridge University Press.
Hasegawa, Yoko (ed.). 2018b. *The Cambridge handbook of Japanese linguistics*. Cambridge University Press.
Hasegawa, Yoko. 2018c. Subjects and topics. In Hasegawa, 2018b, pp. 276–299.
Haspelmath, Martin. 1996. Word-class-changing inflection and morphological theory. In *Yearbook of morphology 1995*, ed. Geert Booij & Jaap van Marle, pp. 43–66. Springer.
Haspelmath, Martin. 2012. How to compare major word-classes across the world's languages. UCLA Working Papers in Linguistics 17:109–130.
Haspelmath, Martin & König, Ekkehard (eds.). 1995. *Converbs in cross-linguistic perspective*. De Gruyter Mouton.
Haugen, Einar. 1950. The analysis of linguistic borrowing. *Language* 26.2:210–231.
Hayakawa, Isamu. 2001. *Methods of plagiarism: A history of English-Japanese lexicography*. Jiyusha.
Hayakawa, Isamu. 2014. *A historical dictionary of Japanese words used in English*. Texnai.
Heinrich, Patrick. 2011. Language choices at Naha airport. In *Language in public spaces in Japan*, ed. Nanette Gottlieb, pp. 21–38. Routledge.
Heinrich, Patrick. 2012. *The making of monolingual Japan: Language ideology and Japanese modernity*. Multilingual Matters.
Heinrich, Patrick; Miyara, Shinsho & Shimoji, Michinori (eds.). 2015. *Handbook of the Ryukyuan languages*. De Gruyter Mouton.
Heycock, Caroline. 2008. Japanese *-wa*, *-ga*, and information structure. In Miyagawa & Saito, 2008, pp. 54–83.
Hibiya, Junko. 1995. The velar nasal in Tokyo Japanese: A case of diffusion from above. *Language Variation and Change* 7:139–152.
Hibiya, Junko. 1996. Denasalization of the velar nasal in Tokyo Japanese: Observations in real time. In *Towards a social science of language. Papers in honor of William Labov, Vol. I: Variation and change in language and society*, ed. Gregory Guy, Crawford Feagin, Deborah Schiffrin & John Baugh, pp. 161–171. John Benjamins.
Hibiya, Junko. 1999. Variationist sociolinguistics. In Tsujimura, 1999, pp. 101–120.
Hinds, John. 1986. *Japanese: Descriptive grammar*. Routledge.
Hinds, John; Iwasaki, Shoichi & Maynard Senko (eds.). 1987. *Perspectives on topicalization: The case of Japanese* wa. John Benjamins.
Hoji, Hajime; Kinsui, Satoshi; Takubo, Yukinori & Ueyama, Ayumi. 2003. The demonstratives in modern Japanese. In *Functional structure(s), form and interpretation: Perspectives from East Asian languages*, ed. Yen-hui Audrey Li & Andrew Simpson, pp. 97–128. Routledge.
Holm, John. 2000. *An introduction to pidgins and creoles*. Cambridge University Press.
Holmes, Janet. 2001. *An introduction to sociolinguistics*. Pearson Education.
Horie, Kaoru. 2018. Linguistic typology and the Japanese language. In Hasegawa, 2018b, pp. 65–86.
Ide, Sachiko. 1982. Japanese sociolinguistics politeness and women's language [sic]. *Lingua* 57:357–385.
Ide, Sachiko & McGloin, Naomi (eds.). 1991. *Aspects of Japanese women's language*. Kurosio.

Bibliography 261

Ide, Sachiko & Yoshida, Megumi. 1999. Sociolinguistics: Honorifics and gender differences. In Tsujimura, 1999, pp. 444–480.
Ide, Sachiko; Hori, Motoko; Kawasaki, Akiko; Ikuta, Shoko & Haga, Hitomi. 1986. Sex difference and politeness in Japanese. *International Journal of the Sociology of Language* 58:25–36.
Ifrah, Georges (trans. David Bello). 2000. *The universal history of numbers: From prehistory to the invention of the computer.* John Wiley & Sons, Inc.
Igarashi, Yosuke. 2015. Intonation. In Kubozono, 2015b, pp. 525–568.
Igarashi, Yosuke. 2018. Intonation. In Hasegawa, 2018b, pp. 181–201.
Inoue, Kazuko. 1969. *A study of Japanese syntax.* Mouton Publishers.
Inoue, Fumio. 2005. Econolinguistic aspects of multilingual signs in Japan. *International Journal of the Sociology of Language* 175/176:157–177.
Inoue, Aya. 2007. Grammatical features of Yokohama Pidgin Japanese. *Japanese/Korean Linguistics* 15:55–66.
Inui, Yoshihiko. Forthcoming. Ritsuryo and the development of the Japanese writing system. In Irwin & Zisk, Forthcoming.
Irwin, Mark. 2009. Prosodic size and rendaku immunity. *Journal of East Asian Linguistics* 18:179–196.
Irwin, Mark. 2011a. *Loanwords in Japanese.* John Benjamins.
Irwin, Mark. 2011b. Mora clipping of loanwords in Japanese. *Journal of Japanese Linguistics* 27:71–81.
Irwin, Mark. 2012. Rendaku dampening and prefixes. *NINJAL Research Papers* 4:2–36.
Irwin, Mark. 2014. Rendaku across duplicate moras. *NINJAL Research Papers* 7:93–109.
Irwin, Mark. 2015. Rendaku lovers, rendaku haters and the logistic curve. *Japanese/Korean Linguistics* 22:37–51.
Irwin, Mark. 2016a. English loanwords. In Kageyama & Kishimoto, 2016, pp. 161–197.
Irwin, Mark. 2016b. Rosen's Rule. In Vance & Irwin, 2016, pp. 107–137.
Irwin, Mark. 2016c. The rendaku database. In Vance & Irwin, 2016, pp. 79–106.
Irwin, Mark. Forthcoming. No English spoken here: The prohibition on English in Japan 1940–45. In Irwin & Zisk, Forthcoming.
Irwin, Mark & Lyddon, Paul. 2016. Rendaku and homophony. *Phonological Studies* 19:11–18.
Irwin, Mark & Zisk, Matthew (eds.). Forthcoming. *Japanese sociohistorical linguistics.* De Gruyter Mouton.
Ito, Junko. 1990. Prosodic minimality in Japanese. In *Papers from the 26th regional meeting of the Chicago Linguistics Society, Vol. 2: The parasession on the syllable in phonetics and phonology*, ed. Michael Ziolkowski, Manuela Noske & Karen Deaton, pp. 213–239. Chicago Linguistics Society.
Ito, Junko & Mester, Armin. 1986. The phonology of voicing in Japanese: Theoretical consequences for morphological accessibility. *Linguistic Inquiry* 17:49–73.
Ito, Junko & Mester, Armin. 1992. Weak layering and word binarity. In *A new century of phonology and phonological theory: A festschrift for Professor Shosuke Haraguchi on the occasion of his sixtieth birthday*, ed. Takeru Honma, Masao Okazaki, Toshiyuki Tabata & Shin-ichi Tanaka, pp. 26–65. Kaitakusha.
Ito, Junko & Mester, Armin. 1995. Japanese phonology. In *The handbook of phonological theory*, ed. John Goldsmith, pp. 817–838. Blackwell.
Ito, Junko & Mester, Armin. 2015. Sino-Japanese phonology. In Kubozono, 2015b, pp. 289–312.
Iwasaki, Shoichi. 2013. *Japanese.* John Benjamins.
Iwasaki, Noriko; Sells, Peter & Akita, Kimi (eds.). 2017. *The grammar of Japanese mimetics: Perspectives from structure, acquisition and translation.* Routledge.
JACET Society of English Lexicography. 2006. *English lexicography in Japan.* Taishūkan.
Jacobsen, W. M. 1992. *The transitive structure of events in Japanese.* Kurosio.
Jacobsen, W. M. 2017. Transitivity. In Shibatani et al., 2017, pp. 55–95.
Johansen, Jorgen. 2002. *Signs in use: An introduction to semiotics.* Routledge.
Johnson, Yuki. 2008. *Fundamentals of Japanese grammar: Comprehensive acquisition.* University of Hawai'i Press.
Jorden, Eleanor & Noda, Mari. 1987–1990. *Japanese: The spoken language*, Part I–III. Yale University Press.
Joyce, Terry. 2013. The significance of the morphographic principle for the classification of writing systems. In *Typology of writing systems*, ed. Susanne Borgwaldt & Terry Joyce, pp. 61–84. John Benjamins.
Joyce, Terry & Masuda, Hisashi. 2018. Introduction to the multi-script Japanese writing system and word processing. In *Writing systems, reading processes, and cross-linguistic influences: Reflections from the Chinese, Japanese and Korean languages*, ed. Hye Pae, pp. 179–199. John Benjamins.
Joyce, Terry; Hodošček, Bor & Nishina, Kikuko. 2012. Orthographic representation and variation within the Japanese writing system. *Written Language & Literacy* 15.2:254–278.
Kageyama, Taro. 1999. Word formation. In Tsujimura, 1999, pp. 297–325.

Kageyama, Taro. 2016a. Lexical integrity and the morphology-syntax interface. In Kageyama & Kishimoto, 2016, pp. 489–528.
Kageyama, Taro. 2016b. Verb-compounding and verb incorporation. In Kageyama & Kishimoto, 2016, pp. 273–310.
Kageyama, Taro & Jacobsen, Wesley (eds.). 2016. *Transitivity and valency alternations: Studies on Japanese and beyond*. De Gruyter Mouton.
Kageyama, Taro & Kishimoto, Hideki (eds.). 2016. *Handbook of Japanese lexicon and word formation*. De Gruyter Mouton.
Kageyama, Taro & Saito, Michiaki. 2016. Vocabulary strata and word formation processes. In Kageyama & Kishimoto, 2016, pp. 11–50.
Kaiser, Stefan. 1994. *The Western rediscovery of the Japanese language*, Vols. 1–8. Curzon Press.
Kaiser, Stefan; Ichikawa, Yasuko; Kobayashi, Noriko & Yamamoto, Hirofumi. 2013. *Japanese: A comprehensive grammar*, 2nd ed. Routledge.
Kakehi, Hisao; Tamori, Ikuhiro & Schourup, Lawrence. 1996. *Dictionary of iconic expressions in Japanese*, Vol. 1 & 2. De Gruyter Mouton.
Kaplan, Robert & Baldauf, Richard. 2008. Language policy and planning in Japan, Nepal and Taiwan and Chinese characters: Some common issues. In *Language planning and policy in Asia, Vol. 1: Japan, Nepal, Taiwan and Chinese characters*, ed. Robert Kaplan & Richard B. Baldauf, pp. 7–37. Multilingual Matters.
Kaplan, David & Dubro, Alec. 2003. *Yakuza: Japan's criminal underworld*. University of California Press.
Kaplan, Abby & Muratani, Yuka. 2015. Categorical and gradient homophony avoidance: Evidence from Japanese. *Laboratory Phonology* 6.2:167–195.
Kasschau, Anne & Eguchi, Susumu. 1995. *A comprehensive guide to using Japanese slang*. Yenbooks.
Kawaguchi, Yuji & Inoue, Fumio. 2002. Japanese dialectology in historical perspectives. *Revue Belge de Philologie et d'Histoire* 80.3:801–829.
Kawahara, Shigeto. 2015. The phonology of Japanese accent. In Kubozono, 2015b, pp. 445–492.
Kawahara, Shigeto & Sano, Shin'ichiro. 2014. Testing Rosen's Rule and strong Lyman's Law. *NINJAL Research Papers* 7:111–120.
Kawashima, Sue. 1999. *A dictionary of Japanese particles*. Kodansha International.
Kay, Paul; Berlin, Brent; Maffi, Luisa; Merrifield, William & Cook, Richard. 2009. *The world color survey*. CSLI Publications.
Kembō, Hidetoshi. 1961. Dictionaries, encyclopedias, and indices of vocabulary. In *Japanese language studies in the Shōwa period: A guide to Japanese reference and research materials*, ed. Joseph Yamagiwa, pp. 32–50. The University of Michigan Press.
Kennedy, George. 1964a. The monosyllabic myth. In *Selected works of George A. Kennedy*, ed. Tien-yi Li, pp. 104–118.
Kennedy, George. 1964b. The butterfly case (Part 1). In *Selected works of George A. Kennedy*, ed. Tien-yi Li, pp. 274–322.
Kess, Joseph & Miyamoto, Tadao. 1999. *The Japanese mental lexicon: Psycholinguistic studies of kana and kanji processing*. John Benjamins.
Kindaichi, Haruhiko (trans. Umeyo Hirano). 2010. *The Japanese language*. Tuttle Publishing.
Kinsui, Satoshi. 2017. *Virtual Japanese: Enigmas of role language*. Osaka University Press.
Kishimoto, Hideki. 2018. Case marking. In Shibatani et al., 2017, pp. 447–495.
Kishimoto, Hideki & Uehara, Satoshi. 2016. Lexical categories. In Kageyama & Kishimoto, 2016, pp. 51–92.
Kiyose, Gisaburo. 1995. *Japanese grammar: A new approach*. Kyoto University Press.
Kobayashi, Noriko. 2016. Japanese language proficiency assessment with the Simple Performance-Oriented Test (SPOT) as a primary focus. In Minami, 2016, pp. 175–198.
Kobayashi, Hideki; Yamashita, Kiyo & Kageyama, Taro. 2016. Sino-Japanese words. In Kageyama & Kishimoto, 2016, pp. 93–131.
Komai, Akira & Rohlich, Thomas. 1988. *An introduction to Japanese kanbun*. University of Nagoya Press.
Komai, Akira & Rohlich, Thomas. 1991. *An introduction to Classical Japanese*. Bonjinsha.
Kondo, Dorinne. 1990. *Crafting selves: Power, gender, and discourses of identity in a Japanese workplace*. University of Chicago Press.
Kondo, Mariko. 2005. Syllable structure and its acoustic effects on vowels in devoicing environments. In van de Weijer et al., 2005, pp. 229–246.
Kubozono, Haruo. 1989. The mora and syllable structure in Japanese: Evidence from errors. *Language and Speech* 32:249–278.

Kubozono, Haruo. 1995. Constraint interaction in Japanese phonology: Evidence from compound accent. *Phonology at Santa Cruz* 4:21–38.
Kubozono, Haruo. 1999. Mora and syllable. In Tsujimura, 1999, pp. 31–61.
Kubozono, Haruo. 2001a. Epenthetic vowels and accent in Japanese: Facts and paradoxes. In *Issues in Japanese phonology and morphology*, ed. Jeroen van de Weijer & Tetsuo Nishihara, pp. 113–142. De Gruyter Mouton.
Kubozono, Haruo. 2001b. On the markedness of diphthongs. *Kobe Papers in Linguistics* 3:60–73.
Kubozono, Haruo. 2002. Prosodic structure of loanwords in Japanese: Syllable, structure, accent and morphology. *Journal of the Phonetic Society of Japan* 6.1:79–97.
Kubozono, Haruo. 2005. Rendaku: Its domain and linguistic conditions. In van de Weijer et al., 2005, pp. 5–20.
Kubozono, Haruo. 2006. Where does loanword prosody come from? A case study of Japanese loanword accent. *Lingua* 116:1140–1170.
Kubozono, Haruo. 2008. Japanese accent. In Miyagawa & Saito, 2008, pp. 165–191.
Kubozono, Haruo. 2012. Varieties of pitch accent systems in Japanese. *Lingua* 122.13:1,395–1,414.
Kubozono, Haruo. 2015a. Diphthongs and vowel coalescence. In Kubozono, 2015b, pp. 215–249.
Kubozono, Haruo (ed.). 2015b. *Handbook of Japanese phonetics and phonology*. De Gruyter Mouton.
Kubozono, Haruo. 2015c. Japanese dialects and general linguistics. *Gengo Kenkyū* 148:1–31.
Kubozono, Haruo. 2015d. Loanword phonology. In Kubozono, 2015c, pp. 313–361.
Kubozono, Haruo. 2018. Pitch accent. In Hasegawa, 2018b, pp. 154–180.
Kunihiro, Tetsuya; Inoue, Fumio & Long, Daniel (eds.). 1999. *Takesi Sibata: Sociolinguistics in Japanese contexts*. De Gruyter Mouton.
Kuno, Susumu. 1973. *The structure of the Japanese language*. MIT Press.
Kuroda, S.-Y. 1965. *Generative grammatical studies in the Japanese language*. Doctoral dissertation, MIT.
Labov, William. 1963. The social motivation of a sound change. *Word* 19:273–309.
Labov, William. 1966. *The social stratification of English in New York City*. Center for Applied Linguistics.
Labrune, Laurence. 2002. The prosodic structure of simple abbreviated loanwords in Japanese. *Journal of the Phonetic Society of Japan* 6.1:98–120.
Labrune, Laurence. 2012. *The phonology of Japanese*. Oxford University Press.
Lange, Roland. 1973. *The phonology of eighth-century Japanese: A reconstruction based upon written records*. Sophia University.
Larm, Lars. 2008. Early uses of the term *chinjutsu*. Lund University, Dept. of Linguistics and Phonetics Working Papers 53:97–115.
Lee, Yeounsuk. 2010. *The ideology of* kokugo*: Nationalizing language in modern Japan*. University of Hawai'i Press.
Lee, Iksop & Ramsey, S. Robert. 2000. *The Korean language*. State University of New York Press.
Li, Charles (ed.). 1976. *Subject and topic*. Academic Press.
Liu, Haitao. 2010. Dependency direction as a means of word-order typology: A method based on dependency treebanks. *Lingua* 120.6:1,567–1,578.
Long, Daniel. 2007. *English on the Bonin (Ogasawara) Islands*. Duke University Press for the American Dialect Society.
Lovins, Julie Beth. 1973. *Loanwords and the phonological structure of Japanese*. Doctoral dissertation, University of Chicago.
Lurie, David. 2011. *Realms of literacy: Early Japan and the history of writing*. Harvard University Press.
Lyman, Benjamin. 1894. *The change from surd to sonant in Japanese compounds*. Oriental Club of Philadelphia.
Maddieson, Ian. 2010. Typology of phonological systems. In *The Oxford handbook of linguistic typology*, ed. Jae Jung Song, pp. 534–548. Oxford University Press.
Maekawa, Kikuo & Kikuchi, Hideaki. 2005. Corpus-based analysis of vowel devoicing in spontaneous Japanese: An interim report. In van de Weijer et al., 2005, pp. 205–228.
Maher, John. 2004. A brief history of pidgins and creoles in Japan. *Educational Studies* 46:173–185.
Mair, Victor. 2016. *ABC dictionary of Sino-Japanese readings*. University of Hawai'i Press.
Maki, Hideki & Uchibori, Asako. 2008. *Ga/no* conversion. In Miyagawa & Saito, 2008, pp. 192–216.
Makino, Seiichi & Tsutsui, Michio. 1986. *A dictionary of basic Japanese grammar*. The Japan Times.
Makino, Seiichi & Tsutsui, Michio. 1995. *A dictionary of intermediate Japanese grammar*. The Japan Times.
Makino, Seiichi & Tsutsui, Michio. 2008. *A dictionary of advanced Japanese grammar*. The Japan Times.
Mandelin, Clyde. 2015. *Legends of localization, book 1: The legend of Zelda*. Fangamer.
Mandelin, Clyde. 2016. *Legends of localization, book 2: Earthbound*. Fangamer.

Martin, Samuel. 1952. Morphophonemics of standard colloquial Japanese. *Language* 28.3 (Part 2, Supplement).
Martin, Samuel. 1975. *A reference grammar of Japanese*. Yale University Press.
Martin, Samuel. 1987. *The Japanese language through time*. Yale University Press.
Masuoka, Takashi. 2018. Topic and subject. In Shibatani et al., 2017, pp. 97–122.
Matsumori, Akiko & Onishi, Takuichiro. 2012. Japanese dialects: Focusing on Tsuruoka and Ei. In Tranter, 2012a, pp. 313–348.
Matsumoto, Yo. 1993. Japanese numeral classifiers: A study of semantic categories and lexical organization. *Linguistics* 31:667–713.
Matsumoto, Yo. 1996. *Complex predicates in Japanese: A syntactic and semantic study of the notion 'word'*. Kurosio.
Maynard, Senko. 1993. *Discourse modality: Subjectivity, emotion and voice in the Japanese language*. John Benjamins.
McCawley, James. 1968. *The phonological component of a grammar of Japanese*. Mouton Publishers.
McCawley, James. 1977. Accent in Japanese. In *Studies in stress and accent*, ed. Larry Hyman, pp. 261–302. University of Southern California Department of Linguistics.
McClure, William. 2000. *Using Japanese: A guide to contemporary usage*. Cambridge University Press.
McCreary, Don. 2013. Japanese lexicography. In *Dictionaries: An international encyclopedia of lexicography*, ed. Rufus Gouws, Ulrich Heid, Wolfgang Schweickard & Herbert Wiegand, pp. 893–900. De Gruyter Mouton.
McCullough, Helen. 1988. *Bungo manual: Selected reference materials for students of Classical Japanese*. Cornell East Asia Series.
Meyerhoff, Miriam. 2006. *Introducing sociolinguistics*. Routledge.
Miller, Roy. 1967. *The Japanese language*. University of Chicago Press.
Miller, Roy (ed.). 1970. *Bernhard Bloch on Japanese*. Yale University Press.
Miller, Roy. 1977. The 'spirit' of the Japanese language. *Journal of Japanese Studies* 3.2:251–198.
Miller, Roy. 1982. *Japan's modern myth*. Weatherhill.
Minami, Masahiko (ed.). 2016. *Handbook of Japanese applied linguistics*. De Gruyter Mouton.
Miyagawa, Shigeru & Saito, Mamoru (eds.). 2008. *The Oxford handbook of Japanese linguistics*. Oxford University Press.
Miyake, Marc Hideo. 2003. *Old Japanese: A phonetic reconstruction*. RoutledgeCurzon.
Moran, Pádraic & Whitman, John. Forthcoming. Glossing and reading in western Europe and East Asia: A comparative case study. ms. National University of Ireland and Cornell University.
Mori, Yuta. Forthcoming. The Japanese social hierarchy and its influence on honorific speech. In Irwin & Zisk, Forthcoming.
Morita, Emi. 2018. Sentence-final particles. In Hasegawa, 2018b, pp. 587–607.
Moseley, Christopher (ed.). 2010. *Atlas of the world's languages in danger*, 3rd ed. UNESCO Publishing. Available at URL40.
Murdock, George. 1970. Kin term patterns and their distribution. *Ethnology* 9.2:165–208.
Murray, Gell & Ruhlen, Merritt. 2011. The origin and evolution of word order. *Proceedings of the National Academy of Sciences* October 2011:17,290–17,295.
Nagara, Susumu. 1972. *Japanese Pidgin English in Hawaii: A bilingual description*. University of Hawaii Press.
Nagashima, Daisuke. 1991. Bilingual lexicography with Japanese. In *Dictionaries: An international encyclopedia of lexicography*, ed. Franz Hausmann, Oskar Reichmann, Herbert Wiegand & Ladislav Zgusta, pp. 3,114–3,120. De Gruyter Mouton.
Nagashima, Heiyō. 2006. *Sha-re*: A widely accepted form of Japanese wordplay. In *Understanding humor in Japan*, ed. Jessica Davis, pp. 75–83. Wayne State University Press.
Nagata, Takashi. 2006. *A historical study of referent honorifics in Japanese*. Hituzi Syobo Publishing.
Nakahara, Tomiko. 2002. *The Japanese copula: Forms and functions*. Palgrave Macmillan.
Nakamura, Wataru. 2018. Case. In Hasegawa, 2018b, pp. 249–275.
Nakanishi, Taro. Forthcoming. Patterns of change in Japanese greeting expressions: Formulization and paradigm optimization. In Irwin & Zisk, Forthcoming.
Nakatani, Kentaro. 2013. *Predicate concatenation: A study of the V-te V predicate in Japanese*. Kurosio.
Nakatani, Kentaro. 2016. Complex predicates with *-te* gerundive verbs. In Kageyama & Kishimoto, 2016, pp. 387–423.
Narrog, Heiko. 2009a. *Modality in Japanese: The layered structure of the clause and hierarchies of functional categories*. John Benjamins.

Narrog, Heiko. 2009b. Modality, *modaritii* and predication: The story of modality in Japan. In *Japanese modality: Exploring its scope and interpretation*, ed. Barbara Pizziconi & Mika Kizu, pp. 9–35. Palgrave Macmillan.
Narumi, Shin'ichi. Forthcoming. Sino-Japanese compounds: The contribution made by kanji orthography to semantic change. In Irwin & Zisk, Forthcoming.
Nemoto, Naoko. 1999. Scrambing. In Tsujimura, 1999, pp. 121–153.
Nishiyama, Kunio. 1999. Adjectives and the copulas in Japanese. *Journal of East Asian Linguistics* 8:183–222.
Nishiyama, Kunio. 2008. V-V compounds. In Miyagawa & Saito, 2008, pp. 320–347.
Nitta, Yoshio. 2017. Basic sentence structure and grammatical categories. In Shibatani et al., 2017, pp. 27–53.
Norman, Arthur. 1955. Bamboo English: The Japanese influence upon American speech in Japan. *American Speech* 30.1:44–48.
Nuessel, Frank. 1992. *The study of names*. Greenwood Press.
O'Neill, P. G. 1972. *Japanese names: A comprehensive index by characters and readings*. Weatherhill.
Ochi, Masao. 2018. *Ga/no* conversion. In Shibatani et al., 2017, pp. 663–699.
Ogi, Naomi. 2017. *Involvement and attitude in Japanese discourse: Interactive markers*. John Benjamins.
Ogi, Naomi & Lee, Duck-Young. 2013. Gender and the sentence-final particles in Japanese. In *Gender-linked variation across languages*, ed. Yousif Elhindi & Theresa McGarry, pp. 50–85. Common Ground.
Okagaki, Hirotaka. Forthcoming. Basil Hall Chamberlain and the study of Japanese as a foreign language in the late 19th to early 20th century. In Irwin & Zisk, Forthcoming.
Okamoto, Shigeko. 2018. Language, gender and sexuality. In Hasegawa, 2018b, pp. 678–697.
Okamoto, Shigeko & Shibamoto-Smith, Janet (eds.). 2004. *Japanese language, gender and ideology*. Oxford University Press.
Oki, Kazuo. Forthcoming. Language stereotypes in Japanese and historical Japanese linguistics. In Irwin & Zisk, Forthcoming.
Olsen, Michael Leon. 1981. *Barai clause junctures: Toward a functional theory of interclausal relations*. Doctoral dissertation, Australian National University.
Onishi, Takuichiro. 2018. Dialects of Japanese. In *The handbook of dialectology*, ed. Charles Boberg, John Nerbonne & Dominic Watt, pp. 559–570. Wiley Blackwell.
Osterkamp, Sven. 2017a. Sino-xenic readings. In *Encyclopedia of Chinese language and linguistics*, Vol. 4, ed. Rint Sybesma, Wolfgang Behr, Yueguo Gu, Zev Handel, C.-T. James Huang & James Myers, pp. 134–138. Brill.
Osterkamp, Sven. 2017b. Sinoform writing. In *Encyclopedia of Chinese language and linguistics*, Vol. 4, ed. Rint Sybesma, Wolfgang Behr, Yueguo Gu, Zev Handel, C.-T. James Huang & James Myers, pp. 115–124. Brill.
Osumi, Midori. 2001. Language and identity in Okinawa today. In *Studies in Japanese bilingualism*, ed. Mary Goebel Noguchi & Sandra Fotos, pp. 68–97. Multilingual Matters.
Ota, Yuzo. 1998. *Basil Hall Chamberlain: Portrait of a Japanologist*. Routledge.
Otake, Takashi. 2015. Mora and mora-timing. In Kubozono, 2015b, pp. 493–523.
Otsu, Yukio. 1980. Some aspects of rendaku in Japanese and related problems. In *Theoretical Issues in Japanese linguistics*, ed. Yukio Otsu & Anne Farmer, pp. 207–227. MIT Press.
Palter, D. C. & Slotsve, Kaoru. 2005. *Colloquial Kansai Japanese: The dialects and culture of the Kansai region*. Tuttle Publishing.
Pardeshi, Prashant & Kageyama, Taro (eds.). 2018. *Handbook of Japanese contrastive linguistics*. De Gruyter Mouton.
Pellard, Thomas. 2015. The linguistic archeology of the Ryukyu islands. In Heinrich et al., 2015, pp. 16–37.
Peppé, Sue. 2012. Prosody in the world's languages. In *Multilingual aspects of speech sound disorders in children*, ed. Sharynne McLeod & Brian Goldstein, pp. 42–52. Multingual Matters.
Plutschow, Herbert. 1995. *Japan's name culture*. Japan Library.
Poser, William. 1990. Evidence for foot structure in Japanese. *Language* 66:78–105.
Preston, Dennis (ed.). 1999. *Handbook of perceptual dialectology*, Vol. 1. John Benjamins.
Qiu Xigui (trans. Glibert Mattos & Jerry Norman). 2000. *Chinese writing*. University of California.
Ramsey, S. Robert. 2004. The Japanese language and the making of tradition. *Japanese Language and Literature* 38.1:81–110.
Ramus, Franck; Nespor, Marina & Mehler, Jacques. 1999. Correlates of linguistic rhythm in the speech signal. *Cognition* 73.3:265–292.

Rickmeyer, Jens. 1986. Verbal inflexion and auxiliary verbs in Classical Japanese. *Bochumer Jahrbücher zur Ostasienforschung* 9:217–28.
Rickmeyer, Jens. 1995. *Japanische Morphosyntax*. Julius Groos Verlag.
Robbeets, Martine. 2005. *Is Japanese related to Korean, Tungusic, Mongolic and Turkic?* Harrassowitz Verlag.
Romaine, Suzanne. 1994. *Language in society*. Oxford University Press.
Rosen, Eric. 2003. Systematic irregularity in Japanese rendaku: How the grammar mediates patterned lexical exceptions. *Canadian Journal of Linguistics* 48:1–37.
Rothaug, Petra. 1991. *Abriß der japanischen Lautgeschichte*. Helmut Buske.
Sampson, Geoffrey. 2015. *Writing systems*, 2nd ed. Equinox.
Sankoff, Gillian. 2013. Longitudinal studies. In *The Oxford handbook of sociolinguistics*, ed. Robert Bayley, Richard Cameron & Ceil Lucas, pp. 261–279. Oxford University Press.
Sapir, Edward. 1931. Conceptual categories in primitive languages. *Science* 74:578.
Sasaki, Kan. 2013. Another look at *sa*-insertion in Japanese. *Studies in Phonetics, Phonology and Morphology* 19.1:179–190.
Sasaki, Kan. 2016. Anticausativization in the northern dialects of Japanese. In Kageyama & Wesley, 2016, pp. 183–214.
Saville-Troike, Muriel. 1985. The place of silence in an integrated theory of communication. In *Perspectives on silence*, ed. Tannen, Deborah & Saville-Troike. Ablex Publishing Corp.
Schourup, Lawrence. 2000. Japanese number mnemonics. *The Journal of the Association of Teachers of Japanese* 34.2:131–158.
Searle, John. 1969. *Speech acts: An essay in the philosophy of language*. Cambridge University Press.
Seeley, Christopher. 1984. The Japanese script since 1900. *Visible Language* 18.3:267–299.
Seeley, Christopher. 1991. *A history of writing in Japan*. Brill.
Shibamoto-Smith, Janet. 1996. Japanese writing. In: *The world's writing systems*, ed. Peter Daniels & Willan Bright, pp. 209–217. Oxford University Press.
Shibamoto-Smith, Janet & Schmidt, David. 1996. Variability in written Japanese: Towards a sociolinguistics of script choice. *Visible Language* 30.1:46–71.
Shibatani, Masayoshi. 1990. *The languages of Japan*. Cambridge University Press.
Shibatani, Masayoshi; Miyagawa, Shigeru & Noda, Hisashi (eds.). 2017. *Handbook of Japanese syntax*. De Gruyter Mouton.
Shimoji, Michinori. 2018. Dialects. In Hasegawa, 2018b, pp. 87–113.
Shimoji, Michinori & Pellard, Thomas. 2010. *An introduction to Ryukyan languages*. Research Institute for Language and Cultures of Asia and Africa.
Shimojo, Mitsuaki. 2018. Word order and extraction: A functional approach. In Hasegawa, 2018b, pp. 404–428.
Shimoyama, Junko. 2008. Indeterminate pronouns. In Miyagawa & Saito, 2008, pp. 372–393.
Shirai, Yasuhiro. 2000. The semantics of the Japanese imperfective -*teiru*: An interative approach. *Journal of Pragmatics* 32:327–361.
Shirane, Haruo. 2005. *Classical Japanese: A grammar*. Columbia University Press.
Shirane, Haruo. 2007. *Classical Japanese reader and essential dictionary*. Columbia University Press.
Shudo, Sachiko. 2002. *The presupposition and discourse functions of the Japanese particle mo*. Routledge.
Sibata, Takesi. 1960. Eastern dialect and Western dialect in Japan. *Zeitschrift für Mundartforschung* 27 H.2:97–100.
Siddle, Richard. 1996. *Race, resistance and the Ainu of Japan*. Routledge.
Skutnabb-Kangas, Tove & Phillipson, Robert. 1995. *Linguistic human rights: Overcoming linguistic discrimination*. De Gruyter Mouton.
Song, Ki-Joong. 2001. *The study of foreign languages in the Choson dynasty (1392–1910)*. Jimoondang International.
Spear, Richard. 2007. *Diego Collado's grammar of the Japanese language*. University of Kansas.
St. Clair, Robert & Murai, Harold. 1974. Codeswitching in Hawaiian creole. *Kansas Journal of Sociology* 10:75–82.
Takagi, Yasaka. 1972. *The works of Inazo Nitobe*. University of Tokyo Press.
Takahara, Kumiko. 1991. Female speech patterns in Japanese. *International Journal of the Sociology of Language* 92:61–85.
Takayama, Tomoaki. 2005. A survey of rendaku in loanwords. In van de Weijer et al., 2005, pp. 177–190.
Takayama, Tomoaki. 2015. Historical phonology. In Kubozono, 2015b, pp. 621–650.
Takezawa, Koichi. 2016. Inflection. In Kageyama & Kishimoto, 2016, pp. 459–486.

Takubo, Yukinori & Kinsui, Satoshi. 1997. Discourse management in terms of mental spaces. *Journal of Pragmatics* 28:741–758.
Tamaoka, Katsuo. 2005. The effect of morphemic homophony on the processing of Japanese two-kanji compound words. *Reading and Writing* 18.4:281–302.
Tamaoka, Katsuo. 2007. Rebounding activation caused by lexical homophony in the processing of Japanese two-kanji compound words. *Reading and Writing* 20.5:413–439.
Tamaoka, Katsuo & Makioka, Shogo. 2004. Frequency of occurrence for units of phonemes, morae, and syllables appearing in a lexical corpus of a Japanese newspaper. *Behavior Research Methods, Instruments & Computers* 36.3:531–547.
Tateishi, Koichi. 1994. *The syntax of 'subjects'*. Kurosio.
Taylor, Insup & Taylor, M. Martin. 2014. *Writing and literacy in Chinese, Korean and Japanese*, Revised ed. John Benjamins.
Teshigawara, Mihoko & Kinsui, Satoshi. 2011. Modern Japanese 'role language' (yakuwarigo): Fictionalized orality in Japanese literature and popular culture. *Sociolinguistic Studies* 5.1:37–58.
Thomason, Sarah. 2001. *Language contact: An introduction*. Georgetown University Press.
Thorpe, Maner Lawton. 1983. *Ryūkyūan language history*. Doctoral dissertation, University of Southern California.
Tomioka, Satoshi. 2016. Information structure in Japanese. In *The Oxford handbook of information structure*, ed. Caroline Féry & Shinichiro Ishihara, pp. 753–773. Oxford University Press.
Tono, Yukio. 2006. Japanese lexicography. In *Encyclopedia of language & linguistics*, 2nd ed., ed. Keith Brown, Anne Anderson, Laurie Bauer, Margie Berns, Jim Miller & Graeme Hirst, pp. 105–109. Elsevier.
Toratani, Kiyoko. 2018. Semantics and morphosyntax of mimetics. In Hasegawa, 2018b, pp. 202–221.
Traill, Anthony. 1994. *A !Xóõ dictionary*. Rüdiger Köppe.
Tranter, Nicolas. 2008. Nonconventional script choice in Japan. *International Journal of the Sociolinguistics of Language* 192:133–151.
Tranter, Nicolas. 2009. Graphic loans: East Asia and beyond. *Word* 60.1:1–37.
Tranter, Nicolas (ed.). 2012a. *The languages of Japan and Korea*. Routledge.
Tranter, Nicolas. 2012b. Typology and area in Japan and Korea. In Tranter, 2012a, pp. 3–23.
Tranter, Nicolas. Forthcoming. Diversity in the Japanese writing system(s): A schematic diachronic analysis. In Irwin & Zisk, Forthcoming.
Tranter, Nicolas & Kizu, Mika. 2012. Modern Japanese. In Tranter, 2012a, pp. 268–312.
Trudgill, Peter. 2000. *Sociolinguistics: An introduction to language and society*, 4th ed. Penguin Books.
Tse, Peter. 1993. *Kansai Japanese: The language of Osaka, Kyoto, and Western Japan*. Tuttle Publishing.
Tsujimura, Natsuko (ed.). 1999. *The handbook of Japanese linguistics*. Blackwell.
Tsujimura, Natsuko. 2014. *An introduction to Japanese linguistics*, 3rd ed. Wiley Blackwell.
Tsukishima, Hiroshi (ed.). 1993. Studies in Sino-Japanese. *Acta Asiatica* 65.
Tsurumi, Patricia. 1977. *Japanese colonial education in Taiwan, 1895–1945*. Harvard University Press.
Twine, Nanette. 1984. The adoption of punctuation in Japanese script. *Visible Language* 18.3:229–237.
Twine, Nanette. 1991. *Language and the modern state: The reform of written Japanese*. Routledge.
Uehara, Satoshi. 1998. *Syntactic categories in Japanese: A cognitive and typological approach*. Kurosio.
Unger, J. Marshall. 1984. Japanese braille. *Visible Language* 18.3:254–266.
Unger, J. Marshall. 1996. *Literacy and script reform in occupation Japan*. Oxford University Press.
Unger, J. Marshall. 1996. *Ideogram: Chinese characters and the myth of disembodied meaning*. University of Hawai'i Press.
Unger, J. Marshall. 2009. *The role of contact in the origin of the Japanese and Korean languages*. University of Hawai'i Press.
Unger, J. Marshall. 2014. No rush to judgement: The case against Japanese as an isolate. *NINJAL Project Review* 4.3:211–230.
van de Weijer, Jeroen; Nanjo, Kensuke & Nishihara, Tetsuo (eds.). 2005. *Voicing in Japanese*. De Gruyter Mouton.
Vance, Timothy. 1980a. The psychological status of a constraint on Japanese consonant alternation. *Linguistics* 18:245–267.
Vance, Timothy. 1980b. Comments on "Some aspects of rendaku in Japanese and related problems" by Yukio Otsu. In *Theoretical issues in Japanese linguistics*, ed. Yukio Otsu & Anne Farmer, pp. 229–236. MIT Press.
Vance, Timothy. 1987. *An introduction to Japanese phonology*. State University of New York Press.
Vance, Timothy. 1993. Are Japanese particles clitics? *The Journal of the Association of Teachers of Japanese* 27.1:3–33.

Vance, Timothy. 2007a. Have we learned anything about rendaku that Lyman didn't already know? In *Current issues in the history and structure of Japanese*, ed. Bjarke Frellesvig, Masayoshi Shibatani & John Smith, pp. 153–170. Kurosio.
Vance, Timothy. 2007b. Reduplication and the spread of rendaku into Sino-Japanese. *Proceedings of the 31st Annual Meeting*, 56–64. Kansai Linguistic Society.
Vance, Timothy. 2008. *The sounds of Japanese*. Cambridge University Press.
Vance, Timothy. 2015. Rendaku. In Kubozono, 2015b, pp. 397–441.
Vance, Timothy. 2018. Moras and syllables. In Hasegawa, 2018b, pp. 135–153.
Vance, Timothy & Irwin, Mark. 2016. *Sequential voicing in Japanese*. John Benjamins.
Vovin, Alexander. 2005–2009. *A descriptive and comparative grammar of Western Old Japanese*, Part 1 & 2. Global Oriental.
Vovin, Alexander. 2003. *A reference grammar of Classical Japanese prose*. RoutledgeCurzon.
Vovin, Alexander. 2010. *Koreo-Japonica: A re-evaluation of a common genetic origin*. University of Hawai'i Press.
Vovin, Alexander. 2017. Origins of the Japanese language. In *oxford research encyclopedia of linguistics*, ed. Mark Aronoff.
Wang, S.-Y. William & Ogura, Mieko. 1999. Explorations in the origins of the Japanese language. In *Interdisciplinary perspectives on the origins of the Japanese*, ed. Keiichi Omoto, pp. 309–334. International Research Center for Japanese Studies.
Webb, Eric. 2013. Pidgins and creoles. In *The Oxford handbook of sociolinguistics*, ed. Robert Bayley, Richard Cameron & Ceil Lucas, pp. 301–320. Oxford University Press.
Wenck, Günther. 1954–1959. *Japanische Phonetik*, Band I–IV. Otto Harrassowitz.
Wenck, Günther. 1973. The Japanese copula: A dummy? *Linguistics* 100:77–86.
Wetzel, Patricia. 1994. A movable self: The linguistic indexing of *uchi* and *soto*. In *Situated meaning: Inside and outside in Japanese self, society, and language*, ed. Jane Bachnik & Charles Quinn, pp. 73–87. Princeton University Press.
Wetzel, Patricia. 2011. Public signs as narrative in Japan. In *Language in public spaces in Japan*, ed. Nanette Gottlieb, pp. 3–20. Routledge.
Whitman, John. 1985. *The phonological basis for the comparison of Japanese and Korean*. Doctoral dissertation, Harvard University.
Whitman, John. 2010. The ubiquity of the gloss. *Scripta* 3:95–122.
Whitman, John. 2011. Northeast Asian linguistic ecology and the advent of rice agriculture in Korea and Japan. *Rice* 4:149–158.
Whitman, John. 2012. The relationship between Japanese and Korean. In Tranter, 2012a, pp. 24–38.
Whorf, Benjamin (ed. John Carroll). 1956. *Language, thought and reality: Selected writings of Benjamin Lee Whorf*. MIT Press.
Wixted, John. 2006. *A handbook to Classical Japanese*. Cornell East Asia Series.
Wolfram, Walt. 2002. Language death and dying. In Chambers et al., 2002, pp. 764–787.
Yamagiwa, Joseph (ed.). 1961. *Japanese language studies in the Shōwa period: A guide to Japanese reference and research materials*. University of Michigan Press.
Yamagiwa, Joseph (ed.). 1965. *Readings in Japanese language and linguistics*. The University of Michigan Press.
Yamaguchi, Toshiko. Forthcoming. Personal pronouns in the history of Japanese: Beyond (inter)subjectivity. In Irwin & Zisk, Forthcoming.
Yamaguchi, Toshiko. 2007. *Japanese linguistics: An introduction*. Continuum.
Zisk, Matthew. 2017. Middle Chinese loan translations and loan derivations in Japanese. *Japanese/Korean Linguistics* 24:315–329.
Zisk, Matthew. Forthcoming. An analysis of Classical Chinese borrowings in Japanese. In Irwin & Zisk, Forthcoming.
Zwartjes, Otto. 2011. *Portuguese missionary grammars in Asia, Africa and Brazil, 1550–1800*. John Benjamins.

麻生 磯次校注. 1958. 東海道中膝栗毛 (日本古典文学大系52). 岩波書店.
あらかわ そおべえ. 1977. 外来語辞典. 角川書店.
有坂 秀世. 1934. 国語音韻史の研究. 三省堂.
飯豊 毅一, 日野 資純, 佐藤 亮一編. 1982–1986. 講座方言学 (全10巻). 国書刊行会.
伊坂 淳一. 1997. 句読法. 日本語学キーワード事典, 小池清治, 小林賢次, 細川英雄, 犬飼隆編, pp. 116. 朝倉書店.
石川 重幸. 1984. 盲人教育：日本訓盲点字説明. 日本図書センター.
石黒 圭. 2018. 接続表現. 日本語学大辞典, 日本語学会編, pp. 569–571. 東京堂出版.

石綿 敏雄. 2001. 外来語の総合的研究. 東京堂出版.
井手 至. 1973. 接続詞とは何か―研究史, 学説史の展望―. 品詞別　日本語文法講座, 鈴木一彦, 林巨樹編, pp. 46–88. 明治書院.
井上 史雄. 2000. 日本語の値段. 大修館書店.
牛山 初男. 1953. 語法上より見たる東西方言の境界線について. 国語学 12:59–63.
楳垣 実. 1963. 日本外来語の研究. 研究社出版.
大河原 欽吾. 1937. 点字発達史. 培風館.
太田 眞希恵. 2010. 若者に多い「ワカシラガ」, 高年層に残る「ワカジラガ」. 放送研究と調査2010年11月: 50–70.
太田 眞希恵. 2011. 女は男よりも「罪作り」. 放送研究と調査2011年11月:26–37.
大野 晋. 1983. 国語政策の歴史(戦前). 日本語の世界16　国語改革を批判する, 丸谷才一編, pp. 5–94. 中央公論社.
大野 晋, 大久保 正編集校訂. 1968. 玉勝間(本居宣長全集 第1巻所収). 筑摩書房.
荻生 待editor編著. 2007. 図説ことばあそび遊辞苑. 遊子館.
加藤 正信. 1977. 方言区画論. 岩波講座日本語11方言, 大野晋, 柴田武編, pp. 1–82. 岩波書店.
角川 =「角川日本地名大辞典」編纂委員会編. 1978–1991. 角川日本地名大辞典(全49巻). 角川書店.
亀井 孝, 河野 六郎, 千野 栄一編著. 1997. 日本列島の言語. 三省堂.
川上 泰一, 末田 統, 加藤 俊和, 有本 圭介, 川上 リツエ. 1999. 川上漢点字. 日本漢点字協会.
北原 保雄. 2008. KY式日本語. 大修館書店.
木部 暢子. 2001. 鹿児島方言に見られる音変化について. 音声研究 5.3:42–48.
清瀬 義三郎則府. 2013. 日本語文法体系新論―派生文法の原理と動詞体系の歴史―. ひつじ書房.
金田一 春彦. 1950. 国語動詞の一分類. 言語研究 15:48–63.
金田一 春彦. 1967. ガ行鼻音論. 日本語音韻の研究, 金田一春彦編, pp. 168–197. 東京堂出版.
金田一 春彦. 1988. 日本語. 岩波書店.
工藤 真由美. 1995. アスペクト, テンス体系とテクスト―現代日本語の時間と表現―. ひつじ書房.
窪薗 晴夫監修, 森 勇太, 平塚 雄亮, 黒木 邦彦編. 2015. 甑島里方言記述文法書. 国立国語研究所.
黒坂 勝美, 国史大系編修会編. 1965. 延喜式(新訂増補国史大系 第26巻所収). 吉川弘文館.
黒坂 勝美, 国史大系編修会編. 1966a. 続日本紀(新訂増補国史大系 第2巻所収). 吉川弘文館.
黒坂 勝美, 国史大系編修会編. 1966b. 日本後紀(新訂増補国史大系 第3巻所収). 吉川弘文館.
国研(=国立国語研究所)編. 1964. 現代雑誌九十種の用語用字第三分冊：分析. 秀英出版.
国研編. 1966–1974. 日本言語地図. 大蔵省印刷局.
国研編. 1983. 現代表記のゆれ. 国立国語研究所.
国研編. 1989–2006. 方言文法全国地図. 大蔵省印刷局.
国研編. 2005. 現代雑誌の語彙調査：1994年発行70誌. 国立国語研究所.
国研編. 2006. 外来語言い換え手引き. ぎょうせい.
国研編. 2007. 公共媒体の外来語―外来語言い換え提案を支える調査研究―. 国立国語研究所.
小林 隆. 2004. 方言学的日本語史の方法. ひつじ書房.
小林 隆, 澤村 美幸. 2014. ものの言いかた東西. 岩波書店.
斎藤 純男. 1997. 日本語音声学入門. 三省堂.
斎藤 純男. 2003. 現代日本語の音声：分節音と音声記号. 朝倉日本語講座3 音声・音韻, 北原保雄監修, 上野善道編, pp. 1–21. 朝倉書店.
阪倉 篤義. 1966. 語構成の研究. 角川書店.
笹原 宏之. 2007. 国字の位相と展開. 三省堂.
笹原 宏之編. 2012. 当て字, 当て読み漢字表現辞典. 三省堂.
笹原 宏之. 2013. 方言漢字. 角川書店.
笹原 宏之, 横山 詔一, エリク・ロング. 2003. 現代日本語の異体字―漢字環境学序説―. 三省堂.
佐藤 知己. 2012. アイヌ語の現状と復興. 言語研究 142:29–44.
真田 信治. 1973. 越中五ケ山における待遇表現の実態―場面設定による全員調査から―. 国語学 93:48–64.
真田 信治. 1990. 地域言語の社会言語学的研究. 和泉書院.
塩野 宏, 前田 庸, 平井 宜雄, 青山 善充編集代表. 1994. 六法全書平成7年版. 有斐閣.
時事新報社編. 1897. 福澤全集緒言. 時事新報社.
柴田 武. 1994. 外来語におけるアクセント核の位置. 明治書院.
柴田 武, W. A. グロータース. 1988–1995. 糸魚川言語地図. 秋山書店.
白川 静. 2012. 常用字解〔第二版〕. 平凡社.
杉本 つとむ. 1978. 異体字とは何か(杉本日本語講座1). 桜楓社.
杉森 久英. 1983. 国語政策の歴史(戦後). 日本語の世界16　国語改革を批判する, 丸谷才一編, pp. 95–167. 中央公論社.
鈴木 重幸. 1972. 文法と文法指導. むぎ書房.
鈴木 重幸. 1996. 形態論, 序説. むぎ書房.

関 正昭. 1997. 日本語教育史研究序説. スリーエーネットワーク.
関 正昭, 平高 史也. 1997. 日本語教育史. アルク.
高田 竹山監修. 2014. 改訂第四版　五体字類. 西東書房.
高橋 留美子. 2007. うる星やつら〔新装版〕第26巻. 小学館.
高松 政雄. 1993. 日本漢字音論考. 風間書房.
東条 操編. 1954. 日本方言学. 吉川弘文館.
土井 忠生. 1971. キリシタン語学の研究. 三省堂.
中山 緑朗, 飯田 晴巳監修. 2013–2015. 品詞別学校文法講座. 明治書院.
野村 雅昭. 1999. 字音形態素考. 国語と国文学 76.5:1–10.
橋本 進吉. 1948. 国語法研究. 岩波書店.
橋本 進吉. 1963. 国文法体系論. 岩波書店.
服部 四郎. 1950. 附属語と附属形式. 言語研究 15:1–26, 103, 104.
比嘉 正範. 1985. ハワイアン・ジャパニーズ. 月刊言語 14.11:72–74.
平山 輝男. 1957. 日本語音調の研究. 明治書院.
藤原 彰. 2008. コンサイス日本人名事典. 三省堂.
古田 東朔, 築島 裕. 1972. 国語学史. 東京大学出版会.
文研＝NHK放送文化研究所. 1998. NHK日本語発音辞典. 日本放送出版協会.
保坂 秀子. 2000. 古代日本における言語接触. 社会言語学 3.1:43–50.
森岡 健二. 1973. 文章展開と接続詞, 感動詞. 品詞別　日本語文法講座, 鈴木一彦, 林巨樹編, pp. 8–44. 明治書院.
森岡 健二. 2004. 日本語と漢字. 明治書院.
文部省編. 1992. 学制百二十年史. ぎょうせい.
文部省編. 1981a. 学制百年史. 帝国地方行政学会.
文部省編. 1981b. 学制百年史　資料編. 帝国地方行政学会.
柳田 国男. 1930. 蝸牛考. 刀江書院.
柳田 征司. 2010. 日本語の歴史I　方言の東西対立. 武蔵野書院.
山田 孝雄解題. 1937. 類聚名義抄. 貴重図書複製会.
山田 雄一郎. 2005. 外来語の社会学. 春風社.
山本 正秀. 1975. チェンバレンから上田万年へ. 新・日本語講座9 現代日本語の建設に苦労した人々, 武藤辰男, 渡辺武編, pp. 127–142. 汐文社.
湯沢 質幸. 1987. 唐音の研究. 勉誠社.
湯沢 質幸. 1996. 日本漢字音史論考. 勉誠社.
湯沢 質幸. 2014. 近世儒学韻学と唐音. 勉誠出版.
吉田 茂樹. 1981. 日本地名語源事典. 新人物往来社.
李 淑子. 1975. 日本統治下朝鮮における日本語教育：朝鮮教育令との関連において. 朝鮮学報 75:97–114.

List of URLs

All URLs cited were live as of late February 2019.

1. ethnologue.com
2. www.stat.go.jp/data/jinsui/new.html
3. www.internationalphoneticalphabet.org/ipa-sounds/ipa-chart-with-sounds
4. kosekimoji.moj.go.jp/kosekimojidb/mjko/PeopleSearch
5. www.seikatubunka.metro.tokyo.jp/passport/documents/0000000485.html
6. glyphwiki.org
7. www.engrish.com
8. www.kuu-kikaku.jp/marld/allow_to_follow/nhk.html
9. www.bunka.go.jp/tokei_hakusho_shuppan/tokeichosa/kokugo_yoronchosa
10. www.netflix.com
11. legendsoflocalization.com
12. www.myoji-yurai.net
13. www.meijiyasuda.co.jp/enjoy/ranking/best100/
14. www.mext.go.jp
15. www.bunka.go.jp
16. www.academie-francaise.fr/la-langue-francaise/terminologie-et-neologie
17. www.mext.go.jp/b_menu/hakusho/hakusho.htm
18. www.nier.go.jp/guideline/
19. www.mext.go.jp/a_menu/shotou/new-cs/
20. www.mext.go.jp/b_menu/hakusho/nc/1299787.htm
21. www.mext.go.jp/a_menu/shotou/new-cs/1385768.htm
22. www.nisshinkyo.org/article/overview.html
23. www.jasso.go.jp/sp/about/statistics/intl_student_e/2018/index.html
24. www.jpf.go.jp/j/project/japanese/survey/result/survey15.html
25. www.jlpt.jp
26. www.jasso.go.jp/en/eju/index.html
27. j-test.jp
28. www.kanken.or.jp/bjt/english
29. www.kanken.or.jp/kanken
30. www.nihongokentei.jp/
31. www.nihongokentei.jp/check
32. www.kanken.or.jp/kanken/outline/degree/example.html
33. archive.org/details/MojikyoCmap400ALL49TTF.7z
34. www.chokanji.com
35. nihongo.monash.edu/cgi-bin/wwwjdic
36. eow.alc.co.jp/
37. apps.ankiweb.net/
38. ocbaxtersagart.lsait.lsa.umich.edu
39. www.dliflc.edu/home/about/command-history-office-3/pictorial-history-of-dli/
40. www.unesco.org/languages-atlas

ENGLISH-JAPANESE GLOSSARY

ablative　奪格
accent　アクセント
accentless　無アクセント
accidental gap　偶然の空き間
accusative　対格
acoustic space　音響空間
acronym　（一語として発音する)頭字語
actor　行為者
addressee　受信者
adjective　形容詞
adjectivization　形容詞化
adjectivizer　形容詞化辞
adnominal　連体的, 連体形
adnominal modifier　連体修飾語
adnominalizer　連体詞化辞
adnoun　連体詞
adposition　接置詞
adverb　副詞
adverbial　副詞的, 連用形
adverbial modifier　副詞的修飾語, 連用修飾語
adverbializer　副詞化辞
adversative　逆接[の]
affirmative　肯定[的], 断定[的]
affix　接辞
affixation　接辞添加
affricate　破擦音
agent　動作主
agentive　動作主格
agglutination　膠着
agglutinative language　膠着語
allative　向格
allomorph　異形態
allophone　異音
alveolar　歯茎音
alveolo-palatal　歯茎硬口蓋音
ambitransitive　自他同形(動詞)
analogical particle　類推助詞
analogy　類推
analytic language　分析的言語

antepenultimate　次々末(音節/モーラ)
anthropomorphism　擬人化
anthroponym　人名
anticausative　逆使役[形]
anti-honorifics　卑罵表現, 俗語的表現
antonym　対義語
apical　舌尖音
apophony　母音交替
applied linguistics　応用言語学
apposition　同格
appositive genitive　同格の属格
arbitrary　恣意的
archaism　古風な語法
areal feature　地域特徴
argument　項
articulation　調音
articulatory phonetics　調音音声学
aspect　アスペクト, 相
aspiration　有気音性
assimilation　同化
attribution　属性付与
auditory phonetics　聴覚音声学
auxiliary　補助用言
auxiliary adjective　補助形容詞
auxiliary verb　補助動詞

babbling　喃語
back-clipping　尾部省略
back-formation　逆成
beautification language　美化語
benefactive　受益表現
bilabial　両唇音
binom　二字漢語
borrowing　借用[語, 形式]
bound form　拘束形式
bronze script　金文
bureaucratese　お役所言葉

calligraphy　書道
calque　翻訳借用[語]

canonical form　基本形
cardinal vowel　基本母音
case　格
case marker particle　格助詞
causative　使役[形]
centralized　中舌化
centrifugal　遠心[的]
centripetal　求心[的]
circumfix　接周辞
circumlocution　婉曲[的]
class　(活用等の)型
classifier　助数詞
clause　節
clerical script　隷書[体]
clipping　短縮[形]
clitic　接語
coda　末尾子音
cognate　同系語
cohort　コーホート, 同時出生集団
coinage　新造語
colloquial　口語[的]
comitative　共格
common noun　普通名詞
competence　(言語)能力
competence continuum　言語能力連続体
complement　補語
complementary distribution　相補分布
complementizer　補文標識
completive　完成相
complex predicate　複雑述語
compound　複合語
compound pictogram　会意文字
concessive　譲歩[の]
conclusive　終止形
conditional　仮定条件, 仮定形
confirmative　確認[の]
conjectural　推量[の]
conjugation　活用
conjugational ending　活用語尾
conjugational form　活用形
conjunction　接続詞
conjunctive particle　接続助詞
connotation　暗示的意味, 言外の意味
consonant　子音
consonant cluster　子音連結

consonant-stem verb　子音語幹動詞
contagious diffusion　伝染的伝播, 接触的伝播
continuative　継続相
contraction　縮約
contrastive　対比[的]
convention　慣例
converb　副動詞
converbalizer　副動詞化辞
coordinate clause　等位節
copula　コピュラ, 繋辞
copularizer　コピュラ化辞
copulative　連結(接続詞)
corpus　コーパス
cosubordinate clause　等位従属節
culminativity　単一頂点
cursive script　草書[体]

dative　与格
deaccent　脱アクセント化
defective　不完全の, 欠如(用言)
definite　特定[の]
defocalization　脱焦点化
defunct　機能を失った
deixis　ダイクシス, 直示
demonstrative　指示詞
depalatalization　非硬口蓋化
deprecative　卑罵表現
derivation　派生
derivational grammar　派生文法
derivational particle　派生助詞
derivational suffix　派生接尾辞
derogatory　軽蔑[的]
descriptive grammar　記述文法
desiderative　意欲[的], 願望[の]
determinative　限定符, 意符
deverbal noun　動詞由来名詞
devoice　無声化する
diacritic　発音区別符号
dialect　方言
dialect accessorization　方言のアクセサリー化
dialect complex　方言コンプレックス
dialect contact　方言接触
dialect continuum　方言連続体

dialect diffusion　方言の伝播
dialect division　方言区画
dialect stigmatization　方言蔑視
dialectology　方言学
diathetic　ヴォイス[の], 態[の]
dictionary form　辞書形
differential object marking　示差的目的語標示
digraph　二重字
diminutive　指小辞
diphthong　二重母音
direct method　直接教授法
direct object　直接目的語
direct translation　直訳
discourse　談話
discourse deixis　談話直示
discourse particle　談話助詞, 終助詞
discriminatory　差別[的]
disjunctive　離接(接続詞)
distal　遠称
distinctive feature　弁別的素性
distribution　分布
donor language　借用元の言語
donor word　借用元の語
dual vowel-stem verb　交替型母音語幹動詞
durative verb　継続動詞
dynamic verb　[外的]運動動詞

economization　経済化
elision　(母音)省略
ellipsis　省略
emphasis　強調
emphatic particle　強調助詞
empirical past　体験過去
endocentric　内心[的]
enunciate　(明瞭に)発音する
epenthesis　音挿入
equipollent　等値[の]
etymology　語源, 語源学
etymon　語源, 原語
euphony　快音, 音便
evidential　証拠性[の], 証拠性表現
evidentiality　証拠性
exclamative　感嘆詞

exclusive　排他[的]
existential verb　存在動詞
exocentric　外心[的]
facilitative　容易さ
filler　フィラー, 言い淀み
final suffix　語末接尾辞
focus　焦点
foot　フット, 韻脚
forced polysemy　強いられた多義性
fore-clipping　頭部省略
formal noun　形式名詞
formulized　定型化した
fossilized　化石化した
free form　自由形式
fricative　摩擦音
front vowel　前舌母音
fusional language　屈折語

geminate　長子音, 重子音
gemination　長子音化, 重子音化
gender　ジェンダー
generative grammar　生成文法
genitive　属格
gerund　動名詞
glide　わたり音
gloss　グロス, 注解, 訓点
glossing　注釈活動, 加点
glottal　声門
glottal stop　声門閉鎖音
glottis　声門
grammar　文法, 文法書
grammatical　文法的(に正しい)
grammatical meaning　文法的意味
grammaticality　文法性
grammaticalization　文法化
graph　字体
grapheme　文字素

habitual　慣習相
hard palate　硬口蓋
head　主要部
head-directionality　主要部方向性
head-final　主要部後行型
head-initial　主要部先行型

headword　見出し語
hearsay　伝聞
hearsay past　伝聞過去
heavy syllable　重音節
heteronym　同綴異音異義語
hierarchical diffusion　階層的伝播
high vowel　高母音
holophrase　一語文
homograph　(同音)同綴異義語
homonym　同音異義語
homophone　(異綴)同音異義語
honorifics　敬語, 待遇表現
hortative　勧告[的]
humble language　謙譲語
hybrid word　混種語
hypercorrection　過剰修正
hyper-polite　過剰敬語

iconicity　類像性, 写像性
idealization　理想化
ideogram　表意文字
idiom　慣用句
idiomatic　慣用[的]
illicit　(音韻的/文法的)違法
imitation　模倣(形式)
imperative　命令形
inchoative　始動相
incompletive　未完成相
indefinite　不定[の]
indicative pictogram　指事文字
indirect object　間接目的語
infinitive　不定詞
infix　接中辞
inflection　屈折
inflectional suffix　屈折接尾辞
initialism　(一字ずつ発音する)頭字語
innovation　刷新, 改新
instrumental　具格
interchangeability　相互交換[可能]性
interference　干渉
interfix　接合辞, 中間接辞
interjection　間投詞, 感動詞
interlocutor　対話者
internal reconstruction　内的再建
interrogative　疑問[の]

intervocalic voicing　母音間有声化
intonation　イントネーション, 音調
intransitive verb　自動詞
intuition　直観
inversion　倒置, 返読
inversion gloss　返り点
irrealis　未然形
irregular　不規則
irreversible completive　不可逆完成相
isochronous　等時間隔[の]
isogloss　等語線
isogloss bundle　等語線の束
isolating language　孤立語
iteration　反復, 再読
iterative　反復相

Japanization　日本語化, 和臭
jargon　専門用語, 職業用語

kanji compound　漢字熟語
kinship term　親族語彙

labourative　困難さ
language contact　言語接触
language death　言語の死
language family　語族
language isolate　孤立[した]言語
language murder　言語殺戮
language policy　言語政策
language revitalization　言語復興
language-as-process theory　言語過程説
language-thought process　言語的発想法
lenition　弱化
lexeme　語彙素
lexical meaning　語彙的意味
lexical strata　語彙層, 語種
lexical stratification　語彙の層化
lexicalization　語彙化
lexicography　辞書学, 辞書編集
lexicon　語彙
licit　(音韻的/文法的)合法
ligature　合字
limitative particle　限度助詞
lingua franca　[混成]共通語
linguicide　言語抹殺

linguistic landscape　言語景観
linguistic universal　言語の普遍的特性
linking verb　連結動詞
loan　借用語, 借用形式
loan creation　借用創作
loan derivation　借用派生語, 転成借用
loan syntax　借用統語
loan translation　翻訳借用[語]
loanword　借用語
locative　所格
logogram　表語文字
long vowel　長母音
longitudinal study　縦断研究, 経年調査
low vowel　低母音

malefactive　受害表現
manner of articulation　調音方法
marked　有標
medial　中称, 語中
merger　融合, 合流
metalinguistic　メタ言語的
mid-clipping　中部省略
mimetic　オノマトペ, 音象徴語
minimal pair　ミニマルペア, 最小対
modal　モダリティの, 法の
modality　モダリティ, 法性
modification　修飾
modifier　修飾語
monomoraic　単モーラの
mononom　一字漢語
monosyllabic　単音節[の]
mood　法
mora　モーラ, 拍
mora consonant　モーラ子音
mora nasal　撥音
mora obstruent　促音
mora-timed　モーラ韻律
moribund　危機に瀕した
morpheme　形態素
morphology　形態論
morpho-orthographic truncation　形態頭
　文字語
morphophonology　形態音韻論
morphosyntax　形態統語論
mutual intelligibility　相互理解[可能]性

nasal　鼻音
nasalization　鼻音化
natural class　自然類
necessitive　当然
negation　否定, 打ち消し
negative　否定形
neologism　新造語
nested structure　入れ子構造
nominal　名詞的, 体言
nominal adjective　名詞的形容詞
nominal suffix　名詞接尾辞
nominal verb　名詞的動詞
nominalization　名詞化
nominalizer　名詞化辞
nominative　主格
non-final suffix　非語末接尾辞
nonpast　非過去
non-verbal communication　非言語コミュ
　ニケーション
norm-consciousness　規範意識
notation　表記
noun　名詞
nucleus　(音節)核
null　ゼロ(形態素)
numeral　数字, 数詞

obsolete　廃語, 死語
obstruent　阻害音
onomastics　名称論, 固有名詞学
onomatopoeia　(1) オノマトペ, 音象徴語;
　(2) 擬音語, 擬声語
onset　頭子音
optative　希求
oracle bone script　甲骨文, 甲骨文字
oral calisthenics　口の体操
oral method　オーラル・メソッド
ordinal　序数詞
orthographic licence　正書法上の許容
orthographic play　文字遊び
orthography　文字論, 正書法

palatal　硬口蓋音
palatalization　[硬]口蓋化
palindrome　回文
paradigm　模範, 語形変化表

paradigm optimization	(表現)体系の最適化
parlance	話しぶり, 話し方
part of speech	品詞
particle	助詞
passive	受身
pattern	(アクセント等の)型
pedagogy	教授法, 教育学
pejorative	卑罵語
penultimate	次末(音節/モーラ)
perfect	完了相
perfective	完結相
pernicious homonymy	同音衝突
personal name	人名
personal pronoun	人称代名詞
phone	単音
phoneme	音素
phoneme inventory	音素目録
phonemic	音素[論]の
phonemicization	音素表記
phonemics	音素論
phonetic	(1) 音声[学]の; (2) 音符
phonetic loan	仮借文字
phonetic value	音価
phonetics	音声学
phonic substitution	(自言語の)音の代用
phonogram	表音文字
phonology	音韻論
phono-semantic compound	形声文字
phono-semantic matching	音義対応翻訳
phonotactics	音素配列[論]
phrase	句
pictogram	象形文字
pitch	ピッチ, 高低(アクセント)
place of articulation	調音位置, 調音点
plosive	破裂音
plural	複数[形]
pluralistic origins	多元[的]発生
pluralizer	複数[形]接尾辞
polite language	丁寧語
polymoraic	多モーラ[の]
polysemy	多義
possessee	所有者
possessive	所有[の], 所有格
post-consonantal glide	拗音
potential	可能形
pragmatic	語用論的
predicate	述語
predication	叙述, 陳述
prefix	接頭辞
preliterate	文字[伝来]以前[の]
prenasalization	前鼻音化
preposition	前置詞
prescriptive grammar	規範文法
prestige	威信, 権威
productivity	生産性
progressive	進行形
prohibitive	禁止形
pronoun	代名詞
pronunciation	発音
proper noun	固有名詞
propositional speech act	命題的発話行為
prosecutive	及格
prosodic prominence	韻律的卓立
prosody	プロソディー, 韻律
prospective	前望相
proto-language	祖語
provisional conditional	暫定的仮定形
proximal	近称
pseudo-anglicism	和製英語
pseudo-sinicism	和製漢語
punctuation	句読法
purposive	目的[の]
qualitative verb	性質動詞
radical	部首
reading	字音, 読み
realis	已然形
reanalysis	再分析
rebus	リーバス, 判じ絵
reconstruction	再建, 再構
rectilinear	直線的
reduction	弱化, 縮約
reduplication	重畳, 重複
reference	参照
reflex	発達形, 派生形
register	使用域, 位相
regular script	楷書[体]
reimportation	逆輸入
representative	代表[的]

respectful language	尊敬語
restrictive particle	限定助詞
resultative	結果相
retrospective	回顧[的]
rhetorical	修辞的, 反語[的]
rhetorical question	修辞疑問, 反語
role language	役割語
romanization	ローマ字化
root	語根
rounding	円唇化
script	(1) 文字体系; (2) 書体
script reform	文字改革
script style	書体
segment	分節[音]
semantic	意味的
semantic bleaching	意味の漂白[化]
semantic borrowing	意味借用
semantic extension	意味拡張
semantics	意味論
semantographic	表意文字的
semi-cursive script	行書[体]
semiotics	記号学, 記号論
semi-vowel	半母音
sentence	文
sentence-final particle	終助詞
signage	標識, 看板
signified	シニフィエ, 所記
signifier	シニフィアン, 能記
similitude	類似
simplified form	新字体, 簡体字
simultaneous	同時並行[の]
single vowel-stem verb	非交替型母音語幹動詞
singular	単数[形]
Sino-Japanese	(1) [日本]漢語; (2) [日本]漢字音
Sino-Korean	(1) 朝鮮漢語; (2) 朝鮮漢字音
sinolingual	中国語圏
sinosphere	漢字文化圏
sinoxenic	非中国漢字音
small seal script	篆書[体], 小篆
sociolinguistics	社会言語学
soft palate	軟口蓋
sonorant	共鳴音
sound symbolism	音象徴
spatial deixis	空間直示
speculative	思索[的]
spelling conceit	綴り上の珍案
spelling convention	綴り上の習慣
spelling device	綴り上の工夫
split intransitivity	分裂自動詞性
spoken language	話し言葉
spontaneous verb	瞬間動詞
standardization	共通語化
static verb	静態動詞
stative	状態相, 既然相
stative verb	状態動詞
stem	語幹
stroke	[字]画
stroke order	筆順
structuralism	構造言語学
style	スタイル, 文体
stylistic	文体的
subject	主語
subject-acting	主体動作(動詞)
subject-acting-and-object-modifying	主体動作・客体変化(動詞)
subject-modifying	主体変化(動詞)
subordinate clause	従属節
subordinator	従属節化辞, 従属詞
suffix	接尾辞
suffix string	接尾辞連結
suffixation	接尾辞添加
suppletive	補充(形)
suprasegmental	超分節音
surname	名字, 姓, 氏
syllabary	音節文字[体系]
syllabeme dialect	シラビーム方言
syllable	音節
syllable structure	音節構造
syllable-timed	音節韻律
synchronic	共時的
synonym	類義語
syntactic particle	統語助詞
syntax	統語[論]
synthetic language	総合言語
systematic gap	体系上の空き間
tap	はじき音

temporal	時間的	unvoiced	無声(音)
tendential	傾向的	utterance	発話
tense	テンス, 時制		
terminative	到格, 達格	variant	変種, 異体字
tetragraph	四重字	velar	軟口蓋音
textual criticism	本文批判	velar nasal	軟口蓋鼻音
thematic particle	提題助詞	verb	動詞
title	敬称	verbal	動詞的, 用言
token	延べ語数	verbal adjective	動詞的形容詞
topic	主題	verbal noun	動詞的名詞
topic marker particle	主題助詞	verbal suffix	用言接尾辞
topicalize	主題化	verbalization	動詞化
topolect	地域語	verbalizer	動詞化辞
toponym	地名	verbosity	口数の多い
traditional form	旧字体, 繁体字	vernacular	自国語, 現地語
transfix	貫通接辞	vocabulary	単語, 語彙
transitive verb	他動詞	vocal cords	声帯
translative	変格	voiced	有声(音)
transliteration	翻字, 転写	voiceless	無声(音)
trigraph	三重字	volitional	意志[的]
trill	ふるえ音	vowel	母音
trinom	三字漢語	vowel alternation	母音交替
truncation	短縮[形]	vowel coalescence	母音融合
type	異なり語数	vowel harmony	母音調和
typographic	活字[の], 印刷上[の]	vowel lengthening	長母音化
typology	類型論	vowel reduction	母音弱化
		vowel-stem verb	母音語幹動詞
unaccented	平板式アクセント[の]		
underlying form	基底形	word class	品詞
undertone	底意	word formation	語構成
ungrammatical	非文法的	word order	語順
union consonant	連結子音	wordplay	言葉遊び
union vowel	連結母音	writing style	文体
unmarked	無標	writing system	書記体系, 表記体系
unproductive	非生産的	written language	書き言葉
unrounded	非円唇(母音)		

Index

accent: see pitch accent
adjectivization 42, 139
adjective: emotive 67; *nar-i* 97;
    no 52, 88, 89; nominal 34, 35,
    41, 42, 50–57, 61–67, 71, 72,
    88–91, 97, 98, 138–140, 167, 186,
    191, 227–229; polite form 56,
    165, 167, 176; stem 5, 51, 52, 56,
    64, 67–70, 96, 100, 121, 140, 165,
    166, 228, 229; suffix: see verbal
    suffix (final and non-final);
    super-polite form 165, 166;
    tar-i 97, 98; verbal 4, 5, 33–35,
    42, 49–58, 61–72, 79–81, 90,
    96–100, 121, 138–141, 144,
    165–167, 172, 176, 206, 215, 219,
    227–229, 245; Western
    Japanese adverbial 32, 165, 175
adnoun 33–36, 39, 40, 50–53, 91,
    97, 98, 227, 244
adverb 34–40, 50–53, 56, 76–78,
    85, 88, 91, 138–140, 155, 186,
    190, 191, 215, 227, 243, 244;
    conjunctive adverb 36, 77, 78
adverbial: see converb and
    modifier
adnominal: see modifier and
    verbal suffix (final)
affix 21, 28, 35, 44, 65, 79, 80, 94,
    136, 138, 139, 151, 152, 171, 186,
    190, 191
affricate 15, 16
agglutination 2, 4–6, 11, 34, 35,
    56, 214, 245
Ainu 114, 182, 190, 195, 196, 247
allomorph 44, 51, 59, 67, 69, 95,
    141, 152
allophone 14, 16, 30, 59
Altaic 2, 247, 248
alveolar 15, 16, 29, 30
analogy 67, 144
Andō Masatsugu 217
anti-honorifics 31, 40, 59, 66–68,
    73–76, 84–86, 147–150, 157, 158,
    161–165, 169–172, 197, 207, 212
apophony 141, 142, 193
Arai Hakuseki 2
archaism 19, 44, 45, 57–59, 61, 62,
    68, 71, 83, 96–98, 109, 147, 150,
    174, 240
Arisaka Hideyo 244
articulation 14–16, 172
aspect 38, 41–50, 60, 69, 70, 141,
    193, 215, 245; classification of

verbs based on 47, 49, 50, 245;
    aspectual auxiliary: see
    auxiliary; perfect 47, 49, 57,
    60–63, 69, 70, 95–97, 163, 171,
    207, 215; progressive 47, 49, 69,
    70, 163, 171, 207, 215; stative 41,
    47–50, 69, 70, 95–97, 215
Aston, William 246, 247
ateji: see kanji reading
Austro-Tai 3
Austroasiatic 3
Austronesian 1, 3
auxiliary: adjective 35, 56, 69–73,
    100, 141; aspectual 69;
    benefactive 35, 69, 71, 73–76,
    167, 169, 171; diathetic 69, 71;
    facilitative 71, 72; labourative
    71, 72; modal 71, 72; negative
    72; perfect-progressive *-te i-ru*
    47, 49, 69–73, 76, 163, 171, 207;
    verb 35, 47, 69–76, 100, 141,
    163, 167, 170, 171, 207, 227–230

beautification: see honorifics
benefactive: see auxiliary
bilabial 14–16, 30, 244
binom: see Sino-Japanese
Bloch, Bernard 222, 247
borrowing: see loanword
boundedness 33–36, 55, 79, 80,
    125, 227, 230
Braille: *tenji* 99, 123–125, 132;
    kantenji 123
bungo: see language, written

calque: see loan translation
Cantonese: see Chinese,
    modern topolects
case 2, 5, 34–39, 53, 79–82, 88, 90,
    98, 113, 114, 138, 174, 193, 195,
    210, 214, 243
case marker particle 36–39,
    79–85, 88–90, 98, 113, 174, 193,
    195, 210, 214; ablative *kara* 24,
    79–83; ablative *yori* 80–82;
    accusative *o* 5, 24, 35, 37, 39,
    80, 82, 113; accusative
    (Tōhoku) *godo~dogo~ba* 210;
    accusative (Kyūshū) *ba* 214;
    allative *e* 80–82, 114, 125;
    allative (Tōhoku) *sa* 177, 210;
    archaic genitive *ga* 24, 98, 105;
    comitative *to* 80–83; dative *ni*
    24, 71, 79–83, 167–170, 210;

genitive *no~N* 53, 80–82,
    88–90; locative *de~nite* 24,
    80–82; nominative *ga* 35, 36,
    39, 80–83, 98; terminative
    made 80–82, 85, 86
Chamberlain, Basil Hall 246,
    247
Chinese: character: see kanji;
    Classical 3, 4, 9, 43, 53, 78, 108,
    110, 111, 122, 129, 180, 185–187,
    198, 218, 226, 231, 232, 237, 239,
    243–245; Middle 3, 6, 106; Old
    103, 185; modern topolects
    10–12, 18, 23, 100, 103, 107, 110,
    114, 132, 133, 150, 186, 189–192,
    195–198, 232
chinjutsu: see predication
Chomsky, Noam 245
Chūtō bunpō 227
classifier 9, 27, 84, 105, 150–152;
    endocentric 151, 152; exocen-
    tric 151
clause: adverbial 60, 77, 78, 90;
    adversative 36, 79, 83; causal
    36, 41, 77, 82, 83, 95; concessive
    41, 57, 62–64, 79, 83, 86, 91, 95;
    cosubordinate 58–61, 90, 91;
    subordinate 36, 38, 42, 58,
    60–62, 77, 90, 91, 120
clipping: back- 145, 146, 155, 156,
    175; fore- 145, 146; mid- 145,
    146
clitic: see particle
coda 19, 212
cognate 2, 3, 196
Collado, Diego 246
compound 6, 9, 16, 24–27, 31, 43,
    55, 61, 69, 135, 140–146,
    150–156, 161, 186, 187, 190–193,
    215, 224, 237, 239; argument
    type 143; clipping 145, 146;
    copulative 26, 141; endocen-
    tric 140; exocentric 140; kanji:
    see kanji; oppositional 141;
    reduction 145, 146; verbal 61,
    140–143
conditional: assertive *nara[ba]*
    62, 63, 79, 83, 84, 98; emphat-
    ic-iterative *-tewa ~ -ča ~
    -kutewa ~ -kuča ~ -kya* 57, 62,
    63; perfective *-tara ~ -kaqtara*
    57, 62–64; provisional *-(r)eba*
    57, 62, 214; temporal *-(r)uto ~
    -ito* 57, 62

Index   281

conjunction 34–36, 55, 77–84, 88, 100, 121, 138, 151, 186, 187, 191, 227, 244
consonant 4, 14–22, 29–32, 43, 44, 65, 94, 112–116, 124, 125, 136–138, 142–144, 152, 188, 190, 205, 206, 212, 213, 228–230; cluster 21, 190; mora 14–16, 19–22, 32, 65, 124, 136, 138, 188, 190, 228; -stem verb: see verb; union 43, 44, 94
contraction: see truncation
converb 38, 44, 45, 57–62, 77, 79, 86, 90, 91, 210; adverbial -(i) ~ -ku 32, 56, 57, 60–64, 66, 69–73, 78, 96, 152, 171, 206, 228; archaic concessive -(r)utomo ~ -kutomo 57, 62, 63; archaic negative -(a)zu[ni] ~ -karazu 44, 45, 57, 61, 95; concessive -temo ~ -kutemo 57, 62–64, 90, 91; concessive-simultaneous -(i)nagara ~ -inagara 57, 62, 64; conditional: see conditional; negative -te form -(a)naide 57, 61, 160; primary 61; purposive -(i)ni 57, 62, 64, 82, 210; representative -tari ~ -kaQtari 57, 61, 64; secondary 61–64, 90; simultaneous -(i)cucu 57, 61, 230; -te form 32, 38, 44, 47, 49, 57, 60–66, 69–74, 76–79, 90, 95, 167, 171, 206, 211, 214, 215, 230; temporal ablative -tekara 57, 62, 63
copula 18, 27, 33–38, 42, 50–58, 61, 62, 69, 72, 79, 81, 88–91, 97–100, 121, 130, 131, 138, 160, 163–165, 207, 234; literary de ar-u 36, 52–56, 89, 98, 130, 131, 164, 207; nar-i 52, 61, 62, 79, 83, 89, 91, 97, 98; neutral da 36, 52–58, 79, 86, 88, 89, 98, 130, 131, 160, 163–165, 205, 207; polite des-u 18, 36, 50, 52, 54–58, 69, 89, 98, 130, 165; similitude goto-si 97, 98; super-polite de gozar-u 54, 55, 164, 165; tar-i 95–98
creole 3, 192–194, 215

dakuon: see sei-daku distinction
demonstrative 34, 38–40, 71, 72
deprecation: see anti-honorifics
derivation 18, 31, 35, 36, 42, 43, 47, 51–57, 62, 65–68, 77, 80–85, 88–91, 98–100, 105, 111, 132,
138–140, 150, 155, 173, 176, 182, 187, 207, 209, 230, 245
derivational particle 36, 42, 80–85, 88–91; adnominalizer na 35, 52, 88–91, 190; adnominalizer no~N 35, 42, 53, 88–91; adverbializer ni 35, 41, 42, 52, 53, 57, 88, 91, 97, 190; complementizer to~Qte 21, 53, 79, 84–88, 91; concessive converbalizer demo 55, 57, 79, 85, 86, 90, 91; converbalizer de 41, 42, 55, 57, 79, 90, 91; emphatic conditional converbalizer dewa~ja 55, 57, 90, 91; nominalizer no~N 87–91, 160
devoicing 18, 193, 206, 208, 212
diacritics 16, 28, 112, 117, 124
dialect: accessorization 204; Chūgoku 194, 202, 203, 206; complex 180, 181; contact 205; continuum 200; diffusion 199, 201–205; division 199–201, 211, 244–246; Eastern 32, 44, 45, 48, 59, 199–207, 245; Eastern-Western differences 199, 200, 205–207; Itoigawa-Hamanako line 203, 205; Kansai 170, 171, 174, 200, 204; Kyūshū 18, 32, 55, 95, 138, 172, 177, 199–207, 209–215, 245; stigmatization 209; survey 200, 245, 246; syllabeme 209, 213; tag 180, 196; Tōhoku 18, 31, 55, 172, 173, 177, 199–215, 245; virtual 173; Western 6, 18, 29, 32, 44, 45, 55–59, 68, 70, 147, 148, 159, 163, 165, 174, 176, 199–207, 211, 245
dictionary 100, 104, 106, 109, 110, 115, 128, 136, 144, 153, 156, 180, 190, 233, 237–244, 246; form of a verb or adjective 24, 43, 58, 96, 140, 234; tradition 190
digraph: see kana
diphthong: see vowel
direct object 4, 5, 11, 33, 35–39, 45–50, 64, 69, 80–82, 93, 210
donor word: see loanword
Dravidian 3
Dutch 10, 135, 189, 190, 193, 199

elision 18, 31, 32, 212
emoji 127, 165, 198
emoticon 127, 128, 165, 198
emphasis 35, 51, 62, 63, 73, 78, 79, 84, 91, 97–100, 104, 120, 121, 139, 152, 155, 160, 235

English 5, 6, 10–21, 28, 32–36, 39, 47, 50, 53, 54, 73, 78, 86, 89, 93, 115, 116–119, 125–128, 132–136, 145, 146, 150, 153–162, 169, 173–181, 183, 186, 189–197, 215, 216, 220–224, 230, 234, 239, 240–243; American 153, 157, 176, 189, 191, 240; British 153, 191, 240; Bonin Creole 194; Hawaii Creole 194, 215
epenthesis 18, 21, 31, 190
etymology 23, 36, 41, 47, 51, 54, 62, 77–79, 83, 84, 98, 158, 169, 182, 183, 239
etymon 111–114, 146, 197, 220, 221
evidentiality 41, 42, 51, 57, 64; hearsay evidential: see nominalizer; visual evidential: see nominalizer

Family Register Character Unification Database 106
feature: areal 7, 38; distinctive 14, 121
female speech 39, 55, 69, 85, 87, 88, 147, 148, 159, 160, 163
filler 35, 86, 87
focus 37, 84, 92, 244
foot 19
free form 33, 227
French 10, 115, 123, 135, 150, 152, 189, 191, 193, 195, 216, 233
fricative 15, 16, 29, 30
Fujitani Nariakira 243
Fujiwara no Teika 9, 183, 219
Fukuzawa Yukichi 104, 114
furigana: see kana

gairaigo: see loanword
gakkō bunpō: see grammar, school
gemination 17, 32, 152
gender 7, 39, 87, 88, 147, 149, 159–161, 163
Genji monogatari 9
German 10, 16, 18, 21, 115, 135, 138, 189, 191, 216, 247
gesture 177–179
glide 14–16, 19–22, 29–32, 112–114, 124, 125, 188, 209, 213, 219; post-consonantal w-glide 19, 21, 32, 114, 209, 213, 219; post-consonantal y-glide 19, 21, 32, 113, 124, 125, 188, 219
glossing: see kanbun kundoku
Goguryeo 2, 3
gojūonzu 229, 238

Index

Grammar Atlas of Japanese Dialects 245
grammar: derivational 245; descriptive 246; generative 245; history of 94–98; prescriptive 122, 227, 229; school 33, 67, 79, 180, 227, 228, 244
grammaticalization 41, 73, 77, 78
Greek alphabet 99, 121
Greenberg, Joseph 5
greeting 161, 175–181, 185, 191, 207
Grootaers, Willem 246

Hachijō 1, 2, 199, 200
Hashimoto Shinkichi 227, 243, 244
Hattori Shirō 244
head-directionality 4, 5
Hepburn, James Curtis 115, 239, 246
Hepburn style: see romanization
heteronomy 153–155
hiragana: see kana
homograph 153
homonymy 67, 71, 153, 154, 206, 236
homophone 25, 132, 133, 144, 153, 187, 208, 209, 241
honorifics 44, 45, 59, 73–75, 139, 150, 162, 165–170, 186, 201, 207, 211, 217, 235, 237, 246; anti-: see anti-honorifics; beautification language 160, 165–169; humble language 19, 70, 73–76, 85, 86, 98, 139, 148, 150, 163, 165–168, 170; polite language 7, 36, 39, 40, 45, 50, 54–56, 61, 66–68, 72, 74, 87–89, 130, 131, 139, 149, 150, 157, 160, 163–169, 175–177, 181, 211, 234; respectful language 61, 66, 67, 70, 71, 74, 75, 163–170, 179, 207; super-polite 54, 73, 74, 76, 90, 160, 165, 166, 177; super-respectful 168
hybrid word 135, 136, 139, 140, 167, 174
hyōjungo: see language, standard

ideogram: see kanji
idiom 6, 52, 57, 107, 108, 117, 118, 147, 148, 178, 186, 239
Ikeda Kikan 244
imitational borrowing: see loan derivation, loan meaning,

loan translation and loan syntax
inanimate 45, 69, 70, 210
indirect object 80, 82
inflection 34, 39, 42, 55–58, 60, 79, 96, 98, 130, 138, 195, 214, 227–230
interjection 34, 35, 55, 100, 114, 119, 121, 138, 160, 161, 191, 227, 244
intonation 58, 85, 160
inversion 37, 54, 93, 232
Ishikawa Kuraji 123, 205
Ishizuka Tatsumaro 244
iteration mark 121, 128
Itoigawa-Hamanako line: see dialect
Japan Kanji Aptitude Test 105, 236
Japanese: Classical 9, 129, 174, 226, 227, 230–232; Early Middle 7–9, 31, 114, 231, 245; Early Modern 7–10, 231; Eastern: see dialect; Late Middle 7–10, 31, 32, 96, 98, 110, 176, 212, 230, 245; Middle 7–9, 29–32, 52, 53, 88, 94–98, 110, 114, 176, 186, 209, 212, 230, 231, 244, 245; Modern 3, 7–10, 29–32, 47, 52, 54, 58, 59, 66, 77, 94–99, 107, 111, 120–122, 181, 182, 186, 212, 224, 226, 231, 232, 239, 244, 247; Near-Modern 7, 8, 10; Old 3, 7–9, 29–31, 43, 94–96, 142, 186, 231, 232, 244, 247; origins and affiliation of 1–4; Sino-: see Sino-Japanese; Standard 11, 15, 17–20, 23, 51, 52, 56, 67, 105, 108, 119, 131, 138, 155, 159, 168, 171, 175, 177, 194, 199, 204–215, 233, 241, 247; Western: see dialect
Japanese Language Through Time, The 247
Japanese Language, The 247
Japanese-Ryūkyūan: see Japonic
Japanische Phonetik 247
Japonic 1–4, 8, 196, 199, 200
jargon 145, 155, 156, 158, 162, 192
Jesuits 10, 30–32, 99, 189, 233, 245, 246
Jorden, Eleanor Harz 222, 247
jōyōkanjihyō 104–110, 184, 217–219, 226, 236

kai-gō distinction 32, 212
Kamo no Mabuchi 218, 247

kana 16, 29, 111–118, 121–128, 132, 154, 155, 175, 213, 228–230, 238, 241–244; digraph 112, 114, 219, 220; *furigana* 122, 127, 184, 240; hiragana 8, 9, 99–101, 111–114, 121, 122, 126–128, 175, 183, 219, 241; *kanazukai* (kana usage) 9, 114, 126, 166, 217, 219, 231; katakana 8, 9, 99, 100, 111–114, 121–123, 126–128, 132, 165, 175, 182, 190, 219, 222, 223, 232, 241; man'yōgana 8, 9, 109, 111, 121; *okurigana* 121, 126, 217, 219; origin of 8, 111; reform 126, 217–219
kanbun kundoku 9, 20, 50, 58, 73, 86, 92, 108, 111, 119, 122, 129, 132, 170, 187, 232, 244, 245
kanbun: see Chinese, Classical
kango: see Sino-Japanese
kanji 3, 7–9, 18, 19, 29, 99–112, 115, 118, 120–123, 126–128, 131, 132, 153, 154, 166, 181–187, 198, 216–219, 223, 226, 232–243; compound pictogram 109, 128; compound 237; educational 226; *jinmeiyō* 184, 218; *kokuji* 106, 109, 110, 236; origin of 101–103; pictogram 102, 103, 109, 128, 131; phono-semantic compound 103, 109; phonetic loan 103; phonographic usage of 3, 8, 109, 182; radical 103, 105, 109, 110, 128, 236, 239, 241; reform 104–106, 108, 110, 184, 217–219, 226, 236; semantographic usage of 3, 8, 109, 121; script: see script (kanji); stroke order 102–104, 128, 241, 243
kanji reading: *ateji* 108, 109, 127, 182, 236; Chinese topolectal 100, 107, 189, 190; *go-on* 106, 107, 216; *kokkun* 110; *kan-on* 107, 216; *kan'yō-on* 107; *kun-yomi* 100, 106–108, 163, 183, 232; *on-yomi* 100, 106–108, 183, 216, 232; sinoxenic 107; *tō-on* 107
kantenji: see Braille
Kasuga Masaji 244
katakana: see kana
Keichū 9
Kindaichi Haruhiko 47–50, 245
Kiyose Gisaburo Norikura 245
kō-otsu distinction 29, 244
Kobayashi Yoshiharu 245
Kobayashi Yoshinori 245
kōgo: see language, spoken

Index 283

Kojiki 8, 107
kokugo 12, 129, 156, 180, 213, 217, 224–227, 239, 244
Kokutai no hongi 180
Konjaku mojikyō 105, 106, 242
Konjaku monogatarishū 9
Korean 2, 3, 6, 11, 14, 50, 99, 100, 107, 124, 132, 133, 158, 182, 186, 190, 195–198, 233, 247
Koreanic 2
kosoado: see demonstrative
Kudō Mayumi 47–50
Kuno Susumu 245
kun-yomi: see kanji reading
kyōiku kanji: see kanji, educational
kyōtsūgo: see Japanese, Standard

L2 learner 11, 12, 16, 18, 24, 25, 36, 39, 103, 106, 136, 144, 152, 159, 233, 239–242
language: age-specific 162; agglutinative: see agglutination; analytic 5; attitudes 179, 180; beautification: see honorifics; common 199; contact 135, 185–198; death 195; derogative: see anti-honorifics; family 1, 2, 200; fusional: see language, synthetic; humble: see honorifics; isolate 1, 195; isolating: see language, analytic; mixed 3; murder 195, 222; national: see *kokugo*; official 216, 233; policy 117, 180, 192, 196, 216, 217; polite: see honorifics; pejorative: see anti-honorifics; revitalization 196; respectful: see honorifics; role 55, 147, 159, 162–166, 171–173; second 217, 233; software 241; spoken 9–11, 129, 131, 219, 234, 245, 247; standard 10, 11, 155, 180, 199, 204, 207, 216, 225; subculture 101, 155, 172, 173, 197; synthetic 5; test 104, 235–237; written 9–11, 59, 61, 80, 88, 129, 130, 132, 247
lexicon 4, 6, 9, 10, 44, 52, 108, 121, 122, 129, 134–136, 141, 144, 159, 162, 166–169, 185, 186, 194, 201, 207, 232, 244
lexicalization 55
lexical meaning 33–35, 41, 42, 56, 65, 70–73, 78, 138, 141, 177
lingua franca 192, 193

Linguistic Atlas of Itoigawa 246
Linguistic Atlas of Japan 200, 245
loan creation 224
loan derivation 187
loan meaning 187, 192, 224
loan translation 187, 192, 224
loan syntax 187
loanword 6, 9–11, 15, 18, 20, 21, 24, 30, 32, 43, 52, 100, 103, 110, 114, 116, 120, 134, 135, 143, 145, 146, 152–156, 174, 181, 185–192, 197, 198, 217–224; Chinese topolects 100, 107, 150, 189, 190; Classical Chinese: see Sino-Japanese; English 145, 146, 154, 175, 181, 187, 190, 191, 220–224; other European languages 10, 18, 135, 150, 152, 189–192; prohibition 187, 222, 223; pseudo-anglicism 191; pseudo-sinicism: see Sino-Japanese; reform 220, 221; Sanskrit 187
Loanword Committee 192, 218, 220
logogram: see kanji
Lyman, Benjamin 142, 246, 247
Lyman's Law 142, 143, 247

Maejima Hisoka 218
male speech 36, 39, 87, 147, 148, 159, 160
man'yōgana: see kana
Man'yōshū 8, 108, 111, 128
Mandarin: see Chinese, modern topolects
Martin, Samuel E. 247, 248
Matsushita Daizaburō 243, 244
Mikami Akira 245
mimetics 23, 26, 27, 31, 32, 53, 88, 91, 99, 100, 114, 134–138, 140, 173–175, 213
minimal pair 14, 18
modality 38, 41–43, 60, 69, 71, 72, 89; modal auxiliary: see auxiliary
modifier: adnominal 36–38, 50–54, 89; adverbial 36–38
mora 4, 8, 9, 14–16, 19–32, 51, 65, 67, 81, 94, 111–116, 121–125, 136, 138, 141, 145, 146, 151, 152, 155, 187–190, 206, 209, 212, 213, 219, 228, 229, 239; -timed 209; nasal 16, 19, 28, 29, 81, 112, 116, 188, 212; obstruent 16, 19, 29, 51, 113, 188, 206, 212, 213, 219
Morohashi Tetsuji 104, 239
morpheme 5, 34, 79, 102, 152, 156, 174, 175, 185–188, 192, 224,

228, 229, 232, 243, 244; bound 33, 227, 230; free 33, 227; null 60, 229
morphology 4–6, 11, 20, 33–36, 39, 43, 47, 60, 67, 106, 122, 136–138, 142, 165, 169, 200, 207, 210, 214, 230, 234, 245, 247; morphological transparency 67, 214; verbal 42–45, 207, 210, 234
morphophonology 42–45, 95, 112
morphosyntax 6, 9, 36, 50, 94, 108, 159, 161, 162, 191, 196, 232, 244
Motoori Haruniwa 243
Motoori Norinaga 201, 218, 243, 244, 247
mutual intelligibility 1, 196, 199, 200

Naganuma Naoe 233
Nagasaki Pidgin 193
Nakada Norio 245
name: personal 6, 8, 24, 34, 96, 99, 100, 105–110, 117, 120, 142, 150, 151, 173, 181–185, 218, 223, 242; place 2, 3, 98, 105, 110, 174, 181–183, 195
nasal 14–16, 19, 28–30, 81, 112, 116, 161, 171, 188, 212
nasalization 16, 31, 32, 208
National Language Council 217, 218
National Language Investigation Committee 216
Nihon shoki 8
nihonjinron 11, 181, 247
nominal 33–35, 38–43, 81, 83, 121, 138, 227, 243, 244
nominal adjective: see adjective, nominal
nominal suffix: see suffix
nominal verb: see verb
nominalization 41, 42, 51, 52, 56–58, 64, 66, 87–91, 139, 160, 167, 187, 232
nominalizer: (de)verbal -*(i)* 56, 57, 64; hearsay evidential *soo* 41; idiomatic -*mi* 51, 52, 57, 64, 139; instrumental -*(i)kata* 57, 64; instrumental -*(i)yoo* 57, 64; particle: see derivational particle; qualitative -*sa* 51, 52, 57, 64, 66, 139; tendential -*(i)gači* 57, 64; tendential -*me* 51, 52, 57, 64, 139, 172; visual evidential -*(i)soo* 57, 64; visual

evidential -*ge* 51, 52, 57, 64, 139; visual evidential *yoo* 41, 42
noun: common 34; deverbal 64, 139, 140; formal 33, 34, 38–42, 100, 244; phrase 5, 33–35, 42, 54, 55, 58, 61, 62, 71, 72, 80, 81, 84, 88–91, 98; proper 34; verbal 64, 143
numeral: Arabic 99, 117–119, 121; bare 143, 150, 151; Chinese 117–119; count 143, 151, 152; native 3, 6, 28, 151; Roman 99, 117

obstruent 15, 16, 19, 22, 23, 29, 51, 112, 113, 138, 143, 187, 188, 206, 209, 212, 213, 219
Okinawan 1, 196
okurigana: see kana
onbin 31, 32, 44, 64, 65, 69, 206
on-yomi: see kanji reading
Ono ga bakamura usojizukushi 128
onomastics: see name
onomatopoeia: see mimetics
orthography: orthographic competence 127; orthographic convention 99, 101, 114, 115, 122, 126, 153, 191–193, 222; orthographic licence 99, 101, 120, 126, 127; orthographic play 28, 101, 126–128; orthographic representation 113; orthographic restoration 30
Ōtsubo Heiji 245
Ōtsuki Fumihiko 216, 239
Ōya Tōru 244

palatalization 209, 213
Palmer, Harold 233
part of speech 33–37, 40, 42, 55, 56, 65, 77, 80, 88, 98, 121, 138–140, 143, 144, 169, 227, 243
particle: case marker: see case marker particle; conjunctive 79–81, 88; definition of 35, 55, 79, 80; derivational: see derivational particle; discourse 41, 55, 58, 59, 85, 87, 88, 160, 162–164, 173, 209, 215; emphatic 78, 79, 84, 97, 98, 152, 160; exclamative 36, 59, 87, 160; interrogative 83, 84, 87, 97, 98; restrictive 84–86; syntactic 80, 82; thematic 81, 84; topic marker: see topic marker particle
Peirce, Charles 131

phone 13, 14, 209
phoneme 4, 13–20, 29, 30, 116, 137, 172, 190, 201, 208, 209, 228, 229, 243
phonemicization 13, 15, 22, 94, 96
phonetics 13, 14, 67, 103, 109–111, 115, 122, 198
phonology 3, 4, 7, 10, 13–32, 35, 80, 94, 142, 153, 159–163, 169, 172, 188–190, 193–196, 200, 205, 208, 211, 216, 217, 245, 247; history of 29–32; phonological play 27–29
phono-semantic matching 108
phonotactics 4, 14, 16, 20–23, 31, 43, 94, 112, 136, 187, 188, 212
pictogram: see kanji
pidgin 191–194
pitch accent 11, 14, 20, 23–27, 64, 141, 153, 201, 204–209, 213, 234, 244; 0-type (accentless) 206, 209, 213; in compounds 25–27; Keihan *n*+1 type 206, 207, 244; *n*-type 206, 213; pattern 23–25, 64, 153, 206, 207, 213; Tokyo *n*+1 type 23–27, 206, 207, 209, 213, 244
plosive 15, 16, 30
plural 6, 39, 139, 140, 148–150, 172, 204
pluralizer: see suffix
politeness: see honorifics
polysemy 153, 154
Portuguese 10, 135, 189, 193, 233, 238
predicate 33–36, 42, 50–54, 69, 84, 87–90, 97, 98, 160, 165, 227
predication 36, 50, 53–56, 243
prefix 7, 124, 125, 138, 139, 143, 150, 152, 156, 160, 166–168, 171, 186
prenasalization 30, 31, 144, 208, 209, 213
pronoun 2, 34, 38–41, 55, 103, 139, 147–150, 159–164, 167, 169, 191, 227; demonstrative: see demonstrative; first person 147–150, 159, 161; interrogative 34, 38–40; personal 34, 39, 40, 103, 139, 147–149, 159, 160, 167, 169; second person 147, 149; third person 149, 150, 159
pronunciation 4, 11, 16–18, 27, 28, 92, 103, 106, 107, 116, 117, 125, 128, 146, 153, 159, 161, 166, 172, 180–184, 193, 194, 198, 205, 208, 209, 212, 213, 231, 240, 244
prosody 4, 19, 27, 51, 52, 92, 93

pseudo-anglicism: see loanword
pseudo-sinicism: see Sino-Japanese
punctuation 99, 119–121, 125, 126, 128, 216

ra-nuki 67, 161
radical: see kanji
Ramstedt, Gustaf 247
reanalysis 43, 58, 79, 160
rebus 28, 107, 108
reduction: see truncation
reduplication 26, 27, 39, 136–138, 140, 141, 150
Reference Grammar of Japanese, A 247
register 9, 10, 37, 39, 82, 88, 96, 147–150, 162–166, 187, 208, 212, 232, 245
rendaku 9, 16, 112, 141–145, 152, 155, 156, 161, 184, 193, 246
rentaishi: see adnoun
respect: see honorific
Rodrigues, João 246
Rōmajikai 115
romanization 10, 30, 32, 115–117, 197, 217, 246, 247; *hebon-shiki* (Hepburn style) 115–117, 197, 241, 246, 247; *kunrei-shiki* 115, 116, 217, 241; *nihon-shiki* 115, 116
Roman alphabet 10, 30, 99, 115, 118, 121, 122, 127, 128, 146, 184, 190, 191, 198, 217, 218, 223, 241
Russian 10, 18, 21, 135, 189, 195
Ryūkyūan 1, 2, 8, 182, 195–197, 199, 200, 245, 247

sa-ire 67, 161
Samguk sagi 2, 3
Sānguózhì 7, 8
Sanskrit 4, 187, 243
Satow, Ernest 246, 247
Saussure, Ferdinand de 131
script (in general): horizontal 117–121; miniscule 113, 114, 219; mixing 117, 121, 122; reform 105; style: see script (kanji); vertical 117–122
script (kanji): bronze 101; clerical 101–104; cursive 102; good fortune 104; old seal 104; oracle bone 101–103; regular 102, 104, 218; seal of fortune 104; semi-cursive 102, 104, 218; small seal 101–104
sei-daku distinction 16, 28, 30, 31, 112, 121, 124, 125, 128, 144, 175
seion: see *sei-daku* distinction

semantics 6, 7, 26, 34, 35, 43, 46, 67, 77, 80, 85, 88, 96, 98, 103, 106, 108, 109, 138, 139, 141, 144, 151–154, 176, 185, 191, 192, 197, 230, 237; semantic bleaching 176; semantic borrowing: see loan meaning; semantic extension 6, 7, 77, 85, 88
semi-vowel: see glide
sentence 4, 8, 27, 33–38, 50, 53–55, 58, 60, 77, 80, 83, 84, 88–93, 119, 125, 130, 131, 138, 160, 164–167, 172, 173, 230–234, 244, 245
sex 7, 159
Shanghainese: see Chinese, modern topolects
Shinmura Izuru 3, 217
Sibata Takesi 246
signage 99, 104, 131, 133, 169, 216, 223
Sino-Japanese 9, 10, 23–28, 31, 32, 43, 52, 79, 99, 100, 107, 117, 120, 126, 134–136, 139–143, 146, 150–156, 166–168, 174–176, 185–192, 198, 209, 213, 220–224, 232, 236, 237, 241, 243; binom 154, 185, 186; morpheme 175, 187, 188; numeral: see numeral, Chinese; pseudo-sinicism 186, 191
Sino-Korean 3, 107, 109, 198
sinosphere 99–102, 107, 109, 120, 132, 180, 182, 197, 235
sinoxenic: see kanji reading
slang 100, 139, 145, 146, 155–158, 162, 169, 240
social class 96, 147, 159, 161
Society for Japanese Linguistics, The 180, 245
sociolinguistics 16, 99, 100, 144, 147, 150, 161
sound change 9, 31, 43, 44, 64, 147
Spanish 10, 11, 16, 17, 172, 189, 193–196, 233
spelling: conceit 114; convention 115, 191, 193; device 112, 113
Spoken Japanese 222
stem: see adjective and verb
style: neutral 130, 131; polite 130, 131; speech 155, 207; writing 54, 129, 130, 160, 166
subject 4, 5, 11, 33–39, 45, 49, 60, 80, 82, 91–93, 98, 169, 214, 227, 245; -acting 49; -modifying 49; dropping 38
suffix 2, 5, 6, 21, 24, 35, 38, 39, 42–47, 51, 52, 55–69, 72, 73, 79, 81, 85, 94–100, 121, 122, 130, 136–140, 150, 151, 157, 163, 165, 171–174, 186, 190, 206, 207, 210, 211, 214, 215, 227–232, 244; derivational: see verbal suffix (non-final); inflectional: see verbal suffix (final); nominal 42, 171; pluralizer 39, 150, 172; string 24, 56, 65, 66, 68, 228; verbal: see verbal suffix (final and non-final)
surname: see name
Swadesh list 2
swearword: see anti-honorifics
syllable 4, 14, 18–20, 23, 26, 31, 32, 111, 123, 146, 175, 190, 209, 213; -timed 209; heavy 19, 32, 146; structure 31, 32
syllabeme: see dialect
syntax 4, 5, 11, 33–98, 138, 141, 164, 169, 187, 214, 247; loan: see loan syntax; syntactic particle: see particle; word order 2–5, 11, 33–37, 187, 193, 195, 232

taboo 40, 157, 158, 183
Tamil 3, 4
Tanakadate Aikitsu 115
Tanikawa Kotosuga 238, 239
-te form: see converb
tekiseigo 222, 224
tenji: see Braille
tense 5, 6, 38, 43, 46, 58, 60, 177, 193, 210, 230; future 46, 58, 59, 193; nonpast 35, 42, 43, 49–51, 55–58, 61, 62, 71, 87, 96, 140, 164, 165, 214, 215, 228, 230; past 5, 6, 38, 40–46, 51, 55–62, 95–97, 165, 177, 210, 230; past-in-future 58, 59; present 46, 58, 59, 210
Tō Teikan 2, 227
Tōjō Misao 200, 201, 244
Tōkaidō-chū hizakurige 176
Tokieda Motoki 243
topic 28, 35–38, 55, 78, 79, 84, 91–94, 114, 214, 245
topic marker particle: *mo* 24, 35, 55, 72, 73, 84, 90, 152; *wa* 24, 28, 35–37, 55, 59, 72, 73, 78, 79, 84, 90–94, 114, 125, 213, 219
topolect: see Chinese, modern topolects
toponym: see name, place
tōyōkanjihyō 217–219, 226
transcription: see romanization
trill 16, 160, 161, 164, 172
truncation 18, 20, 54, 55, 62, 67–78, 81, 84, 86–92, 96, 97, 144–149, 154–156, 171, 175, 177, 187, 190, 191, 197, 215
Tsukishima Hiroshi 245
Tsuzuku Tsuneo 244
typology 2, 4–6, 60

Uchināguchi: see Okinawan
Ueda Kazutoshi 180, 216, 217, 244, 247

velar 15, 16, 30, 161
verb: auxiliary: see auxiliary; class 44–47, 67, 94–96, 207, 214, 228, 229; classification of based on aspect: see aspect; consonant-stem 43–45, 55, 59, 60, 64–67, 122, 210, 228; dual vowel-stem 94–96, 214; existential 36, 45, 54, 207, 210; giving and receiving 35, 73–76, 170; humble form 70, 166, 167; irrealis 67, 228; irregular 42–45, 52, 55, 58, 65–69, 94–96, 227–229; K-irregular 42–45, 58–60, 66, 94, 95, 227–229; linking: see copula; N-irregular 94–96; nominal 43, 52, 166, 167, 171, 186; phrase 5; polite form 66–69, 130, 160, 165, 211, 234; qualitative: see adjective; R-irregular 94–96; respectful form 70, 71, 75, 167, 168, 207; S-irregular 42–45, 58–60, 67–69, 94, 95, 207, 227–229; single vowel-stem 94–96, 214; stem 5, 6, 35, 42–47, 51, 54, 56, 60, 64, 65, 68, 69, 75, 94, 95, 100, 121, 122, 167, 214, 228–230; suffix: see verbal suffix (final and non-final); transitivity 4, 45–50, 211, 214; volition 45–50, 58, 94, 95; vowel-stem 43–47, 58, 67, 95, 122, 204, 207, 214, 229
verbal 2, 5, 24, 33–35, 65, 81, 85, 95, 98–100, 121, 138, 227, 230, 243, 244
verbal suffix (final) 42, 55–63, 66, 68, 79, 96, 98, 228–230; adnominal -(*r*)*u* ~ -*ki* 95–97, 228–230; archaic/Western negative -(*a*)*nu* ~ -(*a*)*N* 44, 57, 59, 66, 68, 163, 174, 205, 207, 214; conclusive -(*r*)*u* ~ -*si* 95–97, 228–230; conditional: see conditional;

conjectural-hortative -(y)oo ~
-karoo 55–59, 66, 69, 96, 214,
229; converb: see converb;
empirical past -(i)ki ~ -(i)si
95–97, 174; imperative -e ~ -ro
~ -yo ~ -i 44, 45, 51, 57, 59, 61,
74, 79, 95, 160, 161, 204, 207,
211, 214, 228, 229; necessitive
-(r)ubeki 44, 57–59, 63, 95, 97;
negative conjectural -(r)umai
~ -mai 44, 57–59; nominalizer:
see nominalizer; nonpast
-(r)u ~ -i 35, 42, 43, 50, 51,
55–59, 96, 214, 228, 230;
nonpast (Kyūshū) -ka 215;
past -ta ~ -kaQta 5, 6, 32, 38,
42–46, 51, 55–66, 95–97, 165,
177, 206, 210, 230; past
conjectural -taroo ~ -kaQtaroo
55–59, 64, 66; prohibitive
-(r)una 57, 59, 160, 161
verbal suffix (non-final) 56,
65–68, 95, 96; abilitative
potential (Kyūshū) -(i)kir-u
215; abilitative potential
(Tōhoku) -e-ru ~ -(r)are-ru
210; adjective verbalizer -kar-i
96, 97; anti-causative
(Tōhoku) -(r)asar-u ~ -(r)ar-u
210; anti-honorific -(i)yagar-u
66–68, 171; archaic negative
-(a)zar-i 97; causative
-(s)ase-ru 35, 38, 44, 47, 51, 56,
66–68, 82, 95, 161, 167, 168, 211;
circumstantial potential
(Kyūshū) -(r)are-ru 215;
circumstantial potential
(Tōhoku) -(r)uEE ~ (r)uE 210;
conjectural -(a)m-u ~ -(a)N
95–97, 174, 207; desiderative
-(i)ta-i 35, 42–44, 66–68, 80,
82, 230; emotive verbalizer
-gar-u 66–68; hearsay past
-(i)ker-i 79, 95, 97; negative

-(a)na-i 42, 44, 51, 56, 58, 62,
63, 66–68, 72, 86, 87, 163, 173,
207, 228; non-volitional
perfect -(i)t-u 95; passive
-(r)are-ru 35, 43–47, 51, 56,
66–68, 82, 95, 167, 168; past
conjectural -(i)kem-u 95;
perfect-stative (Kyūshū)
-tor-u ~ -čor-u 215; polite
-(i)mas-u 18, 44, 45, 55, 66–68,
74, 130, 165, 167; potential -e-ru
~ -rare-ru 44, 45, 51, 66–68,
80–82, 161, 230; progressive
(Kyūshū) -(i)yor-u ~ -(i)or-u
215; stative-perfect -(e)r-i ~
-(i)tar-i 95–97, 230; volitional
perfect -(i)n-u 95
verbalization 56, 66–68, 71, 72,
96, 97, 190; adjective verbalizer: see verbal suffix
(non-final); emotive verbalizer: see verbal suffix
(non-final)
vocabulary: discriminatory 157,
158, 162, 169, 184; foreign: see
loanword; mimetic: see
mimetics; native 9, 22, 30, 43,
114, 120, 134, 135, 143, 154, 166,
185, 187, 188, 213; Sino-
Japanese: see Sino-Japanese;
strata 9, 21–27, 30, 43, 114,
134–140, 143–146, 150, 153, 154,
174, 185–188, 213, 245
voice (grammatical): anti-
causative 47, 48, 210; causative 35, 38, 44, 47, 48, 51, 56,
66–68, 71, 72, 82, 95, 161, 167,
168, 211; diathetic auxiliary:
see auxiliary; passive 35,
43–45, 47, 51, 56, 66–68, 82, 95,
167, 168; reciprocal 71, 72
voicing (phonology) 14–18, 22,
23, 29–32, 65, 112, 124, 138,
141–143, 173, 187, 208, 209, 213

vowel 4, 6, 9, 11, 14–19, 21, 22,
28–32, 43–45, 64, 65, 94–96,
112–117, 120, 124, 125, 136–138,
142, 161, 172, 173, 183, 188, 190,
193, 205–212, 214, 228–230,
244; alternation 6, 96, 142;
cardinal 17; coalescence 31;
diphthong 18, 29, 163, 211;
front 17, 21, 30, 209; harmony
244; high 17, 18, 30, 208, 212;
lengthening 28, 136, 137, 206;
long 18, 19, 29, 32, 114–116, 120,
124, 125, 161, 172, 173, 183, 188,
209; low 17; reduction 18, 31,
32, 77, 166, 212; semi-: see
glide; -stem verb: see verb;
union 43–45, 64, 65, 94, 95,
228

wago: see vocabulary, native
waseieigo: see loanword,
pseudo-anglicism
waseikango: see Sino-Japanese,
pseudo-sinicism
Wenck, Günther 247
word: building 138, 140; class:
see part of speech; definition
of 79; formation 134–146;
order: see syntax; play 128,
165, 175
writing: see orthography

yakuwarigo: see language, role
Yamada Bimyō 239
Yamada Yoshio 53, 216, 217, 243,
244
Yanagita Kunio 202, 244
Yilan Creole 194
Yokohama Pidgin Japanese 193
Yoshizawa Yoshinori 244

zuuzuu dialect: see dialect,
Tōhoku

著者略歴

Mark Irwin（アーウィン マーク）
1967年英国生まれ
山形大学人文社会科学部教授
PhD（シェフィールド大学）
主著：
Loanwords in Japanese（John Benjamins, 2011）
Sequential Voicing in Japanese（ed. T. Vance & M. Irwin. John Benjamins, 2016）
English Loanwords（In *The Handbook of Japanese Lexicon and Word Formation*, ed. T. Kageyama & H. Kishimoto. De Gruyter Mouton, 2016）

Matthew Zisk（ジスク マシュー）
1984年米国生まれ
山形大学工学部国際交流センター助教
博士（文学）（東北大学）
主著：
『日本語大事典』（朝倉書店，2014；共編，欧文監修）
「漢字・漢文を媒介とした言語借用形式の分類と借用要因」（斎藤倫明・石井正彦編『日本語語彙へのアプローチ―形態・統語・計量・歴史・対照―』所収，おうふう，2015）
「義からみた漢字」（沖森卓也・笹原宏之編著『漢字（日本語ライブラリー）』所収，朝倉書店，2017）

The Japanese Language（英語で学ぶ日本語学）1
Japanese Linguistics（日本語学） 定価はカバーに表示

2019年6月1日 初版第1刷

著 者　Mark Irwin
　　　　Matthew Zisk

発行者　朝　倉　誠　造

発行所　株式会社　朝倉書店
　　　　東京都新宿区新小川町6-29
　　　　郵便番号　162-8707
　　　　電話 03(3260)0141
　　　　FAX 03(3260)0180
　　　　http://www.asakura.co.jp

〈検印省略〉

ⓒ 2019〈無断複写・転載を禁ず〉　　中央印刷・渡辺製本

ISBN 978-4-254-51681-4　C 3381　　Printed in Japan

JCOPY <出版者著作権管理機構 委託出版物>
本書の無断複写は著作権法上での例外を除き禁じられています．複写される場合は，そのつど事前に，出版者著作権管理機構（電話 03-5244-5088, FAX 03-5244-5089, e-mail: info@jcopy.or.jp）の許諾を得てください．

宮城教大 西原哲雄編
朝倉日英対照言語学シリーズ1

言　語　学　入　門

51571-8　C3381　　　　Ａ５判 168頁　本体2600円

初めて学ぶ学生に向けて，言語学・英語学の基本概念や用語から各領域の初歩までわかりやすく解説。英語教育の現場も配慮。〔内容〕言語学とは何か／音の構造／語の構造／文の構造／文の意味／文の運用

前筑波大 北原保雄監修　前大東文化大 早田輝洋編
朝倉日本語講座1

世界の中の日本語 (新装版)

51641-8　C3381　　　　Ａ５判 256頁　本体3400円

〔内容〕諸言語の音韻と日本語の音韻／諸言語の語彙・意味と日本語の語彙・意味／日本語の文構造／諸言語の文字と日本語の文字／諸言語の敬語と日本語の敬語／世界の方言と日本語の方言／日本語の系統／日本語教育／他

前立大 沖森卓也編著　拓殖大 阿久津智・東大 井島正博・
東洋大 木村　一・慶大 木村義之・早大 笹原宏之著
日本語ライブラリー

日　本　語　概　説

51523-7　C3381　　　　Ａ５判 176頁　本体2300円

日本語学のさまざまな基礎的テーマを，見開き単位で豊富な図表を交え，やさしく簡潔に解説し，体系的にまとめたテキスト。〔内容〕言語とその働き／日本語の歴史／音韻・音声／文字・表記／語彙／文法／待遇表現・位相／文章・文体／研究

前立大 沖森卓也編著　成城大 陳　力衛・東大 肥爪周二・
白百合女大 山本真吾著
日本語ライブラリー

日　本　語　史　概　説

51522-0　C3381　　　　Ａ５判 208頁　本体2600円

日本語の歴史をテーマごとに上代から現代まで概説。わかりやすい大型図表，年表，資料写真を豊富に収録し，これ1冊で十分に学べる読み応えあるテキスト。〔内容〕総説／音韻史／文字史／語彙史／文法史／文体史／待遇表現史／位相史／他

前立大 沖森卓也・早大 笹原宏之編著
日本語ライブラリー

漢　　　　　字

51617-3　C3381　　　　Ａ５判 192頁　本体2900円

漢字の歴史，文字としての特徴，アジアの各地域で遂げた発展を概観。〔内容〕成り立ちからみた漢字／形からみた漢字／音からみた漢字／義からみた漢字／表記からみた漢字／社会からみた漢字（日本，中国・香港・台湾，韓国，ベトナム）

国立国語研 大西拓一郎編

新　日　本　言　語　地　図
—分布図で見渡す方言の世界—

51051-5　C3081　　　　Ｂ５判 320頁　本体6000円

どんなことばで表現するのか，どんなものを表現することばか，様々な事象について日本地図上にまとめた150図を収録した言語地図・方言地図集。〔本書は「全国方言分布調査」（国立国語研究所，2010-15）に基づいています。〕

前都立大 中島平三編

ことばのおもしろ事典

51047-8　C3580　　　　Ｂ５判 324頁　本体7400円

身近にある"ことば"のおもしろさや不思議さから，多彩で深いことば・言語学の世界へと招待する。〔内容〕I.ことばを身近に感じる（ことわざ／ことば遊び／広告／ジェンダー／ポライトネス／育児語／ことばの獲得／バイリンガル／発達／ど忘れ，など）　II.ことばの基礎を知る（音韻論／形態論／統語論／意味論／語用論）　III.ことばの広がりを探る（動物のコミュニケーション／進化／世界の言語・文字／ピジン／国際語／言語の比較／手話／言語聴覚士，など）

前東北大 佐藤武義・前阪大 前田富祺編集代表

日　本　語　大　事　典
【上・下巻：2分冊】

51034-8　C3581　　　　Ｂ５判 2456頁　本体75000円

現在の日本語をとりまく環境の変化を敏感にとらえ，孤立した日本語，あるいは等質的な日本語というとらえ方ではなく，可能な限りグローバルで複合的な視点に基づいた新しい日本語学の事典。言語学の関連用語や人物，資料，研究文献なども広く取り入れた約3500項目をわかりやすく丁寧に解説。読者対象は，大学学部生・大学院生，日本語学の研究者，中学・高校の日本語学関連の教師，日本語教育・国語教育関係の人々，日本語学に関心を持つ一般読者などである。

上記価格（税別）は2019年5月現在